THE EUROPEAN UNION SERIES

General Editors: Neill Nugent, William E. Paterson

The European Union series provides an authoritative library on the European Union, ranging from general introductory texts to definitive assessments of key institutions and actors, issues, policies and policy processes, and the role of member states.

Books in the series are written by leading scholars in their fields and reflect the most up-to-date research and debate. Particular attention is paid to accessibility and clear presentation for a wide audience of students, practitioners and interested general readers.

The series editors are **Neill Nugent,** Professor of Politics and Jean Monnet Professor of European Integration, Manchester Metropolitan University, and **William E. Paterson,** Honourary Professor in German and European Studies, University of Aston. Their co-editor until his death in July 1999, **Vincent Wright,** was a Fellow of Nuffield College, Oxford University.

Feedback on the series and book proposals are always welcome and should be sent to Steven Kennedy, Palgrave Macmillan, Houndmills, Basingstoke, Hampshire RG21 6XS, UK, or by e-mail to s.kennedy@palgrave.com

---

General textbooks

Published

Desmond Dinan **Encyclopedia of the European Union** [Rights: Europe only]

Desmond Dinan **Europe Recast: A History of European Union** [Rights: Europe only]

Desmond Dinan **Ever Closer Union: An Introduction to European Integration** (4th edn) [Rights: Europe only]

Mette Eilstrup Sangiovanni (ed.) **Debates on European Integration: A Reader**

Simon Hix and Bjørn Høyland **The Political System of the European Union** (3rd edn)

Paul Magnette **What is the European Union? Nature and Prospects**

John McCormick **Understanding the European Union: A Concise Introduction** (4th edn)

Brent F. Nelsen and Alexander Stubb **The European Union: Readings on the Theory and Practice of European Integration** (3rd edn) [Rights: Europe only]

Neill Nugent (ed.) **European Union Enlargement**

Neill Nugent **The Government and Politics of the European Union** (7th edn)

John Peterson and Elizabeth Bomberg **Decision-Making in the European Union**

Ben Rosamond **Theories of European Integration**

Esther Versluis, Mendeltje van Keulen and Paul Stephenson **Analyzing the European Union Policy Process**

Forthcoming

Laurie Buonanno and Neill Nugent **Policies and Policy Processes of the European Union**

Magnus Ryner and Alan Cafruny **A Critical Introduction to the European Union**

Dirk Leuffen, Berthold Rittberger and Frank Schimmelfennig **Differentiated Integration**

Sabine Saurugger **Theoretical Approaches to European Integration**

Also Planned

The Political Economy of European Integration

The major institutions and actors

Published

Renaud Dehousse **The European Court of Justice**
Justin Greenwood **Interest Representation in the European Union (2nd edn)**
Fiona Hayes-Renshaw and Helen Wallace **The Council of Ministers (2nd edn)**
Simon Hix and Christopher Lord **Political Parties in the European Union**
David Judge and David Earnshaw **The European Parliament (2nd edn)**
Neill Nugent **The European Commission**
Anne Stevens with Handley Stevens **Brussels Bureaucrats? The Administration of the European Union**

Forthcoming

Wolfgang Wessels **The European Council**

The main areas of policy

Published

Michele Chang **Monetary Integration in the European Union**
Michelle Cini and Lee McGowan **Competition Policy in the European Union (2nd edn)**
Wyn Grant **The Common Agricultural Policy**
Sieglinde Gstöhl and Dirk de Bievrè **The Trade Policy of the European Union**
Martin Holland **The European Union and the Third World**
Jolyon Howorth **Security and Defence Policy in the European Union**
Johanna Kantola **Gender and the European Union**
Stephan Keukeleire and Jennifer MacNaughton **The Foreign Policy of the European Union**
Brigid Laffan **The Finances of the European Union**
Malcolm Levitt and Christopher Lord **The Political Economy of Monetary Union**
Janne Haaland Matláry **Energy Policy in the European Union**
John McCormick **Environmental Policy in the European Union**
John Peterson and Margaret Sharp **Technology Policy in the European Union**
Handley Stevens **Transport Policy in the European Union**

Forthcoming

Karen Anderson **Social Policy in the European Union**

Hans Bruyninckx and Tom Delreux **Environmental Policy and Politics in the European Union**
Jörg Monar **Justice and Home Affairs in the European Union**

Also planned

Political Union
The External Policies of the European Union

The member states and the Union

Published

Carlos Closa and Paul Heywood **Spain and the European Union**
Alain Guyomarch, Howard Machin and Ella Ritchie **France in the European Union**
Brigid Laffan and Jane O'Mahoney **Ireland and the European Union**

Forthcoming

Simon Bulmer and William E. Paterson **Germany and the European Union**
Brigid Laffan **The European Union and its Member States**
Baldur Thórhallson **Small States in the European Union**

Also planned

Britain and the European Union

Issues

Published

Derek Beach **The Dynamics of European Integration: Why and When EU Institutions Matter**
Christina Boswell and Andrew Geddes **Migration and Mobility in the European Union**
Thomas Christiansen and Christine Reh **Constitutionalizing the European Union**
Robert Ladrech **Europeanization and National Politics**
Cécile Leconte **Understanding Euroscepticism**
Steven McGuire and Michael Smith **The European Union and the United States**
Wyn Rees **The US-EU Security Relationship: The Tensions between a European and a Global Agenda**

The Political System of the European Union

Third edition

Simon Hix

and

Bjørn Høyland

First published 2011 by
PALGRAVE MACMILLAN

Palgrave Macmillan in the UK is an imprint of Macmillan Publishers Limited, registered in England, company number 785998, of Houndmills, Basingstoke, Hampshire RG21 6XS.

Palgrave Macmillan in the US is a division of St Martin's Press LLC, 175 Fifth Avenue, New York, NY 10010.

Palgrave Macmillan is the global academic imprint of the above companies and has companies and representatives throughout the world.

Palgrave® and Macmillan® are registered trademarks in the United States, the United Kingdom, Europe and other countries

ISBN 978–0–230–24981–3 hardback
ISBN 978–0–230–24982–0 paperback

This book is printed on paper suitable for recycling and made from fully managed and sustained forest sources. Logging, pulping and manufacturing processes are expected to conform to the environmental regulations of the country of origin.

A catalogue record for this book is available from the British Library.

A catalog record for this book is available from the Library of Congress.

10   9   8   7   6   5   4   3   2   1
20   19   18   17   16   15   14   13   12   11

Transferred to Digital Printing in 2012

Contents

List of Figures, Boxes, and Tables

Figures

Boxes

Tables

Preface

The third edition of this book is a major rewrite of the previous edition. This is partly due to the significant institutional, political, and policy changes that have taken place in the EU in the five years since the second edition was published. It is also due to the large volume of new research that has been published on the EU, which continues to grow at a fast rate. Much of this new research is of high quality, with new data, careful research designs, and sophisticated methods. Having said that, research on some aspects of the EU remains theoretically, empirically, and methodologically underdeveloped, particularly on the policy outputs of the system and their consequences. Above all, though, this new edition is significantly different from the previous edition because it now has two authors rather than one. We believe the book is markedly improved as a result.

One of the main differences between this edition of the book and the previous two editions is that we have tried to contrast throughout the book two distinct theoretical approaches to EU politics, which we call 'intergovernmentalism' and 'supranational politics'. The first of these terms is shorthand for the most recent version of the intergovernmental approach, as represented by Andy Moravcsik's liberal–intergovernmental theory. The second of these terms is our own description of a range of views which nonetheless share the proposition that supranational institutions, rules, and political interactions need to be treated as independent factors (from national governments) when explaining EU-level politics or policy outcomes. We discuss these two perspectives in the Introduction and also mainly focus on these two theoretical frameworks in the discussions of the explanations of EU policies in Part III of the book.

This edition of the book is also somewhat shorter than the previous two editions. The main reason for this is that we have cut out a lot of basic information about EU institutions, politics, and policies which is easily available on the internet, for example on the Europa website (at: http://europa.eu/).

In writing this new version of the book we would like to thank Sara Binzer Hobolt, Willie Paterson, and an anonymous reviewer for commenting on an early draft of the manuscript, and Vibeke Wøien Hansen and Marianne Dahl for devoted research assistance. We would also like to thank our families, who tolerated our absences during the writing of the book.

List of Abbreviations

ALDE	Alliance of Liberals and Democrats for Europe
CAP	Common Agricultural Policy
CCP	Common Commercial Policy
CFI	Court of First Instance
CFSP	Common Foreign and Security Policy
COREPER	Committee of Permanent Representatives
ECB	European Central Bank
ECR	European Conservatives and Reformists group
EDD	Group for a Europe of Democracies and Diversities
EFD	Europe of Freedom and Democracy group
ECJ	European Court of Justice
ELDR	European Liberal Democrat and Reform group
EMU	Economic and Monetary Union
EPP	European People's Party
EPP–ED	European People's Party–European Democrats
ESDP	European Security and Defence Policy
EUL/NGL	European United Left/Nordic Green Left
G/EFA	Greens/European Free Alliance
GATT	General Agreement on Tariffs and Trade
IGC	intergovernmental conference
IND/DEM	Independence/Democracy group
JHA	Justice and Home Affairs
NATO	North Atlantic Treaty Organization
NGO	non-governmental organization
PES	Party of European Socialists
QMV	qualified-majority voting
S&D	Progressive Alliance of Socialists and Democrats
SEA	Single European Act
UEN	Union for Europe of the Nations group
WTO	World Trade Organization

Chapter 1

Introduction: Explaining the EU Political System

The Institutional and Policy Architecture of the EU
What Is the EU? A Political System but not a State
Two Theories of EU Politics
Structure of the Book

The European Union (EU) is a remarkable achievement. It is the result of a process of voluntary integration between the nation-states of Europe. The EU began in the 1950s with six states, grew to 15 in the 1990s, enlarged to 27 in the 2000s, and is likely to grow even further. The EU started out as a common market in coal and steel products and has evolved into an economic, social, and political union. European integration has also produced a set of supranational executive, legislative, and judicial institutions with significant authority over many areas of public policy.

But, this book is not about the history of 'European integration', as this story has been told at length elsewhere (for example Dedman, 2009). Nor does it try to explain European integration and the major turning points in this process, as this too has been the focus of much political science research and theorizing (for example Moravcsik, 1998; Wiener and Diez 2009). Instead, the aim of this book is to understand and explain how the EU works today. Is the European Commission a runaway bureaucracy? How powerful is the European Parliament? Does the European Court of Justice (ECJ) favour some member states over others? Why do some citizens support the EU while others oppose it? Is there a 'democratic deficit' in the way the EU works? Why are some social groups more able than others to influence the EU? Is the EU single market deregulatory or re-regulatory? Who are the winners and losers from expenditure policies? Does economic and monetary union work? Has the EU extended citizens' rights and freedoms? Can the EU speak with a single voice on the world stage?

We could treat the EU as a unique experiment, which of course in many respects it is since no other continent has progressed so far in the process of supranational integration. However, the above questions could be asked of any 'political system', whether domestic or supranational. Also, political science has an array of theoretical tools to answer

1

exactly these sorts of questions. Instead of a general theory of how political systems work, political science has a series of mid-level explanations of the main processes that are common to all political systems, such as public opinion, interest-group mobilization, legislative bargaining, delegation to executive and bureaucratic agents, economic policy-making, citizen–state relations, and international political and economic relations. Consequently, the main argument of this book is that to help us understand how the EU works, we should use the tools, methods, and mid-range theories from the general study of government, politics, and policy-making. In this way, teaching and research on the EU can be part of the political science mainstream.

This introductory chapter sets the general context for this task. It provides some basic background information about the policy and institutional architecture of the EU, and explains how the EU can be a 'political system' without also having to be a 'state'. The chapter then reviews some of the basic assumptions of political science, and discusses how these assumptions are applied in the two main theories of EU politics.

The Institutional and Policy Architecture of the EU

When six European states decided in the early 1950s to place their coal and steel industries under collective supranational control, few would have expected that this would have led within half a century to a new continental-scale political system. Box 1.1 lists the key stages in this process. A few of the stages are worth highlighting. In the 1960s, Western Europe became the first region in the world to establish a customs union, with an internal free-trade area and a common external tariff, and also the first genuinely supranational public spending programme: the Common Agricultural Policy (CAP). The pace of integration then slowed until in the mid-1980s the then 12 member states agreed to the launch the programme to create the first continental-scale 'single market' by the end of 1992; which involved the removal of internal barriers to the free movement of goods, services, capital, and labour, a single European competition policy, and a single European currency (the euro). As a consequence of the single market, in the 1990s the new 'European Union' adopted common social and environmental policies, common policies on the movement of persons between the member states and across the EU's external borders, and began to coordinate national macroeconomic, justice and policing, and foreign and security policies.

The EU does not have a 'constitution' in the traditional meaning of this term: a single document setting out the basic rules and principles of the organization. A 'Constitutional Treaty' was agreed in 2004, but was rejected by referendums in France and the Netherlands in 2005. Even without the Constitutional Treaty, though, the EU Treaty, and the practices and norms that have evolved around how the EU works, can be thought of as the basic 'constitutional architecture' in that they have established a clear division of policy competences and institutional powers in the EU.

There are five main types of EU policy:

1   *Regulatory policies*: these are rules on the free movement of goods, services, capital and persons in the single market, and involve the harmonization of many national production standards, such as environmental and social policies, and common competition policies.

2   *Expenditure policies*: these policies involve the transfer of resources through the EU budget, and include the CAP, socio-economic and regional cohesion policies, and research and development policies.

3   *Macroeconomic policies*: these policies are pursued in European Monetary Union (EMU), where the European Central Bank (ECB) manages the money supply and interest rate policy, while the Council pursues exchange rate policy and the coordination and scrutiny of national tax and employment policies.

4   *Interior policies*: these are rules to extend and protect the economic, political, and social rights of the EU citizens and include common asylum and immigration policies, police and judicial cooperation, and the provisions for 'EU citizenship'.

5   *Foreign policies*: these are aimed at ensuring that the EU speaks with a single voice on the world stage, and include trade policies, external economic relations, the Common Foreign and Security Policy (CFSP), and the European Security and Defence Policy (ESDP).

Box 1.2 describes how these policies fit together in a 'catalogue of competences'. The EU level has exclusive responsibility for creating and regulating the single market, and for managing the competition, external customs and trade policies that derive from this task. The EU level is also responsible for the monetary policies of the member states whose currency is the euro, the CAP and the common fisheries policy. In these areas, the EU governments no longer have power to make policy at the national level.

Next, a range of policies are 'shared' between the European and national levels, where EU policies generally supplement existing or ongoing policies at the national level, for example in the areas of labour market regulation, regional spending or immigration and asylum. The third area of policies is best described as the 'coordinated competences', in that these are policies where primary competence remains at the national level, but the national governments have accepted that they need to coordinate their domestic policies collectively at the European level because there are spill-over effects on each other from keeping

Box 1.1   *Key dates in the development of the EU*

18 February 1951	Belgium, France, Germany, Italy, Luxembourg, and the Netherlands sign Treaty of Paris, launching the European Coal and Steel Community
23 July 1952	Treaty of Paris enters into force
1 January 1958	Treaties of Rome enter into force, establishing the European Economic Community and the European Atomic Energy Community (Euratom)
30 July 1962	CAP starts
5 February 1963	*Van Gend en Loos* ruling of the ECJ, establishes the 'direct effect' of EEC law
15 July 1964	*Costa* v. *ENEL* ruling of the ECJ, establishes the 'supremacy' of EEC law
29 January 1966	Luxembourg compromise, which effectively means Council must decide unanimously
1 July 1967	Merger Treaty, establishes a single set of institutions for the three communities
1 July 1968	EEC 'customs union' starts
1–2 December 1969	Hague Summit, governments agree to push for further economic and political integration
1 January 1973	Denmark, Ireland, and the United Kingdom join
27 October 1970	Governments start foreign policy cooperation (European Political Cooperation – EPC)
10 February 1979	*Cassis de Dijon* ruling of the ECJ, establishes 'mutual recognition' in the provision of goods and services in the common market
13 March 1979	European Monetary System (EMS) begins
7–10 June 1979	First 'direct' elections of the European Parliament
1 January 1981	Greece joins
26 June 1984	Margaret Thatcher negotiates the 'British rebate' from the annual budget
1 January 1985	First 'European Communities' passports are issued
1 January 1986	Portugal and Spain join
19 May 1986	European flag used for the first time
1 July 1987	Single European Act enters into force, launching the single market programme

→

these policies at the national level. For example, for the states with a single currency there is a need to coordinate macroeconomic policies, and with the freedom of movement of persons there is a need to co-ordinate some policing and criminal justice policies. Finally, all the major areas of taxation and public spending, such as health care, housing, welfare provision, and pensions remain the exclusive preserve of the member states, with very little EU interference in how these policies are managed.

➜

13 February 1988	First multi-annual framework for the EU budget agreed
9 November 1989	Berlin Wall falls
1 January 1993	Single European Market starts
1 November 1993	Maastricht Treaty enters into force, launching the EU and the plan for EMU
21 July 1994	European Parliament rejects a piece of EU legislation for the first time
1 January 1995	Austria, Finland, and Sweden join
1 January 1999	EMU starts
1 May 1999	Amsterdam Treaty enters into force, starting the 'area of freedom, security and justice'
15 March 1999	Santer Commission resigns before a censure vote is held in the European Parliament
24 March 2000	European Council agrees the 'Lisbon strategy' to promote growth and productivity
1 January 2002	Euro notes and coins replace national notes and coins for 10 member states
1 February 2003	Nice Treaty enters into force, launching defence cooperation and reforming the institutions in preparation for enlargement
1 May 2004	Cyprus, Czech Republic, Estonia, Hungary, Latvia, Lithuania, Malta, Poland, Slovakia, and Slovenia join
26 October 2004	European Parliament blocks the election of a new Commission
29 October 2004	Treaty establishing a Constitution for Europe signed
2 December 2004	First EU military operation, in Bosnia and Herzegovina
29 May and 1 June 2005	Constitution rejected in referendums in France and the Netherlands
1 January 2007	Bulgaria and Romania join
1 December 2009	Lisbon Treaty enters into force, establishes inter alia a permanent President of the European Council

Turning to the institutions, Box 1.3 describes the institutional set-up. Most regulatory policies as well as some expenditure policies, macro-economic policies, and interior policies (on asylum and immigration) are adopted through supranational processes: where the Commission is the executive (with a monopoly on policy initiative); legislation is adopted through a bicameral procedure (the ordinary legislative procedure) between the Council and the European Parliament (and the Council usually acts by qualified-majority voting – QMV); and law is directly

Box 1.2   *Policy architecture of the EU*

Exclusive EU competences
Regulation of the single market, including removing barriers and
    competition policy
Customs union and external trade policies
Monetary policy for the member states whose currency is the euro
Price setting and subsidy of production under the CAP
Common fisheries policy

Shared EU and member state competences
Social regulation, such as health and safety at work, gender equality, and
    non-discrimination
Environmental regulation
Consumer protection and common public health concerns, such as food
    safety
Economic, social, and territorial cohesion
Free movement of persons, including policies towards third-country
    nationals (e.g. asylum)
Transport
Energy

Coordinated competences
(where member states coordinate their domestic policies at the EU level
    because of the effects on each other of conducting separate policies)
Macroeconomic policies
Foreign and defence policies
Policing and criminal justice policies
Health, cultural, education, tourism, youth, sport, and vocational training
    policies

Exclusive member state competences
All other policies, for example most areas of taxation and public spending

effective and supreme over national law and the ECJ has full powers of
judicial review and legal adjudication.

Meanwhile, most macroeconomic policies and foreign policies and
some expenditure policies (the multiannual framework programme) and
interior policies (on police and judicial cooperation) are adopted through
intergovernmental processes: where the Council is the main executive
and legislative body (and the Council usually acts by unanimity); the
Commission can generate policy ideas but its agenda-setting powers are
limited; the European Parliament only has the right to be consulted by
the Council; and the ECJ's powers of judicial review are restricted.

Turning to politics in the EU, there are two main types of intermediary associations that connect the public to the EU policy process. First,

political parties are the central political organizations in all modern democratic systems. Parties are organizations of like-minded political leaders who join forces to promote a particular policy agenda, seek public support for this agenda, and capture political office in order to implement this agenda. Political parties have influence in each of the EU institutions. National parties compete for national governmental office, and the winners of this competition are represented in the Council. European Commissioners are also partisan politicians: they have spent their careers in national party organizations, owe their positions to nomination by and the support of national party leaders, and usually seek to return to the party political fray. Members of the European Parliament (MEPs) are elected every five years in 'direct' elections to the European Parliament. Once elected, the MEPs sit as transnational 'political groups' in the European Parliament, which promotes political organization and competition in the EU legislative process.

Second, interest groups are voluntary associations of individual citizens, such as trade unions, business associations, consumer groups, and environmental groups. These organizations are formed to promote or protect the interest of their members in the political process. This is the same in the EU as in any democratic system. National interest groups lobby national governments or approach the EU institutions directly, and like-minded interest groups from different member states join forces to lobby the Commission, Council working groups and MEPs. Interest groups also give funds to political parties to represent their views in national and EU politics. In each policy area, public office holders and representatives from interest groups form 'policy networks' to thrash out policy compromises. And, by taking legal actions to national courts and the ECJ, interest groups influence the application of EU law.

The quasi-constitutional policy and institutional architecture is highly stable. To understand why consider Figure 1.1, which plots the approximate location of the major EU treaties on two dimensions: (1) the x-axis represents the *degree of policy integration* resulting from a treaty, in terms of the number and significance of the policy competences that have been handed to the European level, either as exclusive competences, or shared competences, or coordinated competences; and (2) the y-axis represents the *extent of supranational decision-making* resulting from a treaty, in terms of the proportion of EU policy competences that are governed by supranational decision-making procedures, where the Commission is the agenda-setter, the Council decides by QMV, the Council shares legislative authority with the European Parliament, and the ECJ has jurisdiction.

The Treaty of Rome aimed to be a highly supranational treaty, but after the 1966 Luxembourg compromise between the heads of government of the then six states, in practice the policies that were contained in

Box 1.3 *Institutional architecture of the EU*

Council of the European Union, and the European Council (Brussels)
The Council of the EU is composed of ministers from the member states' governments. The Council is *a legislative and an executive body*. On the legislative side, the Council adopts EU legislation and the budget. On the executive side, the Council coordinates the broad economic policy goals of the member states, concludes international agreements of the EU, co-ordinates CFSP and police and judicial cooperation, and proposes reforms to the EU treaties. On most legislative issues the Council decides by a system of weighted majority voting (QMV), whereas on most executive issues the Council decides by unanimous vote. The highest meeting of the Council is the European Council, which brings together the heads of state and government of the EU and meets four times a year. The Presidency of the Council rotates every six months between the member states, but the President of the European Council is a two-and-half-year appointment, renewable once. Herman Van Rompuy became the first President of the European Council in December 2009.

European Commission (Brussels)
The Commission is composed of one member from each member state and is the *main executive body* of the EU. The Commission is responsible for proposing EU legislation, managing and implementing EU policies and the budget, enforcing EU law (jointly with the ECJ), and representing the EU on the international stage (for example in the WTO). The administration of the Commission is divided into Directorates-General, each of which is responsible for a different area of EU policy. Approximately 25,000 people are employed in the Commission's administration. Following each European Parliament election, the Commission President is nominated by a qualified-majority vote in the European Council and accepted or rejected by a simple-majority vote in the European Parliament. The other members of the Commission are then nominated by each EU government and approved by a qualified majority in the European Council and a simple majority in the European Parliament. José Manuel Barroso, the conservative former Prime Minister of Portugal, was re-elected for a second five-year term as Commission President in 2009.

European Parliament (Brussels, Strasbourg, and Luxembourg)
There are 736 MEPs, who are elected every five years by the EU citizens, and organize together in transnational political groups. The Parliament is

→

the treaty were adopted via unanimous agreement between the heads of government rather than via supranational decision-making. The Single European Act (SEA) was a major step on the other dimension. Rather than adding many new competences, the main innovations in the SEA were on the institutional side: the delegation of new agenda-setting powers to the Commission to initiate over 300 pieces of legislation to half of the EU's **legislative authority** (jointly with the Council). The Parliament amends and adopts EU legislation and the budget, and monitors the work of the other EU institutions. The Parliament has the power to approve or reject the nominated Commission President and the team of Commissioners, and also has the right to censure the Commission as a whole (by a two-thirds majority vote). The Parliament holds committee and party meetings in Brussels and plenary sessions in Strasbourg and Brussels, and part of the Parliament's secretariat is in Luxembourg.

European Court of Justice (Luxembourg)
The ECJ, together with the national courts, is the **judicial authority** of the EU. The ECJ ensures that EU legislation is interpreted and applied in the same way in all member states and undertakes judicial review of the treaties, secondary legislation, and tertiary instruments of the EU. The ECJ is composed of one judge per member state, however it rarely sits as the full court, but instead sits as a Grand Chamber of 13 judges or in chambers of 5 or 3 judges. The ECJ is assisted by 8 advocates general. The judges and advocates general are appointed for a renewable 6-year term by the EU governments. The President of the Court is chosen by the judges to serve for a renewable 3-year term. Vassilios Skouris (from Greece) has been President of the Court since 2003. To help the Court cope with the large number of cases brought before it, it is assisted by the Court of First Instance (CFI).

Other institutions
The **European Central Bank** (Frankfurt) is responsible for monetary policy, including setting interest rates for the European single currency (the euro).

The **European Court of Auditors** (Luxembourg) checks that EU funds are properly collected and spent legally, economically, and for their intended purpose.

The **Committee of the Regions** (Brussels) represents regions and local authorities in the member states in the EU policy-making process.

The EU also has more than 35 other **agencies**, which include the European Investment Bank (Luxembourg), the European Environment Agency (Copenhagen), the European Food Safety Authority (Parma), the European Medicines Agency (London), the European Monitoring Centre on Racism and Xenophobia (Vienna), the European Defence Agency (Brussels), and the European Police Office (The Hague).

complete the single market; the extension of QMV in the Council; and new legislative powers for the European Parliament, under the new 'cooperation procedure'.

The Treaty on European Union (TEU, or the Maastricht Treaty), consolidated the SEA. The new policy competences in the treaty included a three-stage plan for Economic and Monetary Union (EMU), and new

Figure 1.1   *Progress towards equilibrium?*

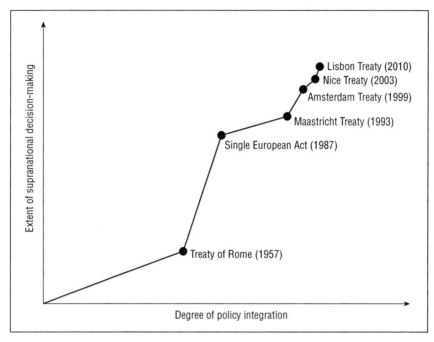

Note: The 'degree of policy integration' is an approximate measure of the number and significance of the policy competences that are covered by the EU. The 'extent of supranational decision-making' is an approximate measure of the proportion of EU policy competences that are governed by supranational decision-making procedures; where the Commission is the agenda-setter, the Council decides by QMV, the Council shares legislative authority with the European Parliament, and the ECJ has jurisdiction.

frameworks for policies on Justice and Home Affairs (JHA) and CFSP. However, this time, the institutional rules in these new policy areas were predominantly intergovernmental, with weak agenda-setting powers for the Commission, decision-making by unanimity in the Council, consultation rather than legislative powers for the European Parliament, and weak or no judicial review powers for the ECJ. The Maastricht Treaty also replaced the cooperation procedure with the co-decision procedure, which further increased the powers of the European Parliament.

The Amsterdam Treaty focused on institutional rather than policy reform: extending supranational decision-making in the new 'area of freedom security and justice', which covered many of the policies on the free movement of persons that were under the intergovernmental JHA pillar in the Maastricht Treaty; and reforming and extending the co-decision procedure, which significantly increased the legislative powers of the European Parliament.

The main objective of the Nice Treaty was to reform the EU institutions in preparation for the accession of 12 new member states from Central, Eastern, and Southern Europe. Nevertheless, the institutional changes in the Nice Treaty were relatively modest, relating mainly to how QMV worked in the Council. Meanwhile, on the policy side, the Nice Treaty added defence policy as an EU competence for the first time, as part of the new ESDP. As with the CFSP provisions, however, decision-making in this area remained intergovernmental.

Finally, the Lisbon Treaty, compared to the previous treaties, is relatively insignificant in terms of institutional or policy reform. On the institutional side, the Nice Treaty simplified the voting system in the Council, introduced a new permanent President of the European Council, and created a new position of High Representative for the Union in Foreign Affairs and Security Policy. The Lisbon Treaty also mad the co-decision procedure the 'ordinary legislative procedure', which is now used for adopting most EU laws. However, unlike the previous EU treaties, these institutional reforms aimed to improve the efficiency of the institutions rather than change the balance of power between the main institutions. For example, the Amsterdam Treaty extended the powers of the European Parliament and QMV in the Council into more policy areas than the Lisbon Treaty.

On the policy side, the Lisbon Treaty incorporated the Charter of Fundamental Rights into the EU Treaty for the first time. However, the ECJ already referred to the Charter before its incorporation by the Lisbon Treaty. The Lisbon Treaty extended supranational decision-making in the area of interior policies, mainly on asylum and immigration. And, in the area of foreign policy, the Lisbon Treaty established a European diplomatic service: the European External Action Service. However, these are relatively modest policy changes compared to the SEA, the Maastricht Treaty and the Amsterdam Treaty, and the only genuinely new policy competence in the Lisbon Treaty is in the area of space exploration!

In sum, every time the EU embarked on a new set of treaty reforms, there were expectations (or fears) that a new agreement would be a major step towards further European integration. The truth is rather different. Broadly speaking, every new treaty has ended up being less ambitious than the previous one. The reason for this is quite simple: the EU has gradually got closer and closer towards a 'constitutional equilibrium'. The basic policy architecture of the EU now has a certain coherent logic. First, the EU level is responsible for creating and regulating a single market on a continental scale, while taxing and spending remain mainly at the national level. Second, the EU governments coordinate a range of policies (from foreign policies, to economic policies, to immigration policies) that affect the free movement of goods, services, capital, and labour in the single market and their collective interests as a continental-scale polity. In the former policy areas, supranational mechanisms, via an independent Commission, QMV in the Council, and the checks and balances of the European Parliament and the ECJ, are the most effective way of making policies for the single market. In the later policy areas, intergovernmental mechanisms ensure the protection of national interests in the adoption of highly salient policies (such as tax issues) and in the coordination of domestic economic and security policies.

As new member states have joined the EU it has become more and more difficult to reach unanimous agreement on which new policies should be added to the EU or how the balance of power between the EU institutions should be changed. However, even if there were fewer member states, the new institutional and policy architecture would be highly stable, as almost no member state wishes to change the basic balance of power between the EU and the member states or between the EU institutions in any major way. As a result, the focus of the EU in the next decade is likely to shift from treaty reform to what can be done within the established institutional and policy framework.

What is the EU? A Political System but not a State

Having described the EU's institutions and policies, what exactly is the EU? Is it an international organization, like the United Nations or the World Trade Organization (WTO), or is it a federal state, like the United States of America? The EU does not fit either of these categories very well. Unlike other international organizations, the EU has delegated significant independent executive, legislative, and judicial powers, rather like a state. However, unlike federal states, the member state governments remain the sovereign signatories of the EU Treaty, the budget of the EU remains small, the EU relies on the voluntary compliance of the member states for the enforcement of EU law, and the member states remain sovereign in many areas of policy, including the ability to sign international treaties.

Thankfully, there is another category we can use to conceptualize the EU: as a political system. Gabriel Almond (1956) and David Easton (1957) were the first to develop formal frameworks for defining and analysing political systems. They defined a political system as having four key characteristics:

1   There is a stable and clearly defined set of institutions for collective decision-making and a set of rules governing relations between and within these institutions.
2   Citizens seek to realize their political desires through the political system, either directly or through intermediary organizations such as interest groups and political parties.

3 Collective decisions in the political system have a significant impact on the distribution of economic resources and the allocation of values across the whole system.
4 There is continuous interaction between these political outputs, new demands on the system, new decisions, and so on.

The EU possesses all these characteristics. First, the degree of institutional stability and complexity in the EU is far greater than in any other international regime, as we have discussed.

Second, as the EU institutions have taken on these powers of government, an increasing number of groups attempt to make demands on the system – ranging from individual corporations and business associations to trade unions, environmental and consumer groups and political parties. The groups with the most powerful and institutionalized position in the EU are the governments of the member states. At face value, the centrality of governments in the system makes the EU seem like other international organizations. However, the governments do not have a monopoly on political demands. As in all democratic polities, demands in the EU arise from a complex network of public and private groups, each competing to influence the EU policy process to protect their own interests.

Third, EU decisions are highly significant and are felt throughout the EU. For example:

- EU policies cover a wide range of areas, including market regulation, social policy, the environment, agriculture, regional policy, research and development, policing and law and order, citizenship, human rights, international trade, foreign policy, defence, consumer affairs, transport, public health, education, and culture.
- Approximately 150 pieces of legislation pass through the EU institutions every year – more than in most other democratic polities.
- Primary and secondary acts of the EU are part of the 'the law of the land' in the member states, and supranational EU law is supreme over national law.
- The EU budget may be small (at about 1 per cent of total EU GDP) compared with the budgets of national governments, but several EU member states receive almost 5 per cent of their national GDP from the EU budget.
- EU regulatory and monetary policies have a powerful indirect impact on the distribution of power and resources between individuals, groups and nations in Europe.
- The EU is gradually encroaching on the power of the domestic states to set their own rules in the highly contentious areas of taxation, immigration, policing, foreign, and defence policy.

In short, EU outputs have a significant impact on the 'authoritative allocation of values' (Easton, 1957) and also determine 'who gets what,
when and how' in European society (Lasswell, 1936).

Finally, the political process of the EU political system is a permanent
feature of political life in Europe. The quarterly meetings of the heads of
government of the member states (in the European Council) may be the
only feature of the system that is noticed by many citizens. This can give
the impression that the EU mainly operates through periodic 'summitry',
like other international organizations. However, the real essence of EU
politics lies in the constant interactions within and between the EU institutions in Brussels, between national governments and Brussels, within
the various departments in national governments, in bilateral meetings
between governments, and between private interests and governmental
officials in Brussels and at the national level. Hence, unlike other international organizations, EU business is conducted in multiple settings on
virtually every day of the year.

What is interesting, nevertheless, is that the EU does not have a
'monopoly on the legitimate use of coercion'. The EU is not a 'state' in
the traditional Weberian meaning of the word. The power of coercion,
through police and security forces, remains in the hands of the national
governments of the EU member states. The early theorists of the political
system believed that a political system could not exist without a state. As
Almond (1956, p. 395) argued:

> the employment of ultimate, comprehensive, and legitimate physical
> coercion is the monopoly of states, and the political system is uniquely
> concerned with the scope, direction, and conditions affecting the
> employment of this physical coercion.

However, many contemporary social theorists reject this conflation of
the state and the political system. For example, Bertrand Badie and Pierre
Birnbaum (1983, pp. 135–7) argue that:

> the state should rather be understood as a unique phenomenon, an
> innovation developed within a specific geographical and cultural
> context. Hence, it is wrong to look upon the state as the only way of
> governing societies at all times and all places.

In this view, the state is simply a product of a particular structure of political, economic, and social relations in Western Europe between the
sixteenth and mid-twentieth centuries, when a high degree of centralization, universality, and institutionalization was necessary for government to be effective. In a different era and context, government and
politics could be undertaken without the classic apparatus of a state.
This is precisely the situation in the twenty-first century in Europe.

The EU political system is highly decentralized, is based on the voluntary commitment of the member states and its citizens, and relies on sub-organizations (the existing nation-states) to administer coercion and other forms of state power.

Table 1.1 provides some basic political data about the EU member

Table 1.1   *Basic data on the EU*

Member state	Date joined	Socio-economic data			Representation in the EU		
		Pop'n, 2009 (mil.)	GDP, ppp, 2008 ($bn)	GDP/cap, ppp, 2008 ($)	Council votes	Commis- sioners	MEPs
Austria	1995	8.4	318.4	38,153	10	1	17
Belgium	1952	10.7	369.2	34,493	12	1	22
Bulgaria	2007	7.6	94.5	12,394	10	1	17
Cyprus	2004	0.8	21.2	29,853	4	1	6
Czech Republic	2004	10.5	257.7	24,712	12	1	22
Denmark	1973	5.5	201.2	36,604	7	1	13
Estonia	2004	1.3	27.7	20,657	4	1	6
Finland	1995	5.3	188.2	35,426	7	1	13
France	1952	64.1	2,112.4	34,045	29	1	72
Germany	1952	82.1	2,925.2	35,613	29	1	99
Greece	1981	11.3	330.0	29,361	12	1	22
Hungary	2004	10.0	194.0	19,329	12	1	22
Ireland	1973	4.5	197.1	44,195	7	1	12
Italy	1952	60.1	1,840.9	30,756	29	1	72
Latvia	2004	2.3	38.8	17,101	4	1	8
Lithuania	2004	3.4	63.2	18,826	7	1	12
Luxembourg	1952	0.5	38.3	78,559	4	1	6
Malta	2004	0.4	9.4	23,971	3	1	5
Netherlands	1952	16.5	671.7	40,850	13	1	25
Poland	2004	38.1	671.9	17,625	27	1	50
Portugal	1986	10.6	245.2	23,073	12	1	22
Romania	2007	21.5	302.7	14,064	14	1	33
Slovakia	2004	5.4	119.4	22,081	7	1	13
Slovenia	2004	2.1	56.3	27,610	4	1	7
Spain	1986	45.9	1,456.1	31,955	27	1	50
Sweden	1995	9.3	344.7	37,383	10	1	18
United Kingdom	1973	61.6	2,176.3	35,445	29	1	72
EU27		499.7	15,271.7	30,563	345	27	736
China		1,333.6	7,903.2	5,962			
India		1,170.3	3,388.5	2,972			
USA		307.7	14,204.3	46,716			
Brazil		192.0	1,976.6	10,296			
Russia		141.9	2,288.5	16,139			
Japan		127.5	4,354.6	34,099			
Turkey		71.5	1,028.9	13,920			

Sources: Compiled from United Nations, Eurostat, and World Bank.

states and their representation in the EU institutions. As the data show, no member state is either physically, economically, or political powerful enough to dominate the EU.

Two Theories of EU Politics

There are two broad theoretical frameworks for understanding EU politics. The first theoretical framework is known as **intergovernmentalism** (especially Hoffmann, 1966, 1982; Moravcsik, 1991, 1993, 1998; Moravcsik and Nicolaïdis, 1999). The core assumption of this framework is that EU politics is dominated by the member state governments, in general, and the governments of the 'big' member states, in particular (especially Germany, France, and Britain). The governments of the member states have clear 'preferences' about what they want to achieve at the European level in each of the main policy areas of the EU. In the 'liberal' version of this approach, developed by Andrew Moravcsik (1991, 1998), member state preferences can vary across policy areas and over time: for example, a member state can be in favour of more EU policy in a particular area in one period, yet opposed to more EU policy in another area in the same period, or in the same area in a different period. The governments also have substantial resources at their disposal, via their large domestic bureaucracies, and so have good information about the positions of the other actors in EU politics and also what is likely to happen as a result of a particular EU decision.

One of the main propositions of intergovernmentalism is that the member states are careful in what they delegate to the three 'supranational' institutions: the Commission, the European Parliament, and the ECJ. Delegation to these institutions only occurs to further the collective interests of the governments. For example, the governments delegate agenda-setting to the Commission to resolve coordination problems in the adoption of policy, legislative power to the European Parliament to improve the legitimacy of EU decisions or to present a check on the Commission, and adjudication power to the ECJ to resolve a collective action problem in the implementation of EU law. Moreover, because delegation is a conscious and careful process, the supranational institutions are in effect 'agents' of the EU governments rather than powerful independent actors.

Another proposition is that every member state is on average a winner from the process of European integration and EU politics. This does not mean that every member state does equally as well out of the EU. Power balances between the member states are asymmetric, and the member state with the most to lose on a particular issue tends to get what it wants. However, this proposition does suggest that if a member state expects to lose from a treaty reform or a policy decision it would either not agree to that decision or would demand compensation (a side-payment) through some other EU policy, such as the EU budget.

The second theoretical framework is perhaps best labelled the **supra-national politics** approach (see Kohler-Koch and Eising, 1999; Marks *et al.*, 1996; Stone Sweet *et al.*, 2001; Stone Sweet and Sandholtz, 1998). This approach encompasses a wide variety of theoretical traditions and ideas in the study of European integration and EU politics, all of which share a central proposition which pits these ideas collectively against intergovernmentalism: that the governments of the member states do not have it all their own way in the EU.

There are three key interrelated reasons why the governments are not all powerful. First, as the early neo-functionalists argued (e.g. Haas, 1958; Lindberg, 1963), the supranational institutions are not simply passive 'agents' of the governments. Instead, the Commission, the European Parliament, and the ECJ have their own institutional interests, policy preferences, and resources and powers. Private interest groups also play a role in shaping the EU policy agenda, bypassing national governments and going straight to Brussels to provide vital information and support to Commissioners, MEPs, and judges (e.g. Sandholtz and Zysman, 1989).

Second, derived from the rational choice institutionalist approach in political science, 'institutions matter' (e.g. Franchino, 2007; Jupille, 2004; Pollack, 2003; Tsebelis and Garrett, 1996, 2001). What this means is that the rules governing decision-making in the EU shape policy outcomes, sometimes in the way governments can predict and at other times in ways they cannot predict as easily. For example, if QMV is introduced in a particular policy area, the set of policies that can be adopted is increased significantly, and governments can then find themselves unexpectedly on the losing side on a key issue. Similarly, extending the legislative powers of the European Parliament under the co-decision/ordinary legislative procedure, gives new veto- and agenda-setting power to a majority in the European Parliament. This majority may sometimes support the Commission against the governments, at other times might support the governments against the Commission, and at other times still oppose both the Commission and the governments.

Third, actors' positions and the nature of the bargaining space can vary issue by issue, even within the same policy area (Thomson *et al.*, 2006). For example, all the actors in EU decision-making – whether governments in the Council or political parties in the European Parliament – not only have preferences over the speed and nature of European integration but also have views about the political direction of EU policy outcomes. And these political views are perhaps better captured by the 'left–right' dimension of politics than the standard 'national sovereignty vs. European integration' dimension of the traditional intergovernmentalist approach (see Hix, 1994).

Putting these ideas together, a key empirical proposition of the supra-national politics framework is that as a result of the autonomous interests and powers of the Commission, the Parliament and the ECJ, and how the decision-making rules and policy bargains play out over time, EU policy outcomes can be different from the original intentions of the govern-ments. For example, the EU single market has led to more environmental and social regulations than some right-wing politicians expected when they signed the SEA. Put another way, the supranational politics approach predicts that a range of factors produce 'unintended consequences' from the delegation of powers to the EU institutions or from the adoption of new policies at the European level (e.g. Pierson, 1996).

A second proposition deriving from these ideas is that the EU has a 'democratic deficit' (e.g. Føllesdal and Hix, 2006). This deficit results from the fact that as the governments have delegated powers to the European level, policy-making in Brussels has become isolated from domestic public opinion and national parliaments, which has led to a degree of 'policy drift' away from the preferences of some notional European wide average citizen. This proposition is disputed by intergov-ernmentalists, who argue that there is a close connection between the preferences of citizens and EU policy outcomes because the governments are elected by their citizens, and it is the governments who run the EU and keep a tight rein on the EU institutions (e.g. Moravscik, 2002).

The differences between these two approaches to EU politics can easily be overemphasized. Both approaches borrow assumptions and argu-ments from the general study of political science. Both also share a common research method: the use of theoretical assumptions to generate propositions, which are then tested empirically. As a result, deciding which theory is 'right' is not a case of deciding which approache's assumptions about actors, institutions, and information are closest to reality. How good a theory is depends on how much and how efficiently it can explain a particular set of facts. Some theories are more efficient, some are more extensive, and all tend to be good at explaining different things. For example, intergovernmentalism uses some simple assump-tions, and from these assumptions produces a rather persuasive explana-tion of the major treaty bargains. But, this theory seems less able to explain the more complex environment of day-to-day legislative politics in the EU. Meanwhile, supranational politics uses a more complex set of assumptions and seems more able to explain specific policy outcomes. Consequently the power of the theories can only really be judged where they produce clearly identifiable and opposing sets of predictions about the same empirical phenomenon.

This may seem a rather arcane debate. However this overview of the main theoretical positions in EU politics is essential for understanding the intellectual foundations of the more empirically based research covered in the following chapters.

Structure of the Book

The rest of this book introduces and analyses the various aspects of the EU political system. Part I looks at EU government: the structure and politics of the executive (Chapter 2), political organization and bargaining in the EU legislative process (Chapter 3), and judicial politics and the development of an EU constitution (Chapter 4). Part II turns to politics: public opinion (Chapter 5), the role of elections, political parties, and the question of the 'democratic deficit' (Chapter 6), and interest representation (Chapter 7). Part III focuses on policy-making: regulatory policies (Chapter 8), expenditure policies (Chapter 9), economic and monetary union (Chapter 10), interior policies (Chapter 11), and foreign policies (Chapter 12). To create a link with the rest of the discipline, each chapter begins with a review of the general political science literature on the subject of that chapter. Finally, in Chapter 13 the underlying arguments and issues in the book are brought together in a short conclusion.

Part I

Government

Chapter 2

Executive Politics

The governments of the member states of the EU have delegated significant powers of political leadership, policy implementation, and regulation to the Commission. As a result, executive responsibilities are shared between the Council and the Commission. This institutionalized separation of powers, or 'dual executive', can sometimes lead to deadlock. However, consensus and stability are secured through a division of labour, with the Council governing long-term matters and the Commission governing short-term ones, via highly developed mechanisms to manage Commission discretion, and careful involvement of national administrations. To help understand how this division of labour came about and how it works we shall first present the standard framework for understanding executive power, delegation, and discretion in political science.

Theories of Executive Politics

In the classic constitutional framework the legislature decides, the executive enacts and the judiciary adjudicates. However, modern governments do more than simply implement law. Their powers are twofold: political and administrative. Governments use their political power of leadership to steer the society through proposals for policy and legislation, and use their administrative powers to implement law, distribute public revenues, and pass secondary and tertiary rules and regulations.

Some systems concentrate these powers in the hands of one set of office holders. Other systems, like the EU, divide these tasks between different actors and bodies. Political scientists use the 'principal–agent' framework to study delegation of responsibilities to specific actors. In this framework, a principal, the initial holder of executive power, decides to delegate certain powers to an agent who is responsible for carrying out the task.

23

The key challenge for the principal is to ensure that the agent executes the task in a neutral fashion. However, agents have their own interests and policy preferences. First, the agent may be targeted by groups lobbying on behalf of segments of the society affected by the task. If the costs and benefits arising from the task are unevenly distributed, interests that stand to gain or lose may either attempt to 'capture' the agent (Lowi, 1969), or make the agent dependent on their information, or tempt the agent with inducements (such as well-paid jobs in the industry after retirement). Second, agencies may want to increase their own influence over the policy process. According to classical rational choice theory, public officials want to maximize their budget (Niskanan, 1971). Larger budgets allow officials to increase their salaries, employ more staff, and raise their profile. Government agencies compete for limited public resources. They hence overestimate budgetary needs and spend as much as possible. The result is growing demands by bureaucrats for public resources. Third, bureaucrats may be more interested in maximizing their independence from their principals and their ability to shape policy rather than maximize the budget (Dunleavy, 1991). All this means that agents may wish to diverge from the principals' original policy intention. It is hence essential to understand the principal's ability and willingness to limit 'policy drift'.

The principal has two means of controlling how the agent executes the task: selection and control. When selecting an agent, the principal often has to make a choice between choosing an agent with similar preferences to the principal and an agent who is highly competent to carry out the task. One problem the principal faces is that the agent may be able to shift policy away from the policy most preferred (ideal point) by the principal towards the agent's own most preferred policy. Another problem is that the agent may not be sufficiently competent to execute the task in line with the request of the principal (Huber and McCarty, 2004). In an ideal scenario, both of these problems can be solved by selecting a competent agent whose ideal point is identical to that of the principal. In practice, an agent with such characteristics may be impossible to find.

The decision to delegate is often made by a collective body whose actors do not have identical ideal points. Depending on the decision rule (see Chapter 3), all or a subset of actors need to agree upon a policy and the level of delegation. This phenomenon is illustrated in Figure 2.1, which shows a two-dimensional policy space in which there are three governments with 'ideal policy preferences' (points A, B, and C). The Commission's ideal policy preference lies outside the 'core' of governmental preferences (depicted by the triangle). The governments and the Commission will each try to secure a policy that is as close as possible to its ideal point. The governments agree on a piece of legislation at position X. The Commission is responsible for implementing this legislation, and during the implementation it is able to shape the final outcome;

Figure 2.1   *Policy drift by the European Commission*

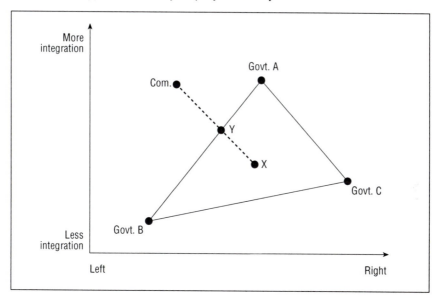

moving the policy away from X towards its ideal policy preference. In fact, the Commission can move the final policy as far as position Y. Governments A and B prefer this policy to the original deal because Y is closer to their ideal preferences than X. If the Commission implements policy Y, governments A and B have no incentive to introduce new legislation to overrule the Commission, and will oppose any attempt by government C to take such action. However, governments A and B will block any moves further towards the Commission's ideal point, as any policy in this direction would be less attractive to these two governments than position Y. Hence, the Commission has discretion to change the original policy outcome, but within the constraints of the preferences of the legislators.

Nevertheless, principals can limit policy drift. When controlling the agent, the principal can employ monitoring devices or constrain the possibility for drift by specifying the delegated task. Monitoring devices may include employing another agent with the task of controlling how the first agent is executing the task. Alternatively, the principal can rely on affected parties, such as interest groups and private citizens, to report such drift. The former approach to control is sometimes labelled 'police-patrol', while the latter approach is sometimes labelled 'fire-alarm' (McCubbins and Schwartz, 1984). By specifying the delegated task the principal can limit the scope for policy drift. The principal can design rules and procedures to minimize agent's discretion (Horn, 1995; Kiewiet and McCubbins, 1991; Moe, 1989). Careful delegation thus implies striking the optimal balance between the cost of policy drift and

Figure 2.2   *Controlling policy drift by restricting discretion*

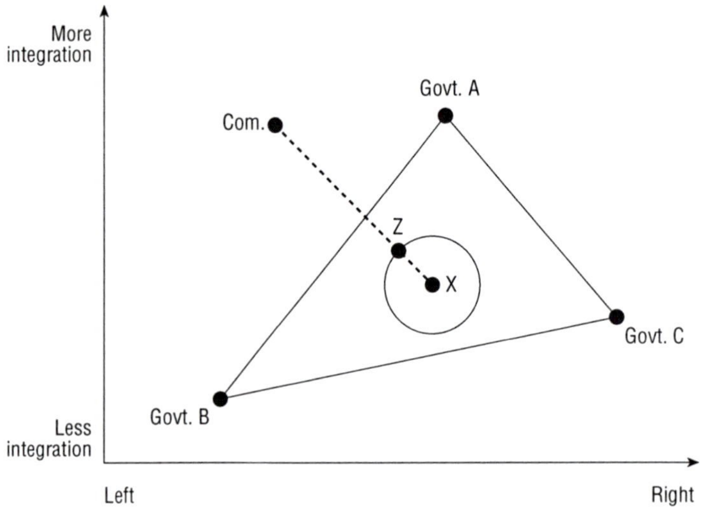

the costs of constraining and controlling the agent (Weingast and Moran, 1983).

The result of such controls is a restriction of the ability of an agent to diverge from the original policy intention. This is illustrated in Figure 2.2. As in Figure 2.1, the governments agree on a piece of legislation at point X, but to limit the ability of the Commission to change the policy outcome, government C, who has most to lose from potential policy drift, forces the other governments to introduce a set of procedures that define exactly how the Commission should go about its job. The result is some drift towards the Commission's ideal point, but only to Z instead of Y.

It can be the case that the agent has access to information which is not available to the principals. This asymmetry is a central feature in recent models of delegation (Epstein and O'Halloran, 1999; Huber and Shipan, 2002). In these models, the agent can use this information to move the policy towards her ideal point when implementing the law, while the principal can limit this possibility by specifying how the law shall be implemented. Once the principal has chosen the policy and the limits for policy drift, the agent decides whether to implement the law or risk punishment for failure to do so.

Franchino (2007) amends this framework to apply it to the dual executive nature of EU. His central premise is that EU legislators can rely on two agents to implement EU legislation: the Commission and the national bureaucracies. When deciding whether to delegate to the Commission or to national administrations, EU governments trade the risk that the Commission may drift away from the agreed policy against the risk that national bureaucracies may implement the legislation differently. The choice is then between a common policy which differs from the policy agreed by the governments and a variation in how EU policies will be implemented in each member state. How the governments decide the balance on this trade-off depends on the complexity of the policy issue as well as the divergence in the policy preferences of the governments. The more complex a policy issue is, the more the governments are likely to favour delegation to national bureaucracies, because they tend to have more administrative resources than the Commission. The more divergent the policy preferences of the governments, the more the governments are concerned that delegation to the Commission will lead to policy drift. As a result, if a policy issue is decided by unanimity (such as taxation), governments prefer to delegate to their national administrations, knowing that once a decision has been made it will be difficult to change. On the other hand, if a policy issue is decided by a qualified majority (such as many of the rules in the single market), governments will be willing to delegate to the Commission, knowing that they will be able to reform the legislation if the Commission changes the policy beyond their original intention.

In sum, the degree of autonomy that executive agents are given by their principals depends on the nature of the tasks in question, the institutional rules under which they operate, the degree of policy disagreement between the principals, as well as the amount of information the principals have on the likely actions of the agents (Tsebelis, 1999, 2002). All these elements are central to the relationship between the Council and the Commission in the EU (Franchino, 2004; Moravcsik, 1999; Pollack, 2003; Tallberg, 2000).

The Member States: Executive Power, Delegation, and Discretion

In this section, we first discuss how the member states have made certain trade-offs in Intergovernmental Conferences. Second, we discuss political leadership in the EU and member states' choices of whether to delegate power to the Commission or national administrations. Third, we explain the pattern of implementation and transposition of EU legislation.

Delegation and intergovernmental conferences

The signing of treaties and their subsequent reform are the result of careful bargaining and agreement between the member state governments in Intergovernmental Conferences (IGCs) (Christiansen and Reh, 2009;

Moravcsik, 1998). The requirement of unanimity in IGCs tends to produce 'lowest common denominator' treaty bargains. However, the process of European integration has been able to proceed because different governments have placed different emphasis on different issues, and hence have been prepared to 'lose' on some issues in return for 'winning' on the issues that are more important to their national interests. The resulting package deals have gradually added new competences to the EU and delegated increasing executive powers to the Commission (Christiansen *et al.*, 2002; Greve and Jørgensen, 2002). In line with the delegation framework presented above, the tasks facing the governments in IGCs are to decide which tasks to delegate to a common agent and to strike a balance between the need to ensure that a common policy is implemented across the EU while limiting the scope for policy drift. Throughout the history of EU integration, governments have struck this balance differently across policies and time, depending on the bundle of issues that were on the negotiating table (Moravcsik, 1993, 1998).

The Treaty of Paris (signed in 1951 and entered into force in 1952), which established the European Coal and Steel Community (ECSC), was essentially a deal between France and Germany. In return for lifting discriminatory rules on German industry, France sought a framework for planned production and distribution in its own coal and steel industry. To secure these aims, the member state governments delegated certain powers to a new supranational body: the High Authority, the precursor of the Commission. Robert Schuman and Jean Monnet were the brains behind this idea. The common production and distribution of coal and steel could have been governed through meetings of ministers of the member governments, but Schuman and Monnet argued that such intergovernmental arenas would suffer from procrastination, indecision and disagreement, as each government would defend its own interests. Consequently, they proposed that decision-making efficiency could best be guaranteed by delegating the responsibility for generating policy ideas and for the day-to-day management of policy to a supranational body (Haas, 1958, pp. 451–85; Monnet, 1978). This combination of intergovernmental decision-making with policy initiation and management by a supranational executive – the so-called 'Monnet method' – provided the model for future treaties (Parsons, 2002; Rittberger, 2001).

The Treaty of Rome (signed in 1957 and entered into force in 1958) established the European Economic Community (EEC) and the European Atomic Energy Community (Euratom). In the EEC, the central bargain was between the German goal of a common market and the French goal of protection for agricultural products, through the Common Agricultural Policy (CAP) (Lindberg, 1963). Again, to achieve these aims the EEC Treaty delegated policy initiation in the common market and administration of the CAP to the Commission. A further innovation of the Treaty of Rome was a legislative procedure – known as the consultation procedure – that made it easier for the Council to accept a Commission proposal than to overturn it. This rule allowed the new supranational executive significant 'agenda-setting' powers in the establishment of rules governing the common market (see Chapter 3). In other words, the governments allowed the Commission a somewhat broader scope for policy drift in order to enable more common policies.

The package in the Single European Act (SEA) (signed in 1986 and entered into force in 1987) centred on the economic goal of establishing a 'single market' by 31 December 1992 in return for new social and environmental 'flanking policies' (Budden, 2002; Garrett, 1992; Hoffmann, 1989; Moravcsik, 1991). This time, the Commission had played an important leadership role by detailing how the single market could be achieved and by preparing the treaty reforms (Sandholtz and Zysman, 1989; Dehousse and Majone, 1994; Christiansen *et al.*, 2002). The reward was new responsibilities for the Commission: to initiate a large body of legislation to establish the single market; to propose and implement common environmental, health and safety, and social standards; to prepare the reform of the structural funds; and to draft a plan for economic and monetary union (EMU). Moreover, to enable the single market programme to be completed by the 1992 deadline, the decision-making rules of the European Community (EC) were amended to strengthen the agenda-setting powers of the Commission: through more QMV in the Council and a new legislative procedure, the cooperation procedure. Finally, the SEA introduced provisions for intergovernmental cooperation in foreign policy, known as European Political Cooperation (EPC), but in this area the member state governments decided that executive authority should be held by the Council. This substantive increase in policies and discretion delegated to the Commission came as a result of the failure to create a functioning common market with the earlier arrangements, and the perceived competitive disadvantage of the European economies vis-à-vis the US and Japan. The governments were hence re-evaluating their trade-off between the need to establish credible common policies and the risk of increased policy drift. The governments needed not only a new initiative, but also a scapegoat for unpopular, but required, policy reforms. By delegating a substantive degree of agenda-setting power and changing the decision-rule to QMV across many policy areas, governments were more concerned with winning the next national election than the long-term policy implications, and could blame the EU for unpopular policy decisions while taking credit for popular decisions.

The Treaty on European Union (the Maastricht Treaty, agreed in 1991 and entered into force in 1993) institutionalized the Commission-brokered plan for EMU. In return, more funds were promised for cohesion policies, EU social policy was strengthened, new health, education, transport, and consumer protection policies were added, and EU 'citizenship' was established (Falkner, 2002; Moravcsik, 1993; Sandholtz, 1993). The Commission was again delegated the responsibility of initiating legislation and managing these policies. However, the Council refused to delegate executive powers to the Commission in two new 'pillars' that were separate from the main EC pillar: the second pillar, on a common foreign and security policy (CFSP), which replaced EPC; and the third pillar, on justice and home affairs (JHA), which aimed to achieve the 'free movement of persons' in the EU. The Maastricht Treaty also introduced a new legislative procedure, the co-decision procedure, which weakened the agenda-setting powers of the Commission (see Chapter 3).

The main policy innovation in the Amsterdam Treaty (signed in 1997 and entered into force in 1999), was the transfer of the provisions for establishing the free movement of persons to the EC part of the EU Treaty (McDonagh, 1998; Moravcsik and Nicolaïdis, 1998). The member state governments accepted that the JHA provisions in the Maastricht Treaty had failed, partly due to the lack of political leadership. To solve this, the governments again agreed to delegate policy initiation rights in this area to the Commission (while allowing policies also to be initiated by the governments). However, similar arguments about the lack of development of CFSP did not result in new Commission powers in this field. Instead, the governments delegated responsibility for policy ideas and the monitoring of CFSP issues to a new 'task force' located in the Council secretariat.

The Nice Treaty (signed in 2001 and entered into force in 2003) mainly aimed to reform the EU institutions in preparation for the accession of Central, Eastern, and Southern European countries (Galloway, 2001). Nevertheless, there were some policy changes, particularly in the area of defence policy. Defence was formally established as an EU competence for the first time, as an integral part of the provisions on a European Security and Defence Policy (ESDP). As with the CFSP provisions, policy initiation, agenda-setting, decision-making, and implementation in the area of defence were kept well away from the Commission.

Finally, the Lisbon Treaty (signed in 2007 and entered into force 2010) formalized the allocation of policy competences between the member states and the EU in a 'catalogue of competences'. The Lisbon Treaty also reformed the decision-making rules within and between the governments and the Commission: such as the weighting of votes in the Council, and two new leadership offices (a permanent President of the European Council and a High Representative for Foreign and Security Policy).

In other words, the development of the EU treaties is a story of selective delegation of political and administrative powers by the governments to the Commission. Treaty reform is a blunt instrument. When signing treaties, governments cannot predict the precise implications of treaty provisions and new decision-making rules, or exactly how the Commission will behave when granted new powers. For example, few member states were able to perfectly foresee the precise implications of the new decision-making rules in the Treaty of Rome and the Single European Act (Tsebelis and Kreppel, 1998). Moreover, once certain powers have been delegated through this mechanism, they may be difficult to overturn in subsequent treaty reforms as at least one member state may benefit from Commission discretion. This, Pierson (1996) argues, leads to long-term 'unintended consequences' of delegation by the member states and policy drift by the Commission.

However, the history of EU Treaty reform suggests that the member state governments are able to rein in the Commission as their evaluation of the trade-off between the need for common policies versus the risk of policy drift changes. With the extensive delegation of agenda-setting to the Commission in the Single European Act, the member states experienced the day-to-day implications of these powers in the construction of the single market. As a result, in Maastricht, Amsterdam, and Nice, the governments were more reluctant to hand over agenda-setting in new or highly sensitive policy areas, and reformed the legislative procedures to restrict the agenda-setting powers of the Commission in those areas where policy initiative had already been delegated to the Commission.

There are several possible explanations of the outcomes of IGCs. First, one approach is to assume that all member states have equal voting power in IGCs (Brams and Affuso, 1985; Hosli, 1995; Widgren, 1994, 1995). A second approach is to assume that only the big member states matter, and hence focus on the preferences of Germany, France, and the UK (Moravcsik, 1998). A third approach, building on the two-level games framework (Putnam, 1988), emphasizes how expected difficulties in the national ratification process binds the hands of some governments to a larger extent than other governments (Hug and König, 2002; König and Hug, 2000). Fourth, spatial models of negotiations suggest that the relative positions of the actors vis-à-vis the existing institutional and policy set-up (status quo) determine who wins and loses in treaty negotiations (König and Slapin, 2004). Because the status quo (the outcome if there is no new agreement) is the current treaty, actors located closer to the status quo tend to win more often than actors who would like more radical policy or institutional change. Slapin (2006) tests these alternative theories of bargaining in IGCs on data from the Amsterdam Treaty negotiations. He finds that all actors are not equally able to 'win', but it is not only the bigger member states who matter. Instead, proximity to the status quo and domestic ratification constraints of certain governments best explain the outcomes in the Amsterdam Treaty.

Political leadership and delegation

The treaties provide the general framework for the division of power and policy competences in the EU (see Chapter 1). Basically, the European Council (the heads of government) sets the guidelines and objectives for the Commission and monitors how the Commission implements these guidelines. The European Council also executes CFSP and macroeconomic policies, agrees the multi-annual budgetary framework, and can adopt new policy competences for the EU. The medium term political leadership of the EU lies in the hands of the European Council in general and the President of the European Council in particular. Meeting at least four times a year, the European Council provides guidance for the work of the meetings of the Council (of ministers) and invites the Commission to develop policy initiatives in particular areas, and monitors the domestic policies of the member states.

The Lisbon Treaty created a separation between the Presidency of the Council and the President of the European Council. While the Presidency of the Council rotates on a six-monthly basis and has a mainly legislative role (see Chapter 3), the European Council elects its President for a renewable two-and-a-half-year term. The first European Council President, elected in December 2009, was Herman Van Rompuy, a former Prime Minister of Belgium. It is not yet clear whether the President is meant to be the chief executive of the EU, or a silent consensus broker, operating behind the scenes at European Council gatherings. Some of the early candidates for the post, such as former British Prime Minister Tony Blair and former Swedish Foreign Minister Carl Bildt would have been suitable for the former type of role, but the choice of Van Rompuy may indicate that some governments prefer the President to take the latter role.

In other words, it is likely that the role of the President of the European Council will be mainly political rather than administrative: focusing on resolving high-profile political disputes among the heads of government, rather than getting involved in day-to-day management of the relationship between the governments and the Commission. In contrast, the Presidency of the Council (of ministers) will continue to play both a political and an administrative role. The member state holding the rotating Council Presidency is responsible for ensuring the smooth running of Council meetings, and providing a six-monthly work programme.

The next chapter focuses in detail on how the legislative process works. From the point of view of executive politics, though, one of the key issues when legislating is who should be responsible for implementing policy: the Commission, or national administrations. Delegation to national administrations benefits individual member states as it allows for control over how legislation is implemented in their own country, and allows them to rely on the policy competences of their national bureaucracies. However, if member states would like to see common EU legislation, the reliance on national bureaucracies increases the risk that a member state will see that it is in its interest to not implement the legislation properly if there is a cost involved. This may be the case for several member states, which leads to a classic coordination problem, where no member state implements the legislation, and nobody reaps the benefit of a common policy. This coordination problem can be solved be delegating more power over the implementation process to the Commission, as the Commission would like to see legislation implemented equally in all member states. A similar justification for involving the Commission in implementation is that, although all member states prefer to implement the legislation, they differ in their preferences over how to implement the legislation.

Transposition of EU legislation

The member states are responsible for transposing EU directives into national law by a certain deadline and in compliance with the adopted statutes. The Commission may take non-complying member states to the ECJ for infringement (see Chapter 4). For member states to comply with EU law they need to have the bureaucratic capacity to implement the legislation in a timely and correct manner (Börzel, 2000). However, despite their comparatively weak administrations, the new member states from Central and Eastern Europe have largely been able to incorporate the full body of EU law into national legislation (Toshkov, 2007). It is, hence, not obvious that it is the capacity of national administrations that is the key factor in explaining varying transposition rates between member states. Across all member states, new EU legislation is more likely to be delayed than legislation which amends existing directives or regulations. Also, deadlines for implementation have a positive effect as it focuses the attention of the national administrations. Policy complexity, however, tends to delay transposition (Luetgert and Dannwolf, 2009).

Several political factors also play a role. Zhelyazkova and Torenvlied (2009) find, for example, that policy conflict within the Council may speed up the transposition process while more freedom to set domestic rules (discretion) slows down the transposition process. On the other hand, König and Luetgert (2009) find that conflict in the Council increases the chance of infringement notification against a member state. Meanwhile, divergent policy preferences between parties in a coalition government in a member state further delays the transposition of directives (*ibid.*; Toshkov, 2008).

The choice of monitoring strategy adopted at the national level also matters. In social policy, for example, Jensen (2007) finds that oversight procedures that concentrate power in the hands of the national bureaucracy (a police patrol mechanism) strengthen the ability of member states to solve infringement cases. He also suggests that member states that reduce their reliance on interest-group participation (a fire alarm mechanism) can improve their ability to solve infringement cases. However, because reliance on interest-group participation is less costly than building up the capacity if national administrations, member states may prefer to risk reduced ability to solve their infringement cases.

In sum, when deciding how and when to implement a directive, the member state governments weigh the costs associated with correct implementation against the costs associated with failure or delays in the implementation process. As the member states would in principle like to see EU law not only correctly implemented but also similar across all the other member states, they have delegated oversight powers to the Commission. But, the executive role of the Commission is not limited to this role. The next section explains the broader role of the Commission in the executive politics of the EU.

Government by the Commission

The Commission has several responsibilities:

- to propose policy ideas for the medium-term development of the EU;
- to initiate legislation and arbitrate in the legislative process;
- to represent the EU in bilateral and multilateral trade negotiations;
- to issue rules and regulations, for example on competition policy;
- to manage the EU budget; and
- to scrutinize the implementation of the primary treaty articles and secondary legislation.

To carry out these responsibilities the Commission is organized much like a domestic government: with a core executive (the College of Commissioners) focusing on the political tasks; a bureaucracy (the directorates-general) undertaking legislative drafting, administrative work and some regulatory tasks; and a network of quasi-autonomous agencies undertaking a variety of monitoring and regulatory tasks.

A cabinet: the EU core executive

Following the Nice Treaty all member states now have only one Commissioner each. The College of Commissioners meets at least once a week (usually on a Wednesday). The President of the Commission chairs the meetings. As far as possible, College decisions are by consensus, but any Commissioner may request a vote. When votes are taken, decisions require an absolute majority of Commissioners, with the Commission President casting the deciding vote in the event of a tie. This absolute majority rule means that abstentions and absentees are equivalent to negative votes. Voting is usually by show of hands (so not by secret ballot). The results of votes are confidential, but how each Commissioner has voted is recorded in the College minutes, and on high-profile issues this information is often leaked to the press from somewhere in the Commission bureaucracy. Nonetheless, the Commissioners are bound by the principle of 'collective responsibility', which is a key norm in most cabinet government systems. This principle means that even if a Commissioner was in a losing minority in a vote, he or she must toe the line of the majority in the outside world.

The political leadership of the Commission operates along the lines of cabinet government in several other ways. The first is the allocation of a portfolio to each Commissioner, as shown in Table 2.1. The most high-profile portfolios are given to the Commission vice-presidents and those who were Commissioners in previous administrations. In the Barroso II Commission, for example, those Commissioners who were in the previous Barroso administration all held key portfolios. Nevertheless any Commissioner is capable of making a name for him- or herself through hard work and skilful manipulation of the media.

The Commission President is the 'first among equals' (Bagehot, 1987 [1865]). The President sets the overall policy agenda of the Commission by preparing the annual work programme, sets the agenda and chairs the meetings of the College, and is in charge of the Secretariat General, which oversees the work of the directorates general). The President also decides which Commissioner gets which portfolio, in consultation with the individual Commissioners and the governments that nominated them. In practice, the member state governments hold agenda-setting power in this relationship as they are responsible for nominating their Commissioners in the first place. Nevertheless, the Commission President can exert some pressure on national governments to propose more high-profile and competent figures (and sometimes more pro-European figures). The President can also ask individual Commissioners to resign if they prove to be corrupt or incompetent.

A further aspect of cabinet government is the system of Commissioners' *cabinets*. The *cabinet* system was imported from the French government system, although it exists in most collective-government systems. The *cabinets* have four main functions: to serve as political antennae and filters for party and interest-group demands; as policy advisers of civil servants in the directorates-general; as mechanisms for inter-Commissioner coordination and dispute resolution; and as supervisors and controllers of the work of the directorates-general responsible to the Commission (Donnelly and Ritchie, 1997). The *chef des cabinets* meet together every week to prepare the agenda for the weekly meeting of the College of Commissioners. They try to resolve most of the items on the weekly agenda, leaving only the more controversial and political decisions to their political masters. The *cabinets* used

Table 2.1   *The Barroso II Commission*

Commissioner	Member state	European political group affiliation	Portfolio
President			
José Manuel Barroso*	Portugal	EPP	
Vice-Presidents			
Catherine Ashton*	UK	S&D	Foreign Affairs and Security Policy
Viviane Reding*	Luxembourg	EPP	Justice, Fundamental Rights and Citizenship
Joaquín Almunia*	Spain	S&D	Competition
Siim Kallas*	Estonia	ALDE	Transport
Neelie Kroes*	Netherlands	ALDE	Digital Agenda
Antonio Tajani*	Italy	EPP	Industry and Entrepreneurship
Maroš Šefčovič*	Slovakia	S&D	Inter-Institutional Relations and Administrations
Members			
Janez Potočnik*	Slovenia	Ind.	Environment
Olli Rehn*	Finland	ALDE	Economic and Monetary Affairs
Andris Piebalgs*	Latvia	EPP	Development
Michel Barnier	France	EPP	Internal Market and Services
Androulla Vassiliou*	Cyprus	ALDE	Education, Culture, Multilingualism and Youth
Algirdas Šemeta*	Lithuania	EPP	Taxation and Customs Union, Audit and Anti-Fraud
Karel De Gucht*	Belgium	ALDE	Trade
John Dalli	Malta	EPP	Health and Consumer Policy
Máire Geoghegan-Quinn	Ireland	ALDE	Research, Innovation and Science
Janusz Lewandowski	Poland	EPP	Financial Programming and Budget
Maria Damanaki	Greece	S&D	Maritime Affairs and Fisheries
Kristalina Georgieva	Bulgaria	EPP	International Cooperation, Humanitarian Aid and Crisis Response
Günther Oettinger	Germany	EPP	Energy
Johannes Hahn	Austria	EPP	Regional Policy
Connie Hedegaard	Denmark	EPP	Climate Action
Štefan Füle	Czech Republic	S&D	Enlargement and European Neighbourhood Policy
László Andor	Hungary	S&D	Employment, Social Affairs and Inclusion
Cecilia Malmström	Sweden	ALDE	Home Affairs
Dacian Cioloş	Romania	EPP	Agriculture and Rural Development

Note: *Member of the previous Commission.
EPP = European People's Party, ALDE = Alliance of Liberals and Democrats for Europe. S&D = Progressive Alliance of Socialists and Democrats, Ind.= Independent

to be handpicked fellow nationals of the Commissioners. This is no longer the case, as the majority members of the *cabinets* are no longer the same nationality as their Commissioner (Egeberg and Heskestad, 2010).

Although the EU Treaty proclaims that the members of the Commission shall serve the general interest of the EU and be completely independent, the Commission is a political body, occupied by actors with backgrounds in national politics. As discussed above, the member states care about two main issues when delegating to the Commission: the gap between the preferences of the Commission and the governments, and the competency of the Commission. Much of the literature on EU politics assumes preference–divergence between the governments and the Commission: the Commissioners prefer more integration than the member states. However, from a principal–agent perspective, it is puzzling that the member states would select a Commission with outlying preferences (Crombez, 1997; Hug, 2003). Commissioners tend to have previously held political positions in parties that are in government at the time of their appointment to the Commission (Wonka, 2007). This suggests a high level of preference–similarity between the governments and the Commission, at least when the Commission is first appointed.

Nevertheless, when choosing Commissions, governments also care about their political competence, and have tended to care more about the competence of prospective Commissioners as the powers of the Commission have increased (Döring, 2007). Put another way, political has-beens with little to offer are now rarely appointed as Commissioners. Also, the allocation of portfolios within the Commission suggests that more experienced and politically moderate Commissioners tend to obtain better policy portfolios (Franchino, 2009).

Comitology: interface of the EU dual executive

The Commission is not completely free to shape policy outcomes when implementing EU legislation. The Council has designed an elaborate system of committees, known as 'comitology', composed of national government officials who scrutinize the Commission's implementing measures. Under some procedures of the comitology system there is a separation of powers, whereby the legislators (the governments) can scrutinize the executive (the Commission). Under other procedures, however, comitology has created a fusion of powers, whereby the member state governments can in some respects enforce their wishes on the Commission, and so exercise both legislative and executive authority.

The comitology system was established by a Council decision in July 1987 and reformed by Council decisions in June 1999 and July 2006. These decisions established four types of committee – advisory, management, regulatory, and regulatory committee with scrutiny – and a set of rules governing their operation. The membership of the committees depends on their role: committees composed of national civil servants monitor the implementation of legislation; temporary committees composed of representatives of private interest groups consider matters for which the Commission feels wider consultation is necessary; and committees composed of scientists and experts give advice on technical issues. This structure of the system dates back to the establishment of the CAP, when the Commission proposed this system, which worked as a powerful focal point for subsequent arrangements (Blom-Hansen, 2008).

Here is how the comitology procedures work. Under the advisory procedure, the Commission has the greatest degree of freedom: although it must take 'the utmost account' of the opinion of the national experts, it can simply ignore their advice. This procedure is used in most areas of EU competition policy, such as Commission decisions on mergers and state aid to industry.

Under the management procedure, if the implementing measures adopted by the Commission are not in accordance with the committee's opinion, the Commission must refer them to the Council, which, within a certain timeframe, may adopt a different decision by QMV. This procedure is mostly used for the CAP and most other areas of EU expenditure, such as regional policy, research, and development aid.

Under the regulatory procedure, if the implementing measures of the Commission are not in accordance with the committee's opinion, the Commission must refer them to the Council and, for information, to the European Parliament. The Council may give its agreement or introduce an amendment within three months. The 2006 amendment to the rules introduced a second variant of the regulatory procedures, known as the regulatory procedure with scrutiny. Under this procedure, the Council and European Parliament can carry out a check prior to the adoption of a measure by the Commission and if there is opposition in either of these institutions the Commission cannot adopt the measure. The regulatory procedure was developed by the Council in the late 1960s to cover areas outside agriculture where the member governments wanted more control over the Commission than they had under the advisory and management committee procedures (Docksey and Williams, 1997). This procedure is now used in such areas as animal, plant and food safety, environmental protection and transport.

The Lisbon Treaty commits the Council and the European Parliament, acting under the ordinary legislative procedure, to adopt a new set of rules to simplify the comitology procedures. In March 2010, the Commission initiated a proposal which aims to simplify the procedures radically.

Given the different degrees of freedom the Commission has under each of the procedures, one would expect the Commission and the Council to be constantly in conflict over which procedure should be used for the enactment of each piece of legislation. However, Dogan (1997, 2001) found that this was not necessarily the case. For example, 29 per cent of all comitology procedures proposed by the Commission between 1987 and 1995 were under procedures where the Commission was weak (such as the regulatory procedure), and contrary to the Commission's rhetoric about the Council's opposition to the advisory committee procedure, the Council accepted 40 per cent of the Commission's proposals for use of this procedure. Dogan consequently argues that 'the Commission is deeply implicated in the pattern of Council comitology preferment' (1997, p. 45). However, as with the seemingly harmonious relationship between the Commission and the committees in the operation of comitology, the figures might reflect the fact that the Commission is strategic in its choice of comitology procedures, and hence only proposes the advisory procedure in cases where it thinks it has a reasonable chance of getting them past the Council.

The European Parliament has been critical of comitology (Bradley, 1997; Corbett *et al.*, 1995, p. 253; Hix, 2000). After the establishment of the system, the European Parliament argued that the system lacked transparency, due to the secretive nature of committee proceedings. It also argued that by allowing the member state governments to scrutinize the executive powers of the Commission, the comitology system undermined the principle of the separation of powers between the legislative authority of the EU (the Council and the Commission) and the executive implementation authority (the Commission). Moreover, the Parliament was critical of the fact that the procedures only allowed for issues to be referred back to one part of the EU legislature (the Council), rather than to both the Council and the European Parliament. The new regulatory procedure with scrutiny established in 2006 was specifically designed to address this concern. Also, the committees are now far more transparent than they used to be, as since April 2008 all committee documents are publicly available in a comitology register.

Some researchers argue that the comitology system enables Commission and national experts to work together to solve policy issues in a non-hierarchical and deliberative policy style (e.g. Joerges and Neyer, 1997). However, the involvement of scientific experts and private interests in the process of policy implementation and regulation is a common feature of most public administration systems. And, on high-profile policy issues, conflicts do arise between the Commission and the national experts, and between experts from different member states.

Administrative Accountability: Parliamentary Scrutiny and Transparency

The administrative and regulatory tasks of the Commission and the Council are subject to parliamentary scrutiny in much the same way as domestic bureaucracies and regulatory agencies are (Rhinard, 2002). First, the President of the Commission presents the Commission's annual work programme to the European Parliament. Second, Commissioners and Commission officials regularly give evidence to European Parliament committees, and certain European Parliament committees have introduced a 'question time' for the Commissioner responsible for the policy areas they oversee. Third, the president-in-office of the Council presents the Council's six-monthly work programme to the European Parliament. Finally, government ministers from the member state that holds the Council Presidency often appear before European Parliament committees, and the President of the ECB and the heads of the EU agencies appear before the European Parliament committees on a regular basis. In contrast, while the President of the European Council is not accountable to the European Parliament, he does appear before the MEPs to report on European Council meetings.

The European Parliament has a highly developed system of presenting oral and written questions to the Council and the Commission (Raunio, 1996). As in national parliaments, these questions enable MEPs to gain information, force the executive to make a formal statement about a specific action, defend their constituencies' interests, and inform the Commission and Council of problems with which they might be unfamiliar. The full texts of the questions and the answers by the institutions are published in the EU *Official Journal*. Proksch and Slapin (2011) show that MEPs from parties in opposition at the national level more actively use questions to scrutinize the Commission and the Council.

Unlike most national governments, however, there are no formal rules governing individual responsibility for Commissioners. Individual Commissioners are often blamed for inconsistencies in the DG in their charge, or for lack of action in the policy area they cover, but no procedure exists for forcing individual Commissioners to resign. Also, the Commission has not developed a culture in which a Commissioner or a senior official would resign out of a sense of obligation, and the European Parliament does not have the right to censure individual Commissioners. Nonetheless, in January 1999 the European Parliament announced it would hold separate votes of no confidence on two Commissioners: Édith Cresson and Manuel Marín, who were in charge of administrative divisions where fraud and nepotism had been alleged. Although these motions would have no legal force, considerable pressure to resign was put on the two Commissioners by the media and several governments. In the event, the motions were defeated.

Despite the above, since the early 1990s the Commission has been eager to promote transparency in its administrative operations. First, in

February 1994 it unveiled a 'transparency package'. This included the publication of its annual work programme in October instead of January, which allows the European Parliament and Council time to debate the draft before the final adoption of the full legislative programme in January. Second, in the initiation of legislation the Commission now makes more use of green and white papers, public hearings, information seminars, and consultation exercises. Third, the Commission's new code of conduct commits it to make internal documents public, with the exception of minutes of its meetings, briefing notes, the personal opinions of its officials and documents containing information that might damage public or private interests. Finally, the Commission submits draft legislation to national parliaments so that their committees on EU affairs can scrutinize the legislation before their government ministers address it in the Council.

Officially the Council supports greater openness in EU decision-making. However, both the Commission and the European Parliament have accused the Council of hypocrisy. First, the majority of member states (and thus the Council) have opposed the Commission's efforts to allow public access to EU documents – many member state governments are keen to prevent private interests and the media from learning more about what they sign up to in the EU legislative and executive processes. Second, the Council has proved reluctant to expose itself to public scrutiny. The EU Treaty (Article 207) specifies that:

> the Council shall define the cases in which it is to be regarded as acting in its legislative capacity, with a view to allowing greater access to documents in those cases. In any event, when the Council acts in its legislative capacity, the results of votes and explanations of vote as well as statements in the minutes shall be made public.

However, this has allowed the Council to remain secretive about matters that come under its executive capacity, and also to define for itself when it is 'acting as a legislature'. The Lisbon Treaty has change this slightly, by defining that the Council acts as a legislature under the ordinary legislative procedure, and so requires the Council to be more open in its legislative activities.

The activities of the governments in the Council are also scrutinized by their national parliaments (Bergman, 1997; Norton, 1996; Raunio, 1999; Saalfeld, 2000). In every national parliament this is primarily conducted by a special EU affairs committee, which receives drafts of legislative initiatives by the Commission, and usually asks national government officials and ministers involved in EU affairs to give evidence and answer questions. Some national parliaments are more effective than others in this role. For example, the EU affairs committee in the Danish Folketing, which was set up in 1972, issues voting instructions to Danish government ministers prior to meetings of the Council. In contrast, the Select Committee on European Legislation in the British House of Commons has very little control over the activities of British ministers in the Council. The extent of national parliament involvement in the transposition of EU legislation is a function of preference–divergence in a national cabinet and the power of the national parliament vis-à-vis the government in a member state (Franchino and Høyland, 2009). In general, member states with single-party majority governments (as in the UK, France, and Greece) tend to have national parliaments which are less involved in EU affairs, whereas member states with minority or coalition governments (as in Scandinavia and the Benelux countries) tend to have national parliaments who are more involved in EU affairs.

As European integration has progressed, and governments have delegated more powers to the EU institutions, several scholars have detected a decline in the ability of national parliaments to scrutinize the executive branch of their national governments effectively (e.g. Andersen and Burns, 1996). For example, Moravcsik (1993, p. 515) argues:

> by according governmental policy initiatives greater domestic legitimacy and by granting greater domestic agenda-setting power ... the institutional structure of the EC strengthens the initiative and influence of national governments by insulating the policy process and generating domestic agenda-setting power for national politicians. National governments are able to take initiatives and reach bargains in Council negotiations with relatively little constraints.

However, since the mid-1990s national parliaments have fought to retrieve at least some of the powers they have lost to the executive as a result of EU integration (Raunio and Hix, 2000). By 1995 all the national parliaments had set up EU affairs committees to scrutinize their governments' activities at the EU level, and developed procedures requiring ministers and national bureaucracies to provide detailed information on new EU legislation and how EU decisions would be implemented in the domestic arena. Furthermore, the Lisbon Treaty establishes an early warning system whereby national parliaments are given six weeks to offer a reasoned opinion on whether a Commission proposal violates the subsidiarity and proportionality principles (the subsidiarity principle means that decisions should be taken at the lowest possible level, and the proportionality principle means that the EU may only act to the extent that is needed to achieve its objectives and not further). If one-third of the national parliaments considers a Commission proposal to be in violation of subsidiarity or proportionality, the Commission has to review the proposal. However, having conducted the review, the Commission is free to amend, redraw, or leave the proposal unchanged. It is thus not clear that this new measure will involve the national parliaments in any meaningful way (Cooper, 2006).

Political Accountability: Selection and Censure of the Commission

In the collective exercise of political leadership in the Council the member state governments can claim legitimacy via national general elections (see Chapter 7). However, the legitimacy of the political leadership role of the Commission is more problematic. Until 1994 the President of the Commission was chosen by a collective agreement among the heads of government in the European Council. The Commission President was regarded as one post in a package deal between governments on the heads of a number of international agencies, such as the secretaries-general of the WTO and the North Atlantic Treaty Organization (NATO). This was more akin to selecting the head of an international organization than to choosing the 'first among equals' in a political cabinet.

However, the Maastricht Treaty introduced a new investiture procedure, whereby the term of office of the Commission was aligned with the term of the European Parliament. Also, the European Parliament would now be consulted on the member state governments' nominee for Commission President, and the members of the full Commission would be subject to a vote of approval by the European Parliament. However, the European Parliament interpreted 'consulted' as the right to vote on the nominee for Commission President (Hix, 2002a). Consequently in July 1994, in the first ever Commission President investiture vote in the European Parliament, Jacques Santer was approved by the European Parliament as Commission President by a margin of only 12 votes (Hix and Lord, 1995). In addition, following the nomination of the individual Commissioners, the European Parliament introduced Commissioner hearings, where the nominees had to give evidence to the European Parliament committee covering their portfolios (consciously modelled on US Senate hearings of the nominees for the US President's cabinet) (Westlake, 1998). Finally, once the committee hearings were complete, the European Parliament took a second vote on the Commission as a whole. The Amsterdam Treaty reformed the procedure, to institutionalize formally the European Parliament's power to veto the nominated Commission President.

Subsequently, the Nice Treaty introduced QMV in the European Council for the nomination of the Commission President and the Commission as a whole. The Lisbon Treaty only slightly amends this combination of QMV in the European Council and veto by the European

Parliament, by requiring that the European Council takes account of the European Parliament election results when nominating a Commission President.

Despite the fact that the European Parliament cannot formally veto individual Commissioners, the Parliament has used its role in the Commission investiture procedure to extract concessions from the governments. In particular, in October 2004, the European Parliament refused to back the investiture of Barroso's first Commission, after the European Parliament's Civil Liberties committee had issued a negative opinion on the appointment of the Italian politician Rocco Buttiglione as the Commissioner for Justice, Freedom and Security. The socialist, liberal, radical left, and green MEPs objected to Buttiglione's views on gender equality and the rights of homosexuals, which were particularly relevant because his portfolio included EU equality provisions. The Italian government initially refused to withdraw Buttiglione, but after the Parliament refused to back the Commission as a whole, Barroso was able to persuade the Italian Prime Minister Berlusconi to nominate Franco Frattini instead.

Then in 2009, Bulgaria's nominated candidate, Rumiana Jeleva, was withdrawn after heavy criticism from a number of MEPs about her alleged connections to organized crime in Bulgaria.

Regarding the removal of the Commission, since the Treaty of Rome the European Parliament has had the right to censure the Commission as a whole by a 'double majority': an absolute majority of MEPs and two-thirds of the votes cast. Motions of censure have been proposed on several occasions, but none has ever been carried. The European Parliament tends to fear that throwing out the Commission would back-fire, as governments and the public would accuse the European Parliament of acting irresponsibly. Also, before the new investiture procedure there was nothing to prevent governments from reappointing the same Commissioners. Above all, the double majority in practice means that a very broad political coalition is required to censure the Commission. This means that the European Parliament's right of censure is more like the right of the US Congress to impeach the US President than the right of a domestic parliament in Europe to withdraw majority support for a government, and therefore it can only be exercised in extreme circumstances – in instances of what the US constitution calls 'high crimes and misdemeanours'.

However, in 1998 and 1999 the European Parliament became more confident about using the threat of censure. In 1998, with widespread public disapproval of the Commission's handling of the BSE crisis, the European Parliament successfully threatened censure to force the Commission to reorganize its handling of food safety issues. In January 1999 the European Parliament demanded that the Commission respond to the high-profile allegations of financial mismanagement, nepotism, and cover-up (the Commission had sacked an official who had leaked a report on fraud and financial mismanagement). On the eve of the censure vote, Commission President Santer promised that an independent committee would be set up to investigate the allegations, and that there would be a fundamental administrative reform of the Commission, including a new code of conduct, rules governing the appointment and work of the cabinets, and restrictions on 'parachuting' political appointees into top administrative jobs. As a result, the censure motion was narrowly defeated, with 232 MEPs in favour of censure and 293 opposed (mostly from the Party of European Socialists and European People's Party).

In a separate motion passed in January 1999, however, the European Parliament put the Commission on probation until the committee of independent experts set up by the European Parliament reported on the allegations of fraud, corruption and nepotism. When the highly critical report was published in March 1999 a new motion of censure was tabled. On Sunday 14 March, the day before the vote, Pauline Green, the leader of the largest political group (the Party of European Socialists), informed Jacques Santer that because the majority in her group would be voting for censure, the motion would probably be carried. Santer promptly called an emergency meeting of the Commissioners, who agreed they should resign en masse. Hence, one can reasonably claim that the European Parliament did in fact censure the Commission in March 1999, even though a vote was never taken – in much the same way as President Nixon was forced to resign in 1974 after a committee of the US House of Representatives had issued an opinion, and before an actual impeachment vote in either the House or the Senate was taken.

Because of the effective censure of the Santer Commission by the European Parliament, the incoming Prodi Commission was much more sensitive to Parliament's concerns. For example during their committee hearings, the prospective Commissioners showed more respect for the opinions and questions of the MEPs than several of the members of the previous Commission had in their hearings. Also, during the debate on the investiture of the next commission, Romano Prodi promised to sack individual Commissioners if the Parliament could prove allegations of corruption or gross incompetence. This effectively gave the Parliament the right to censure individual Commissioners. However, counter-intuitively, this could limit the influence of the European Parliament over the Commission as a whole, as it might undermine the norm of collective responsibility in the Commission – a key weapon of any parliament over a government.

Consequently, the procedures for selecting and deselecting the Commission have become a hybrid mix of the parliamentary and presidential models. The Maastricht and Amsterdam Treaties injected an element of parliamentary government by requiring that the Commission be supported by a majority in the European Parliament before taking office, and that the right of censure allows the European Parliament to withdraw this support. Also, the introduction of QMV in the European Council for nominating the Commission means that the same bicameral majority is now required for electing the executive and passing the legislative initiatives of the executive. Hence, there is a fusion of the executive and legislative majorities, as in a parliamentary system.

However, in the process of selecting the Commission President the member state governments are the equivalent of a presidential electoral college, over which the European Parliament can only exercise a veto. The European Parliament cannot propose its own candidate. And, once invested, the Commission does not really require a working majority in the European Parliament. The right of censure is only a 'safety valve', to be released in the event of a serious political or administrative failure by the Commission.

This design reflects a conscious effort by the member state governments to maintain their grip on who holds executive office at the European level. The European Parliament has gained a limited role in the investiture procedure because the governments had to address the 'democratic deficit' (see Chapter 6). During the Convention on the Future of Europe, which drafted the Constitution, a variety of alternative models were proposed. These included a classic parliamentary model, with a contest for the Commission President in European Parliament elections and the translation of the electoral majority in the European Parliament into the formation of the Commission; and a presidential model, with some form of direct or indirect election of the Commission President. However, neither model was acceptable to the member state governments, which perceived that the benefits of any alternative (democratic) model of electing the Commission would be considerably lower than the potential costs: the loss of their power to choose the members of the other branch of the EU executive, and the likely politicization of the Commission.

Conclusion: the Politics of a Dual Executive

The power to set the policy agenda and implement EU policies is shared between the EU governments in the Council and European Council and the Commission. Basically, the governments set the long- and medium-term agendas, by reforming the EU Treaty and delegating political and administrative tasks to the Commission. In the areas where executive powers have been delegated, the Commission has a significant political leadership role and is responsible for distributing the EU budget, monitoring policy implementation by the member states, and making rules and regulations.

The member state governments have delegated powers to the Commission to reduce transaction costs and produce policy credibility. However, they have been selective in this delegation. For example, they have limited the Commission to certain regulatory matters, such as competition and agricultural policies. They have also retained control of key executive powers, such as treaty reform, policy-making under CFSP, front-line implementation of EU legislation, long-term agenda-setting and the coordination of national macroeconomic policies. In addition, the governments have limited the Commission's discretion through the comitology system and retained their monopoly over the nomination of the Commission President and the selection of the Commissioners.

Meanwhile, the Commission has developed many of the characteristics of a supranational 'government'. At the political level, the College of Commissioners operates along the lines of cabinet government, with collective responsibility and the Commission President as the first among equals. Also, the Commissioners are partisan career politicians and pursue their own political objectives in the EU policy process. At the administrative level, the Commission directorates-general are quasi ministries and many of the directorates-general have direct regulatory powers. Also, like national administrations each service in this Euro-bureaucracy has its own institutional interests, policy objectives, and supporting societal groups. As a result, the Commission has powerful incentives and significant political and administrative resources to pursue an agenda independently from the member state governments.

The member state governments have tried to tilt the balance of power in this dual-executive relationship back to themselves. For example, following the activism of Delors the governments were careful to choose Commission Presidents (Santer, Prodi, and Barroso) who they felt were more sensitive to member state interests. Moreover, the governments have tried to use the European Council to set the medium- and short-term policy agenda, and thereby take away some of the Commission's policy-initiation power. Finally, since the resignation of the Santer Commission, the Commission administration has gone through a period of self-investigation and internal reform, which has bred further insecurity vis-à-vis the governments.

The result is a system with strengths and weaknesses. The main strength is that the dual character of the EU executive facilitates extensive deliberation and compromise in the adoption and implementation of EU policies. This is a significant achievement for a continental-scale and multi-national political system, and it reduces the likelihood of system breakdown. However, there are two important weaknesses. First, the flipside of compromise is a lack of overall political leadership and dual-executive systems tend to be characterized by policy stability. Second, and linked to this issue, there is the problem of democratic accountability. There is no single chief executive whom the European public can 'throw out'. The consequence is a political system that seems remote to most European citizens, as we shall see in Chapter 5.

Chapter 3

Legislative Politics

The EU has a two-chamber legislature in which the Council represents the states and the European Parliament represents the citizens. The Council is more powerful. However, the introduction, revision, and extension of the co-decision procedure to cover most legislative areas have moved the European Parliament towards parity with the Council. In fact, the Lisbon Treaty makes co-decision the ordinary legislative procedure. Although the main actors in the Council are governments and those in the European Parliament are political parties, internal politics and organization of the two chambers share many similarities. To help us understand how the system works, we first look at some general theories of legislative coalitions and organization.

Theories of Legislative Coalitions and Organization

Contemporary scholars of legislatures focus on legislative bargaining, coalition formation, and organization. In Riker's (1962) pioneering theory of 'minimum-winning-coalitions' legislators strive for maximum influence in a winning coalition. This makes coalitions unlikely to include any groups that are not necessary for reaching a majority, as it means fewer interests to appease when distributing the benefits. An actor that is decisive for the formation of a winning coalition can demand a high price in return for participating. The more likely an actor is to be decisive (pivotal), the more 'power' he or she has in coalition bargaining (Banzhaf, 1965; Shapley and Shubik, 1954). An alternative view is that coalition formation is not policy blind but rather policy driven. Actors who care about policy are likely to form 'minimum-*connected*-winning-coalitions', between legislators with similar preferences on a given policy dimension (Axelrod, 1970). The theoretical foundation behind this approach is the spatial model of politics (Hinich and Munger, 1997). In

Figure 3.1   *Legislative bargaining in one dimension*

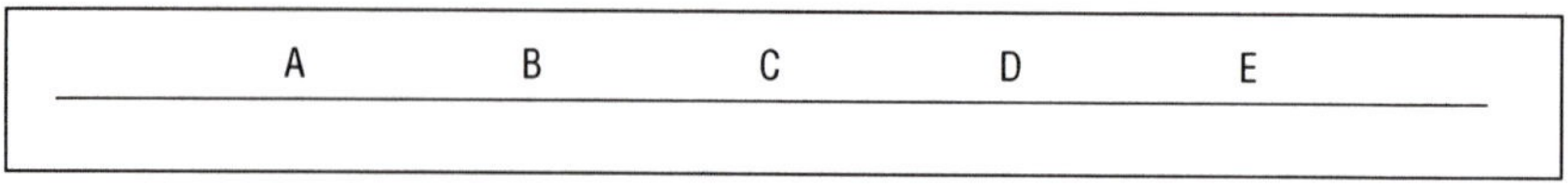

	A	B	C	D	E	

Note: The figure shows the spatial location of 5 actors, labelled A, B, C, D, and E, in a single-dimensional space.

this framework, actors and policies can be represented as points in a policy space. The actors prefer to minimize the distance between their position (their ideal point) and the adopted policy. Consider a simple model with five actors, A, B, C, D, and E, where the ideal point of A is to the left of B, whose ideal point is to the left of C, and so on, as illustrated in Figure 3.1. If a decision is taken by a simple majority and all actors are allowed to make proposals, the outcome will be at C. A and B will not be able to convince D or E to move the policy further to the left, nor will D and E be able to convince A or B of moving the policy further to the right. However, if the policy is to the right (left) of C, she will be able to convince A and B (D and E) to move to policy to C, as this move will make them better off. This is known as the median voter theorem (Black, 1958; Hotelling, 1929). Nevertheless, the outcome might be different if an oversized majority is required. In our example, if a majority of 4 out of 5 is required, any policy between B and D is impossible to move.

The median voter theorem is a useful approximation of bargaining in a single policy dimension. However, many policy issues are multidimensional. Where multiple issues are up for discussion at the same time it is more difficult to find a single policy package which cannot be defeated by an alternative package. This is because in a multidimensional policy space it will always be possible to find an alternative combination of policies which can defeat a policy which a majority has agreed (McKelvey, 1976; Schofield, 1978). Nevertheless, this sort of policy instability is rare. The main reason for this is that legislative institutions generate what is known as 'structured-induced-equilibria': policy outcomes which are stable because of institutional rules (Riker, 1980; Shepsle, 1979).

One set of rules is agenda-setting and veto rights (Banks and Duggan, 2006; Baron, 1989; Romer and Rosenthal, 1978). For example, in Figure 3.1, if actor E is the sole agenda-setter (with the power to make a proposal), and the existing policy (the status quo) is at B, then E can use her agenda-setting power to move the policy all the way to D, since C will be indifferent between having the policy at B and D. However, if A has veto power, it will not be possible to move the policy any further away from A. In general, it is better to be an agenda-setter than a veto-player, as the agenda-setter may be able to move the policy towards her, while a veto-player can only prevent a policy from moving further away from her ideal point (Tsebelis, 2002).

A second set of rules relates to specialization in the legislative process, for example in parliamentary committees. If agenda-setting power on specific policy areas are granted to committees, issues may be prevented from being linked across policies, which can then lead to stable policy outcomes (Shepsle and Weingast, 1987). Another motive for specializing in committees is the need for technical expertise and information in the legislative process. Legislators are often uncertain about the precise relationship between the policy instrument at their disposal and the final policy outcome. There is, hence, an incentive for legislators to grant agenda-setting rights to subsets of legislators on specific policy fields, in return for more precise knowledge about this relationship (Krehbiel, 1991). In turn, this need for information provides opportunities for interest groups to influence committee members (Crombez, 2002).

Third, political parties also facilitate legislative stability by simplifying legislative bargaining (e.g. Aldrich, 1995; Cox and McCubbins, 1993). Because an individual legislator is unlikely to obtain her policy objectives by acting alone, and issue-by-issue coordination is costly, formal relationships that bind individual legislators together reduce the transaction costs associated with coalition formation. With uncertainty about other legislators' preferences and the impact of legislative decisions, legislators with similar policy preferences benefit from institutional arrangements that facilitate information gathering and development of policy expertise (Kiewiet and McCubbins, 1991). The result is a division of tasks: back-bench MPs provide labour and capital, while party leaders distribute committee and party offices and determine the party line on complex legislative issues.

Fourth, legislative stability is also facilitated by the existence of multiple legislative chambers. In bicameral systems, for example, coalitions in both chambers have to be in favour of a proposal before it can become law. This restricts the set of possible policy choices and simplifies legislative bargaining (Riker, 1992; Tsebelis and Money, 1997). The legislative procedures regulating the interaction between the two chambers determines agenda and veto rights, thus determining relative strength of the two chambers in the bicameral bargaining (McCarty, 2000).

Together, these theories help us understand EU legislative politics: what coalitions are likely to form, why the European Parliament and Council are organized in the way they are, and who is more powerful under the EU's legislative procedures.

Development of the Legislative System of the EU

The rules of the EU legislative process have evolved considerably since the Treaty of Rome established that legislation would be adopted through interaction between the Council of national governments, the

Commission and the European Parliament. The Treaty of Rome did not set out a single procedure to govern this interaction. Instead, each article specified what voting rule would be used in the Council – whether the Council should decide by unanimity or qualified-majority voting (QMV), a system of weighted voting – and whether or not the European Parliament should be consulted by the Council.

The right of the Council to make decisions by QMV was challenged in the mid-1960s, when the French President Charles de Gaulle objected to majority voting being used in a number of important areas. De Gaulle insisted that every member state should be allowed to veto legislation, even when the treaty specified that QMV could be used. In 1965 he provoked an 'the empty chair' crisis by refusing to allow his ministers to participate in Brussels business until the other member states accepted his position. The crisis was resolved in 1966 by the so-called 'Luxembourg compromise', which established the principle that if a member state declared that a 'vital national interest' was at stake, the Council should make every effort to reach a unanimous agreement. The Luxembourg compromise was not legally binding, as it was not included in the treaties, but it nonetheless ushered in nearly two decades of intergovernmental bargaining. Any member state faced with being outvoted on a key issue could simply invoke the Luxembourg compromise and halt proceedings. For example, although the Treaty of Rome specified that after 1966 the liberalization of capital movements would be decided by QMV, the Commission did not initiate any proposals as it expected that at least one member state would claim the right to veto a directive (Teasdale, 1993, p. 570).

Nevertheless, by the mid-1990s the EU legislative system had developed into something much closer to a traditional bicameral model. The first major development was the 1980 'isoglucose' ruling by the ECJ. During the first direct elections of the European Parliament in 1979 the Council had adopted a piece of legislation without consulting the European Parliament. The European Parliament challenged the Council before the ECJ, which annulled the legislation on the grounds that the treaty required the Council to 'consult' the European Parliament. In the ECJ's opinion this meant that the Council cannot act until the European Parliament has formally issued an opinion on a piece of legislation. This did not mean that the European Parliament could in future force its opinions on the Council. But, backed by the 'isoglucose' ruling, the European Parliament now had a 'power of delay'. A power of delay is not as strong as an agenda-setting or a formal veto power. Nevertheless, Kardasheva (2009) finds that the European Parliament can substantively influence EU legislative outcomes under the consultation procedure.

The legislative powers of the European Parliament were substantially increased by three subsequent treaty reforms. First, in 1987 the Single

European Act (SEA) introduced a new legislative procedure: the cooperation procedure. This was the first procedure to be set out in a separate treaty article, to which other treaty articles referred. The procedure allowed the European Parliament a second reading, after the Council had adopted a common position, and reduced the ability of the Council to overturn European Parliament amendments made in the second reading. The SEA applied this procedure to only 10 treaty articles, but these included most areas of the single market programme, specific research programmes, certain decisions related to the structural funds, and some social and environmental policy issues. Together these constituted approximately one-third of all legislation. The SEA also introduced an assent procedure, whereby the approval of the European Parliament was required before the Council could act. This applied to association agreements with non-European Community states and the accession of new member states.

Second, in 1993 the Maastricht Treaty extended the assent procedure and introduced a fourth legislative procedure, the co-decision procedure, which was also set out in a separate treaty article. This procedure introduced the rule that if the European Parliament and Council disagreed on a piece of legislation, a conciliation committee would be convened, consisting of an equal number of representatives of the European Parliament and the Council. After a conciliation committee had reached an agreement, the deal would then have to be approved by both the Council and the European Parliament. The co-decision procedure originally applied to most areas of the internal market legislation that had previously been covered by the cooperation procedure, and several new areas introduced by the Maastricht Treaty, such as public health, consumer protection, education, and culture.

Third, in 1999 the Amsterdam Treaty reformed and extended the co-decision procedure. Under the new version of the procedure, legislation could be adopted at first reading if the European Parliament and Council already agreed at this stage. Furthermore, the conciliation committee became the last stage of the legislative process. Also, if the conciliation committee failed to reach an agreement, there would be no legislation. These reforms increased the power of the European Parliament within the procedure. The treaty also extended the procedure to most areas previously covered by the cooperation procedure. As a result, the version of the co-decision procedure established by the Maastricht Treaty is often referred to as 'co-decision I' while the Amsterdam Treaty version is called 'co-decision II'.

Fourth, the 2009 Lisbon Treaty established the Amsterdam version of the co-decision procedure as the ordinary legislative procedure and significantly extended its use to almost all areas of EU law.

Research has shown that despite the complexity of the decision-making rules and the expanding policy agenda of the EU, the EU legislative system had adapted well. Although the involvement of the European Parliament has slowed down the legislative process, this effect has been offset by the increase use of QMV in the Council (Golub, 1999; König, 2007; Schulz and König, 2000). The other reason for the efficiency and effectiveness of the EU legislative system is that both the Council and the European Parliament have developed sophisticated strategies to maximize their influence vis-à-vis each other in the various stages of bicameral bargaining.

Legislative Politics in the European Parliament

In practice the seat of the European Parliament is in Brussels. The Parliament still holds most of its plenary sessions in Strasbourg, and part of its secretariat is in Luxembourg. However, the bulk of the work of the European Parliament is in Brussels, where also an increasing number of plenary sessions are held, the political groups and committees meet, and the offices of the MEPs, the political groups, and the committees are based. The European Parliament operates like any other legislature: organizing and mobilizing to influence EU legislation and the EU executive. The institutional design of the EU – the separation of executive and legislative powers – means that the European Parliament is similar to the US Congress. There is no EU government relying on support from a permanent majority in the European Parliament. The censure procedure is closer to the presidential-style impeachment procedure than a vote of no-confidence in a parliamentary system (see Chapter 2). As a result, the European Parliament is a relatively independent legislature, free to amend legislation proposed by the Commission and agreed by the Council, and the Commission and the Council must build coalitions in the Parliament issue by issue.

The MEPs: agents with two principals

The European Parliament is the only directly elected body of the EU. However, the link to the voters is weak. Because European Parliament elections are fought on national rather than European issues (see Chapter 6), and because few voters know anything about the MEPs, there is very little an MEP can do to improve her chances of re-election. Moreover, most member states use electoral systems in European Parliament elections which enable national party leaders to largely determine which MEPs have a chance of being elected. Consequently, for most MEPs the chance of standing as a candidate and being re-elected is determined not by her political group in the European Parliament or her behaviour on behalf of her voters (Bowler and Farrell, 1993; Farrell and Scully, 2007; Norris and Franklin, 1997). As a result of the way European Parliament elections work, MEPs' behaviour is driven less by re-election than career incentives and policy objectives that can be achieved inside the European Parliament.

Traditionally, a career in the European Parliament was considered either as a training ground for a job in national politics or as a 'retirement home' at the end of a national career. However, as the power of the European Parliament has grown, more MEPs have started to consider Brussels a career in its own right (Scarrow, 1997). MEPs intent on making a career in the European Parliament have two types of goal:

1   office – such as promotion to party leadership, a senior post in the European Parliament such as European Parliament President or a committee chair; and
2   policy – pursuing the ideological views and interests of their constituency through the influence of the European Parliament on the EU legislative and executive processes.

Whereas re-election is usually not dependent on parliamentary performance, the ability to achieve these goals is dependent upon gaining promotion within the European Parliament committees and the political groups, and on being able to form coalitions with the other legislators to secure common policy aims as well as develop relationships with informed interest groups.

In other words, MEPs face a dilemma: to secure reselection and re-election they must cater to national party interests; but to secure promotion within the European Parliament and policy outputs from the European Parliament they must cater to the interest of European Parliament committees and their political group leaderships.

Agenda organization: leaderships, parties, and committees

The European Parliament determines its own organization and writes its own rules. These rules are formalized in the European Parliament rules of procedure. The rules of procedure establish three main organizational structures to facilitate agenda control: the parliamentary leadership, political groups, and the committee system.

Regarding parliamentary leadership

The most senior offices in the European Parliament are the President and the 14 vice-presidents, whose main responsibility is to chair the plenary sessions. There are also three leadership bodies: the Bureau of the Parliament (consisting of the President and the Vice-Presidents); the Conference of Presidents (consisting of the European Parliament President and the leaders of the European Parliament political groups); and the Conference of Committee Chairs. Together these committees involve all the senior figures in the European Parliament. The Bureau deals with the internal organizational and administrative matters, but is also active in political issues and meets almost every week. The Conference of Presidents is traditionally where most political issues are tackled, particularly with regard to the relationship between the European Parliament and the Commission and Council. It normally meets twice a month. The Conference of Committee Chairmen coordinates the committee agendas and tackles inter-committee demarcation disputes, such as which committee is responsible for which legislative report.

European Parliament political groups
These are the central mechanisms for structuring debate and coalition formation in the legislative process (Hix and Lord, 1997; Kreppel, 2002a; Raunio, 1997). The rules of procedure set out how many MEPs are needed to form a party group: at least 25 MEPs from at least one-quarter of all member states. The political groups have certain privileges, such as secretarial and research staff as well as financial resources. Table 3.1 shows the size of the political groups and the national memberships of the groups in the seventh European Parliament 2009–2014. The European People's Party (EPP), on the centre-right, and the Progressive Alliance of Socialists and Democrats (S&D), on the centre-left, are the two dominant groups and together command three-fifths of the MEPs. There are, however, several smaller groups that can also influence legislative outcomes.

The political groups are important because their leaderships determine vital political issues in the European Parliament: such as the choice of the European Parliament President, the allocation of committee positions and legislative reports (*rapporteurships*), the agenda of plenary sessions, and the policy positions of the political groups. If a national party is not a member of a political group, it is unlikely to secure any office or policy goals for its MEPs. National parties are more likely to secure these goals by belonging to one of the two larger groups than to one of the smaller ones. This has led to a reduction in the number of political groups and a consolidation of the two largest groups. However, following the 2009 elections, the EPP split as the British and Czech conservative parties left the EPP–ED to set up a less pro-European and more free market group, together with several smaller conservative parties from Central and Eastern Europe. The British and Czech parties had regularly voted against the EPP–ED on legislative votes prior to this departure (Hix *et al.*, 2007; Hix and Noury, 2009; Høyland, 2010). However, leaving the EPP has resulted in fewer prestigious offices for the British Conservatives and no influence on the formation of policy positions of the largest political group.

In general, individual MEPs try to avoid upsetting their political group leaderships. The party line is enforced through a 'whipping' system, in

Table 3.1   *Membership of the political groups in the seventh European Parliament, October 2010*

	EPP	S&D	ALDE	G/EFA	ECR	EUL/NGL	EFD	NA	Total
Belgium	5	5	5	4	1			2	22
Bulgaria	6	4	5					2	17
Czech Republic	2	7			9	4			22
Denmark	1	4	3	2		1	2		13
Germany	42	23	12	14		8			99
Estonia	1	1	3	1					6
Ireland	4	3	4			1			12
Greece	8	8		1		3	2		22
Spain	23	21	2	2		1		1	50
France	29	14	6	14		5	1	3	72
Italy	35	21	7				9		72
Cyprus	2	2				2			6
Latvia	3	1	1	1	1	1			8
Lithuania	4	3	2		1		2		12
Luxembourg	3	1	1	1					6
Hungary	14	4			1			3	22
Malta	2	3							5
Netherlands	5	3	6	3	1	2	1	4	25
Austria	6	4		2				5	17
Poland	28	7			15				50
Portugal	10	7				5			22
Romania	14	11	5					3	33
Slovenia	3	2	2						7
Slovakia	6	5	1				1		13
Finland	4	2	4	2			1		13
Sweden	5	5	4	3		1	1		18
United Kingdom		13	12	5	25	1	11	5	72
Total	265	184	85	55	54	35	30	28	736

Source: European Parliament.

which votes are designated as 'one-line', 'two-line', and 'three-line' whips, according to the importance of the agenda item to the political group. The result is a high level of group cohesion, even after the 2004 enlargement (Hix *et al.*, 2005; Hix and Noury, 2009). Nevertheless, within groups, the national party delegations remain powerful, with the larger national delegations dominating the key leadership positions. Also, because national parties control the selection of candidates in the elections, if MEPs are ever torn between their national party and their European political group, they almost always vote with their national party (Hix, 2002b, 2004).

The committees

These are the third organizational structure of the European Parliament. It is in the committees that the real scrutiny of EU legislation takes place. The committees propose amendments to legislation in the form of reports and draft resolutions, which are then submitted to the full plenary session. Amendments to the proposed committee resolutions can be made in the full plenary, but without the backing of a committee and political group support, amendments are unlikely to be adopted by the Parliament.

In line with the predictions from the informational theory of legislative organization (Krehbiel, 1990, 1991), MEP membership of committees is largely representative of the European Parliament as a whole in terms of political preferences. Nevertheless, previous committee experience and

Table 3.2   *Distribution of reports in the sixth European Parliament*

	ALDE	EUL/ NGL	IND/ DEM	EPP	PES	UEN	G/EFA	Total
Austria	0	0	3	14	18	0	1	36
Belgium	15	0	0	12	6	0	1	34
Bulgaria	0	0	0	0	0	0	0	0
Cyprus	0	1	0	3	0	0	0	4
Czech Republic	0	3	0	6	0	0	0	9
Denmark	7	0	1	0	6	0	0	14
Estonia	0	0	0	0	1	0	0	1
Finland	6	9	0	9	2	0	2	28
France	50	0	1	55	53	0	5	164
Germany	11	14	0	160	38	0	16	239
Greece	0	5	0	19	14	0	0	38
Hungary	1	0	0	33	10	0	0	44
Ireland	1	1	1	13	1	3	0	20
Italy	59	7	2	52	21	16	1	158
Latvia	0	0	0	0	0	3	0	3
Lithuania	5	0	0	1	0	0	0	6
Luxembourg	0	0	0	6	0	0	2	8
Malta	0	0	0	2	1	0	0	3
Netherlands	9	1	11	10	9	0	1	41
Poland	0	0	0	40	31	2	0	73
Portugal	0	9	0	33	22	0	0	64
Romania	0	0	0	0	0	0	0	0
Slovakia	0	0	0	2	1	0	0	3
Slovenia	4	0	0	6	2	0	0	12
Spain	2	0	0	48	46	0	1	97
Sweden	3	2	0	1	19	0	2	27
United Kingdom	45	0	0	45	33	0	5	128
Total	218	52	19	570	334	24	37	1,254

Source: own calculations based on data from the European Parliament.

policy expertise also matters when committee memberships are assigned (McElroy, 2006; Yordanova, 2009). Within committees, legislative reports are drafted by *rapporteurs*. The allocation of these positions within committees is in general proportional between political groups, although not evenly distributed among nationalities within each political group, as Table 3.2 shows. A small minority of the MEPs write the majority of reports (Mamadouh and Raunio, 2003). It is not clear to what extent the political group leaderships are able to use the allocation of reports as a disciplining tool, given the role national parties play in influencing voting behaviour (Kreppel, 2002a). However, MEPs who oppose political group and national party leaderships are unlikely to write important reports (Hausemer, 2006). MEPs' background and links with interest groups do influence who within the different groups end up writing reports (Kaeding, 2004, 2005), as do links with the Council (Høyland, 2006). *Rapporteurs* and other influential committee members are the target of lobbyists who trade information for influence at the committee stage (Marshall, 2010; see also Chapter 7). When preparing a report, a *rapporteur* has to trade off the interest of her party, advice from lobbyists, and suggestions from other committee members, in order to get the report adopted by both the committee and the plenary (Benedetto, 2005).

Coalition formation

There is no permanent coalition in the European Parliament, and without a government to support, legislative coalitions are formed vote by vote. On many issues the European Parliament behaves as if it were a single actor seeking to promote its own powers and interests against the interests of the second legislative chamber in the EU (the Council) or against the holders of executive power (the Commission). However, an informal 'grand coalition' between the social democrats (S&D) and Christian democrats (EPP) is facilitated by the rules of the EU legislative process. In the adoption of opinions in the early stages of the legislative procedures, when voting on 'own initiative' reports and when adopting amendments to resolutions on legislation, the European Parliament decides by a simple majority of those present at the vote. In contrast, in the second reading under the ordinary legislative procedure (the co-decision procedure until Lisbon) an absolute majority of all MEPs, not just of those turning up to vote, is required to propose amendments. This rule causes a problem due to low attendance. For example, if 75 per cent of all MEPs take part in a vote, then support from 67 per cent of those present is needed to adopt amendments at this stage. This encourages cooperation between the two largest political groups throughout the legislative process.

Coalition formation in the European Parliament is therefore at least partly shaped by whether a simple majority or an absolute is required. Under a simple majority, the EPP and S&D groups can form winning coalitions with various combinations of smaller groups. In contrast, when an absolute majority is required it is almost impossible to form a winning coalition without the EPP and S&D.

Voting in the European Parliament is by show of hands, electronic vote, or by roll-call vote. The latter form occurs if requested by a political group or by at least 37 MEPs (5 per cent). How individual MEPs voted in a roll-call vote is recorded in the minutes, and is now available on the internet (e.g. at: www.votewatch.eu). The records of these roll-call votes have led to a large body of empirical research on voting behaviour and coalition formation in the European Parliament (Hix, 2001; Hix *et al.*, 2005, 2007; Kreppel, 1999). This research shows that MEPs vote more along transnational party lines than national lines, that different coalitions form on different issues, and that the two main political groups do not always vote together.

Figure 3.2 shows the voting patterns in the 2004 to 2009 parliament in a two-dimensional space, as estimated from voting behaviour of MEPs in all the roll-call votes in this period (see also Chapter 6). Note that most MEPs are tightly clustered together with other MEPs from the same political group, except for MEPs belonging to EPP–ED. Within this group, we find two clusters: the main EPP cluster located in the top right on the first dimension; and a second cluster of EPP–ED MEPs low on the second dimension, which mainly consists of British Conservative MEPs. All other political groups are fairly cohesive. Furthermore, the first dimension captures most of the variance in voting behaviour. On this dimension the political groups and the MEPs are located along the standard left–right ideological dimension of politics. On the second dimension, pro-integrationist groups and MEPs are located towards the top of the figure, while more anti-integrationists groups and MEPs are located at the lower end. We see that the PES and (most of) the EPP–ED are close to each other on the second dimension. This grand coalition secures the pro-integrationist stand of the European Parliament in inter-institutional battles, while the first dimension represents the day-to-day ideological battle between left and right, as in most national parliaments.

In sum, the leaders of the main political groups balance the need to present a united front against the Council and the Commission and the need to present competing ideological alternatives for the future of the EU. The absolute majority requirement in the legislative rules of the EU implies that the winning coalitions often need support from the two main political groups. However, as the participation of MEPs has increased, which lowers the *de facto* majority threshold required at second reading, the incentive for the two largest political groups to compete in the legislative process has increased. When the two largest groups vote against each other, the liberal group is often pivotal in deciding whether a majority

Figure 3.2   *Voting in the 2004–9 European Parliament*

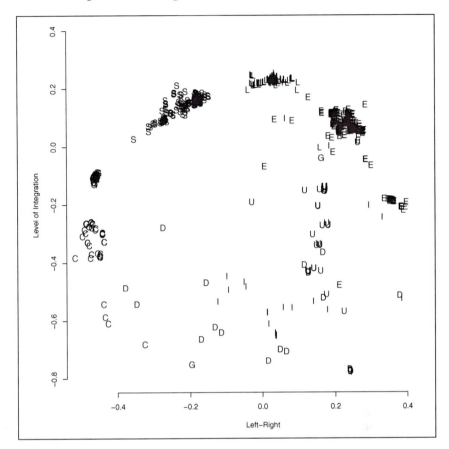

Note: The figure shows the voting coalitions in the European Parliament. Each point is one MEP. MEPs clusters closely together tend to vote the same way. MEPs situated far away from each other tend to vote the opposite way.

Key: E = EPP–ED, S = PES, L = ALDE, G = G/EFA, U = UEN, C = GUE/NGL, D = IND/DEM, I = independent.

coalition in the European Parliament forms on the centre-right or centre-left (Hix, 2001).

Legislative Politics in the Council

The Council is composed of ministers from the governments of the EU member states. Ministers in the Council are like legislators in a parliament in that they weigh potential benefits to the whole of society (the EU) against potential losses to their own constituencies (their voters). This can lead to conflicts of interest between different ministers from the same member state. In coalition governments (which exist in most member states) ministers from different parties have different core electorates, and consequently a policy proposal before the Council might benefit the supporters of one governing party but threaten the supporters of another. This leads to pressure for different ministers to take opposing positions in different Council meetings. Furthermore, different minister-ial portfolios have different functional support groups and budgetary interests. For example, whereas ministers in Ecofin have an interest in constraining public spending, ministers in the Social Affairs Council, the Regional Affairs Council, and the Employment Council have an interest in increasing public spending on their programmes.

Agenda organization: the presidency, sectoral Councils, and committees

The Presidency of the ministerial meetings of the Council, which leads the legislative business of the governments, rotates every six months (recall that the President of the European Council is now chosen for a renewable two-and-a-half year term, but is mainly involved in executive rather than legislative business, as Chapter 2 explains). The Council Presidency has limited agenda-setting powers (Tallberg, 2006; Wantjen, 2008). Each government takes over the Council Presidency with a particular list of policies they would like to see adopted, which they set out in the six-month work programme. For example, Spain held the Council Presidency in January to June 2010. The priorities of the Spanish Presidency were as follows (http://eu2010.es/en/presidencia/programapol/):

- consolidating Europe's social agenda, paying special attention to gender equality and the fight against domestic violence;
- promoting a people's Europe;
- getting out of the economic crisis (which included restoring job creation and achieving a more competitive Europe, as stated in the Lisbon Strategy);
- improving the EU's energy security and the fight against climate change;
- enabling Europe to speak with its own voice on the international scene and promoting its common values, peace and well-being; and
- consolidating a safer Union for its citizens, responding to the chal-lenges of immigration and constructing a shared space with judicial and policy cooperation.

These were ambitious goals and were unlikely to be achieved within the term of the Spanish Presidency. Nevertheless, the work programme guides the Presidency when prioritizing which items to place on the agenda for the various Council meetings. As the Council does not have a right of legislative initiative, the ability of the Presidency to pursue their goals is conditional on the willingness of the Commission to propose legislation on their priority issues. However, if the Presidency does not like the proposals from the Commission, it can simply refuse to put them on the agenda, and so can threaten to delay legislation if the Commission does not cooperate.

Historically, member states have treated their term in office as an opportunity to pursue their own policy objectives. The result has been a rolling addition to the Council agenda of specific national policy issues (Bulmer and Wessels, 1987; Kirchner, 1992). However, member states also like to be seen to have run 'good' presidencies, and not all member states are able to manipulate the agenda to the same extent. Small member states may lack the capacity, and large member states may promote their own interests too hard.

While there is formally only one Council, the attendees at Council meetings change by policy area. Economic and Finance Ministers meet in Ecofin, agricultural ministers meet in the Agriculture Council, and so on. These sectoral Councils are the functional equivalent of the parliamentary committees. Trades across policy areas are facilitated by the fact that the sectoral Councils make final decisions on policies originating from any policy area.

To facilitate the policy trades and to promote pre-legislative agreements, there is a network of committees, working groups, and the Council secretariat. The Committee of Permanent Representatives (COREPER) – which is composed of senior civil servants from the member state governments who are sent to Brussels as 'ambassadors' to the EU for a fixed-time period – is the real engine behind the work of the Council, and is where the majority of issues are decided before legislation is seen by ministers (Lewis, 1998; van Schendelen, 1996). Most Council business is resolved at working groups below the level of COREPER. The EU permanent representatives then deal with remaining issues and pass them onto the Council as either 'A points', issues already resolved which only require formal ministerial approval, or 'B points', issues that remain unresolved.

Hayes-Renshaw and Wallace (2006: 50) report that insiders guess that about 85 per cent of issues are already resolved by the time they reach the Council. However, relying on a large dataset of legislative acts, Häge (2008) estimates that 35 per cent of legislation is resolved at ministerial level, and 48 per cent of legislative issues are discussed by ministers. These numbers vary considerably across policy areas. Issues in salient policy areas are most likely to reach the ministerial level, while policy divergence among the governments makes little difference. Furthermore, legislation adopted by QMV is more often decided below the ministerial level than legislation requiring unanimity. The involvement of the European Parliament in the decision-making process also increases the chance of ministerial involvement. The picture that emerges is that ministers focus on the important and salient legislation and leave the less important decisions to civil servants (Häge, 2007).

Voting and coalition politics in the Council

In the Lisbon Treaty there are two basic voting rules in the Council:

1 Unanimity – where each member state has one vote and legislation cannot be passed if one or more member states vote against the legislation.
2 Qualified-majority voting (QMV) – where the majority of all member states (55 per cent) representing at least 65 per cent of the Union's population is required in order to adopt new legislation. This rule will come into effect in November 2014, and until then the Nice Treaty rules apply, which require a majority of the member states, 74 per cent of the weighted votes (258 out of 345 for the 27 member states), and 62 per cent of the Union's population for legislation to be adopted.

Table 3.3 shows the population size and the number of votes for each member state which will apply until 2014, and the 'voting power' of the member states under the Nice and Lisbon QMV rules (Barr and Passarelli, 2009). Here, voting power means the probability that a member state is pivotal in turning a losing coalition into a winning coalition. Under unanimity, all member states are equally powerful, as a negative vote from any of member states will prevent legislation from being adopted. Under QMV, however, the larger member states are more than twice as likely to be part of a winning coalition than the smaller ones (Brams and Affuso, 1985; Hosli, 1995).

The member states have always been acutely aware of how their voting strength and the QMV threshold will affect their relative power. For example, in the Nice Treaty negotiations the larger member states were concerned that their power in the Council would be reduced after the enlargement of the EU to Central, Eastern, and Southern Europe, as 11 of the 12 prospective members were smaller states. France was also eager to maintain parity with Germany. The result was a rather messy compromise: the total number of votes for each member state was increased, which allowed each to claim that its votes had gone up; the balance of weights between the member states was altered to increase the weights of the larger member states against the smaller ones; the QMV threshold after EU enlargement was increased from 71 to 75 per cent; and a 'triple majority' requirement was established, so that legislation could only be passed if it were supported by a qualified majority of votes as well as a majority of states with at least 62 per cent of the EU population. These changes made the largest and smallest member states better

Table 3.3   *Voting power in the Council*

Member state	Population, 2009	Number of votes	Voting power Nice	Voting power Lisbon
Germany	82,050,000	29	.087	.163
France	64,351,000	29	.087	.110
United Kingdom	61,634,600	29	.087	.111
Italy	60,053,440	29	.087	.107
Spain	45,828,170	27	.080	.073
Poland	38,135,880	27	.080	.070
Romania	21,498,620	14	.040	.042
Netherlands	16,486,590	13	.037	.033
Greece	11,257,290	12	.034	.023
Belgium	10,754,530	12	.034	.022
Portugal	10,627,250	12	.034	.023
Czech Republic	10,467,540	12	.034	.023
Hungary	10,031,210	12	.034	.022
Sweden	9,256,350	10	.028	.020
Austria	8,355,260	10	.028	.020
Bulgaria	7,606,550	10	.028	.020
Denmark	5,511,450	7	.020	.015
Slovakia	5,412,250	7	.020	.015
Finland	5,326,310	7	.020	.015
Ireland	4,465,540	7	.020	.012
Lithuania	3,349,870	7	.020	.012
Latvia	2,261,290	4	.011	.010
Slovenia	2,032,360	4	.011	.010
Estonia	1,340,420	4	.011	.009
Cyprus	793,960	4	.011	.007
Luxembourg	493,500	4	.011	.007
Malta	413,630	3	.008	.007

Note: The Shapley–Shubik voting power indices under the Nice and Lisbon rules are taken from Barr and Passarelli (2009).

off, but made legislation harder to pass (Felsenthal and Machover, 2001; Raunio and Wiberg, 1998; Tsebelis and Yataganas, 2002).

The Nice Treaty deal influenced bargaining over the Lisbon Treaty. Replacing the triple majority from Nice with a double majority of a majority of member states consisting of at least 65 per cent of population has substantively reduced the voting power of Spain and Poland. The Nice Treaty gave Spain and Poland almost as many votes as Germany, France, Italy, and the UK, while the double majority gives them half the influence of Germany and two-thirds of the influence of France, Italy, and the UK. The Spanish and Polish prime ministers hence initially refused to support the double majority, but eventually settled on a compromise, which grants them slightly more chances to block legislation than the original proposal, and also delays the introduction of the new voting rules until 2014.

Barr and Passarelli (2009) compare voting power in the Council under the Nice and Lisbon rules. They present both policy-free Shapley and Shubik (1954) scores and the Owen and Shapley (1989) method for calculating each actor's power as a function of both voting rules and its location in the political space. Relying on positional data extracted from Eurobarometer, Barr and Passarelli (2009) show that policy positions have a large impact on voting power. The Lisbon rules shift power away from governments with extreme policy positions towards more moderate governments. In the policy-blind model, the old 15 member states have 69 per cent of the voting power under the Nice rules, which increases to 75 per cent under the Lisbon rules. When policy positions are taken into account, the voting power of the old 15 states is just 60 per cent under the Nice rules compared to 74 per cent under the Lisbon rules. In other words, the old member states benefit significantly from the introduction of the Lisbon Treaty.

Despite the formal QMV rules and the battles over voting powers, it is well known that some governments are more likely to vote together than others. The Franco-German coalition has been at the heart of Council decision-making since the 1950s. The Benelux countries are more economically and politically integrated than any other grouping in the EU. And there is a general tendency to coalesce with member states that are geographically or culturally similar, and have similar preferences over the EU budget (Carrubba, 1997; Mattila, 2004; Thomson, 2009; Thomson *et al.*, 2004; Zimmer *et al.*, 2005).

Although the Council uses QMV to adopt legislation in most policy areas, decisions are often unanimous (Hayes-Renshaw and Wallace, 2006). This search for unanimous decisions is labelled the 'culture of consensus' (Heisenberg, 2005). During the first two years after the Eastern and Southern enlargement in 2004, 90 per cent of all Council decisions were unanimous (Mattila, 2009). Nevertheless, Council decisions are often taken in the 'shadow of a vote', where opposing governments know that they will be outvoted, and so refrain from recording a negative vote, as their opposition would not change the outcome (Golub, 1999).

Despite the incentives to reach consensus, the analysis of voting in the Council can offer insights into coalition patterns in the Council. Figure 3.3 shows the estimated ranking of governments in the Council on the basis of their voting behaviour between 1999 and 2007 (Hagemann and Høyland, 2008). There is a tendency for governments with similar ideological persuasions to vote together. National interests and policy preferences are interpreted through the ideological lenses of the ministers, causing them to seek different coalition partners in the Council from their predecessors. For example, when the German grand coalition led by

Merkel took over from the Red–Green coalition led by Schröder, Germany altered its closest coalition partners in the Council. However, not all member states change coalition partners in the Council when the national government changes. For example, the positions of the three Portuguese governments are virtually identical despite the changes in party-political colour.

The minutes from the Council meetings only include adopted legislation, which means that if a proposal fails to meet the QMV requirement, there is no public record of any vote that may have taken place. In order words, as we only observe voting on proposals that pass, voting records

Figure 3.3   *Voting behaviour of governments in Council*

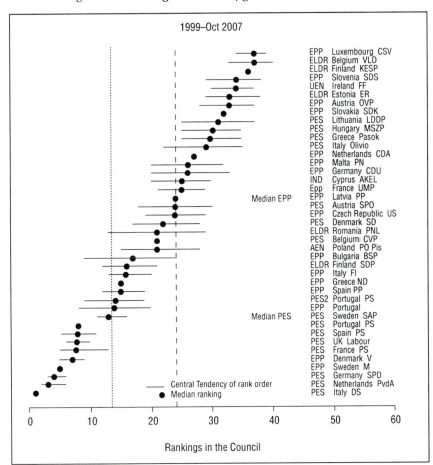

Note: The figure shows the ranking of governments in the Council as a function of their voting behaviour. The dot indicates the rank position. The line indicates the uncertainty surrounding this ranking.

offer only a partial and potentially biased picture of politics inside the Council. Furthermore, politics inside neither the Council nor the European Parliament is conducted in isolation from politics in the other institutions. Under the ordinary legislative procedure, both institutions need to agree for new legislation to be adopted. In the next section, we consequently turn to bicameral politics in the EU.

Bicameral Politics in the EU

Under the Lisbon Treaty, there are three main legislative procedures that regulate the relationship between the Parliament and the Council; *consultation, consent*, and *the ordinary legislative procedure.*

Under *consultation*, the Commission proposes, the Parliament then issues an opinion by a simple majority, and the Council then adopts, amends, or rejects the proposal.

Under *consent*, the Council (acting by QMV or unanimity, and on the basis of a Commission proposal, depending on the policy area) adopts a common position. The Parliament then gives its assent by a simple majority, but an absolute majority of all MEPs is required for admission of new member states and amendment of the rules governing European Parliament elections.

Under *the ordinary legislative procedure*, the Commission submits a proposal to the Parliament and Council, and the Parliament then issues an opinion by a simple majority. The Commission then decides whether to incorporate the amendments from the Parliament and sends the revised proposal to the Council. The Council then either accepts the proposal or adopts a common position by a double majority (QMV before 2014) or unanimity (depending on the policy area). If the Council incorporates all the proposed amendments from the European Parliament, the proposal becomes law. If the Council adopts a common position which differs from the European Parliament proposal, the bill goes to a second reading. In the second reading, the European Parliament can amend or reject the common position by an absolute majority of the MEPs. If there is no absolute majority in favour of amending or rejecting, the common position becomes law. If the European Parliament amends the common position, the Commission issues its opinions on the amendments and sends the proposal back to the Council. The Council then adopts amendments supported by the Commission by double majority (QMV before 2014), but needs unanimity to adopt European Parliament amendments that are not supported by the Commission. Again, if the Council adopts all of the European Parliament amendments at this stage, the proposal becomes law. If the Council and the European Parliament texts still differ, a conciliation committee is established. The conciliation committee is composed of representatives from the 27 member states (usually the permanent representatives), 27 MEPs (which include a vice-president, the chairs of the relevant European Parliament committees, and the *rapporteur*), and a representative from the Commission. The Commission has no voting rights in the conciliation committee. If there is no agreement at this stage, the legislation falls. But, if an agreement is reached, it then has to be adopted by the Council and the European Parliament (by simple majority) in the third reading, otherwise it falls.

These three procedures are the result of several decades of procedural politics in the EU. The European Parliament has managed to increase its power through a series of new legislative procedures introduces in the 1980s and 1990s. This generated a large body of formal models of EU legislative politics (e.g. Crombez, 1996, 1997, 2000, 2001; Moser, 1996; Steunenberg, 1994, 1997a; Tsebelis, 1994; 1997; Tsebelis and Garrett, 1997, 2000, 2001; Tsebelis and Kreppel, 1998; Tsebelis and Yataganas, 2002). The main controversy in this literature relates to the powers of the European Parliament under the cooperation procedure from the Single European Act and the Maastricht version of the co-decision procedure (co-decision I). While Tsebelis and Garrett (Tsebelis, 1994, 1997; Tsebelis and Garrett, 1997, 2000) argue that the European Parliament was more powerful under the cooperation procedure than under co-decision I, Crombez (1996, 1997), Steunenberg (1994, 1997a) and Moser (1996, 1997) find that cooperation did not empower the European Parliament whereas co-decision I did. There is, nevertheless, consensus that the European Parliament and the Council are equal legislators under the Amsterdam version of the co-decision procedure (co-decision II) – which is now the ordinary legislative procedure. However, some scholars point out that the second-reading absolute majority requirement for amending or rejecting still puts the European Parliament at a disadvantage vis-à-vis the Council, as it is easier for the European Parliament to accept the common position of the Council than to reject or amend it (Hagemann and Høyland, 2010).

The best-known model of legislative politics in the EU is developed by Tsebelis and Garrett (2000). Figure 3.4 is a simplified version of their model. The model is based on several assumptions about EU legislative politics:

- for QMV, the Council is deemed to have seven members, and a qualified majority is five out of seven;
- there is a single dimension of legislative bargaining, between 'more' or 'less' European integration;
- the actors have ideal policy preferences on this dimension and want outcomes to be as close as possible to these positions;
- the member states are aligned at different points along this single dimension;
- the Commission and the European Parliament are more pro-integrationist than most member states; and

Figure 3.4   *The Tsebelis–Garrett model of EU legislative politics*

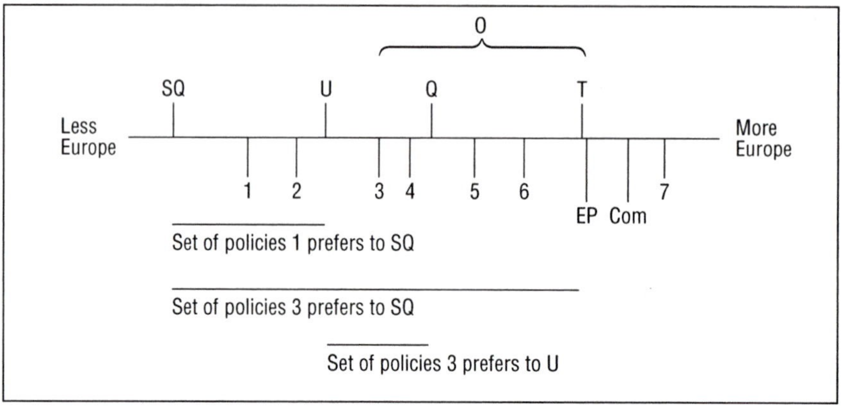

Notes:
Com = European Commission
EP = European Parliament
O = range of outcomes under the ordinary legislative procedure
Q = outcome under QMV in the Council under the consultation procedure
SQ = status quo
T = outcome under the consent procedure
U = outcome under unanimity in the Council under the consultation procedure

- the *status quo* (SQ), the policy outcome if not new policy is adopted, is less integrationist than any member state.

This set of simple assumptions provides a framework for analysing the legislative procedures in the EU.

Under *consultation,* the Commission has agenda-setting power and the Council can accept the proposal with QMV and reject by unanimity. Under these rules, the pivotal member of the Council under QMV, government 3 in Figure 3.4, will only accept policies it prefers to the best policy it can achieve under unanimity, which is at point U in the figure. Knowing this, the Commission can successfully propose Q. The role of the European Parliament is ignorable under this set-up, as it will always prefer the proposal from the Commission to the status quo. The *consultation* procedure only applies to a few areas under the Lisbon Treaty.

Under *consent,* the Council can only adopt legislation if the European Parliament has accepted the proposal from the Commission. Unlike *consultation,* here the European Parliament can reject the proposal from the Commission. Furthermore, the Council cannot adopt policies unanimously. The pivotal government (3) will accept any proposal in the set of policies which it prefers to SQ. The Commission can consequently successfully propose T. Meanwhile, the European Parliament will support a Commission proposal at T, as it is closer to its ideal position than SQ. The inability of the Council to adopt new policies by unanimity under *consent* means that the policy outcome is more integrationist than under *consultation*.

Under the *ordinary legislative procedure* (the Amsterdam version of co-decision), because both the pivotal government in the Council (3) and the European Parliament can amend legislation once the Commission has proposed it, the outcome will be in the range of policies between these two actors, as shown by O in Figure 3.4.

However, these results, and the results of other competing spatial models of EU legislative politics, are highly contingent on the position of actors and the location of the status quo. As a result, the real test of these models is empirical.

For example, early studies demonstrated, in line with the prediction of Tsebelis (1994), that the European Parliament had a significant influence on a number of important pieces of legislation (Earnshaw and Judge, 1997). In the area of health and safety at work the Council accepted several significant European Parliament amendments to the machine directive (89/393/EEC) and the display screen equipment directive (90/270/EEC) that would probably not have been accepted by the Council under the consultation procedure (Tsebelis, 1995). In the area of environmental policy the European Parliament secured significant amendments to the regulation establishing the European Environmental Agency (1210/90/EEC), the directive on genetically modified micro-organisms (90/219/EEC), the directive on the deliberate release of genetically modified organisms (90/220/EEC) and the directive on car emissions (91/441/EEC) (Hubschmid and Moser, 1997; Judge *et al.*, 1994; König and Pöter, 2001; Tsebelis and Kalandrakis, 1999). On all these issues, several member states were opposed to the European Parliament proposals, which were generally aimed at strengthening EU regulation of national regimes. Nevertheless, as the Tsebelis model predicts, on these policy issues there was a qualified majority in the Council who preferred to accept the European Parliament proposals than to see no EU legislation passed.

The European Parliament has also had an impact under the co-decision procedure (Garman and Hiditch, 1998). In July 1994 the European Parliament exercised its third-reading veto for the first time. On the draft directive on open network provision in voice telephony (ONP), the Council and the European Parliament were unable to agree a joint text in the conciliation committee. The Council subsequently reaffirmed its common position, which was then rejected by an absolute majority in the European Parliament. In March 1995 the European Parliament then exercised a third-reading veto on the draft directive on biotechnology inventions (Rittberger, 2000). This time the conciliation committee had agreed to a joint text, but a lobbying campaign by the environmental movement caused rank-and-file MEPs to reject the European Parliament leadership recommendation of the joint text and voted against it in the third reading. It is nevertheless unclear whether these cases are exceptions to the rule. In particular, the vote to veto the ONP directive was held in the first session after the 1994 European Parliament election when there was very high attendance (Earnshaw and Judge, 1995).

Tsebelis and his co-authors found that the key factor explaining the Council's acceptance of European Parliament amendments was Commission support (Tsebelis *et al.*, 2001). Under the cooperation procedure, once the Commission had rejected an amendment by the European Parliament, the probability that it would also be rejected by the Council was 88 per cent, compared to 83 per cent probability of being accepted if the Commission was supportive. Under co-decision I, in contrast, 67 per cent of European Parliament amendments rejected by the Commission were also rejected by the Council, while 73 per cent of European Parliament amendments accepted by the Commission were accepted by the Council. Studies by Kreppel (1999, 2002b) found that the European Parliament is more successful when proposing amendments that clarify a position taken by the Council or Commission than when proposing substantive policy changes. The European Parliament is more likely to get amendments passed when it is united, when the two main party groups vote together. The Parliament is also more able to get amendments passed in the first than in the second reading. Kreppel concludes that this is because the European Parliament tends to reproduce amendments in the second reading that were rejected in the first reading.

The European Parliament's success under the co-decision I procedure can at least partly be attributed to its rules of procedure. In a conscious effort to undermine the ability of the Council to reaffirm its common position in the third reading, Rule 78 of the Parliament's rules of procedures stated that the Parliament would ask the Commission to withdraw the proposal following a breakdown of the conciliation committee. If the Commission refused and the Council decided to reaffirm its common position, the Parliament leadership would automatically propose a motion to reject the Council's text at the next European Parliament plenary session. Faced with a 'take it or leave it' proposal, the Parliament leadership preferred to veto the legislation as a matter of principle, even if the Council's proposal was closer to the Parliament's policy position than the status quo. The rationale for this rule was that the European Parliament was involved in a long-term institutional game to secure a reform of the co-decision I procedure. After the rejection of the reaffirmed common position in the case of the ONP directive and the adoption of rule 78, the Council did not force the Parliament to vote on another reaffirmed common position. Hence, the rule meant that in practice co-decision I stopped with the conciliation committee.

This helps to explain the reform of the co-decision procedure in the Amsterdam Treaty (Hix, 2002a). The removal of the third reading formally strengthens the European Parliament's power to bargain with the Council. However, as the *de facto* operation of the co-decision I procedure was without the third reading anyway, it made no difference to the governments to change the treaty to remove this part of the procedure. As the member states were indifferent between keeping the old procedure and the European Parliament proposal to delete the third reading, the Parliament's proposed reform was accepted. This meant that the European Parliament became substantively closer to being an equal partner with the Council in EU legislative system.

In line with this interpretation, Kasack (2004) demonstrates that the ability of the European Parliament to pass amendments did not increase following the reform of the co-decision procedure. However, a minor, but at the time largely ignored reform of the co-decision procedure in Amsterdam, was the possibility to adopt legislation in the first reading, if the Council accepted the proposal from the European Parliament. While this increased the efficiency of EU legislation, critics warned against lack of transparency as informal vehicles for facilitating early stage negotiation between the European Parliament, the Council and the Commission, so-called *trialoges*, became common (Farrell and Heritier, 2004). In 2009, for example, more than 90 per cent of co-decision legislation was adopted at first reading. To achieve this, the European Parliament and the Council have to pass the same set of amendments to the Commission proposal, which requires considerable behind-the-scenes coordination between the Council Presidency and the *rapporteur*. It is questionable to what extent this volume of first-reading agreements is sustainable, since such deals preclude full deliberation in either the Council or the European Parliament.

To understand EU legislative politics, it is vital to know both the position of actors in both the Council and the European Parliament, as well as their interaction. Thomson *et al.* (2006) collected positional data on all governments as well as the European Parliament and the Commission and used the data to test competing theories of EU decision-making. Their findings highlight the significance of the location of the status quo in legislative bargaining in the EU and also warn against focusing too much on the formal rules of decision-making at the expense of compromises and bargaining. In particular, legislative outcomes from the EU tend to be located closer to the policy position of the average actor in the negotiations rather than to the policy position of a pivotal government in the Council, the European Parliament or the Commission (Achen, 2006).

In the bicameral bargaining between the European Parliament and the Council, the cohesiveness of the chambers also matters. Hagemann and Høyland (2010) find the European Parliament is less likely to meet the absolute majority requirement necessary for amending the common position of the Council when the Council is divided, than when the Council adopts the common position unanimously – which suggests a close connection between the political parties represented across the institutions. Nonetheless, the European Parliament tends to be more successful then the Council in the conciliation committee, in particular if it has the support of the Commission (König *et al.*, 2007).

Conclusion: Bicameral Politics in the EU

The European Union has a sophisticated and effective legislative system. Contemporary theories of legislative behaviour see the internal organization of the European Parliament and the Council and the processes of bargaining and coalition formation as products of the rational self-interests of the EU legislators: the MEPs and political groups in the European Parliament, and the governments in the Council. Both institutions have developed strong systems of specialization to facilitate information gathering, bargaining, and coalition building. There is also an increasingly formalized system of bicameral interaction, which has been capable of coping with an increasing membership of the EU in terms of national party delegations (in the European Parliament) and governments (in the Council).

Consensus and oversized majorities in coalition formation in the European Parliament and the Council are less a response to diverse social interests than a consequence of the institutional rules and policy preferences of the actors. The informal grand coalition between social democrats and the centre-right in the European Parliament is fostered by the absolute majority requirement in the second reading of the ordinary legislative procedure as well as by the similar policy preferences of these two parties on many EU issues. Meanwhile, most governments in the Council are led by social democrats or centre-right parties. This means that both legislative bodies are dominated by representatives with similar policy preferences. The underlying structure of contestation and conflict is hence driven by the relative balance of these policy positions within and across the institutions, as well as by the institutional interests of the actors. The leadership of European Parliament has been particularly successful at defending its institutional interests, often by sacrificing short-term policy gains in exchange for treaty reforms or institutional bargains with long-term consequences. Although the European Parliament has not always been successful, the result has been a development towards a genuinely bicameral system within a relatively short space of time.

Chapter 4

Judicial Politics

No treaty, constitution, piece of legislation, or executive decision can account for all possible developments. They are 'incomplete contracts'. Hence the actors that are responsible for enforcing these contracts, the courts, can use their discretion and shape policy outcomes, sometimes beyond the intention of the decision-makers. This battle between the intentions of decision-makers and the discretion of courts is what political scientists call 'judicial politics'. Judicial politics is particularly interesting in the EU, where the flexible constitutional rules and the nature of the legal instruments allow the European Court of Justice (ECJ) a high degree of discretion. To help explain how judicial politics works in the EU we first look at some general theories of the role and power of courts.

Political Theories of Constitutions and Courts

The rule of law ensures that decisions by political actors are binding. However, judges, who are responsible for enforcing the rule of law, are not neutral actors. Like other political actors, judges have their own preferences, and constitutions and laws are sufficiently incomplete to enable judges to act on those preferences. As the judicial review of legislative acts has evolved and societies have become more litigious, judges have become increasingly involved in making choices between different political positions. Consequently, judicial preferences, and the court judgments that follow from these preferences, are crucial determinants of the final political outcome of the policy process (e.g. Cohen, 1992). This realization has spawned a growing literature on judicial politics and judicial policy-making, of which research on the ECJ is part (for a comprehensive overview, see Whittington *et al.*, 2008).

To explain judicial policy-making, political scientists have developed a range of models to understand the strategic interaction between

Figure 4.1   *Court discretion in a separation-of-powers system*

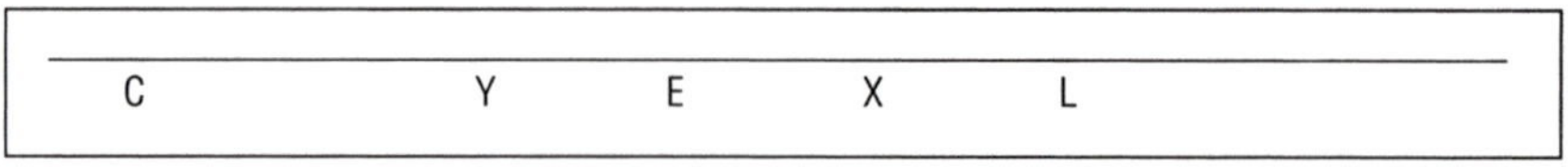

C	Y	E	X	L

Note: L = position of the legislature, E = position of the executive, C = position of the court, X = position of a policy agreement between L and E, X–E = E–Y (i.e. the executive is 'indifferent' between X and Y).

legislators and judges (e.g. Eskridge, 1991; Gely and Spillar, 1992; McCubbins *et al.*, 1990; Miller and Hammond, 1989; Rogers, 2001; Shipan, 2000; Steunenberg, 1997b; Vanberg, 1998, 2001; van Hees and Steunenberg, 2000). One such model, based on the US system of government, is illustrated in Figure 4.1 (see Weingast, 1996, pp. 172–4). The model assumes that the legislature, the executive, and the court are unitary actors in a one-dimensional political space, with symmetrical and single-peaked preferences, and ideal policy positions at points L, E, and C respectively. Legislation X is an agreement between the legislature and the executive, at the mid-point between these two actors. If the court is free to interpret the legislation when cases are brought before it, it will try to move the political outcome towards C. When the opportunity arises, through judicial review and opinions on cases brought before it, the court moves the final policy outcome to point Y. This is as close to the ideal point of the executive as position X, so the executive is indifferent between the original piece of legislation and the new court interpretation. However, if it is relatively costless for the executive to initiate new legislation, it will propose legislation that amends the court's ruling, at position E. The legislature will then agree to this new legislation, as E is closer to L than Y. Hence, because of the court's discretion and the executive's collusion with the court, the final policy outcome is E rather than X.

One implication of this type of analysis is that a court's discretion varies inversely with the probability that new legislation can be introduced to repeal its decisions (Cooter and Ginsburg, 1997; Ferejohn and Weingast, 1992; Vanberg, 1998). A court's power also varies with the amount of information the legislators have about the court's preferences and the probability that it will receive cases that allow it to act on these preferences (Rogers, 2001; Rogers and Vanberg, 2002). As the ease of adopting new legislation and acquiring information about the likely action of the court goes up, the discretion of the court goes down. As a consequence the court has most potential power when there is little information about its likely actions, as at the birth of the European Community.

Courts also have more freedom when there are many veto-players who can block changes to its interpretations, such as multiple political parties, multiple legislative chambers, or a separation of authority between the executive and the legislature (Tsebelis, 2000, 2002). Hence, in separation-of-powers systems, such as the US and the EU, and where legislation must be adopted by oversized and multiple legislative majorities, as in Germany and the EU, a court can reasonably assume that at least one veto-player will prefer the court's interpretation to the original legislative intention, and hence block a repeal of the court's decision.

Conversely, the discretion of courts is restricted under constitutional arrangements where there is a fusion of judicial and legislative powers. For example, in the UK there is not a codified constitution and the doctrine of parliamentary sovereignty asserts that no legislative majority can introduce rules or laws that bind a future majority. As a result, the British House of Commons is relatively free to pass new legislation to overturn court rulings. Similarly, in France the Constitutional Council is composed of ex-politicians who are highly partisan, which makes it more like a third chamber of parliament than an independent 'supreme court' (Stone, 1993, p. 30). Nevertheless, even in these systems the ability of judges to make policy has developed as the practice of judicial review has restrained the legislative authorities (Drewry, 1993; Steunenberg, 1997b; Stone, 1993; Stone Sweet, 2002; Vanberg, 2001).

Until now we have considered the courts as unitary actors. This is too simplifying. First, the judicial system consists of several courts that may not share the same political or institutional preferences. The relationship between courts, in particular the ability of higher courts to enforce lower-courts' compliance with their rulings and ensure that lower courts refer cases to upper courts, are fundamental aspects of the proper operation of any legal system (Segal, 2008).

Second, a court is a collective not a unitary actor. Individual judges have preferences over the outcome of individual cases, but perhaps more importantly, over the policy implications of their rulings. In other words, judges are unlikely to trade-off competing norms identically. Judges may, hence, reach different conclusions when faced with the same evidence. Consequently, the composition of the court matters. The executive, often in combination with the legislature, usually appoints the members of the higher courts. While judicial appointments can be understood as an act of delegation along the principal–agent framework presented in Chapter 2, more emphasis is usually placed on the need to secure the competence and independence of the judges than on their preference concurrencies with the appointing bodies. Nevertheless, it would be naïve to think that the executive does not take the political preferences of the candidates to the higher courts into account when making judicial appointments. For example, work on the US Supreme Court (perhaps one of the more politicized courts in the world) suggests that the pattern of appointments follow a political logic, where the executive tries to move the median in the court towards its ideal point by filling vacant seats with members closer to its ideal point than the median, regardless of the position of the judge vacating the seat (Krehbiel, 2007). The executive is, hence, able to move the median in the court only if somebody on the opposite side of the median vacates a seat on the court. In this 'move the median game' a judge will want to hold on to her seat as long as the executive is on the other side of the median, and only vacate her seat if the executive is on her side of the median.

In sum, there is a paradox at the heart of judicial politics. On the one hand, constitutions, backed by the rule of law and independent courts, are necessary for free citizens to enforce collective agreements. On the other hand, constitutions enable judges to play a role in lawmaking rather than simply apply law. Legislative majorities could design constitutions to limit the power of judges or introduce new legislation to repeal court decisions, but this would undermine the ability of the legal system to preserve property rights and enforce contracts fairly.

The EU Legal System and the European Court of Justice

'EU law' (which here will be use as shorthand for the legal acts of the EC and EU) constitutes a separate legal system that is distinct from but closely integrated with international law and the legal systems of the EU member states. This law derives from three main sources.

First, there are the 'primary' acts between the governments of the EU member states, as set out in the various treaties and the other conventions reforming the basic institutional structure of the EU.

Second, there are the 'secondary' legislative and executive acts of the Council, the European Parliament and the Commission, which derive from the articles in the treaties. The EU Treaty sets out five kinds of secondary act as follows:

1   *regulations*, which have general application and are binding on both the EU and the member states;
2   *directives*, which are addressed to any number of member states, are binding in terms of the result to be achieved, and must be transposed into law by the national authorities;
3   *decisions*, which are addressed to member states or private citizens (or legal entities such as firms) and are binding in their entirety;
4   *recommendations*, which can be addressed to any member state or citizen but which are not binding; and
5   *opinions*, which have the same force as recommendations.

However, these descriptions are somewhat misleading, particularly the distinction between regulations and directives. Directives are often so detailed that they leave little room for manoeuvre in the transposition of the legislation by the member states. Also, through a series of judgments the ECJ has made directives more akin to regulations in terms of their ability to confer rights directly on private citizens.

Added to these two formal sources of EU law are the 'general principles of law'. As in all legal systems, primary and secondary sources of law are unable to resolve all legal issues. The EU Treaty instructs the ECJ to ensure that 'the law is observed', which the ECJ has interpreted to mean that when applying the primary and secondary acts it can apply general legal principles derived from the EU's basic principles (as expressed in other articles in the treaty, such as the preamble) and from the constitutions of the member states. There are four main types of principle:

1   *principles of administrative and legislative legality*, which are drawn from various member states' legal traditions, such as 'legal certainty' (laws cannot be applied retroactively, and litigants can have legitimate expectations about EU actions), 'proportionality' (the means to achieve an end should be appropriate), and 'procedural fairness' (such as the right to a hearing and the right of legal professional privilege);
2   *economic freedoms*, which are drawn from the EU Treaty and include the 'four freedoms' (freedom of movement of goods, services, capital, and persons), the freedom to trade, and the freedom of competition;
3   *fundamental human rights*, which are set out in the Charter of Fundamental Rights of the European Union, which is attached to the treaty; and
4   *political rights*, which have been introduced in declarations by the member states and are referred to in the EU Treaty, such as 'transparency' (access to information) and subsidiarity (the EU can only act in policy areas not included in the treaties if the policy aims cannot be achieved adequately at the national level).

Composition and operation of the European Court of Justice

To apply these sources of law the member states established the European Court of Justice in Luxembourg (not to be confused with the European Court of Human Rights in Strasbourg, which is the court of the Council of Europe). The ECJ has one judge per member state, and eight advocates general. The treaty lays down how the judges are appointed, as follows:

The Judges and Advocates-General shall be chosen from persons whose independence is beyond doubt and who possess the qualifications required for appointment to the highest judicial offices in their respective countries ... they shall be appointed by common accord of the governments of the Member States for a term of six years ... Every three years there shall be a partial replacement of the Judges and Advocates-General ... The Judges shall elect the President of the Court of Justice from among their number for a term of three years. He may be re-elected. (Article 253)

The staggered terms of office of the judges ensures continuity. The other elements of the article are somewhat misleading. In practice, 'by common accord of the member states' means that each member state proposes a judge, whose nomination is then ratified by the other member states. Also, by convention the large member states each appoint one advocate general, with the remaining places rotating between the smaller member states. In addition, the independence and qualifications of the judges are sometimes compromised. There is little evidence of explicitly political appointments to the ECJ. But, several member states have tended to appoint 'academic lawyers' instead of recruiting judges from the senior ranks of the judiciary. To ensure the suitability of judges, the Lisbon Treaty prescribes that candidates have to appear before a panel of former ECJ judges and national courts whose role it is to issue an opinion of the suitability of candidates.

Unlike in the US Supreme Court, there are no provisions for dissenting opinions of judges in the ECJ to be recorded. In fact, the ECJ judges swear an oath to preserve the secrecy of the vote.

The workload of the ECJ has increased dramatically. The number of cases brought before it rose from 79 in 1970, to 279 in 1980, 384 in 1990, 543 in 1999, and 569 in 2009. In 2009, 741 cases were pending. To cope with this increase, the Court of First Instance (CFI) was created in 1989, but the CFI soon became as backlogged as the ECJ.

The ECJ has also established procedures to allow cases to be handled in a chamber of three or five judges instead of the full plenary. The Treaty of Nice extended this practice by formally reversing the precedence between the chamber system and the full court, whereby the ECJ now sits in chamber as the general rule, and the 'Grand Chamber' of 11 judges or the fully plenary of the court only meet on special occasions (Johnston, 2001, pp. 511–12). The Nice Treaty also introduced provisions for the establishment of specialized 'judicial panels' (by unanimity in the Council, following a proposal by the Commission of the ECJ, and after consultation with the European Parliament). The reason for this new practice was the need for a new procedure to deal with EU staff-related cases.

Figure 4.2 shows the proportion of cases heard by the different benches of the court between 2000 and 2009. The most notable trend is that the Full Court went from hearing 10 per cent of all cases in 2000 to not hearing any cases at all after 2005. Meanwhile, the Grand Chamber/Small Plenary kept its proportion of cases stable at about 10 to 15 per cent, while the small Chamber, consisting of only 3 judges, has

Figure 4.2   *Proportion of cases heard by bench type, 2000 to 2009*

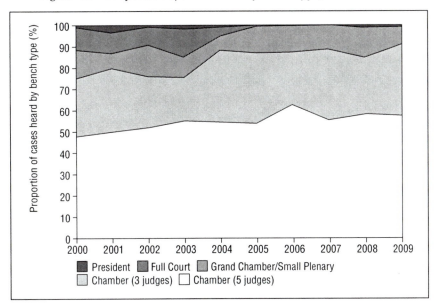

Source: Compiled from data in ECJ annual reports.

increased its share of the cases from 25 to 35 per cent. Meanwhile, the Chamber of 5 judges has kept its share of the cases relatively stable, hearing about 50 per cent of all cases. Hence, the main effect of the introduction of the chamber system is that a larger proportion of cases is heard by only 3 judges rather than the full court. While this change has increased the ability of the ECJ to deal with the increase in the number of cases, it may, to the extent that there is variation in the opinion of the judges, decrease the predictability of the rulings from the court.

Another innovation by the ECJ was the US practice of 'docket control', whereby it could refuse to hear a case that it thought should be resolved by a national court. This was used on an informal basis. The Treaty of Nice introduced a new procedure, whereby the CFI had the right to reject referrals from national courts if they did not fall under the jurisdiction of the treaty article covering preliminary references from national courts. However, the treaty left the wording of the treaty article untouched, thereby rejecting calls by several member states and some members of the ECJ to allow only the domestic courts of last instance to refer cases to the ECJ (see Court of Justice, 1999; Turner and Muñoz, 2000).

Justice via the ECJ is a long and drawn-out process. In 2009 the average length of proceedings was 17 months for both direct actions and references for preliminary rulings. Various suggestions have been made for speeding up this process, such as creating 'circuit courts' modelled on the US federal legal system (see Weiler, 1993). However, further reform would require a substantial overhaul of the EU court system and the national court referrals procedure, which to date the member state governments have refused to contemplate (see Craig, 2001).

Jurisdiction of the European Court of Justice

As defined in the EU Treaty, the ECJ has jurisdiction in three main areas. First, the court hears actions brought against member states for failure to comply with their obligations under the EU treaties and EU legislation. These actions, known as 'infringement proceedings', can either be brought by the Commission under Article 258, by another member state under Article 259, or in the area of state aid by either the Commission or a member state under Article 108. Article 260 also asserts that the member state concerned 'shall be required to take the necessary measures to comply with the judgment of the ECJ'. The ability of the ECJ to enforce rulings against the member states is limited. Until the Maastricht Treaty the Commission was only able to introduce new infringement proceedings against a state in an effort to embarrass it into submission. However, the Maastricht Treaty enabled the ECJ to impose financial sanctions on a member state if the Commission brought an additional action for failing to comply with the ECJ's original infringement judgment.

Second, like many national constitutional courts the ECJ has the power of judicial review of EU legislative and executive acts. Under Article 263 it can review the legality of acts adopted by the Council, the European Parliament, the Commission, the European Council, and the European Central Bank. Under this article any member state, the Council, the Commission, and the European Parliament can bring an action to the ECJ either on the ground of lack of competence, or because of an infringement of the treaty or a procedural requirement. In contrast, the Court of Auditors, the European Central Bank, and the Committee of the Regions can only bring actions to protect their own prerogatives. Finally, private citizens can bring actions against a decision by an EU institution that is of direct concern to them. A further aspect of the ECJ's power of judicial review is hearing actions against EU institutions for failing to act when they have been called upon to do so by the EU Treaty or a piece of secondary legislation (such as the delegation of powers to the Commission) under Article 265. These actions can be brought by any natural or legal person.

Third, under Article 267 the ECJ has jurisdiction to give preliminary rulings on references by national courts. Under this procedure, any national court can ask the ECJ to issue a ruling on a case that relates to any aspect of EU law. The national courts then have some discretion in determining how they should use the ECJ ruling when making their judgment on the case in question. At face value this suggests that it is the national courts that give the final ruling on many cases of EU law, which was probably the intention of the drafters of the Treaty of Rome. In practice, however, the jurisdiction of the ECJ under this article has been far more significant for the development of EU law and the constitutionalization of the EU system than the ECJ's jurisdiction in any other area. The ECJ often interprets EU law in a manner that allows little discretion to be exercised by national courts when applying the ECJ's interpretations. Also, Article 267 rulings constitute the majority of ECJ judgments. On the one hand, this reveals a high penetration of EU law into the national legal systems. On the other hand, by enabling national courts to enforce ECJ judgments, the preliminary references procedure has the effect of making national courts the lower tier of an integrated EU court system, and the ECJ the quasi-supreme court at its pinnacle.

The ECJ has jurisdiction over a number of other miscellaneous areas for which a small number of cases are heard each year. These include actions for damages against the EU institutions by a member state or a private individual (under Article 268), acts of the European Council relating to a breach of fundamental rights by a member state (under Article 269), and employment disputes between the EU and the staff of the various EU institutions (under Article 270).

In sum, the Treaty of Rome created a new legal system and a powerful supranational court to enforce this system. Nevertheless, when signing the treaty the founding fathers probably did not realize the potential long-term implication of their action: the gradual constitutionalization of the EU through the operation of the legal system and the judgments of the ECJ.

Constitutionalization of the EU

In a judgment in 1986 the ECJ described the founding treaties as a 'constitutional charter' (case 294/83, *Parti Écologiste 'Les Verts'* v. *European Parliament* [1986], ECR 1339). This was the first time the court had used the term 'constitution' to describe the treaties, although academic lawyers had been pointing to the constitutional status of the treaties for some time (Green, 1969). Nevertheless, the EU constitution lies less in the founding treaties than in the gradual constitutionalization of the EU legal system (Hartley, 1986; Mancini, 1989; Shapiro, 1992; Stein, 1981; Weiler, 1991, 1997). The two central principles of this constitution are the direct effect and the supremacy of EU law, which are classic doctrines in federal legal systems.

Direct effect: EU law as the law of the land for national citizens

The direct effect of EU law means that individual citizens have rights under EU law that must be upheld by national courts. This makes EU law 'the law of the land' in the member states (Weiler, 1991, p. 2413). The ECJ first asserted the direct effect of EU law in a landmark judgment in 1963 (case 26/62, *Van Gend en Loos* v. *Nederlandse Administratie der Belastingen* [1963], ECR 1). In this case a private firm sought to invoke EC law against the Dutch customs authority in a Dutch court, and the Dutch court consulted the ECJ for a preliminary ruling on whether EC law applied. Four of the then six member states argued to the ECJ that the specific article in the EC Treaty to which the case referred did not have direct effect. Despite the opposition of the majority of the signatories of the treaty the ECJ ruled that individuals did have the right to invoke EC law because 'the Community constitutes a new legal order ... the subjects of which comprise not only member states but also their nationals'. This was accepted by the Dutch court. This ruling meant that direct effect applied to primary treaty articles, and in subsequent judgments the ECJ expanded the doctrine to all categories of legal acts of the EU.

However, direct effect works differently for regulations and directives. Regulations have a vertical and a horizontal direct effect, meaning that citizens can defend their rights against both the state (vertical) and other individuals or legal entities (horizontal). But, in the case of directives the ECJ has taken the view that these only have a vertical direct effect because they must be transposed into national law by the member states (case 152/84, *Marshall I* [1986], ECR 723; case C-91/92, *Faccini Dori* [1994] ECR 1-3325).

To compensate for the lack of a horizontal direct effect of directives the ECJ has developed the doctrine of 'state liability'. This implies that the state is liable for all infringements of EU directives. For example, when an Italian firm became insolvent and failed to make redundancy payments to its employees, the ECJ ruled that the Italian state should foot the bill because it had not properly transposed Directive 80/987, which required the establishment of guarantee funds for redundancy compensation (cases C-6,9/90, *Francovich I* [1991], ECR 1-5357).

The central implication of direct effect is that EU law is more like domestic law than international law. The subjects of international law are states: if a state fails to abide by its obligations under an international convention, individuals cannot invoke the convention in their national courts unless the convention has been incorporated into domestic law. In contrast to international law, the subjects of domestic law and EU law are private citizens who can invoke their rights in domestic courts.

The establishment of the doctrine of direct effect led to a dramatic increase in the number of cases brought by individuals to national courts to defend their rights under EU law. The effect, as Weiler (1991, p. 2414) argues, was that 'individuals ... became the "guardians" of the legal integrity of Community law within Europe similar to the way that individuals in the United States have been the principal actors in ensuring the vindication of the Bill of Rights and other federal law'.

Supremacy: EU law as the higher law of the land

Unlike the US constitution, the Treaty of Rome did not contain a 'supremacy clause' stating that in the event of a conflict between national and EC law, EC law would be supreme. However, shortly after establishing the direct effect of EC law the ECJ asserted the supremacy of EC law, and like direct effect this doctrine was confirmed and reinforced in subsequent rulings.

The landmark judgment on this doctrine was in the case of *Costa* v. *ENEL* in 1964 (case 6/64 [1964], ECR 585). An Italian court asked the ECJ to give a preliminary ruling on a case in which there was a clear contradiction between Italian and EC law. The ECJ duly argued that:

> By creating a Community of unlimited duration, having its own institutions, its own personality, [and] its own legal capacity ... the member states have limited their sovereign rights, albeit within limited fields, and have thus created a body of law which binds both their nationals and themselves. The integration into the laws of each member state of provisions which derive from the Community ... make it impossible for the states, as a corollary, to accord precedence to a unilateral and subsequent measure over a legal system accepted by them on a basis of reciprocity.

In other words, the ECJ held that the doctrine of supremacy was implicit in the transfer of competences to the EC level and the direct effect of EC law.

Formally speaking, EU law takes superiority over national law only in those areas in which EU law applies. But, as the competences of the EU have expanded into almost all areas of public policy, the application of supremacy no longer applies to the 'limited fields' to which the ECJ referred in 1964. Also, through successive judgments the ECJ has established that supremacy applies to all EU norms, be it an article in the treaties, a secondary act by the EU institutions (no matter how minor, such as administrative regulations of the Commission), or even a 'general principle of EU law', as defined by the ECJ.

As a result, the supremacy doctrine has further distanced the EU legal system from international law. Direct effect is insufficient by itself to establish the EU legal system as a system of domestic law. When international conventions are incorporated into domestic law, individuals can invoke them in domestic courts. But, if a domestic legislature subsequently adopts a national law that contravenes the international convention, the provisions of the international law no longer apply. With the supremacy of EU law, in contrast, national legislative majorities are permanently bound by the provisions of EU law. Weiler (1991: 2415) therefore concludes that 'parallels of this kind of constitutional order ... may be found only in the internal constitutional order of federal states'. By establishing the dual doctrines of direct effect and supremacy of EU law the ECJ has transformed the EU from an international organization into a quasi-federal polity.

Integration through law and economic constitutionalism

The application of these basic doctrines has enabled the ECJ to play a central role in the economic and political integration of the EU. For example, in the area of economic freedoms Article 34 states simply that 'quantitative restrictions on imports and all measures having equivalent effect shall be prohibited between the member states'. While this article seems pretty innocuous, through a series of judgments the ECJ has transformed the EU's economic system on the basis of the article (Alter and Meunier-Aitsahalia, 1994).

In 1974, in the *Dassonville* decision (case 8/74 [1974], ECR 837), the ECJ declared illegal any national rule that was 'capable of hindering, actually or potentially, directly or indirectly, intra-Community trade'. Such hindrances included not only quotas and other restrictions on imports, but also internal rules that affected the competitive position of imported goods. The implication of this interpretation became clear with the *Cassis de Dijon* judgment in 1979 (case 120/78 [1979], ECR 837). In this decision the ECJ ruled that a German law specifying that a 'liquor' must have an alcohol content of at least 25 per cent could not prevent the marketing of the French drink *Cassis de Dijon* in Germany as a liquor, despite it having an alcohol content of less than 20 per cent. This is known as the principle of 'mutual recognition': that is, any product that can be legally sold in one member state can be legally sold anywhere in the EU. Mutual recognition subsequently became one of the basic principles in the establishment of the single market (see Chapter 8).

This interpretation of the treaty obligations is inherently deregulatory. It has forced member states to delete numerous social and economic rules that in many cases were established as expressions of particular social, cultural and ideological preferences. The effect is a specific type of 'economic constitution', whereby competition between different national regulatory regimes, has the potential of facilitating a 'race to the bottom' (see Chalmers, 1995; Joerges, 1994; Ehlermann and Hancher, 1995; Maduro, 1997; Streit and Mussler, 1995; and Chapter 8).

State-like properties: external sovereignty and internal coercion

As we discussed in Chapter 1, the EU is not a state. In particular, until the Lisbon Treaty, the EU did not have the right to sign international treaties. And, the EU still does not have a legitimate internal monopoly on the use of coercion to enforce its decisions. Nevertheless, the ECJ has been instrumental in developing state-like properties for the EU in both these areas.

First, on the external side the EU has always had the power to make treaties with third parties under Article 207 (common commercial policy) and Article 217 (association agreements). Even in these limited fields, though, most member states originally considered that the articles merely allowed the Commission to negotiate agreements on behalf of the member states, and that sovereignty remained with the member states. However, in 1971 the ECJ established the principle that when making agreements with third countries the EU would be sovereign over any existing or future acts between the individual member states and the third countries in question (case 22/70, ER TA [1971], ECR 263). In the same judgment the ECJ argued that the jurisdiction of the EU in the international sphere covered *all* areas of EU competence, not just those included in these two treaty articles. In other words, in one stroke the ECJ conferred new treaty-making powers to the EU and deprived the member states of their own independent powers relating to EU competences. In a sense, this ECJ interpretation was a precursor of Article 216 in the Lisbon Treaty, which enables the EU to conclude agreements with any third countries or international organizations which are legally binding for both the EU and its member states.

Second, on the internal side, Article 4 of the treaty instructs the member states to 'take any appropriate measure ... to ensure the fulfilment of the obligations arising out of the Treaties or resulting from the acts of the institutions'. Most member states originally assumed that this article took effect only in relation to the other treaty articles and EU law. However, the ECJ has used it as a substitute for the lack of direct enforcement powers in the EU system (see Shaw, 1996, pp. 208–13; Weatherill and Beaumont, 2004). For example, it ruled that member states must adapt all relevant national rules to the requirements of EU law (cases 205-215/82, *Deutsche Milchkontor GmbH* v. *Germany* [1983], ECR 2633), and that Article 10 should be applied to all state organs at all levels of government (Case C-8/88, *Germany* v. *Commission* [1990], ECR 1-2321).

Furthermore, the ECJ has broadened the definition of the types of action a member state must use to enforce EU law. For instance in 1997 it ruled that the French government should have used the state security forces more effectively to ensure the free movement of goods in the internal market (case C-265/95, *Commission* v. *France* [1997]). The court acknowledged that member states should 'retain exclusive competence as regards the maintenance of public order and the safeguarding of internal security', but it went on to argue that:

> it falls to the Court ... to verify ... whether the member state concerned has adopted appropriate measures for ensuring the free movement of goods ... [In the present case] the French police were either not present or did not intervene ... the actions in question were not always rapid ... [and] only a very small number of persons has been identified and prosecuted.

In other words, the EU did not need a police force of its own in order to exercise coercive power. According to the ECJ, the member states were obliged to take all reasonable measures to enforce EU law, including the use of security forces.

Kompetenz–Kompetenz: **judicial review of competence conflicts**

A key weapon in the arsenal of supreme courts in any multilevel political system is the ability to police the boundary of competences between the states and central government: what German constitutional lawyers call *Kompetenz–Kompetenz*. Prior to the Lisbon Treaty, which sets out a catalogue of competences, the EU Treaty gave no formal powers to the ECJ to undertake this task. The treaty referred to the principle of subsidiarity: meaning that the EU can only act in areas that are not better tackled at the national level. The European Council then agreed a set of rules on how this principle should apply, for example the Commission must prove in the draft of any legislation that the legislation does not breach the principle of subsidiarity. However, it was open to question whether the subsidiarity principle was justiciable before a national court or the ECJ.

In the absence of a catalogue of competences, the ECJ gradually developed a power to police the vertical allocation of competences. Most significant in this respect was the ECJ's decision in 2000 to annul a directive on tobacco advertising and sponsorship (case 376/98, *Germany* v. *European Parliament and Council* [2000]). In 1998, the Council and European Parliament had adopted this directive under Article 114 of the EC Treaty, covering the harmonization of laws for the completion of the single market. However, the ECJ ruled that: 'Article [114] should be available as a legal basis only in cases where obstacles to the exercise of fundamental freedoms and distortion of competition are considerable.' Thus, a ban on tobacco advertising could only be adopted under Article 114 if it allowed products that circulated in the internal market (such as newspapers or magazines) to move more freely than if there were different national tobacco advertising rules. Since the proposed ban was more widespread than simply covering these goods, the ECJ pointed out that 'the national measures affected are to a large extent inspired by public health policy objectives'. However, the public health competences in the treaty (Article 168) only allowed for the adoption of EU legislation on common safety standards in organizations, and hence did not extend to the harmonization of national public health standards more generally.

Some observers were surprised by the judgment to annul the directive as the ECJ had applied Article 114 quite broadly in the past (Hervey, 2001). However, the ruling can be interpreted as a strategic signal by the ECJ to the governments that it could be trusted in competence–conflict decisions: in this case between the harmonization of rules in the single market (an exclusive EU competence) and public health standards (an exclusive competence of the member states). By ruling that the EU could only harmonize rules in the single market if there was a clear case of market distortion, the ECJ effectively defined a boundary between the federal powers of the EU and the rights of the member states.

This was particularly significant because the ECJ judges were aware that the Convention on the Future of Europe was about to begin, and that one of the key issues in the design of an EU constitution would be a catalogue of competences in the EU and who would be responsible for policing such a catalogue. Several member states had already proposed a new quasi-judicial body for this task: a special EU constitutional court composed either of national parliamentarians or judges from the highest courts in the member states. By ruling against the legislative majorities in the Council and European Parliament, the ECJ demonstrated that it could be trusted to protect the rights of states that were on the losing side in the EU's legislative process.

The Lisbon Treaty subsequently established a catalogue of competences, with areas defined as either exclusive competences of the EU (Article 3), shared competences between the EU and the member states (Article 4), areas for coordination of economic and social policies (Article 5), and areas where EU action can supplement the actions of the member states (Article 6). The Lisbon Treaty also established that the ECJ has the sole right to police the boundaries between these competences. In other words, following the tobacco advertising ruling the member states decided to grant exclusive *Kompetenz–Kompetenz* to the ECJ rather than to a new body. Without the tobacco advertising judgment it is unlikely that the governments would have been able to establish formally this important new power.

Penetration of EU Law into National Legal Systems

The penetration of EU law into national legal systems has developed both quantitatively and qualitatively. On the quantitative side there has been a substantial increase in the use of the Article 267 procedure for requesting preliminary rulings from the ECJ by national courts, and on the qualitative side national courts have gradually accepted the existence and supremacy of the EU legal system over national law and constitutions.

Quantitative: national courts' use of ECJ preliminary rulings

Figure 4.3 shows the number of Article 267 references by all member state courts to the ECJ in 1961 to 2009. During this period, while the EU grew from six member states to 27 the number of references to the ECJ rose from one or two a year in the early 1960s to over 250 a year since the late 1990s. The rapid rise in references in the 1970s followed the establishment of the doctrines of direct effect and supremacy, which encouraged national courts to use the references procedure to strengthen their positions in their domestic political systems, and encouraged private litigants to use the procedure to invoke their rights in their domestic courts. Although the number of annual referrals fell in the years

Figure 4.3   *Growth of ECJ referrals, 1961–2009*

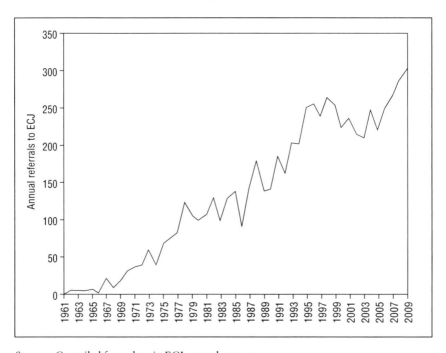

Source: Compiled from data in ECJ annual reports.

Table 4.1   *Average annual number of ECJ referrals, by member state*

	1961–72	1973–85	1986–94	1995–2003	2004–9
Germany	12.7	33.1	42.4	51.4	61.2
Netherlands	3.7	15.3	19.9	18.1	26.8
Belgium	3.3	10.6	18.2	16.6	23.8
Italy	2.8	11.5	22.3	48.0	35.2
France	2.3	18.5	27.1	17.1	21.3
Luxembourg	1.0	2.6	1.8	2.9	2.0
United Kingdom		4.9	14.1	20.9	17.0
Denmark		1.8	4.0	5.3	4.2
Ireland		1.8	2.3	2.0	1.4
Greece			4.6	4.7	11.8
Spain			4.6	11.6	12.8
Portugal			1.8	4.8	2.2
Austria				27.7	16.5
Sweden				5.0	6.0
Finland				4.3	4.0
Poland					4.8
Bulgaria					4.5
Hungary					4.5
Latvia					3.5
Czech Republic					2.4
Estonia					2.0
Lithuania					2.0
Slovenia					2.0
Cyprus					1.0
Malta					1.0
Romania					1.0
Slovakia					1.0
Total	23.5	100.1	163.1	240.4	275.9

Source: Compiled from data in ECJ annual reports.

prior to the Central, Eastern, and Southern enlargement in 2004, the volume of referrals has since increased.

However, not all member states' courts have used the references system to the same extent. As Table 4.1 shows, the number of referrals from most member state has risen over time. The figures suggest a 'learning curve', however, with the original member states making more references in each period than the member states that joined later. Nevertheless, several other factors cross-cut this trend. First, within each wave of EU members, the larger states have made more references than the smaller states: Germany, France, and Italy have made more references than the Netherlands, Belgium, and Luxembourg; the UK have made more than Denmark and Ireland; Spain has made more than Portugal; Austria and Sweden made more than Finland; and Poland has made more than the other member states who joined in 2004 and 2007. Second, despite the learning curve, British courts made fewer references in the early 1990s than did Dutch and Belgian courts, which perhaps reflects the sceptical attitude towards the EU among the public and the elite in the UK (Golub, 1996). However, the courts in Ireland, Portugal, and Luxembourg, where the public and elites are strongly pro-European, also made few references to the ECJ.

Stone Sweet and Brunell (1998a, 1998b, 2000) consequently argue that other factors might explain the variations in member state usage of the referral mechanism. In particular, a significant proportion of the variation is explained by the size and openness of a member state's economy. In other words, the larger the market and the larger the volume of imports, the greater the incentive for importing firms to take cases to the ECJ to guarantee market access for their goods and services. In line with this, the increase in the number of referrals since 2004 cannot be attributed to the arrival of 12 new member states. Instead, it might be due to the fact that Germany, the Netherlands, and Belgium, who are the major net exporters in the EU single market, have substantively increased their number of referrals. Together with Italy and France, these five countries have been responsible for more than 64 per cent of all referrals since 2004.

The subject matter of references to the ECJ by national courts has also changed significantly. In the early period most references related to the Common Agricultural Policy. However, by the early 1990s, issues relating to the operation of the internal market – such as the free movement of goods, the free movement of workers, taxes, freedom of establishment, and the approximation of national laws – comprised over half of all references. This reflects the fact that the majority of laws governing the regulation of the market were set at the European rather than the national level (see Chapter 8).

Finally, there has been considerable national variation in the extent of compliance with EU law. Table 4.2 shows the average number of infringement cases brought before the ECJ in 2005 to 2009. At face value these figures reinforce the conventional wisdom that the southern EU states (except Portugal) are generally less likely to enforce EU law as effectively as the northern states. However, Mbaye (2001) has found that in addition to the efficiency of the domestic bureaucracy (the southern effect), the greater political and economic power of northern member states in terms of their voting weight in the Council and their importance to the European economy reduces the likelihood that they will be subject to infringement proceedings before the ECJ (see Börzel, 2001).

Table 4.2   *Infringement cases declared and dismissed, 2005–9*

	Declared	Dismissed
Italy	72	9
Greece	66	4
Luxembourg	66	0
Spain	59	4
Belgium	48	3
France	40	1
Germany	35	6
Austria	35	0
Portugal	35	1
United Kingdom	25	8
Ireland	23	3
Finland	22	3
Sweden	18	2
Netherlands	14	2
Czech Republic	9	0
Denmark	7	1
Poland	7	0
Malta	3	0
Slovakia	2	0
Estonia	1	0
Lithuania	1	0
Slovenia	1	0
Bulgaria	0	0
Cyprus	0	0
Latvia	0	0
Hungary	0	0
Romania	0	0
Total	589	47

Note: These figures reflect the number of cases in which the ECJ declared that a member state failed to fulfil its treaty obligations, in 2005 to 2009.

Source: Compiled from data in 2009 ECJ annual report.

Qualitative: national courts' acceptance of the EU legal system

Not all national courts have capitulated to the emerging constitutionalization of the EU (Mattli and Slaughter, 1998a, 1998b). In particular, the German Constitutional Court (*Bundesverfassungsgericht*) at first accepted direct effect and supremacy, but more recently has challenged the legitimacy of the EU framework (see Alter, 2001; Kokott, 1998). In the *Brunner* judgment, the German court ruled that the

German Basic Law limited the transfer of powers to the EU, and argued that the EU was a *sui generis* organization and not a state based on democratic norms. The court claimed that because it was commanded by the German constitution to defend the basic rights and principles of democracy set out in the German Basic Law, it had the jurisdiction to declare acts of the EU *ultra vires* (beyond the legal authority of the EU) if they breached the Basic Law (but it would seek to cooperate with the ECJ if faced with such a prospect). Having said this, the court declared that the Maastricht Treaty could be ratified by Germany because the German parliament maintained the right to transfer (or withdraw) German government competences to the EU. The court warned, however, that the EU could only legitimately become a state if it were fully democratic, with the necessary institutions of parliamentary democracy, a clearly defined hierarchy of rights and a single demos (Weiler, 1995).

In the UK, in contrast, the courts accepted direct effect immediately upon the country's accession to the EU in 1973. However, it was difficult for the UK to accept the supremacy of EU law as this conflicted with the central constitutional concept of parliamentary sovereignty – that is, acts of parliament immediately overrode all existing law or legislation (Craig, 1998). Nevertheless, in 1990 the House of Lords found a way to reconcile parliamentary sovereignty and EU supremacy. On a reference from the House of Lords, the ECJ ruled that a 1988 parliamentary act was in breach of EU law, and the House of Lords accepted this judgement on the ground that in passing the 1972 act of accession to the EU the British parliament had voluntarily accepted the EU legal system, of which the supremacy of EU law was a central part. The House of Lords also argued that this did not compromise parliamentary sovereignty, as a future British parliament could repeal the act of accession, and thus withdraw the UK from the EU.

Another interesting case is Sweden, where there was a dispute over whether the domestic constitution would have to be changed if Sweden became a member of the EU (Bernitz, 2001). The constitution had been amended in 1965 to allow for the conclusion of treaties with the then European Community. But most experts in Sweden took the view that because of the development of the EU and its competences in the 1980s and 1990s, this provision was not enough to allow for the substantial transfer of power that would result from accession. The new constitutional provision that was finally agreed upon by the Riksdag (the Swedish parliament) was significantly less extensive than many legal experts had proposed. The constitutional amendment imposed constraints on EU law that flowed directly from the German *Brunner* judgment. If an EU law conflicted with a fundamental right that was protected by the national constitution and backed by a national democratic majority, a Swedish court would be forced to reject the EU law unless it was clear that the relevant right was sufficiently protected at the EU level by a European charter of fundamental rights.

In sum, EU law has been accepted as an integral part of national legal systems and as sovereign over national law. However, in several member states the highest national courts maintain that this is conditional on national constitutional norms: for example that parliaments retain the right to revoke the supremacy of EU law by withdrawing the transfer of sovereignty to the EU (as in Germany, the UK, and France). One could argue that this solution has been driven primarily by the desire of national courts not to renounce their previous positions on the EU, or to declare basic constitutional principles null and void (such as parliamentary sovereignty in the British case). Only in Germany did the national constitutional court withdraw from its previously unconditional acceptance of supremacy, but this had profound effects on the other member states, as in the Swedish case, and forced the EU to address the protection of fundamental rights and the democratic accountability of the EU institutions.

Explanations of EU Judicial Politics: Is the ECJ a Runaway Agent?

Early work from a legal–formalist perspective regarded the ECJ as a heroic promoter of European integration against the wishes of the member states (see Shapiro, 1981; Weiler, 1994). More recently two competing views of the ECJ have emerged (Alter, 2008). Drawing on the intergovernmental approach, one school of thought understands the ECJ as an agent of the member states; empowered to enforce integration on behalf of the governments. In this view, member states are powerful, the judges are national delegates, and the court is sensitive to the interests of the governments, fearing treaty reforms and non-compliance if seen as acting beyond its mandate. The alternative view, derived from the supranational politics approach, argues that the ECJ has been able to work with self-interested lower national courts, integrationist judges, and private interests to move EU integration beyond the intentions of the governments.

Legal–formalist view: the hero of European integration

Legal scholars of the EU have traditionally emphasized the internal logic of law and the legal process. As Weiler (1994, p. 525) explains: 'The formalistic claim is that judicial process rests above or outside politics, a neutral arena in which courts scientifically interpret the meaning of policy decided by others.' In other words, the ECJ simply applies EU law as set out in the EU treaties and in secondary legislation, without any conscious desire to promote its own power or institutional interests. An EU constitution has developed because the EU legal system had its own internal 'integrationist' logic. Instead of a hierarchy of norms, the governments established the goal of 'ever closer union' as the ultimate norm. This forced the ECJ to develop the doctrines of direct effect and supremacy. Furthermore, there was an *effect utile* in the legal workings of the EU, whereby the ECJ preferred to apply EU law in the most efficient and effective way, which compelled the ECJ to promote legal integration to prevent the EU political system from becoming ineffective and unworkable (Cappelletti *et al.*, 1986).

In the same vein, legal–formalist explanations posit that national courts were eager to find ways to reconcile their previous jurisprudence with the emerging EU legal system. Through the preliminary references system, the ECJ provided national courts with the appropriate argumentation and rationale for them to absorb the new doctrines into their national legal systems (see Wincott, 1995). Variations in the use of the preliminary references system and the dates of acceptance of the ECJ doctrines can be explained by variations in national legal cultures and doctrines (Chalmers, 1997; Maher, 1998; Mattli and Slaughter, 1998a, 1998b; Stone Sweet, 1998; de Witte, 1998). On the cultural side, different systems of training judges, different promotion systems and different career paths have produced different patterns of behaviour and reasoning by judges – such as formal versus pragmatic, deductive versus inductive, or abstract versus consensual. Also, each system has a different relationship between administrative, constitutional, and common law courts, and different rules, traditions, and powers of judicial review. On the doctrinal side, the place of fundamental rights in domestic constitutions and how the concept of sovereignty is defined affects the relationship between national legal norms and the EU constitution.

These legal–formalist explanations have some important shortcomings. On an empirical level, the doctrines of supremacy and direct effect are not simply logical extensions of the EU Treaty: if federalization of the EU had been intended from the outset, the treaty would have contained a supremacy clause as in other federal constitutions. Also, many national courts were not immediately convinced of the ECJ's justification of direct effect and supremacy (see Alter, 1998a, pp. 230–4). From the general study of courts and judicial politics we know that the institutional interests of courts and the personal policy preferences of judges drive judges' actions. In a sense, the structural and cultural logic of the law are simply another set of constraints within which courts and judges secure these aims. Consequently, on a theoretical level, explanations of the emergence of the EU constitution must also take into account the institutional and policy incentives of EU and national judges and the strategic motivations of other actors in the system.

Intergovernmentalism: the ECJ as an agent of the member states

From an intergovernmentalist perspective the development of the EU constitution can be understood as a deliberate strategy by national governments (e.g. Cooter and Drexl, 1994; Garrett, 1992, 1995; Garrett *et al.*, 1998; Garrett and Weingast, 1993; Kelemen, 2001). In this view, governments have consciously allowed the ECJ, national courts and transnational litigants to promote legal integration in the EU because it has been in the governments' political or economic interests. If the ECJ or a national court takes an action that is contrary to a government's interests, the government will simply ignore the ruling. High-profile clashes between national governments and the ECJ or national courts over EU legal issues are rare, but not because the governments are powerless in the face of court activism. Instead, courts are careful not to make decisions that threaten government interests, and governments accept decisions that appear to be against them because they are in fact in their long-term interests. Courts are strategic actors. However, they are constrained by the possibility of government threats, such as reform of the treaty or the passing of new legislation. This explains why the ECJ has refused to establish that directives have horizontal direct effect, despite the opinions of several advocates-general and numerous academic lawyers.

Garrett (1995) proposes a simple model to explain why governments often accept ECJ rulings against them. The model posits that governments take two main factors into account: the domestic political clout of the industry that is harmed by the ECJ decision, and the potential gains to the national economy as a whole. If the industry is domestically weak and the general economic gains will be large, the government will accept the ECJ ruling and put up with complaints from the domestic industry. For example, with regard to the *Cassis de Dijon* judgment Garrett argues that the German government accepted a ruling that would damage its (relatively small) spirits industry because the rest of the German economy stood to benefit from the trade liberalization that would result from the principle of mutual recognition. Conversely if the industry in question is domestically powerful and the general economic gains will be small, the government will engage in 'overt evasion' of the ECJ's decision. However, this rarely occurs because the ECJ is careful to avoid such a showdown. The implication is that in the *Cassis de Dijon* case the ECJ waited for the right case to come along to establish the principle of mutual recognition (for a similar model of ECJ behaviour on international trade disputes, see Kelemen, 2001).

By focusing on the centrality of national governments in the EU system and conceptualizing their actions as highly rational, these explanations have some of the same limitations as the general intergovernmentalist approach (see Chapter 1). At an empirical level, there is substantial evidence that the ECJ and national courts have often taken decisions that governments have opposed, and which have had negative effects on the competitiveness of national economies in the single market (Mattli and Slaughter, 1995). At a theoretical level, meanwhile, this can be explained by the fact that governments do not have perfect information about the likely outcome of delegating adjudication to the ECJ and national courts (see Alter, 2001, pp. 182–208; cf. Pierson, 1996). For example, when the Treaty of Rome was signed, few governments realized that the ECJ would establish the doctrines of direct effect and supremacy or could predict the significance of the preliminary reference procedure (Alter, 1998b).

In a later work, Garrett *et al.* (1998) accepted that governments are not completely free to ignore adverse rulings. For example, in cases where the EU treaties are clear and the legal precedent is strong, the costs to a government of ignoring an adverse ruling (in terms of threatening the very foundations of the EU) will be high. In other words, although national governments behave strategically, there are long-term constraints on them as a result of their allowing the ECJ to develop its own legal precedents and norms. However, the main thrust of Garrett *et al.*'s argument remains: the ECJ is heavily constrained if the potential costs to a powerful domestic constituency are high or if a large number of governments are likely to be adversely affected by an ECJ ruling. For example, the *Barber* judgment on equal pension rights for men and women imposed substantial costs on all governments. In response, the governments added a protocol to the treaty that prevented the retroactive application of the judgment, and subsequently the ECJ moderated its activism in this area – although it extended its activities in other areas of pension rights (see Pollack, 2003, pp. 360–72).

Supranational politics: the ECJ as an independent but constrained actor

An alternative explanation depicts the ECJ as an explicitly powerful political actor capable of using its discretion to forward its interests by catering to the interests of national courts and private interests against the interests of the member states. Karen Alter (2008) highlights four steps that are crucial for understanding the development of judicial politics in the EU.

First, since the ECJ can only rule on specific cases, it relies on other actors to provide cases it can rule on. The main non-state actors that have sufficient resources to bring cases to the ECJ are private firms and interest groups. Stone Sweet and Brunell (1998a, 1998b) argue that firms involved in the import and export of goods are the dominant private litigants in the EU legal system. These interests have a particular incentive to secure effective application of the free movement of goods and services, and have sufficient resources to take actions all the way through to the ECJ. Regarding interest groups, Conant (2002) argues that variations in the incentives of groups explain why EU law has developed in areas other than those of direct interest to the ECJ or national governments. Concentrated interests (who potentially face large costs/benefits from EU law) tend to be better organized than diffuse interests (who potentially face small costs/benefits from EU law) (see Chapter 6). But, the relatively low cost of gaining access to the ECJ means that EU law has been a vehicle for the promotion of some interests that are underrepresented in several domestic systems of interest representation (Pollack, 1997).

Second, the ECJ can only rule on cases that get referred to it. Most cases involving EU law are not referred. Unlike the ECJ, national courts are not interested in the emergence of an EU constitution to promote the goal of European integration. Instead, national courts use the EU legal system to secure their interests and policy preferences within their national contexts (e.g. Weiler, 1991, 1994). In many domestic political systems judicial review is weak, parliaments are sovereign, and governments have substantial administrative and political resources at their disposal. Consequently, national courts welcome the direct effect and supremacy of EU law and actively use the preliminary references system to strengthen their hand in the national policy process. However, Alter (2001) and Golub (1996) argue that national judges are selective in the cases they bring to the ECJ.

Also, lower and higher courts have different incentives vis-à-vis the EU legal system. Alter (1996, 1998a) contends that lower courts can use the preliminary references procedure to play higher courts and the ECJ off against each other to influence legal developments in their preferred direction. As a result, lower courts have made more use of the preliminary references procedure than higher courts (Stone Sweet and Brunell, 1998b).

Third, however, activism by the ECJ has not been linear (Chalmers, 1997). Rather, it has responded to the pace of the integration process, and has been sensitive to anti-ECJ feelings among certain national governments. Carrubba *et al.* (2008) show that the ECJ takes member states' preferences into account in their judicial rulings. Specifically, as the number of governments contributing observations in support of an accused government increases, the probability of the ECJ ruling in favour of the accused government also increases. This effect is substantively larger when a government is the litigant rather than the Commission or a private individual. This suggests that the ECJ responds to the strength of feeling among the member states on a case-by-case basis. This helps explain why the ECJ seems inconsistent in its attempts to promote European integration.

Fourth, rulings in the ECJ must be followed through by other political actors. Different national political and institutional settings affect the way in which national courts respond to the EU (e.g. Alter, 2000, 2001; Golub, 1996; Mattli and Slaughter, 1998a, 1998b). There are different levels of public support for European integration, awareness of the ECJ, satisfaction with the ECJ, and general satisfaction with courts and judges (Caldeira and Gibson, 1995; Gibson and Caldeira, 1995, 1998). If courts ignore these mass sentiments they risk provoking parliamentary challenges to their judicial autonomy and undermining public acceptance of courts and the judicial system. In addition, each national system has a different structure of legal institutions, court procedures, powers of judicial review, cost of access for litigants, and legal training of judges (Alter, 2000).

Nevertheless, this explanation suffers from some of the same weaknesses as the general supranational politics approach. In particular, it overemphasizes the autonomy of supranational institutions and transnational interests in the promotion of EU legal integration. These scholars argue that once transnational activities and supranational institutions have been unleashed there is little that national governments can do to stop them (Pierson, 1996). However, national governments are the signatories of the treaties, and if provoked they can restrict the powers of the ECJ and redefine the nature of the EU judicial system.

Conclusion: a European Constitution?

The EU has a legal–constitutional framework that contains two of the basic doctrines of a federal legal system: the direct effect of EU law on individual citizens throughout the EU, and the supremacy of EU law over domestic law. Also, in the ECJ the EU has a powerful constitutional and administrative body to oversee the implementation of EU law and keep the EU institutions in check.

How this came about is a matter of contention. Courts have more discretion under certain institutional designs than others. The ECJ has substantial room for manoeuvre because there is only a small probability that the EU Treaty will be reformed to reduce the ECJ's powers or that new legislation will be passed to overturn one of its decisions. Because there are many veto-players in the EU system, at least one member state, the Commission, the European Parliament or a group of powerful transnational economic actors is likely to be able to block a reduction of the ECJ's powers or the overturning of one of its decisions.

However, the ECJ has imperfect information on how other actors will react to its decisions. Governments have shorter time horizons than courts because they face general elections every few years. This means that they are less interested in the long-term implications of delegating powers to the ECJ than in the immediate political salience of a decision. But it also means that the ECJ is uncertain about what issues will become politically salient in which member state.

This judicial politics game has produced an incomplete constitution. The precise constitutional architecture is not fixed, particularly following the rejection of the draft Constitutional Treaty. In a sense, as Weiler (1993) argues, the EU still has an 'unknown destination' (see Shonfield, 1973).

However, the current quasi-constitutional set-up in the EU already constitutes a relatively stable equilibrium: a balance between the discretion of the ECJ/national courts on the one hand and the conscious decisions by national governments to construct a rule of law to enable economic integration on the other. This goes hand in hand with the emerging equilibrium in the vertical allocation of competences (discussed in Chapter 1). Put this way, the constitutional settlement relating to the allocation of market regulation competences to the European level relies on a stable structure for the enforcement of contracts in these policy areas.

Nevertheless, this equilibrium could be upset by changes in public opinion, party competition and ideology, interest group politics, and so on, which could push the EU towards a full federal constitutional arrangement or result in a constitutional step backwards, as happened with the German Constitutional Court ruling on the Maastricht Treaty. It is to the political context of institutional politics that we turn in Part II of this book.

Politics

Chapter 5

Public Opinion

Theories of the Social Bases of Politics
End of the Permissive Consensus
Explaining Support for the EU at the National Level
Explaining Support for the EU at the Individual Level
Political Context Matters: the Role of Ideology, Parties, and the Media
Conclusion: from Consensus to Conflict?

Citizens' attitudes towards the European Union now matter. As the EU institutions have gained more powers and the policy agenda of the EU has expanded, the publics have become more questioning. Europe's political leaders, at both the national and European levels, operate in a political environment where actions at the EU level are constrained by citizens' attitudes. Hence, understanding how citizens' attitudes towards the EU are formed is essential to understand both the possibility of further integration and the lines of political conflict in EU policy-making. We first discuss some general theories of people's attitudes towards politics, before looking at the patterns and determinants of attitudes towards the EU.

Theories of the Social Bases of Politics

Each individual has a set of beliefs, opinions, values, and interests which shapes their attitude towards politics and the political process. These political 'preferences' often derive from deep historical or cultural identities, such as nationality, religion, or language. Political preferences also stem from economic interests, such as whether a policy will increase a person's income. Inevitably, different individuals and social groups have different preferences and this produces conflicts in the political process.

The 'cleavage model' of politics posits that political divisions derive from 'critical junctures' in the development of a political system (Lipset and Rokkan, 1967). For example, at the national level in Europe, the democratic revolution in the eighteenth and early nineteenth centuries produced a conflict between church and state (between liberals and conservatives), and the industrial revolution of the nineteenth century divided workers and the owners of capital (between socialists and liberals/conservatives). Using the Lipset–Rokkan model to conceptualize the social bases of politics at the European level, there are two main cleavages in EU politics: (a) national–territorial; and (b) transnational–socio-economic.

First, the combination of a common territory, history, mass culture, legal rights, and duties, and a national economy constitute a powerful force for individual attachment to the nation-state (Smith, 1991, p. 14). The EU is segmented along national lines: that is, between the EU member states, within which the bulk of individual social interactions and experiences take place and interests and identifications are formed (see Lijphart, 1977). This national–territorial cleavage emerges in EU politics when an issue on the agenda puts individuals from different nations on different sides of the debate, for example when one national group appears to gain at the expense of another.

Second, cross-cutting these national divisions are transnational interests. On certain issues a group of citizens in one nation-state may have more in common with a similar group in another nation-state than with the rest of society in their own nation-state. For example, Danish and Hungarian farmers have a common interest in defending the Common Agricultural Policy (CAP) against the interests of Danish and Hungarian consumers. Transnational cleavages can be mobilized around traditional social divisions, such as class, but can also emerge around newer 'issue divisions', such as post-materialism, age, education, and information. These transnational divisions tend to be less salient in EU politics than national divisions, but they become increasingly important when the EU agenda shifts to questions of economic redistribution between functional rather than territorial groups (such as EU labour market policies) and questions of social and political values (such as EU environmental policies).

These ideas explain why different countries and social groups have different interests in EU politics, but they do not explain how these attitudes change over time. For this, David Easton's (1965, 1975) theory of 'affective' and 'utilitarian' support for political institutions is useful. Affective support is an ideological or non-material attachment to a political institution, while utilitarian support is the belief that the institution promotes an individual's economic or political interests. Rather than seeing these two types of support as competing or contradictory, Easton saw them as related. His idea was that a citizen's affective support for an institution provides a basic reservoir of goodwill towards a set of institutions. Some citizens have a high reservoir of affective support, while others have a low level. If a citizen then perceives that an institution promotes (acts against) her material interests or policy preferences, this basic level of support will go up (down). Hence, utilitarian cost–benefit calculations determine whether the underlying ideological level of support goes up or down over time. This process can operate at both the national and individual level, explaining how countries' and individuals' support for the EU changes over time.

This chapter starts by plotting the general pattern of support for European integration over time. It then looks at what factors explain variations in support for the EU, first across member states, then at the level of individual citizens, and then how the national political context shapes individual-level attitudes towards the EU and its policies.

End of the Permissive Consensus

According to Lindberg and Scheingold (1970), following the signing of the Treaties of Paris and Rome, there was a 'permissive consensus' among European citizens in favour of European integration. This term came from V.O. Key (1961), who had used it to describe support by the American public for certain government actions, particularly in foreign affairs. On the whole, on foreign policy issues citizens tended to have the same opinions and hence were willing to trust the government to get on with business, without questioning too much, regardless of the political colour of the government of the day. The same phenomenon was apparent among the publics of the founding members of the European Communities. As Inglehart (1970b, p. 773) explained:

> There was a favourable prevailing attitude toward the subject, but it was of low salience as a political issue – leaving national decision-makers free to take steps favourable to integration if they wished but also leaving them a wide liberty of choice.

In other words, most people in Europe were either not interested in European integration, and therefore had no opinion about their government's actions on the issue, or generally supported their government's efforts to promote further integration.

These ideas could not be tested without survey data. Since 1973 the European Commission has commissioned Europe-wide opinion polls every six months, conducted by private polling agencies in each member state and involving a sample of approximately 1,000 interviewees in each country. These Eurobarometer surveys provide a large dataset for the study of citizens' attitudes towards European integration, among other things. As with national governments and national opinion polls, the European Commission, the EU governments, the MEPs, and perhaps even the judges in the ECJ study these polls carefully to gauge the level of support for or opposition towards further EU integration or specific EU policies.

One question which has been asked in all Eurobarometer surveys is about a person's attitude towards his or her country's membership of the EU, as follows:

> Generally speaking, do you think [your country's] membership of the Common Market/European Community/ European Union is a 'good thing', a 'bad thing', 'neither good nor bad', 'don't know'.

This is a simple question for citizens to understand, and is probably a more accurate barometer of attitudes towards the EU than some of the more abstract questions in the Eurobarometer surveys, such as the questions about support for European integration, or whether a person has a European identity.

As the solid line in Figure 5.1 shows, in the early 1980s just over 50 per cent of citizens were in favour of their country's membership of the then 'European Communities'. Throughout the 1980s support for European integration rose steadily, perhaps as a result of public interest in, and enthusiasm for, the '1992 programme' – the project of completing the single market by the end of 1992 (Inglehart and Reif, 1991; see also Chapter 8). Up to this point, it appeared that support for European integration was a 'fair-weather phenomenon': support rose in economic good times and declined in bad times (see Eichenberg and Dalton, 1993). The average annual economic growth rate is also plotted in Figure 5.1, and seems to follow a similar pattern to support for EU membership until

Figure 5.1   *Public support for European integration and economic growth*

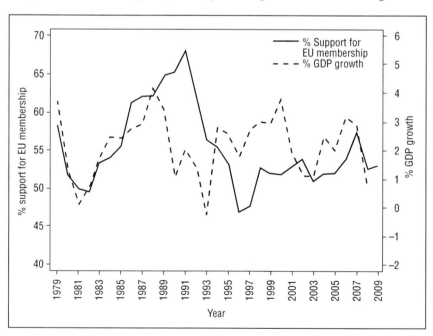

Source: Calculated from Standard Eurobarometer polls and Eurostat data.

the late 1980s. This made sense, since until the Single European Act European integration largely meant 'economic integration' for most people in Europe.

Something happened in the early 1990s, however. Support for the EU peaked in 1991, with 71 per cent being in favour of their country's membership of the EU, and then declined rapidly after that, and has remain at a relatively low level since then – just above 50 per cent.

Widespread opposition to the EU first emerged during the process of ratifying the Maastricht Treaty, in 1992 to 1993, in the wake of referendums in France, Denmark, and Ireland, the defeat of the government in the British House of Commons on the Maastricht Treaty bill, and a Constitutional Court challenge in Germany. This opposition continued in the form of votes for anti-European parties in the 1994 European Parliament elections, in the 1994 referendums on EU membership in Austria, Finland, Sweden, and Norway, and in the European Parliament elections in 1995 and 1996 in Austria, Sweden, and Finland. Anti-EU sentiment then continued throughout the 1990s and early 2000s, culminating in the defeat of the proposed EU Constitution in referendums in France and the Netherlands in 2005 and the defeat of the Lisbon Treaty in a referendum in Ireland in 2008.

Part of the collapse in support for European integration in the early 1990s can be attributed to changing geopolitical relations in Europe, as a result of the collapse of the Berlin Wall, the end of the Cold War and the reunification of Germany. However, another element is that with the Maastricht Treaty, the 'European Union' was now clearly something more than just economic integration. For the first time, many citizens now paid attention to what was happening in Brussels and started to question whether they agreed with everything their governments were doing in their name. For example, as Figure 5.2 shows, when asked what the EU means to people they name a wide variety of economic as well as political factors. By far the most commonly mentioned issue in 2008 was the individual freedom to travel, study, and work in the EU, as a result of the free movement of persons in the single market. The second most commonly mentioned issue was 'the euro'. However, significant proportions of people also associate the EU with non-economic issues such as peace, democracy, having a stronger voice in the world, cultural diversity, bureaucracy, crime, a waste of money, not enough control of external borders, social protection, and a loss of cultural identity.

If a permissive consensus existed in the first few decades of European integration, as a result of the perceived benign economic benefits of European integration, it certainly no longer exists today. As Franklin *et al.* (1994) elegantly put it: the anti-European 'bottle' has been 'uncorked'. Citizens are now more aware of policies and events at the European level, and their attitudes towards the EU and its policies are now influenced by a range of economic as well as political factors, and

Figure 5.2   *What the EU means to citizens*

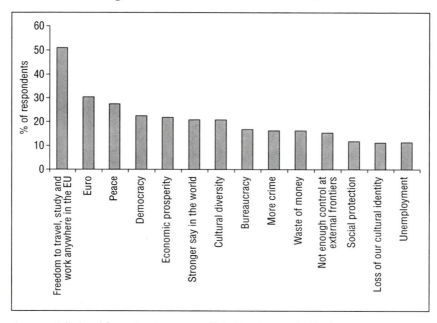

Source: Calculated from Eurobarometer 69.2 (March–May 2008) data.

Note: The survey question was: 'What does the European Union mean to you personally? (Multiple answers possible).'

these attitudes shape the way governments, Commissioners, MEPs, and ECJ justices behave when making decisions at the European level (see Hooghe and Marks, 2009).

Explaining Support for the EU at the National Level

Citizens in Latvia, the United Kingdom, Austria, and Hungary tend to show the lowest levels of support for the EU in recent Eurobarometer polls, with only 30 to 40 per cent of respondents in these countries saying that they support their country's membership of the EU. At the other end of the scale, citizens in Luxembourg, the Netherlands, Ireland, Belgium, Spain, and Denmark tend to show the highest levels of support for EU membership, in the 65 to 80 per cent range. The remaining 15 member states have levels of support in the 40 to 65 per cent range. Moreover, it is worth remembering that two of the more pro-European states have had referendums in the last five years where a majority of their citizens voted against an EU Treaty: the Netherlands on the EU constitution in 2005, and Ireland on the Lisbon Treaty in 2008. So, even a high level of popular support for the EU does not guarantee that a public will support everything their government does in Brussels in their name.

There are a wide range of interests and traditions that differ across the nation-states of Europe which could explain these national-level variations. These include:

- *Political differences*, such as weak versus strong national identities, Catholic versus Protestant, North versus South, East versus West, long versus short democratic traditions, majoritarian versus consensual systems of government, liberal versus social/Christian democratic welfare states, and liberal versus coordinated versions of capitalism (Esping-Andersen, 1990; Hall and Soskice, 2001; Lijphart, 1984; Rokkan, 1973).
- *Economic differences*, such as rich versus poor, exporters versus importers, industrial versus agricultural, services versus manufacturing, high versus low unemployment, large- versus small-income inequalities, energy producers versus energy consumers, high versus low levels of public debt, and so on (Cole and Cole 1997; Gourevitch, 1989; Krugman, 1991).

Figure 5.3 illustrates the relationship between some of these political factors and national levels of support for EU membership, using survey data from spring 2008. Citizens in countries with high levels of trust in their national governments tend to be more pro-EU than citizens in countries with lower levels of trust in their governments. Similarly, higher levels of satisfaction with national democracy go hand in hand with support for the EU. Interestingly, the perception is often the reverse: that people in countries with untrustworthy politicians or failing national institutions are thought to support the EU because they trust the EU more than their national leaders. For example, concerns about a 'democratic deficit' at the European level have had a larger impact on support for the EU in countries with strong democratic institutions (Rohrschneider, 2002). However, strong democratic institutions can also shape citizens' attitudes to the EU, in that citizens who trust what their national leaders are doing in Brussels are more likely to support European integration.

In contrast, there is no relationship these days between the length of EU membership and support for the EU. The citizens of the original member states were neither clearly pro- nor anti-European in the 1950s, but there was a high level of trust between these societies and a sense of community (Inglehart, 1991; Niedermayer, 1995). This allowed the national elites to begin the process of European integration. Building on this, the integration process had a socializing effect as the citizens grew used to the idea of integration and were more willing to accept its consequences, which led to increased support for the project (Anderson and Kaltenthaler, 1996). Consequently, in the Eurobarometer polls in the

Figure 5.3 *Some political determinants of national-level support for the EU*

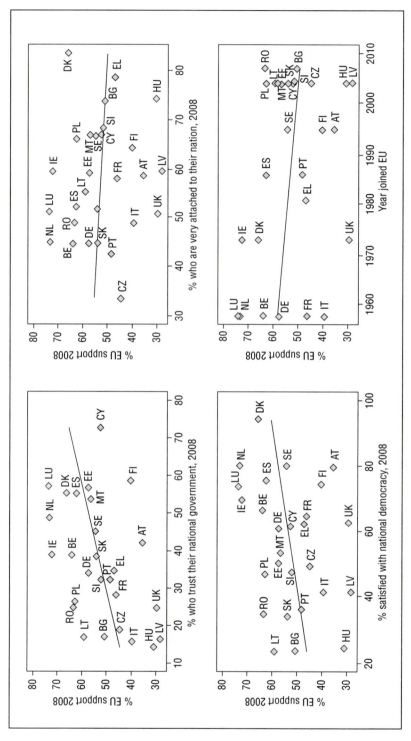

Source: Calculated from Eurobarometer 69.2 (March–May 2008) data.

1980s the citizens of the 'original six' – Germany, France, Italy, Belgium, the Netherlands, and Luxembourg – were on average more supportive of European integration than the citizens in the states which joined later – Ireland, Denmark and the UK (in 1973), Greece (in 1981), Spain and Portugal (in 1987), and Austria, Sweden, and Finland (in 1995). However, the effect of the length of membership has now disappeared. In 2008 there was considerable divergence in attitudes towards the EU among the 'original six' member states, among the nine states who joined between 1973 and 1995, and among the 'new 12' who joined in 2004 and 2007.

Also, at the aggregate level there does not appear to be any relationship between attachment to the nation and support for the EU. Some countries with strong national attachments, such as Denmark, have high levels of support for the EU, whereas other countries with strong national attachments, such as Hungary, tend to be more opposed to the EU. Attachment to one's country may be positively or negatively related to support for the EU, depending on whether European integration is perceived to strengthen or weaken a country's national identity (Diez Medrano and Gutiérrez, 2001; Schild, 2001) or its national political or policy-making institutions (Martinotti and Stefanizzi, 1995; van Keesbergen, 2000). So, for example, some Danish citizens feel that European integration has not undermined Danish identity and instead has enabled Denmark to play a more prominent role on the European and international stage.

Having seen that political differences are not fully capable of explaining different national levels of support for the EU, do economic differences do any better? Figure 5.4 illustrates the relationship between some economic factors and national-level support for the EU, also from the spring 2008 surveys. As citizens have learned more about the EU they have become more aware of how much their country stands to gain or lose economically from European integration or particular EU policies. One issue is whether a national economy has gained or lost from trade liberalization through the EU single market (Anderson and Reichert, 1996; Eichenberg and Dalton, 1993; Gabel and Palmer, 1995; see also Chapter 8). Richer countries tend to be slightly more pro-European than poorer countries, perhaps revealing that citizens in richer countries feel that they are gaining more from economic integration in Europe. Countries which are net exporters to the rest of the EU tend to be more supportive of the EU than countries which are large net importers. If a country imports more than it exports from the rest of the EU, then European economic integration is likely to lead to increased competition for domestic goods and services providers, whereas if the reverse is the case, then national producers are likely to feel that they benefit from economic integration in Europe.

Regarding public finances, countries with higher budget deficits tend to be more supportive of the EU than countries with lower public deficits.

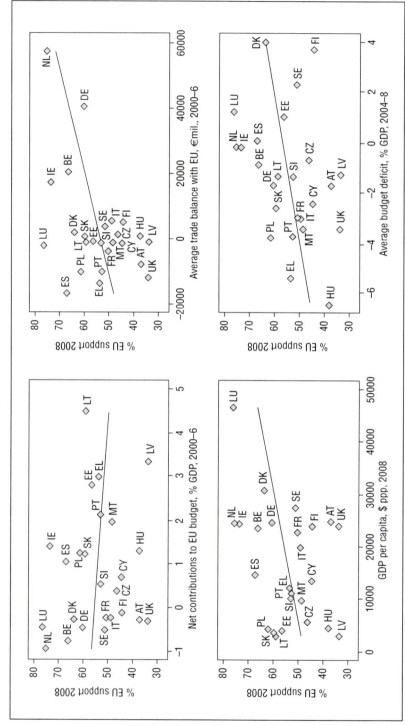

Figure 5.4   Some economic factors and national-level support for the EU

Source: Calculated from Eurobarometer 69.2 (March–May 2008) and Eurostat data.

This perhaps suggests that citizens in high-borrowing states favour economic integration in Europe as a way of constraining profligate politicians.

Nevertheless, as with the political factors, none of these relationships are particularly strong at explaining variations in national levels of support for the EU. For example, there does not seem to be a clear relationship between contributions to the EU budget and support for the EU, with some net contributors (such as the Netherlands and Belgium) being strongly pro-European and other net contributors (such as the United Kingdom and Austria) being less pro-European.

However, economic factors do explain some of the variation over time in the levels of support for European integration among the original member states and the states that joined later (see Gabel, 1998; Gabel and Whitten, 1997). For example, the German and Dutch economies benefit hugely from the single market because these states are large net exporters to the rest of the EU, but the citizens of Germany and the Netherlands have become increasingly aware that they are also the major contributors to the EU budget, which has led to declining levels of support for the EU in these states in recent years. Conversely, between the early 1980s and early 1990s the citizens of Greece, Ireland, Portugal, Spain, and Italy, whose national economies benefited from EU cohesion policies, saw significant increases in their support for the EU. In addition, the economic boom in Ireland in the 1990s was fuelled by foreign direct investment, attracted by Ireland's integration with and relative competitiveness in the wider European single market. When Ireland and Britain joined the EU in 1973 they had similar levels of support for the EU. By the mid-2000s, however, Ireland had become one of the most pro-European countries in Europe, largely as a result of the direct economic benefits to Ireland from EU membership, while Britain remained one of the most anti-European, where many citizens do not identify specific economics benefits from EU membership.

Explaining Support for the EU at the Individual Level

Part of the reason that variations in the national levels of support or difficult to explain is that the real story is at the individual level. The process of economic integration in Europe affects individuals' economic interests in a variety of ways (Gabel, 1998). First, the introduction of free movement of goods in the single market has presented opportunities for citizens connected with export-oriented manufacturing and service industries in the private sector. Entrepreneurs, business owners and company directors can now market their products elsewhere in the EU, and reap economies of scale from a higher turnover. On the other hand, trade liberalization has brought new competition for sectors that are either non-tradable (such as the public sector), or cater to national markets (for example small businesses in the retail sector) or compete with imported goods (such as local manufacturers). Furthermore, EU state aid policies have presented new challenges to jobs in industries that rely on government subsidies or protectionist trade policies (see Frieden, 1991; Smith and Wanke, 1993).

Second, the free movement of capital and the single currency have created new investment opportunities for citizens with capital to invest. Capital liberalization has also led to cross-border competition for investments. Skilled workers attract investment by offering advanced skills, while manual workers attract investment by offering lower wages. Consequently, capital liberalization has increased the opportunity of low-wage manual workers (in Eastern Europe, for example) to attract investment, but threatens manual workers in high-wage regions (primarily in Western Europe) who might become victims of capital flight. Also, the fiscal policy rules of EMU have forced governments to restrict their public expenditure, thus threatening welfare programmes that support low-income citizens and the unemployed (see Chapter 10).

Third, the free movement of persons has increased competition for jobs in all sectors of the economy, as citizens move between member states to seek better economic opportunities. Citizens with considerable human capital, such as a high level of education and employment in professional or management positions, are likely to see this as a chance to improve their status. On the other hand, low-skilled manual workers in Western Europe are likely to see it as threatening their jobs, as immigrants from other EU countries (mainly from Eastern Europe) move to other states, and so suppress wages for some low-skilled sectors of the economy (in the service sector, for example).

Fourth, the CAP is the only clearly distributive EU policy (see Chapter 9). The benefits of CAP subsidies are concentrated on farmers, whereas the costs are spread among all EU taxpayers and consumers. However, some farmers benefit from the CAP more than others. In general, farmers with high incomes, particularly in Western Europe, are likely to perceive that the CAP helps them to secure markets for their products and subsidizes their production, whereas farmers with low incomes are likely to perceive that the CAP does not benefit them.

Figure 5.5 consequently shows attitudes towards EU membership in 2009 by social group and whether a person is from an old 15- or a new 12-member state. In general, social groups with high incomes and high-skill levels are more supportive of the EU than social groups with lower incomes and lower-skill levels. Professionals (such as doctors, lawyers, accountants, architects, and university professors!), with highly mobile skills in the single market are most supportive of integration, as are company directors and senior managers, who can benefit from new profit opportunities.

Figure 5.5   *Social group and EU support*

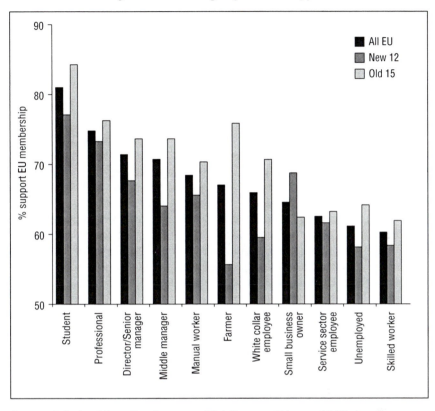

Source: Calculated from Eurobarometer 71.1 (January–February 2009) data.

In contrast, white-collar employees (who make up 15 per cent of EU citizens) are less supportive of the EU, as are small business owners, who are predominantly in non-tradable sectors, and so face more competition in the single market. Similarly, skilled workers and workers in the service sector (who together comprise over 20 per cent of EU citizens) are also less favourably disposed towards European integration. These groups of workers are the most threatened by the free movement of labour, which creates more competition for relatively low-skilled jobs. In contrast, manual workers, who are mainly in manufacturing jobs, are the most supportive of EU membership among the lower-skilled social groups, perhaps as they feel protected from labour market competition by restrictive hiring-and-firing practices in many manufacturing contracts.

Of the two social groups in Figure 5.5 which are not active in the labour market, students are highly supportive of integration, while the unemployed are far more sceptical. In addition to students' immediate opportunities for subsidized education elsewhere in the EU, through such programmes as Erasmus and Socrates, many students aspire to enter the professions or take up senior management positions, and hence their attitudes are similar to those held by these social groups. At the other end of the social spectrum, the unemployed may have lost their jobs as a result of competitive pressures in the single market or government cutbacks to meet the convergence criteria for EMU, and also face more competition for jobs in the labour market.

When comparing the attitudes of social groups in the old 15 and new 12 member states, on average within a social group, citizens in the old 15 states are more supportive of EU membership than citizens in the new 12. This could reflect socialization, as a result of a longer history of membership of the EU. However, it might also reflect the fact that within each social group, citizens in the old 15 are on average more highly paid than comparable people in the new 12, and so can benefit more from the freer circulation of goods, services, and labour in Europe's single market.

When comparing attitudes in the two groups of member states, two social groups are particularly interesting. First, the biggest difference in support levels between the old and new member states is among farmers: with farmers in the old 15 showing very strong support for EU membership while farmers in the new 12 showing very low levels of support. This clearly reflects the effect of EU agricultural subsidies via the CAP, which farmers in the old 15 states have directly benefited from for many decades, while farmers in the new 12 states may feel that they have not done as well out of the CAP as they expected, as a result of the budgetary bargain that was struck between the old and new member states in the enlargement negotiations.

Second, owners of small businesses in the new 12 states are more supportive of the EU than owners of small businesses in the old 15 states. In fact, this is the only social group where support is higher in the new member states than in the old member states. This perhaps reflects the new market opportunities for small businesses in the new member states, either to attract capital investment or to seek to expand their businesses. In contrast, small businesses in the old member states, who are mainly providing goods and services for domestic markets, face more competition in their sectors as a result of economic integration in Europe and EU enlargement.

Social group is, of course, not the only significant division between individual citizens in Europe. Indeed, since the 1960s, social class has declined as an indicator of general political attitudes. For example 'class voting', whereby working classes vote for socialist parties and middle classes vote for liberal, Christian or conservative parties, has declined throughout Europe (Dalton, 1988; Franklin, 1992). Class identity has also eroded as different patterns of production, consumption, and educational and life experiences have produced new and cross-cutting socio-economic attitudes, interests and values (Bell, 1960; Dahrendorf, 1959). These social changes, together with economic prosperity and peace, led Ronald Inglehart (1977a) to argue that a 'silent revolution' had taken place in advanced industrial societies: whereby class-based materialist values of economic and political security were being replaced through generational-change by post-materialist values, such as environmentalism, women's and minorities' rights, democratic participation, and nuclear disarmament.

Applying his theory of post-materialism to European integration, Inglehart (1977b, p. 151) argued that:

> we would expect post-materialists to have a significantly less parochial and more cosmopolitan outlook than materialists ... First, the post-materialists are less pre-occupied with immediate concrete needs than are materialists; other things being equal they should have more psychic energy to invest in relatively remote abstractions such as the European Community. Moreover ... the relative priority accorded to national security has fallen ... [hence] one of the key symbols of nation-alism has lost much of its potency – especially among post-materialists.

Because Inglehart expected that younger-age cohorts would be more post-materialist, he proposed that support for European integration should be stronger among younger people (Inglehart, 1970b, 1977b). He also developed several related hypotheses: for example that individuals with greater cognitive skills, as a result of higher levels of education, are more able to understand the abstract process of European integration (Inglehart, 1970a; Inglehart and Rabier, 1978; Janssen, 1991). The opposite might also be the case, however, in that the more someone understands the process of European integration the more they might realize that they personally do not benefit or perhaps even lose from this process.

There are other non-economic factors which might play a role at the individual level. One such factor is religion. As Nelson and Guth (2003, p. 89) explain:

> The very idea of a united Europe reaches back to early medieval con-ceptions of Christendom united under the spiritual and temporal authority of the Roman pontiff. Moreover, integration in the postwar period was largely a Christian Democratic project led by Catholic politicians – such as Konrad Adenauer, Robert Schuman and Alcide de Gasperi – who enjoyed unwavering support from the church hier-archy. On the other side of the Reformation divide, Protestant politi-cians in Britain and Scandinavia feared joining a European project dominated by 'wine-drinking Catholics'.

And what about the other major religions in Europe: Orthodox Christianity, Islam, and Judaism? In contrast to the national churches of

Figure 5.6   *Education, age, migration, and religion and EU support*

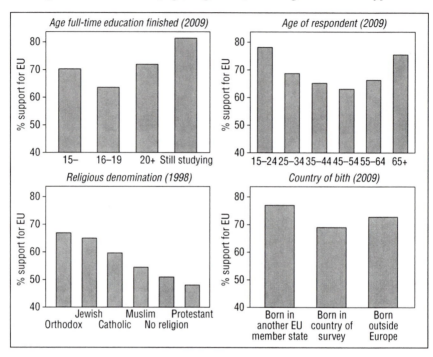

Source: Calculated from Eurobarometer 71.1 (January–February 2009) data, for the education, age, and migration questions, and Eurobarometer 50.0 (autumn 1998) data, for the religious denomination question.

the Protestant faith, these other faiths are based on transnational religious organizations and identities, as is Catholicism, and might hence be considered to be anti-nation-state in their ideologies.

Figure 5.6 consequently illustrates the effects of some of these non-economic factors on support for the EU. As Inglehart predicted, below the age of 55, age seems to be negatively related to support for the EU: the older a person is, the less likely she is to support the EU. Interestingly, though, people in the 55 to 64 and 65+ age groups are more supportive of the EU than people in the 45 to 54 age group. This is probably because people in these older age groups more closely relate European integration to peace and the prevention of war than the younger generations, all of whom were born after the Second World War and so might see the EU as primarily an economic project.

Regarding education and support for the EU, people with university degrees are significantly more supportive of the EU than people with only secondary school education. It is impossible to know before whether this effect is due to higher cognitive skills, as Inglehart predicted, or whether it is due to the fact that people with university degrees have more social and economic capital that they can trade in the single market. Somewhat surprisingly, people who left school before 15 are more supportive of the EU than people who completed secondary school. However, this is probably a result of the fact that most people who left school before 15 are in the older generational groups (since the expansion of education in the 1960s fewer people left school at such a young age) and the older generations are more supportive of the EU.

Inglehart (1977b) concluded that his theory would bode well for European integration, as successive generations and higher levels of education would lead to greater support for European integration. However, the opposite has happened. Despite an increasing proportion of every generational cohort going to university, support for the EU has declined since the early 1990s rather than increased. Also, rather than Inglehart's generational cohort effect, the evidence suggests that while younger people are generally more supportive of European integration, as they get older they become more critical.

There is also some evidence that a person's religious affiliation has a stronger influence on their attitudes towards European integration than her age or education, in that there are larger variations in the levels of support for the EU across religious groups than across age or educational-level groups (Nelson *et al.*, 2001), although this result is contested (e.g. Boomgaarden and Freire, 2009). Catholics are considerably more pro-European than Protestants, as are Orthodox Christians, Muslims, and Jews. Atheists and agnostics are more critical of the EU than all citizens who declare a religious affiliation, except Protestants. Nelson and Guth (2003) also find that the degree of devoutness of a person – as measured, for example, by how frequently a person attends a religious service – affects support for the EU in opposite ways for different faiths. More devout Catholics and Orthodox Christians are more pro-European than less devout Catholics, while more devout Protestants are less pro-European than less devout Protestants. In general, Europe is an increasingly atheist or agnostic continent (compared with the US for example), and because less devout people and people of no religious faith are less likely to support the EU, declining religiosity may be one factor behind declining support for the EU, at least in the Catholic parts of Europe.

The final panel in Figure 5.6 looks at a different personal experience of European citizens, relating to migration. Immigrants, both into the EU from third countries, as well as from one EU member state to another, make up increasing proportions of the populations of the EU member states (see Chapter 11). Immigrants are more pro-European than non-immigrants. This is true both for migrants from one EU member state to another as well as immigrants into the EU from third countries. These attitudes reflect the fact that migrants directly experience the economic and social benefits of being able to move freely into and around the EU (see Favell 2008a). They also reflect the fact that migrants tend to be 'self-selecting', in that they are generally more highly motivated and skilled than the resident population of a country, and so are on average more likely to benefit from market integration in Europe than less skilled or motivated citizens (e.g. Geddes 2003).

Another political factor which shapes individual attitudes towards European integration is a person's attachment to his or her nation-state (Carey, 2002b; Hooghe and Marks, 2005, 2009; Kaltenthaler and Anderson, 2001). On average, the stronger a person's attachment to her nation, the more likely she is to support the EU. This might seem counter-intuitive, in that one might expect people who have strong national identities to feel threatened by European integration. However, as Figure 5.7 shows, the relationship between attachment to the nation and support for the EU works differently in different countries. In Italy, Hungary, and Germany, people with strong national attachments are more supportive of the EU than people with weak national attachments, while the reverse is the case in Denmark and Sweden, and the strength of a person's national attachment does not seem to have much of an effect in the UK. This might be because European integration is more compatible with national identity is some countries than in others. For example, many

Figure 5.7   *National attachment and support for the EU*

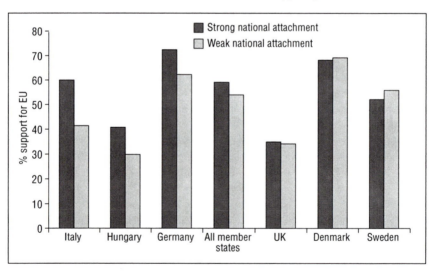

Note: The survey question was: 'People may feel different levels of attachment to their village, town or city, to their country or to the European Union. Please tell me how attached you feel to (your country).' The figure shows support for EU membership among respondents who answered 'very attached' compared to respondents who answered 'fairly attached' or 'not very attached' or 'not at all attached'.

Source: Calculated from Eurobarometer EB 68.1 (September–November 2007) data.

Italians feel both strongly Italian and strongly European, whereas many Swedes feel either Swedish or European. However, McLaren (2002, 2004) finds that fear of the threat to national identity is a weaker factor in explaining opposition to the EU than utilitarian calculations about national economic costs and benefits from the EU.

Finally, Europe's elites are more pro-European than are European citizens (see Hooghe, 2003; Katz, 2001; Slater, 1982). In February to May 1996 the Commission undertook the only Eurobarometer survey of elite attitudes towards European integration; the so-called Top Decision-Makers Survey. In every member state, interviews were conducted with 200 to 500 senior elected politicians, senior civil servants, business and trade union leaders, leading media owners and editors, public intellectuals, and leading cultural and religious figures. Figure 5.8 shows support for EU membership among these elites compared with support for EU membership among the general public, as revealed in the general Eurobarometer survey in the same period in 1996.

The data reveal three things. First, in all member states elites are more supportive of the EU than is the public. For example, 94 per cent of all elites see EU membership as a good thing, compared with only 48 per cent of the general public, at that time. Second, there is considerable variation

Figure 5.8   *Elites compared to mass support for the EU*

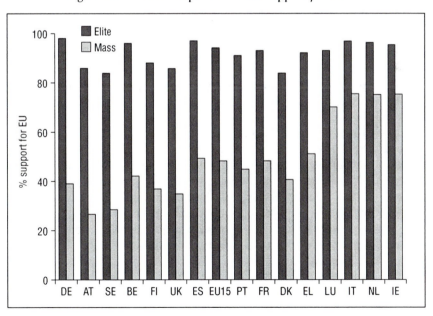

Sources: Calculated from Eurobarometer 45.1 (spring 1996) and Top Decision-Makers Survey (spring 1996) data.

in the elite–public gap across the member states. The gap is much larger in Germany, Austria, Sweden, and Belgium than in Luxembourg, Italy, the Netherlands, and Ireland. Third, there is a higher degree of cohesion among elites from different nations than among the publics – as indicated by the lower variation in the elite scores compared to the higher variation in the opinions among the national publics.

The gap between elite and mass attitudes towards the EU might offer some insights into why some referendums on European integration have not always turned out as governmental and party elites have hoped (see Chapter 6). It might also explain why mass-based anti-European protest movements have emerged, with demonstrations being held on an almost weekly basis outside one or other of the EU institutions in Brussels, by citizens who feel that their domestic elites are not properly representing their views at the European level (Imig 2002; Imig and Tarrow, 2001; Marks and McAdam, 1996; Tarrow, 1995).

Political Context Matters: the Role of Ideology, Parties, and the Media

In general, citizens are not well informed about the EU. This does not mean that if citizens were more informed about the EU that they would be more supportive of the project. Indeed, more information can lead to a better understanding of why some people are winners of European economic integration while others are losers. What the low level of information does mean, though, is that citizens' attitudes can be influenced by other actors: such as political parties, interest groups, and the media. Put another way, the 'information deficit' means that citizens' attitudes towards the EU are influenced by their national context (Anderson, 1998; Brinegar and Jolly, 2005; Hooghe and Marks, 2005; Sánchez-Cuenca, 2000).

To understand how national context shapes attitudes towards European integration, let us first consider what citizens with different political views might want the EU to do, irrespective of their national contexts. On average, citizens who have left-wing views tend to favour equality of outcomes: intervention to promote equitable outcomes in the market, but liberty to promote social and political equality before the law. Citizens who have right-wing views, on the other hand, tend to favour equality of opportunities but not outcomes, thus allowing the inequalities inherent in the free market and the privileges of authority and tradition to be protected (Bobbio, 1996). This does not preclude intermediate positions: intervention–authority (the traditional stance of Christian democrats), and laissez-faire–liberty (such as liberals). However, these positions were less common in the 1990s than those of the oft-observed 'left-libertarians' (such as greens and social democrats) and 'right-authoritarians' (such as conservatives and contemporary Christian democrats) (see Finer, 1987; Kitschelt, 1994, 1995).

Irrespective of national political context, then, in EU politics we should expect individuals on the left to favour economic intervention by the EU (such as social policies, tax harmonization, aid to poorer regions, and aid to the developing world), and EU policies to promote social liberty (such as environmental regulation, consumer rights, minority rights, and gender equality). Conversely we should expect individuals on the right to favour EU policies which promote economic freedoms (such as the single market, deregulatory policies, and a single currency), and social authority (such as EU policies on drug trafficking, organized crime, immigration and asylum, and security and defence) (see Hix, 1999; Hooghe and Marks, 1998).

Figure 5.9 shows what citizens on the left and right think should be the priorities for the EU in the coming years (see Gabel and Anderson,

Figure 5.9 *Ideology and support for EU policies*

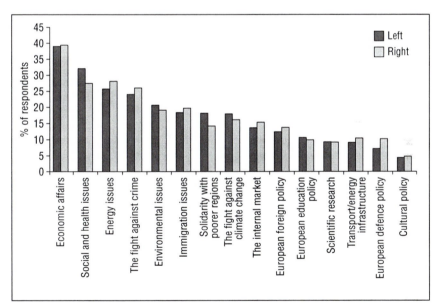

Note: The survey question was as follows: 'European integration has been focusing on various issues in the last years. In your opinion, which aspects should be emphasized by the European institutions in the coming years, to strengthen the European Union in the future? (maximum of three answers)'. Citizens were allocated to 'left' and 'right' according to their answers to the question: 'In political matters people talk of "the left" and "the right". How would you place your views on this scale? (Left) 1–2–3–4–5–6–7–8–9–10 (Right)'. Answers 1 to 5 were coded as 'left' and 6 to 10 as 'right'.

Source: Calculated from Eurobarometer EB 71.1 (January–February 2009) data.

2002; de Winter and Swyngedouw, 1999). Data on citizens' self-placement on a left–right scale and their attitudes towards EU policy priorities shows that there are not huge differences on the issues citizens on the left and right would like the EU to address. There are, nevertheless, some interesting differences. Citizens on the left are more in favour than citizens on the right of the EU promoting social and health issues, environmental issues, solidarity with poorer regions, and the fight against climate change. In contrast, citizens on the right are more in favour than citizens on the left of the EU promoting energy issues, the fight against crime, immigration, the internal market, EU foreign policy, and EU defence policy. So, in general, this pattern fits what one would predict.

However, several national contextual factors shape how these political views about what policies individuals would like translated into attitudes towards the EU. One key factor is the role played by political parties. On low-salience issues, such as European integration, voters take 'cues' from party leaders about what positions to take on these issues. So, in the UK, for example, the switch in the positions of the Labour Party and the Conservative Party towards European integration in the mid-1980s affected the attitudes of the supporters of these parties, with Labour voters becoming more pro-European than Conservative voters for the first time (Carey, 2002a). In this context, voters did not change their basic ideological views, but fundamentally changed their opinions about whether the EU would promote their political views or not as a result of the changing positions of the British political parties on this issue.

There is evidence that the relationship between parties and their supporters on the issue of Europe is a two-way interaction: with parties responding to voters and voters responding to parties (Hellström, 2008; Mattila and Raunio, 2006; Steenbergen *et al.*, 2007). Interestingly, the ability of parties to shape voters' preferences on EU issues seems to be declining (Steenbergen *et al.*, 2007). This might be because of weaker leadership by political parties. A more likely explanation, though, is that citizens have increasingly stable positions on European integration, which are more difficult for parties to shape.

In addition, an increasing number of parties are divided on European issues. For example, Gabel and Scheve (2007) find that dissent within parties reduces party voters' support for Europe. One way of interpreting this finding is that dissent within a party reveals that the party's leadership is uncertain about the consequences of European integration, which leads to a split among the party's supporters. Alternatively, party supporters receive mixed signals from their party, which leads them not to trust the party leaders on this issue. Either way, citizens are less responsive to cues from divided parties on what to think about European integration.

Even if the ability of parties to shape citizens' attitudes towards Europe may be declining, the relative position of domestic policies compared to the EU shapes how parties, interest groups, and citizens see the EU (Hix, 2007). As a result of the multiple checks and balances in the EU system, the policy mix of the EU single market – a mix of deregulation plus common social and environmental standards (see Chapter 8) – is relatively centrist, and perhaps not too far from some notional European-wide average voter (Crombez, 2003). However, the EU-level policy mix is considerably different from the policy mix in several member states (Brinegar *et al.*, 2002). For example, the EU's regulatory framework is considerably to the left of the United Kingdom's more liberal and deregulated economy. On the other hand, the deregulatory side of the EU single market is considerably to the right of France's more highly regulated and managed economy.

From the perspective of the British Conservatives, EU policies can seem like 'socialism through the back door', or as Margaret Thatcher famously put it in her 1988 speech to the College of Europe in Bruges: 'We have not successfully rolled back the frontiers of the state in Britain, only to see them reimposed at a European level.' In contrast, from the perspective of the French Socialists, the liberalizing effects of the single market programme and the associated privatization and state aids policies seem like an Anglo-Saxon plot to undermine protected French workers. In other words, despite the same general ideological positions and policy preferences, the different domestic policy context explains why the British right are more critical of the EU while the French right are more supportive, and the British left are more supportive while the French left are more critical.

Figure 5.10 illustrates this intuition further, showing the different attitudes of citizens in the old 15 and new 12 states towards EU membership at different points on the left–right dimension. The two lines in the figure illustrate the general patterns shown by the two sets of bar charts. On average, in the old 15 states, citizens with centrist political views are more supportive of the EU than citizens with more extreme political views (e.g. Taggart, 1998). Meanwhile, in the new member states, citizens on the right (who support the free market), expect to benefit more from the economic transition process, and hence tend to be more supportive of European integration than those on the left, who fear further economic transformations (Christin, 2005; Cichowski, 2000; Tucker *et al.* 2002).

Related to the significance of domestic political context, Garry and Tilley (2009) look at how the domestic economic context shapes citizens attitudes towards the EU. They specifically focus on two factors – national identity and attitudes towards immigration – and how these affect support for the EU under different national economic contexts. They find that having a strong national identity only moderately

Figure 5.10   *Political ideology and EU support*

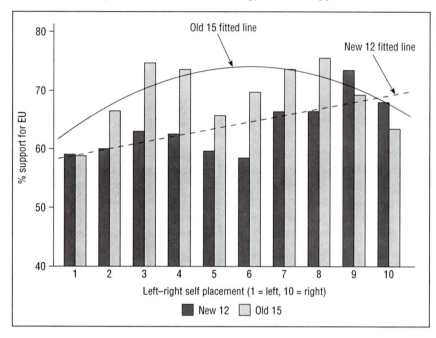

Note: The lines in the figure are fitted regression lines. The quadratic relationship fits best for the old 15 member states whereas a linear relationship fits best for the new 12 member states.

Source: Calculated from Eurobarometer 71.1 (January–February 2009) data.

decreases citizens' support for the EU in member states that are net beneficiaries from the EU budget, whereas having a strong national identity leads to a lot less support for the EU in member states that are net contributors into the EU budget. Equally, in richer countries, which are more attractive to economic migrants, if an individual is generally anti-immigrant, then he or she is also likely to be opposed to the EU, whereas in poorer countries, which are less attractive to economic migrants, anti-immigrant attitudes have a much weaker effect on individual attitudes towards the EU.

Finally, the domestic media play a significant role. Several member states, in particular the UK and Austria, have populist national newspapers which are vehemently anti-European, and which some people believe has contributed to the low levels of support for the EU in these two countries (see Diez Medrano, 2003). In addition to the variation in the way the EU is portrayed in the national media, there is considerable variation in the volume of coverage of EU politics and events in national newspapers and on television news broadcasts (esp. Peter *et al.*, 2003).

The effects of the variations in the volume and content of the coverage of the EU in the national media on individual attitudes towards the EU is difficult to identify. Pro-European citizens tend to consume pro-European media, and anti-European citizens tend to consume anti-European media. But, which way round is the relationship: are media outlets shaping voters, or are the media simply reflecting the opinions of their readers and viewers? On the one hand, with low information about the EU, there is considerable room for newspapers and TV news programmes to influence what people know about the EU, and hence how they feel about the EU – and there is some evidence that this occurs (e.g. Maier and Rittberger, 2008; de Vreese and Boomgaarden, 2006; de Vreese and Kandyla, 2009). On the other hand, newspaper and TV news programme editors are competing in an ever more competitive media market, and hence have strong incentives to tailor their news coverage to fit the attitudes of their core readers and viewers, otherwise they risk their readers/viewers switching to other news sources.

Conclusion: from Consensus to Conflict?

Until the early 1990s the EU was essentially a consensual system of governance (see Taylor, 1991). The result was the so-called 'permissive consensus', whereby citizens were content to delegate responsibility to their leaders to tackle the European integration project. However, this permissive consensus collapsed in the early 1990s, which has resulted in much more contested attitudes towards the EU among Europe's citizens. European integration no longer commands widespread support and a complex web of economic interests, social values, political preferences and national contexts shape individuals' attitudes towards the EU.

In this new post-consensus environment, Europe's elites are faced with a dilemma. They can continue the practice of consensus politics, but this risks provoking more public opposition to the EU and a wider gap between the attitudes of the public and the elites. Alternatively, Europe's elites could abandon consensus politics and seek to politicize the question of Europe in domestic politics and at the European level: with different national politicians and political parties taking up different positions on issues on the EU political agenda. This would make politics at the European-level more conflictual and less amendable to consensus, but might close the gap between the increasingly divisive attitudes of citizens across Europe and the currently disconnected elites at the national and European levels.

Chapter 6

Democracy, Parties, and Elections

Democracy: Choosing Parties, Leaders, and Policies
The 'Democratic Deficit' Debate
Parties: Competition and Organization
Elections: EP Elections and EU Referendums
Conclusion: Democratic Politics in the EU?

This chapter looks at how the two central processes of 'democratic politics' – party competition and elections – operate in the EU. At the domestic level in Europe, parties and elections operate hand in hand in the 'competitive party government' model. There is also an emerging party system at the European level. European-wide elections to the European Parliament are held every five years, and competitive and cohesive political parties exist in the European Parliament. But genuine democratic politics in the EU remains some way off.

Democracy: Choosing Parties, Leaders, and Policies

Elections are the central mechanism of representative democracy and operate in two interlinked ways (King, 1981). First, elections allow voters to choose who governs. Voters' choose between rival candidates for public office, and the winning candidate becomes the head of the executive branch of government. Elections consequently allow voters to 'throw the scoundrels out' if they flout their electoral promises, prove incompetent, or become less popular than a rival group of elites. Second, elections allow voters to choose policies. Political parties and political leaders present citizens with rival policy proposals, and the parties or leaders who emerge as the winners from the democratic process then have a mandate to implement their policies. In this conception, democracy only exists if there is a choice between competing politicians and policies, and if there is a reasonable chance of alternation in government (Downs, 1957; Schumpeter, 1943; Przeworski *et al.*, 2000).

In most democratic systems, competition over policies and for public office are combined in a single model of 'competitive party government' (see McDonald and Budge, 2005; Weber, 1946 [1919]). In this model the leader of the party that wins the election becomes the head of the executive (the prime minister), and the party acts cohesively in the legislative arena to implement the policy agenda presented in the election manifesto. Meanwhile, the losing opposition parties try to demonstrate the failings of the politicians in government. In this model voters exercise an indirect influence on policy outcomes.

Alternative models allow voters to exercise a direct choice over office holders or the policy agenda. First, in the presidential model, voters directly elect the head of the executive. Parties may play an important role selecting presidential candidates and running their campaigns, but presidential elections tend to be dominated by the policies and personality of the individual candidates rather than by the manifestos of the parties. Second, through referendums voters can choose policies directly. Again, parties play a role, advocating one side in a referendum, and the (un)popularity of the parties on each side of the debate (particularly those in government) will affect the way citizens vote in the referendum.

So, which model is right for the EU? Following the logic of the competitive party government model, in the past most commentators on the EU's so-called 'democratic deficit' argued that: (a) the European Parliament should be directly elected; and (b) it should be given greater powers in the EU legislative process and the selection of the EU executive (that is, the Commission). 'Direct elections' to the European Parliament were introduced in 1979 and have been held at five-yearly intervals ever since. And, in a series of treaty reforms the European Parliament has been given a greater power in the EU legislative process vis-à-vis the Council and the Commission and also in the selection of the Commission (see Chapter 3).

In purely procedural terms, the election of the European Parliament and the new legislative and executive-appointment powers of the European Parliament suggest that the democratic deficit in the EU has been overcome. In substantive terms, however, the EU lacks genuine 'democratic politics'. Democratic politics in the EU would require:

- a genuine contest between political parties and leaders for control of the policy agenda at the European level and for the main political offices in the EU (such as the President of the Commission);
- choices by voters in European Parliament elections on the basis of these rival policy platforms or candidates for political office; and
- that the winning electoral choices are translated into legislative and executive action at the European level via cohesive political parties.

If this pattern of behaviour does not exist in the EU, then the EU cannot be considered to be a democratic polity in the way political science normally understands this concept.

The 'Democratic Deficit' Debate

Articles on the so-called democratic deficit in the EU started to be published in academic journals in the mid to late 1980s. More widespread discussion of this issue in the media soon followed, in response to the collapse in support for the EU in the early 1990s (see Chapter 5). There is no single definition of the democratic deficit in the EU. However, Joseph Weiler and his colleagues described what they called a 'standard version' of the democratic deficit in 1995, which is a set of widely-used arguments by academics, practitioners, media commentators and ordinary citizens (Weiler *et al.*, 1995). Adding some elements to Weiler's original definition, the current 'standard version' of the democratic deficit involves five main sets of claims (Føllesdal and Hix, 2006):

1 *Increased executive power–decreased national parliamentary control.* EU decisions are made primarily by executive actors: national ministers in the Council and the Commissioners. As powers have shifted to these actors at the European level there has been a reduction of the power of national parliaments, since governments can ignore their parliaments when making decisions in Brussels or can be outvoted in the Council (where QMV is used), and the European Commission is beyond the control of national parliaments.

2 *The European Parliament is too weak.* Increases in the powers of the European Parliament have not sufficiently compensated for the loss of national parliamentary control, since the Council still dominates the European Parliament in the passing of legislation and the adoption of the budget, and citizens are not as well connected to their MEPs as to their national parliamentarians.

3 *There are no 'European' elections.* Citizens are not able to vote on EU policies, except in periodic referendums on EU membership or treaty reforms. National elections are fought on domestic rather than European issues, and parties collude to keep the issue of Europe off the domestic agenda. And, European Parliament elections are not about Europe either, because national parties and the media treat them as mid-term polls on the performance of national governments and parties.

4 *The EU is too distant.* Citizens cannot understand the EU. The Commission is neither a government nor a bureaucracy, and is appointed through an obscure procedure rather than elected directly by the people or indirectly by a parliament. The Council remains a largely secretive legislature. The European Parliament is impenetrable because of the multilingual nature of the debates. And, the EU policy process is highly technocratic, which prevents actors and citizens from easily identifying political preferences.

5   *Policy drift*. As a result of all these factors, the EU adopts policies that are not supported by a majority of citizens in many (or even most) member states, such as a neo-liberal regulatory framework for the single market, a monetarist framework for EMU and massive subsidies to farmers through the CAP (see especially Streeck and Schmitter, 1991; Scharpf, 1999).

However, these arguments are not universally accepted. For example, Giandomenico Majone and Andrew Moravcsik – two of the biggest names in the study of the EU – have contested many of these claims.

Giandomenico Majone argues that the EU is essentially a 'regulatory state', which should not produce redistributive or value-allocative outcomes, and so does not require democratic legitimation in the same way that domestic 'welfare states' do (Majone, 1993, 1996, 1998, 2002; see also Chapter 8). Regulatory policies in the EU, Majone contends, should mainly aim to correct market failures, and so should be designed to benefit everyone (produce 'pareto-efficient' policy outcomes) rather than to make some people better off at the expense of others (which is the explicit aim of redistributive policies). As a result, Majone argues that EU policy-making, which primarily involves the regulation of goods, services, capital, and labour in the single market, should be isolated from the standard processes of majoritarian democratic politics. During the single market programme, for example, because the Commission was independent from direct political control, either by the governments or from the majority in the European Parliament, the Commission was able to develop and propose social, economic, and environmental standards that were in the interests of all of Europe, rather than in the interests of a particular member state or political majority. If 'normal democratic politics' had set the basic framework for the internal market, instead of an internal market that balanced deregulation of national markets with common environmental and social standards, the EU would have had either an overtly neo-liberal framework, with few social and environmental standards, or an overtly social democratic framework, with high costs for business and consumers. In either of these situations there would have been widespread opposition to the internal market programme from the supporters of the losing side. Majone consequently argues that a more politicized EU during this period would have undermined rather than reinforced the legitimacy of the project.

In Majone's view the main problem facing the EU is less a democratic deficit than a 'credibility crisis' (Majone, 2000). The solution to this problem, he believes, is largely procedural. What the EU needs is more transparent decision-making, *ex post* review by courts and ombudsmen, greater professionalism and technical expertise, rules that protect the rights of minority interests, and better scrutiny by private actors, the media, and parliamentarians at both the EU and national levels. In this view, an EU dominated by the European Parliament or a directly elected Commission would politicize regulatory policy-making. Politicization would result in redistributive rather than pareto-efficient outcomes, as political majorities will inevitably promote the interests of their supporters against minority or European wide interests, and therefore undermine rather than increase the legitimacy of the EU (Dehousse, 1995; Majone, 2002).

Andrew Moravcsik (2002, 2008) goes further, presenting a critique of all the main claims in the standard version of the democratic deficit. Against the argument that power has been centralized in the executive, Moravcsik points out that national governments are the most directly accountable politicians in Europe. Against the critique that the executives are beyond the control of representative institutions, he argues that the most significant institutional development in the EU in the past two decades has been the increased powers of the European Parliament in the legislative process and in the selection of the Commission. Moravcsik also argues that EU policy-making is more transparent than most domestic policy-making, that the EU bureaucrats in the Commission and the Council are forced to listen to numerous European and national societal interests, that there is extensive judicial review of EU actions by both the European Court of Justice and national courts, and that the European Parliament and national parliaments have increasing powers of scrutiny that they are not afraid to use. Finally, against the so-called 'social democratic critique' that EU policies are biased against the median voter, Moravcsik argues that the EU's system of checks and balances ensures that a consensus is required for any policy to be agreed. As a result, radical free marketeers (such as the right wing of the British Conservative Party) are just as unhappy with the moderate policy outcomes of the EU as radical left-wingers (such as the left wing of the French Socialist Party).

Moravcsik's arguments fit with the intergovernmental theory of EU politics (see Chapter 1). In this theory, because the member state governments run the EU and the Commission is simply an agent of these governments, there are no unintended consequences of intergovernmental bargains. As a result, since the governments are accountable to their electorates, and there is no gap between the preferences of the elected governments and final EU policy outcomes, then the EU is not undemocratic because policy outcomes from the EU broadly reflect the preferences of European voters (see Crombez, 2003).

Regarding Majone's argument, it might have been reasonable to isolate the EU from democratic politics during the market-creating stage of the EU's development, to ensure that the basic political and economic architecture was in the interest of virtually all European citizens. Also, where there were potential redistributive consequences of market integration in Europe, unanimous agreement between the governments ensured that budgetary polices were used as side payments to compensate potential losers from the process: such as the doubling of EU regional spending in the late 1980s (see Chapter 9).

However, now that the EU has moved beyond market-creating to deciding what social and economic policies should be pursued in the internal market and how European economic and social policies should be reformed, most new EU policies have identifiable winners and losers. As a result, most questions facing the EU today are explicitly political, where citizens, interest groups, political parties, and governments find themselves on different sides in the policy process. For example, should the internal market be more liberal or more regulated? Should governments be able to protect their domestic service providers from market entrants from other member states? Should incumbent workers be protected in labour markets or should firms be allowed to hire and fire employees more easily? Should the costs of reducing carbon emissions be borne by producers or consumers? Should there be full or restricted free movement of workers from the new EU member states? And so on. Whereas the creation of the internal market and the adoption of market-correction regulations as part of the internal market programme probably benefited most social groups in one way or another, whatever choices the EU makes on these questions, some groups will gain while others will lose, at least in the short term. So, growing political conflict at the European level is inescapable as the EU begins to face up to the new policy challenges.

Turning to Moravcsik's argument: claiming that as a result of the accountability of national governments and the EU's checks and balances that policy outcomes from the EU are close to the views of the average European citizen is not sufficient to demonstrate that the EU is democratic. In the absence of political debate and democratic competition about the direction of EU policies we do not know *a priori* that the current views of the average EU citizen on a subject would in fact be different had a debate taken place (see Bellamy, 2010).

Citizens' views on most policy questions are only partially formed. This is because most citizens have limited information about the likely consequences of policy change, and so are uncertain about how a particular policy proposal will affect their interests. This is particularly true of highly complex issues. Without open political debate, citizens' views are easily manipulated by political entrepreneurs, such as newspaper editors, leaders of political parties, or activists in single-issue lobby groups. If there is more open debate between the main political leaders, the protagonists are forced to set out their positions and confront their opponents in the media or outside mainstream politics. The result would be a process of policy learning, whereby citizens' original opposition to a particular policy proposal can evolve into qualified support as they understand the costs, benefits, and tradeoffs involved in the adoption of new policies.

There are a number of other reasons why democratic politics in the EU might be desirable (see Hix, 2008a). First, competitive democratic elections guarantee that policies and elected officials respond to the preferences of citizens. Electoral contests provide incentives for elites to develop rival policy ideas and propose rival candidates for political office. They also allow citizens to punish politicians who fail to keep their electoral promises or are dishonest or corrupt (Fearon, 1999). Where the EU is concerned, policies might be in the interests of citizens when they are first agreed, but without electoral competition there are few incentives for the Commission or the member state governments to change these policies in response to changes in citizens' preferences.

Second, democratic politics promotes the formation of cross-institutional coalitions, which would help overcome policy gridlock. The EU's system of checks and balances are not a problem when policies are adopted for the first time, as large majorities in the Commission, the Council, and the European Parliament usually prefer a range of potential policies to no common policies – as was the case in the creation of the internal market. However, once an EU policy has been adopted or if a piece of legislation involves reforming an existing set of national or European policies, the result is often policy gridlock. This is because only a few actors are needed to prevent an overwhelming majority from undertaking policy reform (see Chapter 3). Under the ordinary legislative procedure, for example, policy change can be blocked either by a majority of Commissioners, or by a blocking minority of governments in the Council, or by one of the main political groups in the European Parliament. With more open political coalition formation, both within and between the EU institutions, policy gridlock is more likely to be overcome.

Third, democratic politics provides incentives for the media to cover what goes on in Brussels. There is little coverage of EU politics on national TV news and in newspapers. This is partially because political editors of newspapers and TV news programmes operate in highly competitive markets, which forces editors to cover political events not because they are important in and of themselves but rather because they are 'infotainment' for their viewers or readers. National capitals, not Brussels, are the centres of political news for editors, and there are few incentives for them to give up precious time or space to cover EU politics. The problem, though, is that citizens will not be able to understand EU politics or take sides in EU debates unless news editors cover Brussels. So, until there is genuine political drama in Brussels, with identifiable winning and losing personalities, news editors will not have an incentive to cover EU politics, and citizens will not be able to gain sufficient information to form opinions about what goes on in at the European level.

Fourth, democratic political competition can produce a mandate for policy change. A mandate involves the public recognition of the winners of a political contest. On the one hand, the politician or political coalition that emerges victorious from a contest is recognized by the public as having the right to try their policy agenda. On the other hand, the politicians and their supporters on the losing side accept that they have lost, for the time being, and so are willing to allow the other side to govern. This is crucial for what political scientists call 'losers' consent': where the losers of a political contest peacefully accept the outcome rather than engaging in obstruction, protest, or even violence. Without a mandate, the losers of a contest or from a particular set of policies have an incentive to challenge the outcome. But, if a mandate does emerge, any challenge by the losers is deemed illegitimate and will cost them popular support.

Finally, democratic politics has a powerful formative effect, promoting the gradual evolution of political identities. For example in the evolution of the American and European democracies, the replacement of local identities by national identities occurred through the process and operation of mass elections and party competition (Key, 1961; Rokkan, 1999). The current political majority in the EU – in the Commission, the Council, and the European Parliament – is on the centre-right, which means that the current policies of the EU are in a more free-market direction. Without open democratic politics, this particularly 'governing coalition' is not recognized by most citizens. So, rather than recognizing that the current right-wing policies are the product of this particular governing coalition and would change if a different coalition emerged as the governing majority, those parties and citizens on the losing side in the current policy battles (on the left) believe that free market policies will be a permanent feature of the EU. This explains why many citizens on the left, particularly in Western Europe, currently oppose the EU. If these citizens expected that the political majority at the European level could change in the near future, they would be more willing to accept the EU as legitimate. Then, over time, as the European level governing coalition shifts from the moderate right to the moderate left and back again, a European-wide democratic identity would begin to emerge.

In other words, even if one accepts most of the arguments of Majone and Moravcsik – for example about the need to isolate the implementers of some regulatory policies (such as competition policy) from democratic competition, or about the existing openness of the EU policy process – the EU polity cannot be considered to be democratic unless there is some form of democratic political contestation over the direction of the EU policy agenda. Hence, the rest of this chapter focuses on the electoral processes in EU politics and the behaviour of political parties.

Parties: Competition and Organization

EU politics is party politics. This may not seem obvious to a casual observer of the EU. But on closer inspection party organizations, labels, ideologies, policies, coalitions, and interests take centre stage. All politicians at the domestic and European levels are party politicians who owe their current positions and future careers to the electoral success and policy positions of 'their' parties. Parties are the main actors in domestic elections, European Parliament elections, and referendums. They are the main organs connecting governments to parliaments and parliaments to voters. As a result, they provide vital links between the national and EU arenas and between the EU institutions themselves. To understand how EU politics works, then, we need to understand how parties compete and organize in the EU.

National parties and Europe

No single party family dominates EU politics. The social democrats are the main force on the centre-left in all member states, whereas the mainstream right is split; with Christian democrats being the largest force in some countries and conservatives the largest in others. Also, in terms of the main political blocs, the combined forces of the centre-right currently command approximately 10 per cent more electoral support across the EU than the combined forces of the centre-left. The liberals hold a pivotal position between these two forces and are available to form coalitions with the left or the right. However, in 2010 the liberals are more often in coalition at the national level with centre-right parties (either conservatives or Christian democrats) than with parties on the centre-left.

On the question of European integration, however, whereas the party families on the mainstream centre-left (the social democrats and greens) are moderately pro-European, there is a split in the centre-right: between parties which are predominantly pro-European (such as the Christian democrats), and more anti-European conservative parties (such as the British and Czech conservative parties), who favour a looser association of independent nation-states to a more federal structure for Europe. However, pro-European parties from the centre-left, centre-right, and the liberals win almost 80 per cent of the votes in national elections. In other words, despite the fact there is growing opposition to European integration among the European electorates (see Chapter 5), at the elite level almost all mainstream parties in Europe are pro-European, and anti-European parties are largely located on the radical right or radical left (Taggart, 1998). For example, all mainstream parties supported the EU Constitutional Treaty, with the exception of the British conservatives and some more nationalist conservative parties in Central and Eastern Europe (Crum, 2007). This, of course, did not prevent the Constitutional Treaty from being rejected by voters in France and the Netherlands in 2005, and the Constitutional Treaty would probably have been rejected in several of the other member states who were due to hold referendums on the document.

Figure 6.1 *Party policy positions in EU politics*

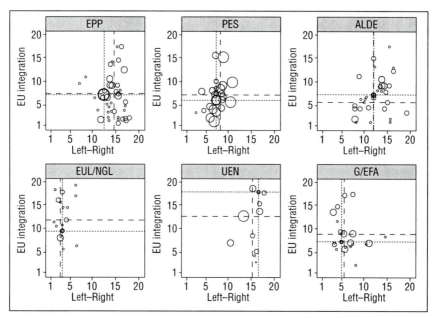

Note: This figure plots the positions of the member parties of the six largest political groups in the 2004 to 2009 European Parliament on the two main dimensions in EU politics, using expert surveys of where national parties and EP groups are located on 20-point left–right and pro-/anti-Europe scales (where 1 = left or pro-European and 20 = right or anti-European). The long dashed lines are the two-dimensional positions of the median national parties in each EP group, and the short dashed lines are the two-dimensional positions of the EP political groups. The grey circles indicate the size of each national party's vote share and the black circles each EP group's seat share.

Key: EPP = European People's Party
PES = Party of European Socialists
ALDE = Alliance of Liberals and Democrats for Europe
EUL/NGL = European United Left/Nordic Green Left
UEN = Union for a Europe of the Nations
G/EFA = Greens/European Free Alliance.

Source: McElroy and Benoit (2010).

Figure 6.1 shows the location of the member parties of the six main political families in European politics on the two main dimensions of EU politics: the left–right dimension, and the EU integration dimension (see Hix and Lord, 1997; Ray, 1999). The locations of the party families suggest several possible alliances in EU politics. The clearest natural allies are the Christian democrats, conservatives, and liberals, all of whom are moderately centre-right and pro-European. The socialists, in contrast, are faced with a choice: a potential alliance with these centre-right forces on a common pro-European platform, or an alliance with the greens and the radical left in a common left-wing bloc. However, the latter alliance would be divided on the question of European integration, since the radical left are considerably anti-European.

But, the locations of the grey circles in the figure – which represent the positions of the national member parties of these six European political groups – reveals that while most party families are relatively homogeneous on the left–right dimension they are more internally divided on Europe integration. Party families are historically defined in relation to the left–right dimension and not on the question of European integration. As a result, parties in the same party family have similar policy preferences on left–right issues. However, European integration affects these national political preferences differently. In some countries EU policy outcomes tend to change domestic policies in a leftwards direction, by introducing new social regulations (as in the UK, for example), whereas in other countries EU policies tends to move policies rightwards, by liberalization of domestic markets (as in France, for example) (Hix, 2008b). Hence, there is considerable variation on attitudes towards European integration among political parties in both the mainstream right and left (see Aspinwall, 2002; Hooghe *et al.*, 2003; Marks *et al.*, 2002; Marks and Wilson, 2000).

The dominance of the centrist pro-EU alliance in European politics, which has effectively prevented the mainstream parties from competing on European issues in domestic electoral campaigns, means that anti-European positions among the electorate have not had much of an impact on national party systems (see Gabel and Hix, 2003; Mair, 2000; Tillman, 2004; de Vries, 2007). There is little evidence that the main national parties are disconnected from the majority of their supporters on the question of Europe (Carrubba, 2001; van der Eijk *et al.*, 2001). However, within most parties there are significant minorities who are opposed to European integration, and there are parties to the left and right of this centrist/pro-European bloc who cannot challenge the dominance of this coalition. As a result, anti-European voters express their frustration at this pro-European 'cartel' in electoral arenas where the normal structure of party competition is not so dominant: that is, in European Parliament elections and referendums on European questions.

Parties at the European level

There are two-party organizational structures at the European level. The most prominent of these are the political groups in the European Parliament. These groups were first formed in the Assembly of the European Coal and Steel Community in 1953; the precursor of the modern European Parliament (Hix *et al.*, 2003). Since then, the political groups in the European Parliament have evolved into highly developed organizations, with their own budgets, leadership structures, administrative staff, rules of procedure, committees, and working groups.

The second organizational structure consists of the transnational party federations outside the European Parliament, which were formed in the run-up to the first direct elections in the mid-1970s. The Confederation of Socialist Parties of the EC was the first to be established, in April 1974, followed by the Federation of Liberal and Democratic Parties of the EC, in March 1976, and the European People's Party (EPP) of Christian democratic parties in April 1976. Despite their names, these were rather loose organizations, did not have highly sophisticated organizations at the European level, and did not have a clear and coherent policy orientation, despite biannual European party conferences. Nevertheless, at the instigation of the three secretaries-general of the party federations, a new 'party article' was introduced in the Maastricht Treaty, which stated that:

> Political parties at the European level are important as a factor for integration within the Union. They contribute to forming a European awareness and to expressing the will of the citizens of the Union.

Following this article, the party federations established new and more coherent organizations. The Party of European Socialists (PES) was launched in November 1992, the EPP adopted a set of new statutes in November 1992, a new European Federation of Green Parties (EFGP) was set up in June 1993 and the European Liberal, Democratic and Reform Party (ELDR) was established in December 1993. These party organizations strengthened their links with the political groups in the European Parliament, and also with the representatives of these party federations in the Commission, Council, and European Council, mainly via quarterly party federation leaders' summits. Instead of being umbrella organizations for fighting European Parliament elections, these federations have gradually developed into genuine 'Euro-parties', albeit with limited power over their constituent national member parties or the political groups in the European Parliament.

Figure 6.2 shows the party political make-up of the EU institutions in January 2005 and January 2010. At the end of the 1990s, the centre-left dominated EU politics, with the socialist group the largest group in the European Parliament until the 1999 elections and centre-left parties running 13 of the then 15 member state governments. By 2005 there had already been a considerable shift rightwards, and this trend has continued until 2010. So, the European People's Party (EPP) is now the largest political group in the European Parliament (with 265 of the 736 MEPs), 14 of the 27 Commissioners in the second Barroso Commission are affiliated to national parties who belong to the EPP, and 12 of the EU heads

Figure 6.2   *Party make-up of the EU institutions in 2005 and 2010*

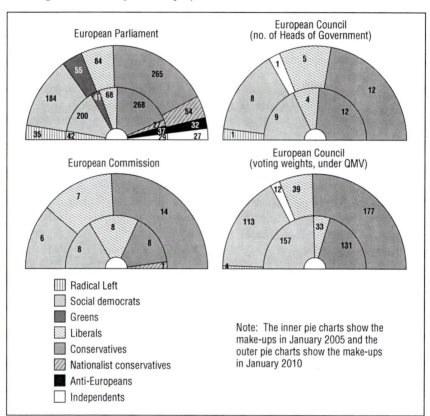

European Parliament

European Council
(no. of Heads of Government)

European Commission

European Council
(voting weights, under QMV)

▥ Radical Left
☐ Social democrats
◼ Greens
▨ Liberals
▦ Conservatives
▨ Nationalist conservatives
■ Anti-Europeans
☐ Independents

Note: The inner pie charts show the
make-ups in January 2005 and the
outer pie charts show the make-ups
in January 2010

of government in the European Council belong to the EPP, who together command 177 of the 345 votes under QMV in the Council.

If democratic politics works in the EU, this rightward shift in the make-up of the EU's legislative and executive institutions should produce a concomitant shift in the EU policy agenda towards more market liberalization and deregulation (see Manow *et al.*, 2008; Warntjen *et al.*, 2008). However, this translation from party strengths to policy outputs requires party actors in the same political family to cooperate within and across the three institutions, which is not always the case in EU politics. There is some evidence that Commissioners and governments are influenced by their party affiliations as well as their nationality when acting in the EU policy process (Hagemann and Høyland, 2008; Tallberg and Johansson, 2008; Wonka, 2008). However, the transnational party linkages are still weak in the Commission and the Council. In the European Parliament, in contrast, political behaviour is dominated by supranational party organization and competition.

Research on roll-call (recorded) votes in the European Parliament has revealed that voting along supranational party lines has increased while voting along national lines has decreased (Attinà, 1990; Hix *et al.*, 2005, 2007; Hix and Noury, 2009). This growing voting cohesion of the political groups cannot be explained by increasing internal ideological homogeneity of the groups. The national member parties of the main political groups have quite diverse policy positions, and the internal heterogeneity of the main groups has grown as the groups have expanded their membership as a result of enlargement of the EU. For example, the EPP is now a broad alliance of Christian democrats, conservatives, and various other mainstream centre-right forces from the new EU member states. The British and Czech conservative parties left the EPP group in 2009, as they were critical of the strongly pro-EU integration position of the EPP party, and formed a new group to the right of the EPP with several smaller non-EPP-affiliated parties on the right, in the European Conservatives and Reformists (ECR) group. Despite these departures, the EPP remains a broad coalition of relatively corporatist parties from the Benelux, France, Germany, and Austria and more free-market parties from Iberia, Scandinavia, and Eastern Europe.

The growing party-based voting in the European Parliament is more a result of the increased powers of the European Parliament than the internal ideological coherence of the groups (especially Hix *et al.*, 2007; Kreppel, 2002a; Raunio, 1997). As the European Parliament has gained more influence over policy outcomes from the EU, the stakes have raised for the MEPs. More at stake means more incentives to strengthen the division of labour inside the political groups, to try to win votes and shift outcomes in a particular policy direction. The political groups have consequently strengthened their leaderships and established mechanisms for rewarding and punishing 'backbenchers' who toe the group line: via the system of party whips (who monitor group voting) and committee assignments, party coordinators in committees, and the allocation of the *rapporteurships.*

However, the political groups are rarely able to prevent particular national delegations of MEPs from defecting in key votes (e.g. Gabel and Hix, 2002; Hix, 2002b; Lindberg, 2008; Ringe, 2005). For example, between 1999 and 2009, the British conservative MEPs, who belonged to the EPP group in that period, voted differently from the majority of their European political group about 30 per cent of the time. The political groups may control rewards inside the parliament, but national parties still control the selection of candidates for European Parliament elections and hence whether MEPs will be reselected as MEPs. As a result, if MEPs have conflicting voting instructions from their political group and their national party, they will usually follow the instructions of their national party (especially Ringe, 2009). MEPs from member states with candidate-centred electoral systems (such as open-list proportional representation or single transferable vote) tend to be freer from their national parties (Hix, 2004). Nevertheless, the growing cohesion of the political groups, despite the power of national parties over their MEPs, suggests that national parties rarely instruct their MEPs to vote differently from their groups, either because they share the same preferences as their group on most issues on the EU agenda, or because issues in the European Parliament are not salient in domestic politics. Also, repeated interactions in the European Parliament provide strong incentives for national parties to support their political group, since voting against the group rarely changes the policy outcome yet risks the withdrawal of important positions for national parties, such as a committee chair or a key *rapporteurship* (especially Hix *et al.*, 2007).

Competition between the European political groups has also grown (Hix *et al.*, 2003, 2005). Unlike in national parliaments in Europe, there is no governing majority in the European Parliament. The separation of executive and legislative powers in the EU means that coalitions in the European Parliament are built issue by issue – rather like in the US Congress. This is illustrated for the sixth directly elected European Parliament (2004–9) in Table 6.1.

Table 6.1 shows the percentage of times the majority in each political group voted the same way as the majority in another group in roll-call votes in the sixth European Parliament, in all votes, and in three policy areas. The top panel in the table shows that the main dimension of coalition formation and political competition in the European Parliament is the left–right: since a group is more likely to vote with groups that are closer to it on the left–right dimension than groups that are further away (see Hix *et al.*, 2006). The only case where this does not hold is for the Independence/Democracy group (IND/DEM). This is because this group is aligned on the pro-/anti-Europe dimension rather than the left–right dimension, and hence votes more with the European United Left (EUL/NGL) (at the other end of the left–right spectrum) than with the groups in the centre-left (who are pro-European).

Second, the 'grand coalition' between the EPP and PES occurred 69 per cent of the time in roll-call votes in the sixth Parliament. There are two main reasons why the two main groups often vote together. First, under the rules of the ordinary legislative procedure, an absolute majority (of all MEPs) is required for the European Parliament to propose amendments in second reading (see Chapter 3). This forces the two biggest groups to work together across the whole legislative procedure, even at first reading. Second, in many issues the European Parliament sees itself as united against the Commission or, more often, against the governments in the Council (Kreppel, 2000). Nevertheless, the two main groups vote less often together now than they did in the late 1980s and early 1990s, when they had common views on the single market programme. In fact, in the sixth parliament, both the EPP and the PES voted more frequently with the liberals (ALDE) than they did with each other.

Table 6.1   *Issue-by-issue voting coalitions in the 2004 to 2009 Parliament*

All roll-call votes (6,149 votes)

	EUL/NGL	G/EFA	PES	ALDE	EPP–ED	UEN
EUL/NGL						
G/EFA	74					
PES	62	70				
ALDE	52	62	75			
EPP–ED	41	50	69	77		
UEN	45	49	63	71	81	
IND/DEM	41	39	40	45	51	54

Environment, public health, and food safety (794 votes)

	G/EFA	EUL/NGL	PES	ALDE	EPP–ED	UEN
G/EFA						
EUL/NGL	88					
PES	74	75				
ALDE	57	61	76			
EPP–ED	41	41	60	70		
UEN	47	46	61	69	82	
IND/DEM	43	41	46	51	52	54

Civil liberties, justice, and home affairs (509 votes)

	EUL/NGL	G/EFA	PES	ALDE	EPP–ED	UEN
EUL/NGL						
G/EFA	80					
PES	73	82				
ALDE	70	83	86			
EPP–ED	44	54	64	65		
UEN	34	40	50	50	79	
IND/DEM	29	27	25	29	50	58

Internal market and consumer protection (260 votes)

	EUL/NGL	G/EFA	PES	EPP-ED	ALDE	UEN
EUL/NGL						
G/EFA	85					
PES	62	66				
EPP–ED	34	40	67			
ALDE	33	36	65	85		
UEN	40	41	64	82	87	
IND/DEM	50	50	49	49	48	54

Note: Each cell shows the percentage of times the plurality of any two political groups voted the same way in all the roll-call votes in a particular policy area in the European Parliament in 2004 to 2009. Frequencies above 70 per cent are shaded. The political groups are sorted within each policy area from left to right according to the coalition patterns on that policy area, and the arrows show how the groups' coalition behaviour shifts by policy issue. See the note to Figure 6.1 above for the party abbreviations, except IND/DEM = Independence/Democracy group.

Source: Calculated from data on www.votewatch.eu.

Third, as the bottom three panels in Table 6.1 show, different coalitions came together on different policy issues in the 2004 to 2009 Parliament. In the 794 votes on environment, public health and food safety issues, there was a pro-environment majority on the centre-left, of the socialists (PES), radical left (EUL/NGL), liberals (ALDE) and greens (G/EFA), against a more pro-business minority block of the Christian democrats/conservatives (EPP) and the more nationalist conservatives (UEN). A similar centre-left coalition voted together and dominated on civil liberties and justice and home affairs issues. Meanwhile, on internal market and consumer protection issues, a centre-right coalition formed a majority, between EPP, ALDE, and UEN.

In sum, parties at the European level are underdeveloped compared to national parties, and national parties remain the key actors at the European-level party organizations. However, the political groups in the European Parliament do behave like national parliamentary parties: MEPs vote increasingly along political lines, and coalition formation in the European Parliament is driven by left–right policy positions. Also, the transnational party federations are beginning to serve as arenas for linking key party actors at the European level: the national party leaders, the European political group leaders, and the European Commissioners. But, do voters choose between rival policy agendas for European action in European electoral contests?

Elections: EP Elections and EU Referendums

There are two types of EU-related electoral contest: European Parliament elections, and referendums on EU Treaty reforms or other major changes to the EU. Whereas European Parliament elections are held throughout the EU according to a fixed schedule, referendums on EU-related issues have only been held sporadically in some member states.

EP elections: national or European contests?

Direct elections to the European Parliament were first held in June 1979, and since then have been held every five years. In the run-up to the first elections many scholars expected that elections to the European Parliament would provide a new legitimacy for the EU (e.g. Marquand, 1978; Pridham and Pridham, 1979). According to Walter Hallstein (1972, p. 74), a former President of the European Commission:

> Such a campaign would force those entitled to vote to look at and examine the questions and the various options on which the European Parliament would have to decide in the months and years ahead. It would give candidates who emerged victorious from such a campaign

a truly European mandate from their electors; and it would encourage the emergence of truly European political parties.

After seven rounds of these elections it is clear that this optimistic prediction is a long way from the reality.

This is because European Parliament elections are fought not as 'European' elections but rather as 'second-order national contests'. Karlheinz Reif and Hermann Schmitt (1980) came up with this concept having observed that the first elections in 1979 tended to be about national political issues, national parties, and national government office. The main goal of national parties throughout the EU is to win and retain national government office. Elections that decide who holds national executive office are therefore 'first-order contests', and parties consequently treat all other elections – which includes European Parliament elections, regional and local elections, second chamber elections, and elections to choose a ceremonial head of state – as beauty contests fought in the shadow of the ongoing first-order election contest.

The second-order and national character of European Parliament elections has two effects. First, because second-order elections are less important than first-order elections, there is less incentive for people to vote in European Parliament elections, and hence there is a lower turnout in these elections than in national elections. Turnout in European Parliament elections has always been approximately 20 per cent lower than in national parliamentary elections. Participation in European Parliament elections has also declined over time: from 63 per cent in 1979 to 43 per cent in 2009. Mark Franklin (2001) demonstrates, however, that most of the decline in turnout in European Parliament elections can be explained by falling turnout in national elections, the fact that voting is compulsory in fewer member states, that national elections are held on the same day as European Parliament elections in a declining proportion of member states, and that the EU has enlarged to countries that have generally had lower levels of turnout in national elections. Once these factors have been controlled for, turnout in European Parliament elections has in fact been relatively stable.

Second, because European Parliament elections are really about the performance of national governments, many people vote differently in a European Parliament election than they would if it were a national election. There are two reasons for this (Oppenhuis *et al.*, 1996). First, some citizens use the opportunity to vote sincerely rather than strategically, by voting for a (small) party that is closest to their preferences and which has a chance to win a seat under the electoral system used in a European Parliament election, rather than for a (large) party that is more likely to form a majority or be pivotal in the formation of government. Second, some people express their dissatisfaction with the party or parties in government, by voting for an opposition party. Either way,

Figure 6.3   *Second-order effects in European Parliament elections*

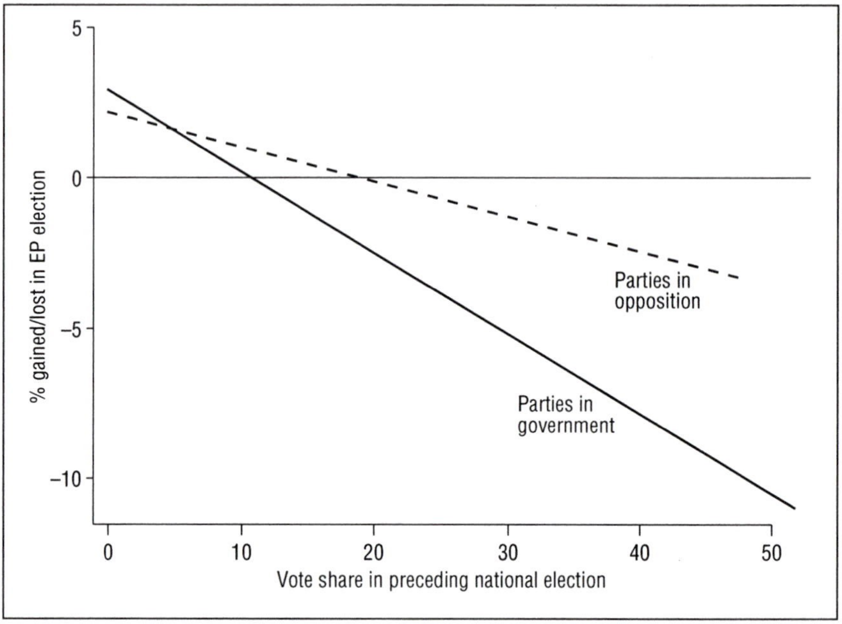

Note: The graph shows bivariate regression lines of the relationship between a party's vote share in the national general election immediately preceding the European Parliament election and the percentage of votes gained or lost in the subsequent European Parliament election, for parties in government compared to parties in opposition, for all parties in all member states in all European Parliament elections between 1979 and 2009.

Source: Calculated from data in Hix and Marsh (2011).

the consequence of such 'vote switching' is that large governing parties lose votes in European Parliament elections while opposition parties and small parties gain votes (van der Eijk and Franklin, 1996; Hix and Marsh, 2007; Marsh, 1998; Reif, 1984). This effect is illustrated in Figure 6.3: which shows that large governing parties – for example, who won 40 per cent of the vote in a preceding national election – on average lost 8 per cent of their vote share in the next European Parliament election, while small governing parties and small and medium-sized opposition parties increased their vote share in European Parliament elections. If anything, the second-order nature of European Parliament elections has increased over time, as the novelty factor in the first elections has worn off (Hix and Marsh, 2011).

The second-order national elections model consequently suggests that lower turnout in European Parliament elections and the outcome of these elections has nothing to do with 'Europe'. There is some contrary evidence.

First, focusing on the motivations for voting, Blondel *et al.*, (1997, 1998) find evidence that voters' attitudes towards Europe are relevant in explaining participation in European Parliament elections. Individuals who are opposed to their country's membership of the EU, have a negative attitude towards the European Parliament or lack knowledge of the European Parliament or the EU are less likely to vote in these elections.

Second, there is some evidence that voters' attitudes towards European integration influence which parties they support in European Parliament elections also (Hobolt *et al.*, 2009; Tilley *et al.*, 2008; Weber, 2007). This affects which parties win and lose. Some political families have systematically done better than others in these elections, irrespective of their size or governing status, which cannot be explained by the standard second-order national elections model (especially Hix and Marsh, 2011). For example, anti-European parties did particularly well in Denmark in 1979 and 1994, France in 1999, and the UK in 2004 and 2009. Green parties also performed well in the 1989 elections (Curtice, 1989). Furthermore, as Figure 6.4 illustrates, socialist parties, both in government and opposition, did particularly badly in the 2009 elections compared to the other main political families.

Also, the standard second-order model does not fit the post-Communist states in Central and Eastern Europe as well as the Old 15 member states in Western Europe: in that there has not been such a general anti-government swing in European Parliament elections in these new member states (Koepke and Ringe, 2006). And, Ferrara and

Figure 6.4 *Main party families and the 2009 European Parliament elections*

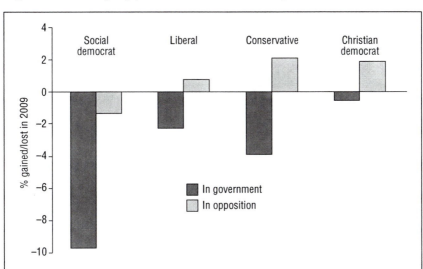

Source: Calculated from data in Hix and Marsh (2011).

Weishaupt (2004) demonstrate that while the general position of parties on the issue of Europe may not have an effect on whether they gain or lose votes in European Parliament elections, whether a party is divided on the question of Europe does seem to matter, in that parties whose elites are divided over European integration have performed worse than parties who have a united pro- or anti-European position, other things being equal.

Third, at the level of individual MEPs and candidates in European Parliament elections, the elections work differently in different member states. For a start, there is not a uniform electoral system in European Parliament elections, as Table 6.2 shows (especially Farrell and Scully, 2005). Since the 1999 elections, when the UK replaced its single-member constituencies with regional list-proportional representation (PR), all member states have used some form of PR. However, there are two major differences in the type of PR that are used. First, many member states have some form of preferential voting – either 'open'-list PR or single-transferable vote – which allows citizens to choose between politicians from the same political party, rather than simply to choose between political parties. Second, while most member states elect their MEPs in one single national constituency, several member states elect their MEPs in several sub-national constituencies.

Comparative political science research has found that preferential voting and the number of politicians elected in each constituency have a significant effect on how candidates campaign in elections and the relationship between politicians and their parties (e.g. Carey and Shugart, 1995; Chang and Golden, 2006; Shugart *et al.*, 2005). In particular, preferential voting systems encourage politicians to campaign directly to voters, to persuade voters to support them rather than other politicians from the same party. Also, larger constituencies under preferential voting systems produces more competition between candidates and hence more direct campaigning and candidate recognition by the citizens. There is some evidence that there are similar effects in European Parliament elections (Hix and Hagemann, 2009; Farrell and Scully, 2007). For example, evidence from the 2009 European Elections Study shows that citizens in countries that have small multi-member constituencies and preferential voting systems – as in Estonia and Ireland – were far more likely to be contacted by parties or candidates during the election campaign than citizens in countries where non-preferential voting systems are used – such as Poland, Greece, Portugal, or Germany.

Despite these factors, the basic claims of the second-order theory of European Parliament elections remain intact because these 'European' or candidate-level aspects of the elections only affect voting behaviour at the margins. This has consequences for the ability of European Parliament elections to reduce the democratic deficit in the EU. Despite the increased powers of the European Parliament in both the legislative arena (vis-à-vis

Table 6.2 Electoral systems used in the 2009 European Parliament elections

Member state	No. of MEPs	Electoral system type	Preferential voting	No. of constituencies size	Average constituency	Voting days
Austria	17	List PR	Yes	1	17	Sunday 7 June
Belgium	22	List PR	Yes	3	7	Sunday 7 June
Bulgaria	17	List PR	Yes	1	17	Sunday 7 June
Cyprus	6	List PR	Yes	1	6	Saturday 6 June
Czech Republic	22	List PR	Yes	1	22	Friday 5 June & Saturday 6 June
Denmark	13	List PR	Yes	1	13	Sunday 7 June
Estonia	6	List PR	Yes	1	6	Sunday 7 June
Finland	13	List PR	Yes	1	13	Sunday 7 June
France	72	List PR	No	8	9	Saturday 6 June & Sunday 7 June
Germany	99	List PR	No	1	99	Sunday 7 June
Greece	22	List PR	No	1	22	Sunday 7 June
Hungary	22	List PR	No	1	22	Sunday 7 June
Ireland	12	STV	Yes	4	3	Friday 5 June
Italy	72	List PR	Yes	5	14	Saturday 6 June & Sunday 7 June
Latvia	8	List PR	Yes	1	8	Saturday 6 June
Lithuania	12	List PR	Yes	1	12	Sunday 7 June
Luxembourg	6	List PR	Yes	1	6	Sunday 7 June
Malta	5	STV	Yes	1	5	Saturday 6 June
Netherlands	25	List PR	Yes	1	25	Thursday 4 June
Poland	50	List PR	No	13	4	Sunday 7 June
Portugal	22	List PR	No	1	22	Sunday 7 June
Romania	33	List PR	No	1	33	Sunday 7 June
Slovakia	13	List PR	Yes	1	13	Saturday 6 June
Slovenia	7	List PR	Yes	1	7	Sunday 7 June
Spain	50	List PR	No	1	50	Sunday 7 June
Sweden	18	List PR	Yes	1	18	Sunday 7 June
UK–Great Britain	69	List PR	No	11	6	Thursday 4 June
UK–N. Ireland	3	STV	Yes	1	3	Thursday 4 June
Total	736			66	11	

Note: List PR = party-list proportional representation; STV = single-transferable vote.

the Council) and the executive arena (vis-à-vis the selection and account-ability of the Commission), European Parliament elections are still fought by national parties on national issues, and not on the performance and the policy agendas of parties or politicians at the European level.

Since 1994, when the European Parliament won the right to veto the governments' choice for Commission President, there has been a possibility of connecting the European Parliament elections to the process of selecting the President of the Commission. Unfortunately, we have not yet had rival candidates for the Commission President, either nominated individually or proposed by the European level parties prior to the European Parliament elections. The Party of European Socialists is committed to putting up a candidate to be the next Commission President prior to the 2014 elections, at the end of Barroso's second term. If the EPP, the liberals, and the greens support other candidates, then we might for the first time see a genuine contest for executive office in the EU. This would add a European flavour to the election campaigns and also change the way the media cover the contests (see Hix, 2008a). Without a genuine contest for executive office in the EU, European Parliament elections will never be more than second-order national contests.

Referendums on EU membership and treaty reforms

Do referendums on European issues do better than European Parliament elections in terms of enabling citizens to express their preferences on European issues? Table 6.3 shows that there have been 48 referendums on EU-related issues in 25 different countries or territories. Over 30 per cent of these referendums have been in just two states: Denmark and Ireland, who together have had 15 referendums. While the pro-EU side has won in most of these referendums, it has not done so well recently. For example, of the 13 referendums that were won by the anti-EU side, two were before 1990, four were in the 1990s, and seven have been since 2000. In fact, if one only counts referendums among EU member states (either on treaty reforms or membership of EMU), then since 2000 the pro-EU side has only won in a minority of cases (5 out of 11), and two of these victories were rerun referendums in Ireland, after Irish voters had initially rejected a treaty reform and were then asked to vote again on a slightly amended version.

But, are these referendums really about the EU? Mark Franklin and his co-authors argue that most EU referendums work much like European Parliament elections: in that the European issues in an EU referendum are of such low salience that the popularity of the government of the day dominates in the campaign and the outcome (Franklin, 2002; Franklin, Marsh, and McLaren, 1994; Franklin, Marsh, and Wlezien, 1994; Franklin *et al.*, 1995). For example, looking at the Danish, Irish, and

French referendums on the Maastricht Treaty in 1992 and 1993, they find that the determining factor in these cases was not attitudes towards the EU but support for or opposition to the party or parties in government at the time of the referendums. In the case of the 1992 French referendum, polls showed overwhelming support for the EU, but voters used the referendum to punish the unpopular Mitterrand presidency. In the opposite direction, when the government changed in Denmark from a liberal–conservative coalition to a social democrat government, the new government was able to win the second referendum on the Maastricht Treaty because its popularity was high in the 'honeymoon period' that followed its national election victory. Siune and Svensson (1993) also find that an individual's level of knowledge about the EU had no effect on whether the individual participated or how he or she voted in the 1992 Danish referendum, thus supporting the notion that the referendum was less about Europe than domestic politics.

Nevertheless, there is evidence that attitudes towards the EU and the positions taken by various political actors towards Europe in the referendum campaigns have played a significant role. For example, Siune *et al.* (1994) and Svensson (2003) show that in the Danish case, parties that were opposed to the EU were more able to mobilize voters against the EU than parties that were in favour of the EU (see Justesen, 2007). Downs (2001) offers a similar explanation of the Danish rejection of membership of the single currency in 2000. In this case, the popularity of the prime minister, Poul Nyrup Rasmussen, did not affect the result. Instead, the No campaign and the anti-European media successfully framed the debate around the issue of protecting national sovereignty, foiling the attempt by the government and the main opposition parties to focus on the alleged positive economic benefits of adopting the euro. Saglie (2000) finds that voters' perceptions of the EU were crucial in how they voted in the Norwegian referendum on EU membership in 1994. Looking at the two votes in Ireland on the Nice Treaty in 2001 and 2002, Garry *et al.* (2005) find that despite a comparatively popular government and unity among the main parties in support of the treaty, attitudes of voters on European issues (particularly enlargement of the EU) played a dominant role in the two campaigns. Finally, Lubbers (2008) and Glencross and Trechsel (2011) find that attitudes towards the EU were stronger predictors of voting behaviour than attitudes towards parties in government in the referendums in 2005 on the EU Constitutional Treaty.

Hence, EU referendums tend to be about both domestic politics and EU issues. Schneider and Weitsman (1996) present a theory of the conditions under which domestic politics will dominate in an EU referendum campaign. Because voters cannot be certain about the consequences of a major constitutional change, such as a treaty reform or membership of the EU, how they vote will depend on how much they trust the protagonists on each side of a referendum campaign. If both sides are trusted, the

Table 6.3 Referendums on European integration, 1972–2009

Date	Member state	Topic	Result (% yes)	Turnout (%)
23 April 1972	France	Enlargement	68.3	60.7
10 May 1972	Ireland	Membership	83.1	70.9
24–5 September 1972	Norway	Membership	46.5*	79.2
2 October 1972	Denmark	Membership	63.3	90.1
3 December 1972	Switzerland	Treaty (EC–EFTA)	72.5	52.0
5 June 1975	United Kingdom	Membership (continued)	67.2	64.0
23 February 1982	Greenland	Membership (continued)	46.0*	75.4
26 February 1986	Denmark	Treaty (Single European Act)	56.2	75.4
6 May 1987	Ireland	Treaty (Single European Act)	69.6	44.0
18 June 1989	Italy	Mandate for Spinelli Treaty	88.1	85.4
3 June 1992	Denmark	Treaty I (Maastricht)	47.9*	82.9
18 June 1992	Ireland	Treaty (Maastricht)	68.7	57.3
20 September 1992	France	Treaty (Maastricht)	51.1	69.7
6 December 1992	Switzerland	Treaty (EEA)	49.7*	78.0
13 December 1992	Liechtenstein	Treaty (EEA)	55.8	87.0
18 May 1993	Denmark	Treaty II (Maastricht)	56.8	85.5
12 June 1994	Austria	Membership	66.6	82.4
16 October 1994	Finland	Membership	56.9	70.4
13 November 1994	Sweden	Membership	52.3	83.3
20 November 1994	Aland Islands	Membership	73.6	49.1
28 November 1994	Norway	Membership	47.8*	89.0
9 April 1995	Liechtenstein	Membership (EEA)	55.9	82.1
8 June 1997	Switzerland	Membership (open negotiations)	25.9*	35.0
22 May 1998	Ireland	Treaty (Amsterdam)	61.7	56.3

Date	Country	Subject		
27 May 1998	Denmark	Treaty (Amsterdam)	55.1	76.2
21 May 2000	Switzerland	Treaty (EU–Switzerland agreement)	67.2	48.0
28 May 2000	Denmark	Membership of EMU	46.9*	87.5
4 May 2001	Switzerland	Membership (resume negotiations)	23.2*	55.0
7 June 2001	Ireland	Treaty I (Nice)	46.1*	34.8
19 October 2002	Ireland	Treaty II (Nice)	62.9	49.5
8 March 2003	Malta	Membership	53.6	90.9
23 March 2003	Slovenia	Membership	89.6	60.2
12 April 2003	Hungary	Membership	83.8	45.6
10–11 May 2003	Lithuania	Membership	89.9	63.4
16–17 May 2003	Slovakia	Membership	92.5	52.2
7–8 June 2003	Poland	Membership	77.5	58.9
13–14 June 2003	Czech Republic	Membership	77.3	55.2
14 September 2003	Estonia	Membership	66.8	64.1
14 September 2003	Sweden	Membership of EMU	42.0*	82.6
20 September 2003	Latvia	Membership	67.7	72.5
20 February 2005	Spain	Treaty (Constitution of the EU)	76.7	42.3
29 May 2005	France	Treaty (Constitution of the EU)	45.3*	69.3
1 June 2005	Netherlands	Treaty (Constitution of the EU)	38.5*	63.3
5 June 2005	Switzerland	Membership of Schengen Area	54.6	55.9
10 July 2005	Luxembourg	Treaty (Constitution of the EU)	56.5	87.8
25 September 2005	Switzerland	Treaty (free movement of persons)	56.0	54.4
12 June 2008	Ireland	Treaty I (Lisbon)	46.6*	53.1
2 October 2009	Ireland	Treaty II (Lisbon)	67.1	59.0

Note: * = pro-EU side lost the referendum.

Sources: Compiled from data in Hug (2002) and European Elections Database www.nsd.uib.no/european_election_database/election_types/eu_related_referendums.html).

referendum is less likely to be purely about the popularity of the government. However, if the government is not trusted, the voters may decide to punish the government. Nonetheless, voters may be torn between voting to punish/reward the government and voting sincerely on the issue before them.

Building on the work of Schneider and Weitsman, Simon Hug predicts how the institutional context of a referendum determines whether voters act sincerely or strategically (Hug, 2002; Hug and Sciarini, 2000). First, a referendum is less likely to be a pure popularity contest between domestic parties and leaders if it is constitutionally required rather than initiated by a group of opposition parties, the media, or a protest movement. From the perspective of the government, submitting an issue to the voters in a non-required referendum and suffering a defeat is more likely to damage the government irreparably than suffering a defeat in a required referendum. The latter may still be damaging, but it will not be the result of a serious miscalculation by the government. Second, a referendum is less likely to be about domestic parties and leaders and more likely to be about Europe if the result of the referendum is binding on the elites rather than simply consultative. In a consultative referendum, citizens are free to use their vote to protest against the government, in the knowledge that the parliament will ultimately decide on the issue in the referendum. Hence, there is less opportunity for voters to use referendums strategically to punish the government in binding referendums than in non-binding referendums.

Similarly, Sara Hobolt (2009) shows that information also plays a role in determining whether Europe matters in an EU-related referendum. Voters act on their preferences towards European integration when more information is available. At an aggregate level, EU attitudes matter more when the campaign environment is more intensive. At the individual level, European issues have a bigger impact on better informed voters. This suggests that when provided with sufficient information, voters are able to make educated choices about EU issues. Hence, it is probably a mistake to assume that the anti-EU votes in recent referendums are because voters were ill informed about the EU or the issues at stake. The opposite might in fact be the case.

Finally, EU referendums affect national governments' behaviour and voters' attitudes towards the EU, and therefore have policy consequences for the EU as a whole. Where governments are concerned, having to hold a referendum on an EU Treaty reform increases the risk that the reform will be rejected. This strengthens the negotiating position of those member states which have to hold referendums and whose voters are more critical of the EU, compared with those member states in which treaty reforms only require a parliamentary vote and a single party controls a clear parliamentary majority (Hug, 1997, 2002; König and Hug, 2000).

Where voters are concerned, referendums have a more powerful 'inducing effect' than do European Parliament elections (Christin and Hug, 2002; Hug, 2002). Holding a referendum on the EU forces the elites to debate the associated issues in public and to explain the EU institutions and complex treaty reforms to their citizens. As a result, citizens in member states that have had referendums tend to be significantly better informed about the EU than citizens in member states that have never had a referendum, or only had referendums several decades ago. Furthermore, EU referendums affect the level of support for European integration by increasing public acceptance of government decisions related to the EU, and hence the legitimacy of the EU, as the case of Denmark has shown.

Overall, the existing electoral contests related to Europe do not allow citizens to express their preferences on European integration in a clear way or to choose between particular policy packages for the EU or candidates for EU executive office. Despite the increasing powers of the European Parliament to influence EU policy outcomes, there are few incentives against national parties using European Parliament elections as mid-term polls on the performance of a national government. EU referendums give voters more of an opportunity to express their views on the EU, but most institutional and political contexts encourage citizens to vote strategically on domestic issues rather than to express their sincere views on EU matters. Also, EU referendums are about big constitutional issues rather than whether the EU policy agenda should move in a particular direction, and are hence rather crude instruments for connecting citizens to EU level politics.

Conclusion: Democratic Politics in the EU?

The EU is not a particularly democratic political system. In procedural terms, the EU ticks all the necessary boxes for a state to be considered to be democratic. We elect our governments, who negotiate on our behalf in Brussels and decide who forms the EU executive. We elect the MEPs, and we indirectly elect the Commission. Moreover, European Parliament elections are free and fair, and freedom of association and a free press are guaranteed by the European Convention on Human Rights, to which all EU member states are signatories. In other words, the EU would be allowed to join the EU!

However, in substantive terms – where the substance of democratic politics is a competition between rival elites for political power which allows citizens to make educated choices about who should govern them and the direction of the policy agenda – the EU is far from democratic. National government elections are about *national* issues, fought by *national* parties, and about who controls *national* government office.

European Parliament elections, moreover, are by-products of these national electoral contests: fought on domestic issues rather than the EU policy agenda or executive officeholders at the European level. In no sense, therefore, can Europe's voters choose between rival policy programmes for the EU or 'throw out' those who exercise political power at the European level.

The political consequences of this indirect system of representation and elections are not all bad. Voters have an impact on EU policies via national elections, and have increasingly used referendums on EU issues to constrain their governments' actions at the European level. Also, because European Parliament elections tend to be lost by parties in government and won by parties in opposition, 'divided government' (where one political family dominates the Council while the other side dominates the European Parliament) has until recently been the norm in the EU (Manow and Döring, 2008).

The problem, however, is that without a more directly democratic system there are few incentives for Europe's leaders to tackle some of the fundamental problems facing Europe: such as structural economic reforms, energy security, the place of the EU in the world, and how to deal with Europe's multi-ethnic society. In a genuinely democratic polity, tough policy decisions are resolved through the process of competitive elections, which forces elites to debate issues and allows voters to form opinions in response to this debate.

Given the opportunity, Europe's voters and the nascent European-level parties would be up to the challenge of EU democracy. Since the battle for control of the policy agenda is the crucial contest in any political system, how the Commission President is elected and the political fall-out of such a contest for this office on the workings of the EU will probably determine the viability of a more directly democratic system of government for Europe.

Because the power of the member states in the EU would be challenged by either a more powerful European Parliament or an elected Commission President, many governments are reluctant to allow a more open contest for the Commission President or a more central role for the political groups in the European Parliament in the election of this office. However, we may be getting close to the point when governments are punished by their voters for failing to take key decisions at the European level and the very existence of the EU is under threat. Faced with this situation, some governments might consider that a more democratic EU is the lesser evil. Until such time, it will be rational for citizens to be sceptical of the European integration process, and therefore not to take European Parliament elections too seriously or trust their governments too much when making decisions in the EU.

Interest Representation

This chapter looks at the representation of societal interests at the European level. Interest groups play a central role in all democratic political systems, where private organizations represent 'civil society' in the policy-making process. Whereas political society at the European level, in terms of supranational democratic politics, may be comparatively weak compared to the national level (as we saw in the previous chapter), civil society in Brussels is more developed, dense, and complex than in most national capitals in Europe. In a sense Brussels is more like Washington, DC than Paris, London, Warsaw, Berlin, or Prague. But is EU policy-making open to some of the popular criticisms of American pluralism, in which the best-organized and funded special interests appear to reap the biggest rewards? Or is the EU more like national European polities, where policy-makers take an active role in balancing private and public interests? We first look at several different theories of interest-group politics before turning to how far these theories apply to interest representation in the EU.

Theories of Interest-Group Politics

Pluralism is the classic model of interest-group politics in democratic systems. The central idea in this model is that open access by private citizens and organized groups to policy-makers provides checks and balances against powerful state officials or the capture of policy by a particular group (Bentley, 1908; Truman, 1951). The main assumption behind pluralism is that for every group pressing on one side of a debate, another group will present the opposing view. If there are cross-cutting (rather than reinforcing) social divisions, there will be 'multiple oppositions' to any particular group (Lipset, 1959). Put another way, there is always 'countervailing power' against any well-organized group which tries to promote its own private interests against a broader 'public interest'. A central requirement of the pluralist model, therefore, is that opposing interests have equal access to the political process. For example, environmentalist groups should have equal influence as the industrial lobby. If this is the case, all governmental officials need do to promote the public interest is to act as neutral referees of the interest-group game.

But the pluralist theory naïvely assumes that opposing groups will naturally have equal access to power (Galbraith, 1953; Schattschneider, 1960). Mancur Olson (1965, pp. 127–8) provided a powerful explanation of why this is not always the case:

> Since relatively small groups will frequently be able voluntarily to organize and act in support of their common interests, and since large groups normally will not be able to do so, the outcome of the political struggle among the various groups in society will not be symmetrical ... The smaller groups ... can often defeat the larger groups – which are normally supposed to prevail in a democracy. The privileged and intermediate groups often triumph over the numerically superior forces in the latent or large groups because the former are generally organized and active while the latter are normally unorganised and inactive.

The reason for this disparity, Olson argued, was a 'logic of collective action': where there are high incentives to join a group that seeks benefits only for the members of the group (private interests), and low incentives to join a group that seeks benefits for all of society (public interests). Where public interests are concerned, people can simply 'free ride' on the actions of others: reap the benefits of higher environmental protection, for example, without helping an environmentalist group to lobby the government. Related to this idea, 'concentrated interests', such as groups which represent particular producer interests, are more likely to be able to organize than 'diffuse interests', which represent the interests of society as a whole (Wilson, 1980). These logics suggest that rather than a pluralist level playing field, open access to government could lead to heavy lobbying of public officials by concentrated well-organized groups, and policy outputs that benefit special interests at the expense of society as a whole.

To overcome such potentially biased outcomes, two alternative models of interest-group intermediation have emerged. In each of these models the state actively promotes a particular structure of interest-group politics, with the aim of producing more balanced representation and policy outcomes.

First, in the *corporatist* model, the state assumes that the main division in society is between business and labour (Schmitter 1974; Schmitter and Lehmbruch, 1979). To promote an equal balance of power between these two forces the state recognizes, licenses, and grants representational monopolies to the two sides of the class divide: the 'social partners'. Instead of open policy networks, representatives from business and trade unions participate in closed 'tripartite' meetings with state officials. If an agreement can be brokered in these meetings, which is either implemented voluntarily or leads to new legislation, the assumption is that policy will reflect a broad social consensus.

Second, *neo-pluralists* argue that the inherent biases in pluralism can be overcome if state officials cease to be neutral arbiters (Dunleavy and O'Leary, 1987; Petracca, 1994). In this model, bureaucrats deliberately seek out, subsidize, and give access to underrepresented public interests (Lindblom, 1977). Unlike corporatism, however, neo-pluralism does not involve privileging a particular set of social interests. Instead, on each policy issue the state promotes the group that represents the particular public interest at stake. For example, environmental groups are asked to give evidence on industrial standards, consumer groups to look at product standards, women's groups to speak on gender equality legislation, trade unions to provide information on labour market policies, and so on.

Nevertheless, each of these alternative models of interest representation has its problems. First, corporatist systems arbitrarily privilege particular social groups while excluding others. As societies have evolved, old class divisions have eroded and new social movements have emerged (such as environmental groups, women's groups, and consumer groups) outside the traditional representational structures of labour and business (Dalton and Kuechler, 1990). Second, in the corporatist system, big business and industrial labour share similar 'producer interests' and hence often promote these interests at the expense of the 'diffuse interests' of consumers and taxpayers. Third, requiring consent from both sides of industry, or from all cultural/national interests, reduces the ability of policy-makers to undertake policy change. Fourth, even in neo-pluralism, providing state funds to public interest groups introduces a perverse incentive for groups to organize for the purpose of securing state subsidies for their organizations rather than to promote the policy views of their members.

In addition, Olson's (1965) critique of pluralism may be overblown. For example, Becker (1983) argues that as the level of policy supplied to a concentrated interest rises, the incentives for the losing group to organize to oppose these policies will also rise. Hence, at a certain level of capture by a particular group, diffuse interests – such as consumers or taxpayers – will start to mobilize. As a result, an equilibrium balance of interests will emerge, and will act as a constraint against policy-makers supplying unlimited benefits to concentrated interests.

In addition, information may be more important than organization power. Information provided by interest groups is valuable for making good policy, and information from a group that has incurred high costs to gather and provide information is probably more credible than information from a group that has found it cheap to provide. Hence, policy-makers are more likely to use information from groups that represent diffuse interests than groups that represent concentrated interests (Austen-Smith, 1993; cf. Lohmann, 1998). Moreover, where demand for interest-group access is concerned, Austen-Smith and Wright (1994) argue that because groups will secure greater returns from lobbying policy-makers who have opposing policy views than from policy-makers with similar views, there are greater incentives for 'counteractive lobbying' than is often assumed in the classic critiques of pluralism (cf. Baumgartner and Leech, 1996).

In general, a perfect model of interest-group representation does not exist, and what explains the structure of interest-group politics in a policy area is the nature of the incentives and the interests of interest groups and policy-makers in that particular policy area. Hence, more interesting questions for our purpose are which interest groups are best organized in Brussels, and why? And how does the structure of interest representation in Brussels affect the policy outcomes, operation, and legitimacy of the EU?

Lobbying Europe: Interest Groups and EU Policy-Making

The number of private individuals and groups seeking to influence the EU policy process has increased dramatically since the 1980s (Coen and Richardson, 2009a; Greenwood *et al.*, 1992; Greenwood and Aspinwall, 1998; Mazey and Richardson, 1993; Pedlar, 2002; Pedlar and van Schendelen, 1994;). In the mid-1980s researchers estimated that there were approximately 500 interest groups with offices in Brussels (e.g. Butt Philip, 1985). By the mid-2000s this number had quintupled. Table 7.1 shows the number and types of interest group seeking to influence the EU policy process in 2001, as calculated by Greenwood (2007a) from a variety of sources, such as the annual *European Public Affairs Directory* (Haxell, 2010).

According to Greenwood's figures, groups representing business, producer and professional interests are most numerous. To start with, 295 individual companies have offices in Brussels. There are also 267 EU-specialist public affairs consultancies and law firms. These 'lobby firms' specialize in advising interest groups on EU policy-making and legislation, and mounting 'advocacy campaigns'. The clients of these commercial consultancies are mainly private firms, and these consultancies serve as an alternative and more direct route for businesses to influence the EU institutions than taking action through a European industrial or trade association (Lahusen, 2002, 2003).

In addition, there are over 800 European-level trade and professional

Table 7.1   *Types and numbers of interest groups at the European level, in 2006*

Type of interest group	Number	
European interest-group associations	1,296	
EU trade and professional associations		843
Citizen interest associations (e.g. NGOs)		429
EU and international trade unions		24
Brussels-based public affairs organizations	371	
Commercial public affairs consultancies		153
Law firms, specializing in EU law		115
Think-tanks and EU training organizations		103
Individual companies in Brussels (with public affairs offices geared towards the EU)	295	
National interest-group associations	200	
National trade and professional associations		122
Employers' federations		38
Chambers of commerce		40
Offices of member states' regions in Brussels	198	
International organizations	118	
Total	2,478	

Source: Compiled from data in Greenwood (2007a).

associations, 122 national trade and professional associations with offices in Brussels, 38 national employers' federations, and 40 national chambers of commerce. These figures include a large number of associations who represent professional groups, such as accountants, doctors, lawyers, teachers, and journalists, who are neither clearly on the side of big business nor on the side of 'the little people'.

Organizations that represent broader public (diffuse) interests are less numerous in Brussels, but are nevertheless present. In fact, there are more than 400 different interest groups and non-governmental organizations (NGOs) who represent the interests of a broad array of 'citizens interests', such as consumer groups, environmental groups, and women's groups, and so on. There are also 24 groups representing international, European, and national trade unions.

In November 2005, Commissioner Siim Kallas launched the European Transparency Initiative (ETI), in response to growing concerns about the relationships between 'lobbyists' and the EU institutions. The ETI included, among other things, a voluntary register of interests for groups who would like to gain access to the Commission, which was launched in June 2008. Inclusion in the register requires acceptance of a Code of Conduct for Interest Representatives, which sets out specific financial,

Figure 7.1   *Interest groups in the Commission registry, by policy area*

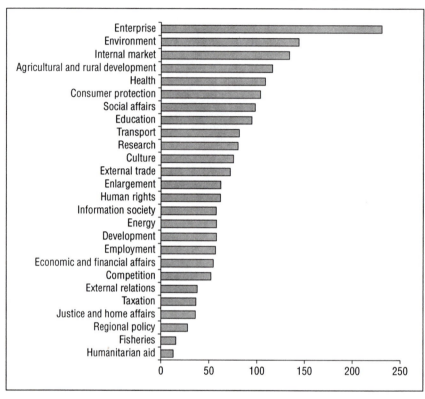

Source: Compiled from data in Coen (2007).

transparency, and behaviour obligations for groups and individuals. The European Parliament has a similar register of interests and the two institutions are working towards a common register and code of conduct. For example, the two registries can already be accessed via the same internet page (http://europa.eu/lobbyists/interest_representative_registers/index_en.html).

The Commission's register of interests provides a useful indicator of the volume of interest-group activities in Brussels by policy area, as Figure 7.1 shows (Coen, 2007). As one would expect, a large number of groups are registered in the main policy areas of interest to business and producer interests, such as enterprise, internal market, and agriculture. However, a large number of groups are also registered in the policy areas where citizens' groups and NGOs are the primary actors, such as environment, health, consumer protection, social affairs, education, research, culture, human rights, development, employment, and justice and home affairs. A similar picture is obtained from the European Parliament's register of interests, which includes over 5,000 groups, of which approximately 70 per cent are business oriented and 30 per cent represent other interests (Coen and Richardson, 2009b, p. 6).

As Greenwood (2007a: 49) summarizes:

> Around 1,000 formally constituted business associations are organized at, and addressed to the EU level, accounting for approximately two-thirds of all EU groups. Available indicators suggest that their numbers have reached a plateau since the mid-1990s, and that the proportion of business groups in Brussels has declined relative to citizen groups.

Finally, regarding the number of people employed by interest groups in Brussels, estimates range from 15,000 to 20,000 (Greenwood, 2007a; Haxell, 2010). Put another way, while political society in Brussels, in terms of supranational party politics, may be underdeveloped relative to national political systems, civil society in the EU, as represented by EU interest-group activities, is more developed than in any national capital in Europe.

Business interests: the large firm as a political actor

Lobbying of the political process by private firms took off at the national level in Europe in the 1970s and 1980s, when governments began to set standards for the marketplace through new forms of economic and social regulation. However, with the European single market these standards are now set almost exclusively at the European level, and business interests are thus naturally drawn to the new political centre.

Business interests have not only responded to the emergence of regulatory competences in Brussels, they have also actively promoted this development. Even if certain European industries have been opposed to global free trade, most sectors of the European economy have been in favour of removing barriers to the free movement of goods, services, capital, and labour within Europe. This observation was at the heart of neo-functionalist theories of European integration in the 1950s, when business interests promoted new European competences in sectors that were originally excluded from the agreements between the governments (Haas, 1958, pp. 162–213). The situation was similar with the European single market, when European multinationals urged national governments and the Commission to pursue further market integration to help Europe recover from the recession of the 1970s (Middlemas, 1995; Sandholtz and Zysman, 1989).

Business interests are well organized in Brussels, and have considerable financial and personnel resources behind them. The main umbrella organization for business is Business Europe, which until 2007 was called UNICE, the Union of Industrial and Employers' Confederations of

Europe (www.businesseurope.eu). Business Europe, which was established in 1958, is a confederation of 39 national federations of business from 33 EU member states plus accession and aspirant countries. The Business Europe office in Brussels has 40 permanent staff, but the bulk of its work is done in a network of committees and working groups that involve over 1,000 officials from the member organizations. Business Europe plays a high-profile role in EU policy-making, and its officials meet regularly with officials from the Commission, the Council, and the European Parliament. It also regularly makes formal submissions to the EU institutions such as Commission and Council working groups and European Parliament committees, but these submissions are usually only bland statements of business interests that are designed to include the views of as many member organizations as possible. One problem for Business Europe is that member businesses and national associations have several exit options through their own private channels of representation if they think Business Europe is not representing their interests effectively enough.

Business Europe is just one of ten business associations in Brussels who employ at least 20 full-time staff, the others being: the European Chemicals Industry Council (CEFIC), which is the only group which employs more than 100 staff (www.cefic.org); the Committee of Agricultural Organizations in the EU/General Committee for Agricultural Cooperation in Europe (COPA–COGECA) (www.copa-cogeca.be); the European Federation of Pharmaceuticals Industries and Associations (EFPIA) (www.efpia.org); the Association of European Insurers (CEA) (www.cea.eu); the Union of Electricity Industry (EURELECTRIC) (www2.eurelectric.org); the European Automobile Manufacturers' Association (ACEA) (www.acea.be); the European Confederation of Iron and Steel Industries (EUROFER) (www.eurofer.org); the European Cement Industry Association (CEMBUREAU) (www.cembureau.be); and the EU Committee of the American Chamber of Commerce (AMCHAM-EU) (www.amchameu.eu) (Greenwood, 2007a, p. 53).

In addition to these sector-specific associations, business interests are represented by a variety of other groups in Brussels. One particularly influential group is the European Round Table of Industrialists (ERT) (www.ert.be). The ERT was established in 1983 by a select group of chief executives of some of the largest firms in Europe, and membership of the group has always been by invitation only. The primary focus of ERT in the 1980s was the single market project: promoting the removal of technical barriers to trade in Europe while preventing the introduction of high social and environmental standards that would impose costs on business (Cowles, 1995). Since the establishment of the single market, the ERT members have maintained their personal contacts at the highest political level in national capitals and Brussels, and are therefore uniquely placed to make the case for business at the European level (van

Apeldoorn, 2002). Since the 1980s the ERT has clubbed together with AMCHAM–EU and UNICE in the 'big business troika' (Cowles, 1997, 1998), and in the 1990s and 2000s the ERT has been a central player in the formation of global business networks, such as the Transatlantic Business Dialogue, which brings together CEOs from Europe, the US, and Canada (Cowles, 2002).

In 2010 the ERT comprised 45 chief executives and chairmen of major multinational companies from a variety of sectors, who collectively have a turnover of over €1,000 billion and employ more than 6 million people. Around half of the ERT members are among the largest 100 transnational corporations in the world, and anyone with only a cursory knowledge of major European companies would recognize many of the names in the list of current members, in Table 7.2.

However, one should not think of business interests as a monolithic block in the Brussels policy process. Individual firms in pursuit of their own private interests lie at the heart of the Brussels lobbying system. Individual firms often have competing policy interests, such as different domestic regulatory frameworks and competitive advantages. As a result, individual firms will only participate in umbrella organizations if the benefits of cooperating with other firms are greater than the costs competing with each other to gain influence (Coen, 1998). The growth in the membership of the cross-sectoral organizations hence suggests that these groups have been able to produce results: EU policies that promote individual firms' interests.

To find out where firms go to influence EU policy-making, and how these strategies have evolved, David Coen (1997, 1998, 2010) has conducted a series of surveys of private firms. In the surveys, Coen asked the public affairs directors of approximately 100 large firms how they would allocate a hypothetical 100 units of resources between various channels to influence EU policy outcomes. As Figure 7.2 shows, the data from three waves of the survey, in 1984, 1994, and 2004, reveal some significant shifts in the lobbying behaviour of business interests in Brussels. In general, over the past 20 years, there has been a significant shift in lobbying resources by large firms away from national level actors (such as governments, national MPs, and national civil servants) to European level actors (such as the Commission, the European Parliament, and individual MEPs). Interestingly, between 1994 and 2004 there was a slight decline in the amount of resources devoted to lobbying the Commission and a dramatic increase in the amount of resources devoted to lobbying the European Parliament. In fact, in 2004 the firms said that they allocated similar amounts of resources to lobbying the Commission (21 per cent) and the European Parliament and the MEPs (19 per cent, combined). Nevertheless, when asked which strategy produced the highest pay-offs, the Commission was still the clear winner. Perhaps surprisingly, the employment of specialist lobby firms in Brussels

Table 7.2   *Members of the European Round Table of Industrialists*

CEO or Chairman	Company
Leif Johansson (Chairman)	Volvo
Gerard Kleisterlee (Vice-Chairman)	Royal Philips Electronics
Peter Löscher (Vice-Chairman)	Siemens
Paul Adams	British American Tobacco
César Alierta Izuel	Telefónica
Nils S. Andersen	A.P. Moller-Maersk
Paulo Azevedo	SONAE
Jean-Louis Beffa	Saint-Gobain
Franco Bernabè	Telecom Italia
Carlo Bozotti	STMicroelectronics
Peter Brabeck-Letmathe	Nestlé
Svein Richard Brandtzaeg	Norsk Hydro
David Brennan	AstraZeneca
Martin Broughton	British Airways
Antonio Brufau	Repsol YPF
Vittorio Colao	Vodafone Group
Gerhard Cromme	ThyssenKrupp
Rodolfo De Benedetti	CIR
Bülent Eczacibaşi	Eczacibaşi Group
John Elkann	Fiat
Carlos Ghosn	Renault
Jürgen Hambrecht	BASF
Antti Herlin	KONE Corporation
Zsolt Hernádi	MOL
Franz Humer	F. Hoffmann-La Roche
Pablo Isla	Inditex
Olli-Pekka Kallasvuo	Nokia
Bruno Lafont	Lafarge
Thomas Leysen	Umicore
Ian Livingston	BT
Gary McGann	Smurfit Kappa Group
Gérard Mestrallet	GDF SUEZ
Aloïs Michielsen	Solvay
René Obermann	Deutsche Telekom
Jorma Ollila	formally of Nokia
Dimitri Papalexopoulos	Titan Cement
Paul Polman	Unilever
Benoît Potier	Air Liquide
Norbert Reithofer	BMW Group
Wolfgang Ruttenstorfer	OMV
Güler Sabanci	Sabanci Holding
Paolo Scaroni	Eni
Carl-Henric Svanberg	BP
Jean-François van Boxmeer	Heineken
Ben Verwaayen	Alcatel-Lucent
Peter R. Voser	Royal Dutch Shell
Jacob Wallenberg	Investor
Hans Wijers	AkzoNobel

Source: Compiled from information on www.ert.be, 17 June 2010.

Figure 7.2 *How large firms lobby the EU*

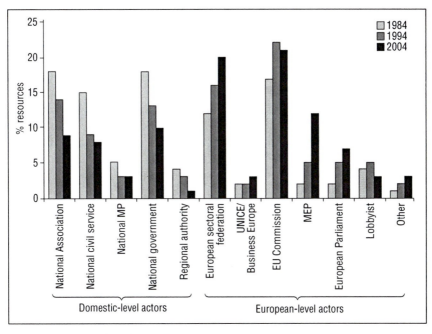

Source: Calculated from data in Coen (2010).

was not seen as a particularly rewarding strategy. Instead, firms tend to use public affairs consultants to provide specialist information and monitoring services as a supplement to, rather than a substitute for, direct approaches to the EU institutions.

In sum, business interests and the owners of capital are powerfully represented in the EU policy process. Regulation of the market at the European level provides a strong incentive for firms to spend valuable resources to ensure that policy outcomes do not harm their interests. Also, individual firms have become increasingly sophisticated in their lobbying strategies, using multiple channels and diversifying their public affairs expenditure. The easy access of these interests to the Commission and the multiplicity of actors involved suggest a pluralist model of intermediation of business interests. But, for pluralism to work, groups with opposing interests to those of the business community must be equally well organized.

Countervailing power: public interests, social movements, and trade unions

Groups with interests often diametrically opposed to the owners of business were not well represented in Brussels until the early 1990s.

Representatives of a variety of societal interests have been formally represented in the Economic and Social Committee since its establishment following the Treaty of Rome, in an early attempt to establish an element of corporatism in the EU policy process. But, this committee is purely consultative: mainly to provide reports on legislation, which are then considered by the European Parliament, the Council, and the Commission. A wide variety of social interests, such as trade unions, environmentalists, and consumer groups, then became interested in Brussels as a result of the new EU policy competences in such areas as health and safety at work, environmental policy, consumer protection and social policy, in the wake of the Single European Act and Maastricht Treaty. However, it was not until the 1990s that these groups really began to compete on a more equal basis with business groups.

The European Trade Union Confederation (ETUC) was founded in 1973. Like Business Europe, ETUC is an umbrella organization, comprising 82 national trade union federations in 36 EU and non-EU states, as well as 12 affiliated European Industry Federations (see www.etuc.org). The ETUC has 58 full-time staff, so in terms of personnel resources is larger than Business Europe. The national trade union federations who are members of the ETUC together account for more than 60 million individual trade union members. Like Business Europe, the number and diversity of the ETUC members make it difficult to construct a coherent European-level trade union strategy (e.g. Dølvik and Visser, 2001). Also like Business Europe, ETUC is part of a network of like-minded 'public' interest groups, even though its members have limited resources and fewer opportunities to pursue alternative lobbying strategies compared to private business interests.

Nevertheless, ETUC has increasingly been able to gain a place at the bargaining table as the legitimate 'social partner' of Business Europe and the European Centre of Employers and Enterprises providing Public Services (CEEP), which represents nationalized industries and services providers in the public sector (www.ceep.eu). In 1984 the President of the Commission, Jacques Delors, announced that no new social policy initiatives would be forthcoming without the prior approval of both sides of industry, as represented by Business Europe and ETUC. In the early years of this 'social dialogue' little progress was made since Business Europe insisted that its members would not be bound by any agreement reached with ETUC. However, persistent Commission sympathy for the ETUC's interests ensured that the social dialogue did not dissolve. Delors launched the Commission's strategy for a European social policy at an ETUC meeting in May 1988, and the Commission supported the ETUC's proposal for a European Social Charter, which was signed in 1989 by all the member states except the UK. As a result of further Commission pressure, in 1990 the social dialogue produced three joint proposals that the Commission duly proposed as legislation (Story, 1996).

A boost for ETUC came with the Maastricht Treaty, which institutionalized the social dialogue in the area of social policy. The Maastricht Social Agreement extended the competences of the EU in the social policy field for all member states except the UK (although the British Labour government signed up to the Social Chapter of the Maastricht Treaty immediately after winning the 1997 election). Under the rules of the agreement, the Commission is now statutorily obliged to consult both business and labour before submitting proposals for social policy legislation (see Chapter 8). In addition, a member state may request that business and labour seek to reach an agreement on the implementation of directives adopted under the Social Agreement. Moreover, and most significantly, if business and labour reach a collective agreement on a particular policy issue, this can serve as a direct substitute for EU legislation. These rules provide the social partners with a considerable degree of agenda-setting power in the area of social policy (Boockmann, 1998). In other words, this is a classic model of corporatism in a central area of EU socio-economic policy (Falkner, 1996; Obradovic, 1996).

However, the social dialogue has not been a complete success from the point of view of labour interests (Falkner, 2000; Pochet, 2003). In the late 1990s, institutionalizing corporatism in the social policy area has given business interests a veto over legislation that they may not have been able to block in a centre-left-dominated EU Council or European Parliament at that time (Branch and Greenwood, 2001). The ETUC has also become reliant on the Commission's Directorate-General for Employment and Social Affairs for information, expertise and resources (Dølvik and Visser, 2001). And despite the quasi-corporatist EU decision-making on European-wide labour rights, there are few signs of a genuine transnational industrial relations system developing. There are no European-wide collective agreements in any major industrial sector or even within multinational firms (Martin and Ross, 2001). As a result, labour interests are on average less influential at the European level than business interests and also less influential than they have traditionally been at the national level. Defenders of labour interests often complain about the gradual erosion of national corporatism by the process of EU economic integration and the passing of labour market regulation competences to the European level (Streeck and Schmitter, 1991; Treib and Falkner, 2009).

Nevertheless, while labour interest may have been weakened by the transfer of policy-making powers to the EU, other diffuse interests have been more successful at challenging the dominance of business interests in Brussels. For many of these groups, EU integration has opened up new channels that have enabled them to go directly to Brussels, over the heads of national politicians and bureaucrats. Although few public interest groups had a voice in Brussels before the late 1980s, by the mid-1990s they were playing a central part in many EU policy debates.

For example, in the environment field, ten groups make up the so-called 'Green 10' environmental NGOs: the European Environmental Bureau (EEB) (www.eeb.org), the World Wide Fund for Nature (WWF) (wwf.panda.org), the Friends of the Earth Europe (FoEE) (www.foeeurope.org), Greenpeace (www.greenpeace.org/eu-unit), the Transport and Environment (T&E) (www.transportenvironment.org), Birdlife International (http://europe.birdlife.org), Climate Action Network Europe (CANE) (www.climnet.org), Friends of Nature International (NFI) (www.nfi.at), Central and Eastern Europe Bankwatch Network (www.bankwatch.org), and Health and Environment Alliance (www.env-health.org). Together these groups employ over 100 full-time staff and claim to have more than 20 million individual members between them. The individual membership basis of these groups enables their leaderships in Brussels to act more quickly and decisively than labour interests. Moreover, their scientific and resource base means that these groups provide reliable information to EU policy-makers, which has strengthened their position against corporate interests on many issues of EU environmental law (Long and Lörinczi, 2009; Rootes, 2002; Rucht, 2001; Webster, 1998).

In the area of consumers' interests, the main interest group is the European Consumers' Organization (BEUC), which was founded in 1962, employs 25 full-time staff and has a corporate membership structure, involving 43 national consumer organizations from 31 EU and non-EU countries (www.beuc.org). There are several other smaller groups representing consumers' interests, such as the European Association for the Coordination of Consumer Representation in Standardization (ANEC), the Association of European Consumers (AEC), the Confederation of Family Organizations in the European Union (COFACE), and the European Community of Consumer Cooperatives (EUROCOOP). However, unlike the environmental groups, these groups are all umbrella organizations of various national consumer associations, and are hence less capable of developing innovative lobbying strategies.

A large number of 'social NGOs' represent a wide variety of other public interests, which are brought together in the Social Platform (www.socialplatform.org). Social Platform was established in 1995 and now has 40 member organizations which cover a wide range of social interests, as Table 7.3 shows. Most of these organizations are themselves federations of national NGOs, and constitute a considerable numerical force in the corridors of Brussels.

As with the labour movement, the key source of power and influence for these public interests is the Commission. Virtually all environmental, consumer, and other public interest groups in Brussels derive their main source of funding from the EU budget, via the various directorates-general of the Commission. For example, a four-year action programme between 2002 and 2006 for promoting NGOs in the environmental field was allocated a budget of €32 million from EU funds (Greenwood, 2007a, p. 132). And, one example of funding social NGOs was the €7 million the Commission spent in 1997 on anti-racist activists as part of the European Year Against Racism, most of which was channelled through European-level interest groups (Guiraudon, 2001).

The Commission has also been instrumental in setting up fora that provide these groups with access to the EU policy process. For example, the EEB has often been invited to attend meetings of the Environment Council, and has even been a member of the Commission's delegation to the Earth Summits. In the area of consumer interests, the Consumers Contact Committee (CCC) was set up by the Commission in 1961, but was plagued by a lack of commitment on the part of the Commission and the rival interests of the various European-level consumer associations. In 1995 the Commission transformed its Consumer Policy Service into a proper directorate-general, and reorganized the CCC into the Consumers' Committee (CC). The CC has a more streamlined structure, consisting of a small number of representatives (one from each of the main European-level consumer associations) and chaired by a Commission official (Young, 1997, 1998).

A similar process is taking place with the social NGOs. There has been much talk of a 'civil dialogue' between the Commission and these NGOs. Several groups as well as EU officials, including the Employment and Social Affairs DG and the Social Affairs Committee in the European Parliament, lobbied unsuccessfully for a legal reference to civil dialogue in the Amsterdam Treaty, in line with the model for the social dialogue. But even without a formal reference in the treaty, the Social Platform emerged as the de facto forum for bringing together social NGOs and Commission officials on a regular and structured basis (Geyer, 2001).

There are several potentially negative consequence of these corporatist and neo-pluralist strategies by the Commission. One is that by funding interest groups, the Commission may be reducing the credibility of the information it receives from these groups, as the groups have an interest in providing information to the Commission which they think will help them continue to be funded. Another consequence is that the Commission's has in effect created 'insider' and 'outsider' groups. The ETUC, BEUC, and the EEB are clearly insiders in the EU policy process. Other groups are not sufficiently represented by the formal structures of representation in the EU or in the network of European associations with links to the Commission, while some NGOs have failed to socialize their members into acting inside rather than outside the emerging European-level organizational structures (Warleigh, 2001).

One result of the exclusion of some interests from the elitist structure of interest-group representation in the EU is the growing use of more direct forms of collective action against the EU institutions, for example in the

Table 7.3 *Members of Social Platform*

Abbrev.	Name	Website
AGE	European Older People's Platform	www.age-platform.org
ATD	Quart Monde – ATD Fourth World International Movement	www.atd-quartmonde.org
–	Autism Europe	www.autismeurope.org
–	Caritas Europa	www.caritas-europa.org
CEBSD	Combined European Bureau for Social Development	www.cebsd.org
CECODHAS	European Liaison Committee for Social Housing	www.cecodhas.org
CECOP	European Confederation of Workers' Cooperatives, Social Cooperatives and Participative Enterprises	www.cecop.coop
CEDAG	European Council for Non-Profit Organizations	www.cedag-eu.org
CEV	European Volunteer Centre	www.cev.be
COFACE	Confederation of Family Organizations in the EU	www.coface-eu.org
EAEA	European Association for the Education of Adults	www.eaea.org
EAPN	European Anti-Poverty Network	www.eapn.eu
EASPD	European Association of Service Providers for Persons with Disabilities	www.easpd.eu
EBU	European Blind Union	www.euroblind.org
ECDN	European Consumer Debt Network	www.ecdn.eu
EDF	European Disability Forum	www.edf-feph.org
ENAR	European Network Against Racism	www.enar-eu.org

EPHA	European Public Health Alliance	www.epha.org
EPR	European Platform for Rehabilitation	www.epr.eu
ESAN	European Social Action Network	www.esan.eu
EURAG	European Federation of Older Persons	www.eurageurope.org
EUROCHILD		www.eurochild.org
EURODIACONIA	European Federation for Diaconia	www.eurodiaconia.org
EWL	European Women's Lobby	www.womenlobby.org
FAI	International Federation of the Christian Associations of Italian Workers	www.aclifai.org
FEANTSA	European Federation of National Organizations working with the Homeless	www.feantsa.org
FEFAF	European Federation of Unpaid Parents and Carers at Home	www.fefaf.be
ICSW	International Council on Social Welfare	www.icsw.org
IFSW	International Federation of Social Workers	www.ifsw.org
ILGA	Europe – European Region of the International Lesbian and Gay Association	www.ilga-europe.org
INCLUSION EUROPE	European Association of Societies of Persons with Intellectual Disability and their Families	www.inclusion-europe.org
MHE	Mental Health Europe	www.mhe-sme.org
SOLIDAR		www.solidar.org
WAGGGS	World Association of Girl Guides and Girl Scouts Europe Region	http://europe.waggsworld.org
—	Workability Europe	www.workability-europe.org
YFJ	European Youth Forum	www.youthforum.org

Source: Compiled from information on www.socialplatform.org.

form of demonstrations in Brussels and other types of protest against the EU institutions (Imig and Tarrow, 2001; Tarrow, 1995). For instance farmers from several member states have often taken to the streets of Brussels to protest against the reform of the CAP or other farming issues, often against the explicit instructions of COPA, their European association (Bush and Simi, 2001). Numerous other groups have protested in the streets of Brussels or outside the European Parliament in Strasbourg, ranging from bikers protesting against limits on the size of motorbike engines to animal rights campaigners protesting against the transportation of live animals. However, the Europeanization of social protest through non-formal channels of representation is dependent on the pan-European politicization of an issue as well as the resources of the groups concerned. As a consequence, compared with the growing participation by insider groups such as the ETUC, the ability of outsider groups to mobilize in Brussels varies enormously (Marks and McAdam, 1996).

Territorial interests: at the heart of multilevel governance

Another set of non-business interests that has established an important role in the EU policy process is sub-national regions. Almost 200 sub-state authorities have offices in Brussels (Greenwood, 2007a). These include the offices of the state governments of the German, Belgian, and Austrian federal systems, regional councils and other official organs of the decentralized states of Italy, France, and Spain, local government bodies of the unitary states of the other EU member states, and various intermediary associations of local authorities, communities, municipalities, towns, cities, regions, and sub-national units from inside and outside the EU.

Some of these sub-national groups have been represented in Brussels since the start of the 1970s, but the majority only began to mobilize in the late 1980s following the reform of EU regional policies (see Chapter 9). The 1988 reform of the structural funds led to efforts to outflank national governments by the Commission and the regions (Pollack, 1995). On the one hand, the Commission consciously sought the involvement of regional interests in the initiation, adoption, and implementation of regional policy. On the other hand, regional interests made the most of the opportunity to bypass national governments, many of which were of opposing political hues or were cutting back on national regional spending. 'Partnership' between the Commission and regional government became the guiding principle in this policy area. Regional bodies were invited to submit funding applications directly to the Commission, and funds were forwarded directly to regional authorities rather than passing through central government treasuries. In addition, regional bodies were responsible for implementing their own framework programmes, monitored by Commission officials.

The formal involvement of regions in EU policy-making was further institutionalized by the creation of the Committee of the Regions (CoR) by the Maastricht Treaty. The CoR replaced the Consultative Council of Regional and Local Authorities (CCRLA) which had been set up by the Commission in 1988 as part of the new regional policy regime. The members of the CCRLA had been appointed by two European-wide sub-national associations: the Assembly of European Regions and the Council for European Municipalities and Regions. In the new CoR, these transnational associations were replaced by representatives of regional and local governments in each member state. Some of these were nominated by the central government, as in the UK, but most were independently nominated by sub-national bodies, such as the French regional assemblies and the German states. The Maastricht Treaty specified that the CoR had the right to be consulted not only in the adoption and implementation of EU regional policies but also in all policy areas that had implications for European economic and social cohesion. This included all policies that affect the level of economic and social disparities in Europe, such as the CAP and the Common Transport Policy.

The existence of EU competences in the area of regional policy, and the deliberate funding and promotion of regional representation by the Commission, are not the only explanations of the different levels of regional mobilization. Another important factor is whether the member state of which a region is part has a tradition of private/pluralist or state-funded/corporatist interest representation (Jeffery, 2000; Marks *et al.*, 1996). In other words, regions tend to establish offices in Brussels not because of the competences of the EU, but because of their own competences and incentives vis-à-vis national governments. So, those sub-national governments with the broadest range of policy competences, such as the German and Belgian states, all have offices in Brussels. Furthermore, backed by constitutional statutes the German and Belgian states have forced their national governments formally to include them in the German and Belgian delegations in the Council when the agenda touches on sub-national competences. Nevertheless, there are more regional interest groups in Brussels from the UK and France, which are two of the most centralized states in Europe, than from Germany, Spain, or Italy.

The consequence, some scholars claim, is an emerging system of 'multilevel governance', whereby policies are made through interaction between regional, national, and European-level authorities. Because of the role of regional authorities in the operation of the structural funds, the multilevel governance approach was developed first in research on EU regional policy (especially Hooghe, 2002; Marks, 1993). As regional interests have been incorporated into other EU policies, and as EU policy deliberation and implementation has involved a growing number of participants at the regional and local levels, the multilevel governance conception has gradual evolved into a general model of EU decision-making (Hooghe and Marks, 1996).

Nevertheless, it is difficult to extrapolate a general theory of the EU from the structure of interest-group representation in the particular area of regional policy-making. And because the CoR has remained marginalized in the EU policy process, regions are considerably less influential in most other policy areas than are the various business, labour, or social interests. In response, proponents of multilevel governance have argued that this conceptual framework refers to the emergence of multiple levels of bargaining outside the dominance of the national governments, and not only to the notion that the EU is a three-level system (Bache and Flinders, 2004; Hooghe and Marks, 2001, 2003; Marks *et al.*, 1996).

In sum, since the start of the single market project in the mid 1980s, Brussels has become more like Washington, DC than any other national capital of Europe, in terms of the volume and intensity of interest-group lobbying of the political process. The bulk of this activity is by individual firms and national and European associations that represent business interests. However, responding to the new EU policy competences and fostered by the EU institutions, public interests, social movements and sub-national governmental bodies have begun to fight back. The result is a sophisticated and complex system which combines elements of pluralism, corporatism and neo-pluralism.

Explaining the Pattern of Interest Representation

This system of European-level interest representation has evolved through an interaction between the growing demand for access by non-state actors in the EU policy process and the supply of access by officials in the EU institutions: particularly *fonctionnaires* and political advisers in the Commission, and MEPs, their assistants and bureaucrats in the administration of the European Parliament. The goals of these actors have remained stable: for interest groups, policy outcomes close to their interests; and for EU governmental actors, more power and influence in the EU decision-making process. However, the strategies of the actors have evolved in response to the changing structure of opportunities in the EU and how these structures vary across policy sectors (cf. Eising, 2008; Princen and Kerremans, 2008).

Demand for access: the effects of globalization and European integration

On the demand side, public and private interests in Europe have faced a transformation of economic and political institutions since the 1960s. First, globalization of the economy – through the expansion of cross-border trade and capital movements – has challenged the traditional patterns of capital–labour relations in Europe. The removal of tariff barriers, and the resultant globalization of product markets, has forced individual firms that compete in international markets to pursue new competitive strategies. Freed from restraints on capital mobility, these strategies have included cross-border relocation, merger, joint ventures, specialization, and diversification. As a result, companies have had to become multinational to survive.

This has produced new relationships between economic and governmental actors. On the one hand, globalization and market integration in Europe create new competitive pressures on domestic economic interests, which turns some national interests, particularly producers for domestic markets, to turn to their national governments to protect them (Grossman, 2004). On the other hand, multinational firms are less interested in securing national protection of their products and markets than in securing transnational policies that will enable them to increase their market opportunities and the productivity of their assets. Instead of lobbying for national protection, companies are increasingly lobbying politicians and regulators to secure neo-liberal and deregulatory policies. From an individual firm's point of view, the rewards from national corporatist bargaining with governmental and labour actors, and even from membership of national business associations, have receded as the benefits of private action have increased. As discussed above, in the last two decades individual companies in Europe have become less interested in national policy processes and national business associations, and are more interested in approaching market regulators privately and directly, whether at the regional, national, European, or international levels and even in other national systems. Hence, globalization has undermined the ability of national state officials to incorporate business actors into corporatist models of interest intermediation in the national system (Crouch and Menon, 1997; Streeck and Schmitter, 1991).

Second, the opportunity structure for social and economic interests in Europe has been transformed by the accumulation and concentration of market regulation functions at the European level, most notably in the Commission. Firms are not interested in the large public spending priorities, such as health, education and welfare, which are still controlled by national governments. What they are interested in, and why they began to take an interest in politics at the domestic level in the first few decades of the post-war period, are rules governing the production, distribution, and exchange of goods and services in the marketplace (Coen, 1998). Multinational corporations were quick to realize that the centralization of market regulation in the EU institutions would significantly reduce the transaction costs of doing business in Europe. Consequently, individual companies were some of the most vocal proponents of the single market, and since the establishment of the single market, Brussels' position at the centre of multinational lobbying strategies have been confirmed.

Having said that, the incentives for business interests to lobby the EU vary by industrial sector (Weber and Hallerberg, 2001). Firms' preferences for European-level market regulation depend on the size of the threat of competition from firms outside the EU, and on the transaction costs of moving assets and changing production levels in their particular industry. Industries with strong competition and high transaction costs, such as the car and aerospace industries, were the first to mobilize to try to persuade EU policy-makers to introduce European-wide market integration and regulation in their sectors, to promote industrial consolidation in the European single market. Also, how far a firm's sector is exposed to EU regulatory policies increases the likelihood that a firm will set up an office in Brussels and lobby the Commission and the European Parliament (Bernhagen and Mitchell, 2009). For example, during the passage of the REACH directive, which set up a new framework for regulating chemicals production, usage and disposal, there were ferocious lobbying campaigns in Brussels by competing chemicals firms within different parts of this industrial sector, as well as rival campaigns by environmental and consumer groups (Lindgren and Persson, 2008). Furthermore, Eising (2007a, 2007b) finds that well-resourced business interests tend to have better access to EU policy-makers than poor-resourced groups, given the same level of incentive to mobilize – such as the pending adoption of a piece of EU legislation which will affect a particular industrial sector.

In terms of countervailing interests to those of private firms, with a single political centre regulating the European market, the cost of mobilizing oppositions to business interests has also reduced. Instead of trying to prevent industry-wide cost-cutting in several EU states, public interests with a coordinated transnational plan of action can go straight to Brussels to campaign for their causes. For example, in response to the deregulatory policies of the British Conservative governments in the 1980s the British trade union movement became one of the strongest financial sponsors and political backers of the activities of the ETUC. Similarly, it is much cheaper for environmental and consumer groups to defend their interests in Brussels than in each national capital separately.

Hence, similar factors influence the demand for access to EU policy-makers by private and public interests. Driven by economic globalization, private companies have abandoned national interest intermediation in favour of direct action at the European level to promote market liberalization. Driven by political Europeanization, and the expansion of EU policies to a broad range of social and economic issues, diffuse interests have turned to Brussels as the new political centre in which to pursue European-wide interests as an adjunct to and sometimes substitute for national structures of interest intermediation (Geddes, 2000; Imig and

Tarrow, 2001; Warleigh, 2000). Nevertheless, Poloni-Staudinger (2008) finds that domestic opportunity structures also shape the incentives for diffuse interests to mobilize at the European level, with groups which are marginalized by national governments more eager to pursue their interests in Brussels than groups which have high levels of domestic public, party, and government support.

Furthermore, the agenda-setting powers of the Commission and the European Parliament vary across policy areas and legislative procedures, which in turn influences the lobbying incentives for both private and public interest groups. For example, Broscheid and Coen (2007) find higher levels of lobbying activity of the EU institutions on regulatory policies, where the Commission has a powerful agenda-setting role, than on EU spending policies, where the Commission's agenda-setting powers are weaker as a result of intergovernmental decision-making rules on these policies.

In general, though, once there are incentives to mobilize at the European level, the rules of the game of EU policy-making provide plenty of opportunities for private or public interests to influence EU policies. The EU legislative procedures (as we saw in Chapter 3) grant agenda-setting and veto powers to multiple actors. As a result, interest groups are likely to find someone somewhere in the EU system who will listen to their arguments or will want to receive information that they can use to shape policy outcomes (Crombez, 2002). Contrast this with policy-making at the domestic level in Europe, where majority support for governing parties in parliaments usually means that there are few opportunities to change legislation or budgets dramatically once they have been proposed. Hence, at the domestic level, interest groups are forced to focus their efforts on the pre-legislative stage of policy-making. At the EU level, interest groups are able to influence the direction of policy at any point in the legislative process, from pre-legislative preparation through amendment during legislative adoption, to post-adoption implementation and judicial adjudication.

Supply of access: expertise and information means legislative power

Without adequate response by EU decision-makers, the new interest-group strategies would have been ineffectual. The fact that all forms of EU lobbying have increased suggests that the demand for access has been met with a concomitant supply of access by actors in the EU institutions (Beyers, 2004, 2008; Bouwen, 2002, 2004b; Cram, 1998; Michalowitz, 2007; Pollack, 1997).

The key institution in the supply of access to non-state interests is the Commission, which has an incentive to grant private interest groups access in exchange for specialized information and expertise (Broscheid and Coen, 2003). Given the size and complexity of the task of regulating a single market of over 500 million people and 27 national regulatory systems, the Commission is an extremely small bureaucracy. 'Not surprisingly, officials often lack the necessary detailed expertise and knowledge of sectoral practices and problems' (Mazey and Richardson, 1997, p. 198).

As early as 1992 the Commission developed what it called an 'open and structured dialogue with special interest groups' (European Commission, 1992; McLaughlin and Greenwood, 1995). As the Commission put it in the paper which set up this dialogue:

> The Commission has always been an institution open to outside input. The Commission believes this process to be fundamental to the development of its policies. This dialogue has proved valuable to both the Commission and to interested outside parties. Commission officials acknowledge the need for such outside input and welcome it.
>
> (European Commission, 1992)

The relationship between the Commission and interest groups has developed considerably since the 1990s. The Amsterdam Treaty required the Commission to 'consult widely before proposing legislation, and, wherever appropriate, publish consultation documents'. Adapting a practice from British government the Commission publishes Green and White Papers, to facilitate the process of communication and consultation. Green Papers set out the basic ideas behind a potential piece of legislation, while White Papers contain a formal set of proposals which, if approved inside the Commission, will result in a draft directive or regulation or a group of legislative proposals. In the explanatory memoranda to the White Papers the Commission likes to explain how it took into account the views of various interest groups in the consultation process.

In addition, before formally proposing legislation the Commission must undertake individual impact assessments (IAs). Each IA sets out the process and timetable for consultation on a particular piece of legislation, and the particular target groups which the Commission intends to consult. In other words, rather than employing private consultancies to undertake these impact assessments, which can be extremely costly, the Commission prefers to allow the organized and mobilized groups in Brussels to assess the impact of a proposed law on their members' interests or the issues they care about. The assumption of this approach, which fits a classical pluralist idea, is that there are so many groups organized in Brussels who have access to the EU policy process that if a proposed law is likely to have an unintended negative effect on any economic or social interest a group somewhere in Brussels will bring this to the attention of the Commission in the pre-legislative consultation process.

The European Parliament has pursued a similar strategy to the Commission. Although it is not responsible for policy initiation, its legislative powers have increased, making it an increasingly popular target for interest groups (e.g. Earnshaw and Judge, 2002). From the European Parliament's point of view, more power means a greater need for detailed policy expertise to enable it to compete effectively with the Council and the Commission in the legislative process. Whereas the Council has national public administrations to supply information, individual MEPs have limited staff resources or research budgets (unlike Congressmen in the US legislative system). Consequently, when preparing legislative reports, *rapporteurs* seek out key interest groups to canvass their views. From the other side, interest groups have very good information about which MEPs are most influential when scrutinizing legislation, and some interest groups even supply carefully worded amendments to *rapporteurs* and other influential committee members, which often end up in the final laws adopted by the European Parliament and the Council (Marshall, 2010).

Figure 7.3 shows the results of a survey of MEPs in 2006 about their links with interest groups (cf. Kohler-Koch, 1997; Wessels, 1999). Over 95 per cent of MEPs who responded to the survey stated that they had contacts with interest groups at least once a month. Contrary to Austen-Smith's theory of 'counteractive lobbying', as discussed in the introduction, the survey reveals that MEPs are more likely to be in contact with groups with similar policy preferences than with groups with divergent preferences. MEPs on the centre-right, in the EPP group, are more likely to be in contact with groups representing industry, trade/commerce and banking/insurance. Meanwhile, MEPs on the left, in the socialists, greens and radical left, are more likely to be in contact with groups representing trade unions, environmental interests, and human rights. And, liberal MEPs, in the centre of the European Parliament, talk to a range of different groups. The fact that MEPs in general talk to sympathetic groups more than other groups suggests that information from political allies is more useful to MEPs than information from potential enemies. This might be because MEPs need to know the positions of their supporters, so that they do not act against the interests of these groups. It might also be because MEPs are not sure what position to take on a particular policy issue, and are more likely to trust groups with similar political views on issue specific questions.

The primary motivation to supply interest-group access to the policy-making process by the Commission and the European Parliament is for these actors to increase their influence in the EU legislative process (see Beyers, 2008; Bouwen, 2002, 2004a, 2004b; Cram, 1998). Commissioners and MEPs are under-resourced compared to national government officials. Hence, using interest groups to supply information and expertise increases the chance that Commission officials and MEPs will be able to secure the policies they want. Interest groups possess a

Figure 7.3   *MEPs' contacts with interest groups*

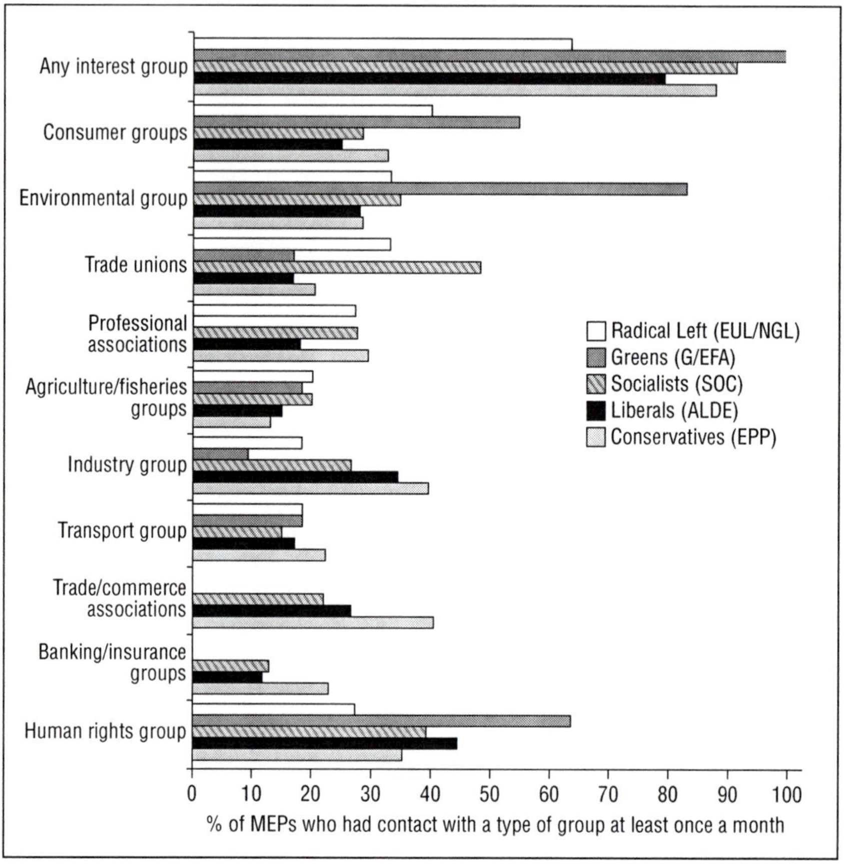

Legend:
- Radical Left (EUL/NGL)
- Greens (G/EFA)
- Socialists (SOC)
- Liberals (ALDE)
- Conservatives (EPP)

X-axis: % of MEPs who had contact with a type of group at least once a month

Categories:
- Any interest group
- Consumer groups
- Environmental group
- Trade unions
- Professional associations
- Agriculture/fisheries groups
- Industry group
- Transport group
- Trade/commerce associations
- Banking/insurance groups
- Human rights group

Notes: Not enough MEPs from the other political groups answered the survey questions to produce reliable results for these groups.

Source: Calculated from European Parliament Research Group data, see Farrell *et al.* (2006). Field research conducted in March to June 2006.

range of resources which they can offer Commission officials and MEPs. In addition to information and expertise, interest groups can influence their national member organizations, and can help in the implementation of policy. These resources can be used by the Commission and the European Parliament to undermine opposition to a proposal from particular governments in the Council. For example, the German government will be reluctant to oppose a legislative initiative if the Commission or the European Parliament can demonstrate that key German interest groups support the initiative and are willing to facilitate the transposition of the policy into national practice.

Whereas the mobilization of mass public opinion and national interests can strengthen the position of national governments in the Council, the mobilization and incorporation of interest groups can strengthen the hand of the supranational institutions. As a result, the institutional structure of the EU system provides an incentive for the Commission and the European Parliament to supply negotiating space and resources to groups that represent transnational socio-economic constituencies, including the labour movement, environmentalists, consumers, and social NGOs as well as individual companies and business organizations.

Conclusion: Competing Interests on a Level Playing Field

The system of interest representation at the European level is highly dense. Business interests, who have more incentives and substantially more financial and political resources than public interests, are particularly good at playing the Brussels game. At face value this makes interest-group politics in the EU look like primitive US pluralism, in which there is little countervailing power to block manipulation of the political process by the owners of capital. Without cohesive European political parties to promote wider public interests, diffuse interests might struggle to compete with the more highly organized and resourced business lobby. This vision of a Europe dominated by an alliance of big business against the people of Europe was a common criticism by left-wing parties and Marxist scholars in the 1970s and early 1980s (for example Holland, 1980).

However, business interests do not have it all their own way. On the one hand, the centralization of market regulation in Brussels provides a focus for public interests, such as trade unions and environmental groups, to organize at the European level. On the other hand, institutional competition between the EU institutions provides an incentive for the Commission and the European Parliament to grant access to and even fund underrepresented groups. The promotion of transnational alliances spanning both sides of a policy debate strengthens the information capacity and the credibility of these supranational actors against the Council. Also, by fostering the emergence of socio-economic allegiances that cut across national divisions, these strategies increase the public support bases for the Commission and the European Parliament.

Finally, at the national level interest representation exists side by side with mass democratic politics. As the previous chapter has shown, the EU is not a fully democratic system. Some scholars and activists believe that a vibrant civil society in Brussels may be a way of bringing the EU closer to the citizens (such as Schmitter, 2000). However, others are more sceptical, pointing among other things to the inevitable elitism of the interest-group community in Brussels (see Greenwood, 2007b; Kohler-Koch, 2010; Saurugger, 2008). Also, as discussed in Chapter 5, public support for the EU has declined while the volume and density of interest-group activity in Brussels has increased. Clearly citizens are not convinced that a vibrant civil society in Brussels is sufficient to legitimatize government at the European level. As at the domestic level in Europe – where for decades the decline of parties and the rise of interest groups has been predicted but has never materialized – interest groups are unlikely ever to be more than (vital) lubricants of the EU policy-making machine.

Part III

Policies

Chapter 8

Regulation of the Single Market

Theories of Regulation
Deregulation: Market Integration and Liberalization
Re-regulation: Common Standards
Explaining EU Regulatory Policies
Conclusion: Mostly Winners, But Some Losers

Studies of public policy differentiate between three types of economic policy: regulatory, expenditure, and macroeconomic policies (Lowi, 1964; Musgrave, 1959). The EU supplies all three of these policy types. This chapter consider EU regulation. Chapter 9 looks at EU expenditure. Chapter 10 investigates macroeconomic issues related to EMU. With the increased delegation of economic, social, and environmental regulatory policy competences to the European level, the EU has been described as 'a regulatory state' (Egan, 2001; Majone, 1996). This chapter contrasts deregulatory with re-regulatory aspects of this regulatory state, and explains regulatory policy-making in the EU. We start by investigating general explanations of regulation and regulatory policy-making.

Theories of Regulation

Economic policies have two possible effects: redistribution and efficiency. The difference between these two effects is illustrated in Figure 8.1. This hypothetical society consists of two citizens, A and B, with a government policy X. Policy X produces benefits of AX and BX for the two citizens. The government considers two possible policy changes, Y and Z. Policy Y has a 'redistribute' effect as it makes citizen A better off (by AY–AX) and citizen B worse off (by BY–BX). In fact, any policy change along the line that goes through X and Y implies redistribution from one citizen to the other. In contrast, a move to policy Z would benefit both citizens (by AZ–AX and BZ–BX, respectively). In fact, any policy change from X to somewhere in the shaded area would make one citizen better off without making the other worse off. This is known as a 'pareto-efficient' outcome.

Producing outcomes that are in the interests of everyone – the 'public interest' – is the traditional aim of regulatory policies (Mitnick, 1980). In

Figure 8.1   *Difference between redistributive and efficient policies*

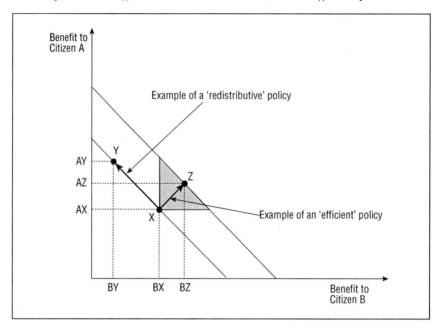

neoclassical economic theory, free markets are naturally pareto-efficient, but in the real world there are numerous 'market failures'. Regulation can be used to correct these failures:

- *technical standards* and *consumer protection standards* enable consumers to acquire information about the quality of products that would otherwise not be publicly available;
- *health and safety standards* and *environmental standards* reduce the adverse effects of market transactions on individuals who do not participate in the transactions;
- *competition policies* prevent the emergence of monopolistic markets, market distortions (through state subsidies), and anticompetitive practices (such as price collusion); and
- *industry regulation,* through such instruments as price controls, ensure that natural monopolies operate according to market practices.

However, economic policies made by traditional democratic (majoritarian) institutions such as parliaments and governments tend to be redistributive rather than efficient. Parliaments and governments are controlled by political parties, which will try to achieve policy outputs that benefit their supporters. Majoritarian democratic government consequently tends to lead to policies that redistribute resources from the losing minority to the winning majority in a particular electoral contest (Lijphart, 1994). For example, in the case of expenditure policies, governments on the left usually raise taxes imposed on the wealthiest members of society and increase public spending on social benefits, whereas governments on the right tend to reduce taxes and cut benefits. If democratic majorities are allowed to govern regulatory policies, similar redistributive outcomes will result. The left may use regulation to improve the rights of workers and protect the environment thereby imposing costs on business, while the right may do the opposite.

This traditional 'public interest' justification of regulation is essential normative (Joskow and Noll, 1981). Policy outputs can also be analysed using positive theories, which seek to explain policy outcomes through deductive reasoning. The first positive approach to the study of regulation was Stigler's (1971) 'economic theory of regulation', in which regulation is demanded by private interests and supplied by politicians. On the demand side, applying Olson's (1965) theory of interest-group organization, certain interests groups are more able to mobilize to influence regulators. Compare the cost to a monopolistic firm of a price control with the benefit to an individual consumer or taxpayer. As there is more at stake for the monopolistic firm, the firm will be willing to supply more lobbying efforts and thus exercise more influence than the diffuse public interests of consumers, taxpayers, environmentalists, and employees. On the supply side, meanwhile, using Down's (1957) theory of electoral politics, Stigler assumes that politicians primarily seek re-election. Politicians recognize that regulators impose costs on some voters and provide benefits to others, and that groups that are the subject of regulation tend to have more available resources to finance politicians' campaigns. The average voter tends to be 'rationally ignorant' about the details of specific regulatory policy proposals, and as a result politicians have an incentive to supply regulatory policies to those voters who have most at stake, namely producers. Stigler (1971, p. 94) consequently concludes that 'as a rule, regulation is acquired by the industry and is design and operated primarily for its benefits'.

The positive and normative theories of regulation have opposite prescriptions of how regulations should be made. From the normative perspective, if regulatory policies are meant only to correct market failures, and achieve pareto-efficient outcomes, these policies should be made by 'non-majoritarian', independent, institutions (Majone, 1996). In contrast, the positive theory suggests that it is unlikely that independent regulators will produce pareto-efficient policies as they are more likely to be 'captured' than democratic/majoritarian institutions, such as parliaments and governments. In practice, no single producer, industry, or profession is ever able to capture a regulatory agency completely, and regulations invariably provide at least some benefits to consumers and other diffuse interests (Jordan, 1972; Peltzman, 1989; Stigler and Friedland, 1962). Also, as the losses to consumers increase, their incentive to mobilize to prevent regulatory capture grows (Becker, 1983; Peltzman, 1976).

Furthermore, these theories generally ignore the role played by institutions in shaping how regulators behave. Regulations are made in a complex institutional environment, involving legislators, courts, executives, and competing regulatory agencies on multiple levels of government. In multilevel political systems such as the EU, for example, regulation can be produced at both the national and European levels (Kelemen, 2000). Given a choice, producers would prefer market regulations to be produced at the highest level of government. This is because it is more expensive to organize at a higher level, which makes it harder for diffuse interests to mobilize against producers (Cawson and Saunders, 1983; Dunleavy, 1997). Also, at the higher level there may be competition between different local regulatory regimes which would force governments to introduce deregulatory policies to attract capital (Scharpf, 1997).

Institutional rules can also limit the discretion of regulatory agencies. For example, legislators can use a variety of institutional mechanisms to ensure that a regulator does not supply policies that are solely for the benefit of the subject producer. A parliament can specify the public interest criteria in a regulator's contract, choose a new head of the agency every few years, and require the regulator to consult diffuse interests and report to a parliamentary committee and the media (Fiorina, 1982; Horn, 1995; Moe, 1987; Weingast and Moran, 1983). Nevertheless, if a regulatory agency is tightly controlled by a legislative majority, we are back to where we started: with a parliamentary majority using regulation as a means to redistribute benefits to a particular electoral majority rather than to society as a whole.

Deregulation: Market Integration and Liberalization

The deregulation of Europe can be divided into four elements: the single market programme, a common competition policy, services integration, and the open method of coordination.

The single market programme

At the Milan European Council in June 1985 the member state governments adopted the Single European Act (SEA) and the Commission's white paper *Completing the Internal Market*. The SEA set the deadline of 31 December 1992 for the implementation of the Commission's proposals, and introduced new institutional mechanisms to achieve this goal: QMV in the Council and the cooperation procedure with the European Parliament (see Chapter 3). The Commission's white paper set out approximately 300 pieces of legislation that would be necessary to complete the single market. This legislation covered three main areas: physical barriers, technical barriers, and fiscal barriers (Pelkmans and Winters, 1988).

First, with regard to physical barriers, the Commission proposed lifting controls on the movement of goods and persons. By the end of 1991 the Council had agreed to abolish customs formalities, paperwork, and inspections at borders between member states. The Commission issued the Common Customs Code, and customs barriers were finally abolished on 31 December 1992. By the end of 1992, 81 measures had been adopted on issues relating to the movement of agricultural produce and the compensation of farmers at borders under the CAP. Less progress was made on barriers to the movement of persons. The UK, Ireland, and Denmark refused to agree to the abolition of passport controls and the introduction of common visa requirements, while the other member states signed the Schengen Accord, to remove their border controls (see Chapter 11).

Second, the Commission used the heading 'technical barriers' as a catch-all category. The *Cassis de Dijon* ruling in 1979 had already prepared the ground for common product standards: any product that met the standards of one member state could be legally sold in another (see Chapter 4). Building on this principle of 'mutual recognition', the Commission proposed a 'new approach to technical harmonization' (Pelkmans, 1990). This involved establishing mutual recognition as a basic principle in the single market: restricting harmonization to minimum technical and health and safety standards; contracting with pan-European standards organizations – such as the CEN (European Standardization Committee) and CENELEC (European Electrotechnical Standardization Committee) – to develop voluntary European standards; and introducing the 'CE mark' for products that met the required standards.

On public procurement, governments were prevented from favouring domestic companies in government contracts. On the free movement of persons, residency rights were extended to non-workers (such as students and retirees), non-nationals gained access to state subsidies and social benefits, and rules were established for comparing educational and professional qualifications. On services, a host of directives were passed on the liberalization of financial services, air, water and road transport, and the opening up of national telecommunications and television markets. On the movement of capital, controls on the free flow of capital between the member states were abolished. Finally on company law, various rules governing cross-border company activities were harmonized, and common rules on the protection of intellectual property were agreed.

Third, to remove fiscal barriers the Commission proposed the harmonization of value added tax (VAT) and excise duties on goods such as alcohol and tobacco. After protracted negotiations, the Council adopted a framework for harmonizing VAT in October 1992. This included a standard minimum VAT of 15 per cent in each member state, the abolition of luxury rates (and lower rates on special items for a transition period), and rules on where VAT should be paid. In the case of cross-border trade, VAT would be paid in the country of destination. The Council also agreed a harmonized structure for excise duties, with the elimination of restrictions on cross-border purchases of goods such as alcoholic drinks and tobacco (for personal use), and the eventual abolition of duty-free sales on planes and boats (in 1999).

The single market programme did not stop at the end of 1992. The implementation and transposition of the legislative programme was still under way, and many pieces of single market legislation needed reforming and updating. In March 1992 the Commission set up the High Level Group on the Operation of the Internal Market, chaired by Peter Sutherland, a former Commissioner. The group's report, the so-called Sutherland Report, proposed greater consultation with the actors affected by single market regulation, greater access to the EU decision-making process, and better cooperation between the Commission and national administrations to ensure that uneven implementation of legislation would not create barriers to trade. Acting on these recommendations the Commission drafted an action plan for the single market, which was adopted at the Amsterdam European Council in June 1997. The action plan promised progress on two levels: a rolling programme of simplification of single market legislation (the SLIM programme), and a coordinated effort by the Commission and the member states to ensure the implementation of existing legislation.

Also, to shame the member states into action, in November 1997 the Commission launched a 'single market scoreboard'. This was a record of the member states' efforts to implement single market legislation and the frequency of single market infringements by each member state. Table 8.1 compares the 2003 and 2009 scoreboards. The table reveals three things. First, the average amount of single market legislation not transposed into national law fell from 2.4 to 1.0 per cent between 2003 and 2009. These figures compare to an average of 6.3 per cent in 1997. Second, while the number of infringements proceedings launched by the Commission increased from 242 to 1,597 between 1997 and 2003, it fell to 1,271 in 2009, despite the accession of 12 new member states. Third, there is considerable variation in implementation rates across member states. The Northern and Eastern European member states generally have a better transposition record than the member states in Southern Europe. The good track record of the new member states is a function of their effort to implement EU legislation prior to joining the EU. Five member states – Spain, Belgium, France, Greece, and Italy – accounted for 30 per cent of all open infringement proceedings in 2009.

Table 8.1   *The Single Market Scoreboard, 2003 and 2009*

	Percentage of single market legislation not transposed into national law		Total open proceedings	
	2003	2009	2003	2009
Italy	3.9	1.7	200	110
Spain	1.2	0.8	153	96
Belgium	1.8	1.2	138	88
Greece	3.3	2.1	144	88
France	3.3	0.8	220	85
Germany	3.0	0.8	136	73
Ireland	3.5	0.8	132	63
Portugal	3.7	2.0	57	63
Poland		2.1		60
United Kingdom	1.5	1.1	121	58
Netherlands	2.0	0.6	68	57
Austria	3.4	0.9	79	48
Sweden	1.0	0.6	32	41
Slovakia		0.4		35
Luxembourg	3.2	1.7	34	33
Finland	1.0	0.4	47	30
Czech Republic		1.9		30
Malta		0.2		28
Hungary		0.6		28
Estonia		1.4		28
Denmark	0.6	0.2	36	26
Bulgaria		0.3		21
Latvia		0.7		20
Slovenia		0.4		19
Lithuania		0.4		17
Cyprus		1.0		15
Romania		0.3		11
EU average/total	2.4	1.0	1,597	1,271

Source: Compiled from Eurostat data.

Competition policies

For the single market to function properly, competition is essential. The EU has empowered the Commission with a series of policy tools to prevent anti-competitive practices from distorting free trade and competition in the single market, including the ability to impose fines. There are three main strands to EU competition policy:

1 *Antitrust regulation:* Articles 101 to 106 of the treaty outlaw a variety of agreements between companies that would restrict competition (such as cartels, price fixing, or predatory pricing agreements, exclusive sales agreements and discrimination on the grounds of nationality by a firm in a 'dominant position' in a national market) and ensure that publicly owned industries abide by the EU competition rules.

2 *Regulation of state aids:* Articles 107 to 117 of the treaty outlaw subsidies to industry that threaten competition and trade between member states, unless the subsidies promote the interests of the EU as a whole, or specific sectoral or regional objectives.

3 *Merger control:* in 1989 the Council adopted the first Merger Regulation, delegating substantive powers to the Commission. The reform of this regulation in 2004 created a bigger role for national regulators.

EU competition policy is based on the US model of antitrust regulation. Eager to prevent European cartels, US competition lawyers helped to draft the competition articles in the Treaty of Rome. However, unlike US competition policy, which is concerned with anti-competitive practices in the private sector, EU competition policy also deals with anti-competitive practices by government-owned and government-subsidized businesses.

The directorate-general for Competition has not always pursued a policy of 'perfect competition', particularly in the regulation of public sector industries. The Competition DG is constrained by the Commission's lack of political power against certain member states, especially in the face of potentially high economic and sectoral costs of competition policy decisions. Furthermore, until the mid-1980s most Commissioners responsible for competition policy were ideologically in favour of promoting 'Euro-champions'.

However, the Commission's status in competition policy was as a result of the political commitment behind the liberalization aspects of the single market programme. Also, a series of Commissioners responsible for competition policy – Peter Sutherland (1985–9), Leon Brittan (1989–93), Karel van Miert (1993–9) and Mario Monti (2000–4) sought to apply antitrust principles more strictly and were not afraid to confront member states and multinationals. The appointment of Neelie Kroes (2004–9), a Dutch conservative-liberal, was criticized for risking breaking this trend as she had close ties with big business. But, during her term in office she confronted several large firms, including Sony, Apple, and Microsoft. The Commissioner for competition in the second Barosso Commission (2009–14), Joaquín Almunia, who is a Spanish social democrat, is expected to continue the firm stand against anti-competitive practices. As a result, the competition policy portfolio has become one of the most powerful and prized positions in the Commission.

Responding to the rise in cross-border mergers in anticipation of the single market and to heavy lobbying by multinational firms, the member states adopted the merger regulation in 1989, after 15 years of negotiations. This created a 'one-stop-shop' for cross-border mergers in the EU. The Commission was given the power to assess and veto mergers between companies that would have a combined worldwide turnover of €5 billion and an EU-wide turnover of €250 million. The regulation also set up a procedure and timetable for reviewing mergers. In the first stage of the procedure the Commission was granted one month to decide either that the merger was within the scope of the regulation, to approve the merger or to initiate proceedings. The Commission then undertook a detailed appraisal and had to decide (within four months) whether to approve a merger, conditionally approve a merger, or prohibit a merger. If the Commission blocked a merger, the companies concerned had two months to appeal against the decision in the ECJ.

Although the merger procedure worked well, with the Merger Task Force in DG Competition evaluating 2,430 cases and only blocking 18 (one by Brittan, 10 by van Miert, and 7 by Monti), it became clear that reform was needed. First, due to the growing number of cross-border mergers in Europe, the workload of the Merger Task Force grew dramatically, from 60 cases per year in the early 1990s to over 300 per year between 1999 and 2004.

Second, companies on the receiving end of negative decisions became increasingly vocal in their criticism of the Commission. The procedures were seen as less transparent than the equivalent procedures of the US Federal Trade Commission. The Commission was also accused of not giving sufficient economic justification for its decisions. Moreover, the mechanism for appealing to the ECJ after a merger had been blocked was anachronistic, since an appeal to the court could take several years, by which time the conditions for the original merger would have passed, and one or more of the companies might have even ceased to exist. This mechanism also compared unfavourably with the US merger control system, whereby the US Federal Trade Commission had to seek *a priori* court approval for a decision to block a merger.

Third, smaller member states argued that market concentration should be treated differently in their case as their companies were really competing in European-wide markets.

Fourth, unlike the division of powers between the US Justice Department and the Federal Trade Commission, or between the German Industry Ministry and Federal Cartel Office (*Bundeskartellamt*), there was no clear separation of powers in the application of EU merger controls, with the Merger Task Force acting as 'policeman, judge and jury' (McGowan and Cini, 1999, p. 193).

Finally, the political stakes rose as the extra-territorial impact of the Commission's merger decisions grew (Damro, 2001). Two of the 18 vetoes by the Commission involved mergers between two US companies whose economic activities were mainly conducted in the US market: the merger between Boeing and McDonnell-Douglas, which the Commission blocked in 1997; and the merger between General Electric and Honeywell, which was blocked in 2001. Both these mergers had been approved by the US Federal Trade Commission, and in both cases the US federal government intervened at the highest political level to try to persuade the Commission to give in. However, the Commission stood firm, much to the fury of the US government and the powerful US industrial interests involved.

As a result of these pressures there were three major developments in EU competition policy between 2002 and 2004: (a) the reform of the EU's cartel policy in 2002; (b) the reform of the merger regulation in 2004; and (c) the adoption of the takeover directive in 2004.

Starting with the reform of the cartel policy, the key changes were that the centralized (EU-level) *ex-ante* authorization was replaced by decentralized (member-state level) *ex-post* control system. The new regulation relies on firms' self-assessment of inter-firm relations with subsequent administrative control, instead of prior notification and Commission approval. Furthermore, national competition authorities (NCA) and national courts were given the right to grant EU-wide exemptions from general cartel prohibition. National authorities must inform the Commission and other NCAs. In case of parallel proceedings, national authorities may, but are not required to, suspend or close investigations. However, national bodies are required to use EU law when deciding in these cases. Furthermore, the Commission can pre-empt national rulings by opening its own investigations (Budzinski and Christiansen, 2005, pp. 318–19; McGowan, 2005; Wilks, 2005).

Second, the reform of the merger regulation aimed to reinforce the 'one-stop-shop' principle. More flexibility was introduced into the time frames to improve the ability of companies to respond to Commission concerns. A new code of conduct for the Merger Task Force was introduced to increase the transparency of Commission decision-making. A set of new guidelines was introduced specifying the criteria by which the Commission would approve or reject a proposed merger. And, the Commission appointed a chief competition economist and set up an independent panel to scrutinize the Merger Task Force's conclusions. Nevertheless, these changes neither introduced *a priori* judicial review nor provided a clear separation of powers between politicians (the competition Commissioner and the other members of the Commission) and the antitrust regulators (in the Merger Task Force).

Third, the takeover directive, which was finally agreed in 2004 after more than ten years of negotiations, included neutralization measures designed to strengthen minority shareholders rights in the event of hostile takeover bids. The directive also made takeovers more expensive by introducing minimum bid requirements and privileged rights to the existing shareholders. It introduced so-called 'poison pills', which allow existing shareholders to buy additional shares from or sell back to the target company in the event of a hostile takeover. However, the directive also included a 'breakthrough rule' designed to increase the chances of success for hostile takeover bids in the face of multiple voting rights. In effect, the final compromise agreement gave each member state the right to decide whether neutralization or breakthrough rules should apply. This outcome was due to the fact that the battle between the member states and in the European Parliament ended up being about different models of capitalism, namely Anglo-Saxon versus continental, which split governments and MEPs along national lines as well as ideological lines (Cernat, 2004; Clift, 2009; Hix *et al.*, 2007, pp. 200–15; Ringe, 2005).

Services integration

Despite the completion of the single market and the EU's new deregulatory policy framework, large segments of the economies of the member states remained highly regulated, in particular the service sectors. On the deregulation of services, the EU has followed a different strategy for financial services compared to non-financial cross-border provision of services. While financial services have been deregulated through the Lamfalussy process, which involves most stakeholders in the shaping and implementing of directives, non-financial services have been regulated using the standard legislative framework of the EU.

To promote faster integration and liberalization of European financial markets, in July 2000 the EU set up a 'committee of wise men', chaired by Alexandre Lamfalussy, a former President of the European Monetary Institute (the precursor of the European Central Bank). The committee concluded its deliberations in February 2001 and proposed a list of legislative and regulatory measures and a new legislative procedure for adopting these measures and regulating European financial markets. The procedure works as follows:

- A directive or regulation is adopted through the usual ordinary legislative procedure, but only setting out the 'framework principles' in a given area.
- A new regulatory committee, the European Securities Committee (ESC), then fills in the legislative details in cooperation with the Commission, and the European Parliament is 'kept fully informed'.
- After this, a second new committee, the Committee of European Securities Regulators (CESR), is responsible for the technical implementation, monitoring, and application of a measure.

- The Commission then enforces the regulatory rules in the usual way, that is, by issuing warnings and taking member states to the ECJ when required.

The Commission duly established the two committees in June 2001. The ESC met for the first time in September 2001 and has since met almost every month. However, it was not until February 2002 that the European Parliament agreed to the use of the new Lamfalussy process. The European Parliament was initially concerned about the lack of transparency and control of the new process, but accepted an assurance by the Commission that in any referrals back for new legislation for political approval the European Parliament would be treated equally with the Council. Nevertheless, as the politicians in the Council and the European Parliament are only involved in drawing broad policy guidelines, while policy experts representing the views of their respective governments and industries are responsible for establishing the detailed rules, the procedure can be seen as strengthening the hands of the member states at the expense of the European Parliament, and at the same time strengthening the role of the Commission and expert committees (Quaglia, 2007, 2008).

The Lamfalussy procedure has increased the pace of liberalization of financial services (Alford, 2006; de Visscher *et al.*, 2008). As transposition was a potential bottleneck, the Internal Market DG established a Lamfalussy League Table, showing the progress of implementing the directives. By the end of 2008, the Lamfalussy League Table included nine directives: the directive on market abuse (MAD) and three MAD-implementing directives; a directive on prospectuses; a directive on markets in financial instruments (MIFID) and a MIFID-implementing directive; and a transparency directive (TD) and a TD-implementing directive. As of the end of 2008, Poland had not transposed three of these nine, the Netherlands, Hungary, and Czech Republic had not transposed two, France, Italy, and Slovenia had transposed all but one of the directives, while the other 20 member states had transposed all nine directives.

Two key developments for the integration of financial services are Solvency II, for the insurance/securities sector, and the transposition of Basel II, a non-legally binding international agreement, into the capital requirement directive. Aimed at creating a single market for insurance services, the capital requirement directive takes a risk-based approach when assessing the assets and liabilities of insurance providers, the directive is expected to come into effect in 2012. As with Basel II for the banking sector, the directive focuses on quantitative requirements, governance, and risk management of insurers, as well as disclosure and transparency.

In contrast to the new push towards a single market in financial services, which was accommodated with a new procedure, the new effort towards a single market in non-financial services proceeded within the standard legislative framework. Originally included in the single market programme, a genuine free movement of services had proved harder to achieve than the free movement of goods. One reason for this was the fear from some member states and social groups that deregulation and mutual recognition would lead to a 'race to the bottom' or 'social dumping' as service providers from member states with low levels of workers' protection could undercut providers from states with high levels of workers' protection, and hence higher labour costs. The proposal of a services directive highlighted the tension between mutual recognition as a weapon against protectionism and as a legitimizing tool for social dumping. The timing of the directive, in the aftermath of the 2004 Eastern enlargement, exaggerated this tension. The original directive was based on three pillars: freedom of establishment, the 'country of origin' principle, and mutual assistance by the member states. Freedom of establishment meant that anyone that is allowed to provide a service in one member state should be allowed to provide the same service in another member state. The country of origin principle means that the rules of the home country of the service provider would regulate the provision of a service. For example, a Polish plumber can work in France under Polish labour law. And, mutual assistance was meant to harmonize consumer protection regulation across member states. The country of origin principle created particular controversy, with unions in several of the old 15 member states fearing for the jobs of their members.

The Council was deeply divided over the directive, with the French government, in particular, refusing to support the proposal. However, a compromise deal was brokered between the two main groups in the European Parliament. In the compromise, the country-of-origin principle was replaced by the more generic principle of the 'freedom to provide services'. In return for watering down a key deregulatory element of the directive, the groups in the European Parliament added some additional measures which would force the member state governments to demonstrate what measures they had taken to open up their markets to new service providers. This deal was duly backed in the Council, and the watered-down directive came into effect at the end of 2009. It is unclear whether the comprised directive will be able to create a genuine single market in services in the coming years (Nicolaïdis and Schmidt, 2007).

Open method of coordination

Conscious of the fact that the EU's performance was lagging behind that of the US, the so-called 'Lisbon Agenda' adopted at the European Council in March 2000 called for an ambitious reform agenda to make the EU 'the most competitive and dynamic knowledge-based economy of the world'. The governments highlighted three means for achieving this goal:

1   better policies at the European and national levels for the informa-
    tion society, including investments in the 'knowledge-economy' and
    completing and deepening the internal market in the service sector
    (see above);
2   modernizing the European social model, by structural reform of
    domestic labour markets and welfare states in parallel with policies
    to tackle social exclusion and increased investment in education and
    training; and
3   macroeconomic policies to secure sustainable growth while under-
    taking the necessary structural reforms to the domestic economy.

The vagueness of these goals reflected a political compromise. The
governments on the centre-right, plus the British Labour government,
wanted to concentrate on structural, labour market, and welfare state
reforms, while the governments on the left, led by the French and
German administrations, wanted to emphasize investment in human
capital, education, and the new knowledge economy. With such competing views on how structural changes in the EU economy should be
achieved, and because many of the reforms would be highly sensitive, the
governments accepted that it would be difficult to agree a coherent package of legislation to promote structural reform through the normal EU
legislative procedures.

The Commission was also reluctant to initiate controversial new legislation that might provoke a backlash from some of the large member
states. Ironically, by weakening the Commission's power to initiate legislation in the Maastricht and Amsterdam Treaties, and by choosing an
amenable Commission President in Romano Prodi, the governments
were no longer able to use the Commission to force each other to honour
the collective commitments they had made – as they had done with the
Delors Commissions and the single market programme and EMU.
Consequently, the governments and the Commission decided to by-pass
the normal method of EU legislation and try a new mode of policy coordination, called 'open method of coordination' (OMC).

OMC involved the agreement on a set of goals, which the EU governments have promised to achieve independently and without recourse to
the EU's legal instruments. The method also involves 'naming and sham-
ing', whereby the governments monitor each other's progress towards
the agreed goals, and publicly congratulate or admonish each other
accordingly. This has force to the extent that governments do not like to
be embarrassed for failing to honour commitments made to their EU
colleagues. However, faced with opposition from voters and organized
interests against reforms, governments have been reluctant to honour
their promises. As a result, the absence of enforcement mechanisms has
meant that OMC has contributed very little towards realizing the Lisbon
Agenda.

Re-regulation: Common Standards

The EU has also developed a series of policies to supplement the single market programme, most significantly environmental policy and social policy. These policies are re-regulatory rather than deregulatory, in that they involve replacing separate national rules with new common EU rules. Unlike competition policies and rules designed to integrate the single market, EU environmental, and social regulation is not intended primarily to secure pareto-efficient outcomes. These policies involve choosing values that are preferred by some citizens but not others. As Easton (1965, p. 50) explains:

> An allocation may deprive a person of a valued thing already possessed, it may obstruct the attainment of values which would otherwise have been attained, or it may give some persons access to values and deny them to others.

EU environmental and social policies do not redistribute resources directly, but they do lead to a 'reallocation of values' in European society: with some citizens' values being promoted at the expense of those of others.

Environmental policy

Although not covered in the Treaty of Rome, in 1972 the heads of government agreed to launch a series of environmental action programmes. These culminated in the sixth action programme for the environment in 2002, which set out the priorities for the EU up to 2012. The programme highlights four areas: climate change, nature and biodiversity, environment and health, and the management of natural resources and waste. Environmental policy became a full competence of the EU with the implementation of the Single European Act, and was strengthened and extended by the Maastricht Treaty, which introduced QMV in the Council and co-decision with the European Parliament on environmental legislation, as well as the principle of sustainable development as a central aim of the EU. While allowing member states to apply higher environmental protection standards if they wished, the treaty requires the EU to develop a common environmental policy to achieve 'a high level of protection' and to rectify environmental damage at source, based on the 'polluter pays' principle.

To this end, the main EU actions in the environmental field have been as follows:

* *Air and noise pollution:* since 1970 the EU has adopted ever-stricter directives on air pollution by vehicles, large combustion plants, and

power stations; the Commission has proposed measures to phase out chlorofluorocarbons and introduce an energy tax on carbon dioxide emissions; and EU rules have been laid down on noise pollution by motor vehicles, aircraft, lawnmowers, household equipment, and building-site machinery. The EU was a strong supporter of the global effort to combat climate change, supporting the 2009 'Copenhagen Accord' as a first step towards legally binding international accords to succeed the 1997 Kyoto Treaty. The EU has also committed itself to cut 20 per cent of 1990 emission levels by 2020.

- *Waste disposal:* since 1975 a series of directives have established EU regulations on toxic and dangerous waste, the transport or shipment of hazardous waste, and the disposal of specific types of waste and manufactured products (for example the end-of-life vehicles directive, adopted in September 2000).
- *Water pollution:* since 1976 a number of directives have established common standards for surface and underground water, bathing water, drinking water, fresh water, and the discharge of dangerous chemicals, and providing for a European inventory of all chemical substances on the market.
- *Chemical products:* after the industrial disaster in Seveso in 1977 the EU adopted a series of directives regulating the use, storage, handling, packaging, and labelling of a wide variety of dangerous chemicals, and providing for a European inventor of all chemical substance on the market.
- *Nature protection and biodiversity:* between 1982 and 1992 the EU adopted directives related to the International Convention on Trade in Endangered Species (CITES), which established rules on the conservation of wild birds, the protection of natural habitats, and scientific experiments on animals. The EU also offers financial support for projects to conserve natural habitats.
- *Environmental impact assessment:* in 1985 the Council adopted a directive, which has subsequently been extended, requiring environmental impact assessments of all public and private industrial and infrastructure projects above a certain size. The directive also requires that the public be consulted.
- *Eco-labelling and eco-audits:* in 1992 the Council adopted a regulation that lays down rules for granting EU eco-labels to environmentally friendly products, and in 1993 the Council adopted a regulation that established a voluntary environmental auditing scheme.
- *European Environment Agency* (EEA): set up in 1994 in Copenhagen, the EEA is responsible for collecting data and supplying information for new environmental legislation, developing forecasting techniques to enable preventive measures to be taken, and ensuring that EU environmental data are incorporated into international environmental programmes.

- *Natural and technological hazards:* the EU adopted an action programme on civil protection in 1998, is a signatory of the UN Convention on the Transboundary Effects of Industrial Accidents, protection against radiation and the management of radioactive waste, and has issued two directives on the potential impact of genetically modified organisms (GMOs) – one on the release of GMOs into the environment and the other regulating the use of GMOs.

As is clear from this list, the EU uses a variety of instruments to promote environmental protection. In addition to the EU-level environmental regulations, these instruments include an expenditure programme (LIFE), participation in international treaties and cooperation with third countries, and the provision of incentives for public and private actors to protect the environment, ranging from voluntary systems such as eco-labelling and the EU system of environmental auditing to compulsory systems such as the environmental impact assessment of public and private projects.

Furthermore, there is more EU legislation in the area of environmental policy than in almost any other policy area, and environmental legislation tends to be adopted more quickly than legislation in most other areas (Jordan *et al.*, 1999). However, there is some variation in the effectiveness with which environmental legislation is implemented by the member states (Bailey, 1999; Grant *et al.*, 2000; Knill and Lenschow, 2000). Börzel (2000, 2003) argues that the existing level of environmental protection in a state is not what determines how effective the state is at implementing EU environmental legislation, but rather the structure and power exerted by industrial interests (cf. Knill and Lenschow, 1998; Mastenbroek, 2005). This contrasts with EU social regulation, where the existing national welfare regime and model of capitalism influences how much discretion a state exercises when implementing EU rules.

From a normative perspective, the reason why the EU is able to act so easily and effectively in this policy area is that most EU environmental regulations address market failures arising from the integration of the single market, and so are pareto-efficient in their goals (Majone, 1996). First, environmental pollution is an unwanted side effect of most economic activities, affecting many people who are not involved in the transactions that produce the pollution. Second, without environmental standards and environmental labelling, consumers lack the necessary information to make judgements about the quality and environmental friendliness of the goods they buy. To limit these two types of market failure, the EU has established environmental standards at all stages of the economic process: from production (such as chemical emissions), to distribution (such as eco-labelling), consumption (such as vehicle emissions). and disposal (such as waste management).

However, EU environmental policy does not always fit this pareto-efficiency justification (McCormick, 2001; Weale, 1996). EU environmental legislation covers far more than cross-border pollution. The EU sets standards for both the national and EU levels, and these standards are almost universally based on the high standards of the most environmentally advanced member states, such as Denmark, Germany, Sweden, and the Netherlands, rather than on the lower standards of the UK, Ireland, and Southern and Eastern Europe. In many cases the lower standards might have been sufficient to protect against negative externalities and provide information to consumers.

Environmental policy at the EU level is primarily driven by the desire to prevent a distortion of competition in the single market – which is an ideological argument that is disguised as a need to address market failure. EU environmental legislation invariably involves intense battles between industry and environmentalists. If these policies were purely pareto-efficient, such lobby campaigns would be unnecessary. For example, the REACH directive, which was adopted in 2006 and is designed to regulate the production and use of chemical substances, involved one of the most expensive lobbying campaigns by industry groups and environmentalists in the history of the EU, and hence highlights the ideological nature of EU environmental policy-making (Lindgren and Persson, 2008). There are clearly winners and losers of many EU environmental acts.

Social policy

The Treaty of Rome provided for an EU social policy through:

- a general objective of promoting 'social progress and a high level of employment';
- a section allowing for closer cooperation in the improvement of living and working conditions;
- a requirement that the member states ensure equal pay for men and women;
- a European Social Fund to help occupational and geographical mobility; and
- the free movement of workers, with rights to residence, social security, and non-discrimination in employment.

Little progress was made on these issues in the 1960s and 1970s, except in respect of the coordination of social security systems for migrant workers and equal pay for women. EU social policy received a new impetus in the 1980s. Fearing that the single market would primarily benefit capital rather than labour, François Mitterrand and Jacques Delors argued for a 'social dimension' of European integration. As a result, the Single European Act provided for the harmonization of health and safety standard at work using QMV in the Council. Then in December 1989, all member states except the UK signed the Commission's Charter on the Fundamental Rights of Workers (the Social Charter), which listed 47 actions for the establishment of the single market programme. The Commission then turned these obligations into legislative proposals in the subsequent Social Action Programme. During the negotiations on the Maastricht Treaty in 1992, a majority of member states proposed incorporating the aims of the Social Chapter into the EU Treaty and using QMV in the Council on most social policy issues, but, the British Conservative government vetoed this proposal. This resulted in a separate agreement on social policy signed by the other 11 member states. This Social Protocol provided for QMV in areas such as working conditions and workers' consultation, and unanimity voting in more sensitive areas such as social security.

The Maastricht Social Protocol also strengthened the social dialogue between European-level representatives, management, and labour: the European Trade Union Confederation (ETUC), the Union of Industrial and Employers' Confederations of Europe (UNICE), and the European Centre of Enterprises with Public Participation (CEEP) (Compston and Greenwood, 2001). The protocol made it mandatory for the Commission to consult the 'social partners' before initiating legislation in the social policy field. Furthermore, the protocol allowed the social partners to initiate their own agreement (so-called 'Euro-agreements'), which could either be implemented in the member states by the member associations of the social partners or be turned into formal EU legislation by a decision to the Council, on the basis of a proposal to do so by the Commission.

In 1997 the new British Labour government agreed to the Amsterdam Treaty, which incorporated the Social Protocol into a new Social Chapter of the treaty, including the provisions related to the social dialogue. The Amsterdam Treaty also included provisions for cooperation between member states to combat unemployment. Despite these legislative provisions, examples of EU social legislation have been few and far between compared with environmental legislation.

The main recent developments in EU social policy are as follows:

- *Free movement of workers:* the right to reside has been extended to students, retirees, ex-employers, and the self-employed, but here have been repeated problems with the application of movement of persons, particularly in the case of nationals from third countries, and migrant workers from other EU member states still do not have fully equal social rights throughout the EU.
- *Health and safety at work:* directives have been passed to establish a general health and safety framework covering all the main sectors,

specialized rules for particular industries, and health and safety protection for part-time workers.

- *Working conditions and workers' rights:* the series of measures adopted in this area include directives on the protection of pregnant women at work (1991), working time (1993 and 2003), parental leave (1996), equal rights for temporary workers (1997), fixed-term work (1999), and the protection of workers in the event of insolvency of their company (2008).

- *Worker consultation:* despite repeated proposals by the Commission since the 1970s on the right of workers to be consulted and participate in company decisions, the work councils was not adopted until 1994 (1997 in the UK). A directive establishing a general framework for informing and consulting employees was then passed in 2002, and directive setting out how workers should be consulted in EU-wide companies was adopted in 2009.

- *Equally between men and women:* little new legislation has been adopted on sexual equality since the mid-1980s, but the main piece of legislation governing equal pay and treatment in the workplace (adopted in 1976) was amended in 2002, significantly shifting the burden of proof from the employee to the employer.

- *Anti-discrimination:* after the addition of the so-called 'general non-discrimination clause' in the Amsterdam Treaty, the EU adopted some of the most advanced pieces of legislation anywhere in the world on equality in the workplace: in June 2000 a directive on equal treatment irrespective of racial or ethnic origin, and in December 2000 a directive establishing a general framework for the equal treatment, covering non-discrimination on the grounds of religion, disability, age, and sexual orientation.

- *Employment:* based on the employment chapter in the treaty, EU action plan for employment, on the basis of which the Commission and the Council issue a series of non-binding recommendations in the form of a joint employment report, and the establishment of the European Employment Services (EURES) – a network of public employment agencies, trade unions and employers organizations, to promote the cross-border recruitment of employees.

As the above list shows, social legislation at the European level is far from the traditional social policy of domestic welfare states, in which the state is responsible for supplying social goods such as social insurance, health care, welfare services, education, and housing (Titmus, 1974). These core redistributive powers remain in the hands of national administrations. EU social policy, in contrast, is social regulation, which is primarily designed to address market failures rather than to redistribute resources between employers and workers or between rich and poor citizens (Majone, 1993).

The most developed areas of EU social policy are social security rights for migrant workers, health and safety standards, and product safety standards (Eichener, 1997; Leibfried and Pierson, 1996). The provision of social security to migrant workers increases the efficiency of the labour market as part of the general single market goal, whereas health and safety and product standards reduce information costs to consumers and the effects of production processes on the health of workers. The costs of these standards are spread among all producers and consumers, and the benefits are received by all consumers and industrial workers. Hence, both the costs and the benefits are diffuse.

The EU has been much less successful in adopting common rules on working conditions and industrial relations, and in pursuing common labour market policies. In the case of working conditions, some EU-wide standards have been agreed, for example on working time, rights for part-time and temporary employees, maternity and paternity leave, and fixed-term contracts. But, in contrast to health and safety standards, these rules tend not to conform to the standards that prevail in the most advanced member states; rather they set out minimum basic require-ments and there is a high degree of flexibility in terms of how the member states apply the rules (Streeck, 1996). With regard to industrial relations, the rules on workers' consultation and information only apply to large multinational firms and allows a high degree of flexibility in the applica-tion (Falkner, 1996). Finally, despite the employment chapter in the EU Treaty, the EU lacks the power to force member states to adopt common labour market policies. Furthermore, recent developments towards social inclusion in the Lisbon Agenda have been conducted within the Open Method of Coordination, where much of the focus has been on sharing information and discussing best practices rather than on common binding rules, hence leaving the member states with substantive discretion (Dali, 2006).

Explaining EU Regulatory Policies

These developments in EU regulatory policies need explaining:

- Why has the EU been more able to adopt more deregulatory than re-regulatory policies?
- Why has the EU been more able to adopt product standards (such as environmental standards) than process standards (such as labour market regulations)?
- Why has the EU been more able to adopt gender equality and general non-discrimination legislation than legislation governing working conditions and workers' rights?

There are two sets of explanations to these questions. The first focuses on national preferences and bargaining between member states, while the second focuses on rules for interaction between member states and non-state actors shape outcomes.

National preferences and bargaining over EU regulatory policies

The decision to create a single market was the result of the emergence of an ideological compromise between the governments in the mid-1980s (Cameron, 1992; Garrett, 1992). On one side, the British Conservative government, led by Margaret Thatcher, saw the single market as a way to export the British deregulatory model to the rest of Europe. On the other side, the failure of Mitterrand's 'socialism in one country' experiment in the early 1980s led the French socialist government to see the single market as a means to develop Europe's industrial competitiveness and capacity vis-à-vis the US and Japan. For the French and other social democratic governments, liberalization of intra-EU trade and deregulation of national markets were necessary evils to achieve the long-term benefits of lower transaction costs, higher economies of scale and the creation of European-wide 'industrial champions'. Once consensus was reached regarding the pareto-efficiency of the single market project, the perceived benefits of collective action outweighed the costs (Moravcsik, 1991, 1993). The EU governments consequently agreed to delegate to the Commission the task of proposing a plan to complete the single market.

The social democratic governments also argued for EU environmental and social policies to be developed in tandem with the deregulatory single market programme. But it became clear that consensus on *product* standards were more easily agreed upon than *process* standards (Scharpf, 1996). Product regulations are standards governing how a good or service is packaged, labelled and marketed (such as environmental packaging rules, technical standards and product safety codes), while process regulation are standards governing how goods and services are produced (such as working conditions and industrial relations rules). Richer member states (such as the Scandinavian countries) tend to have higher product and process standards, while poorer member states (such as those in Southern and Eastern Europe) tend to have lower product and process standards.

Both rich and poor states may prefer to have common product standards in order to reap the benefits of the single market. Governments therefore agreed to delegate agenda-setting powers in this field to the Commission and were prepared to risk being outvoted under QMV in return for common standards, provided that this facilitated the function of the single market (Majone, 1996). The Commission has thus been able to propose successfully comparatively high consumer protection and environmental packaging and labelling standards as these were preferable to no standards as all (Egan, 2001).

This is not the case for process regulations. While richer states, with high process standards (such as labour market rights to protect workers in the event of redundancy) would like to export these to the EU as a whole, poorer states would like to be able to offer cheaper unit labour costs to attract investments from richer states. This leads to regulatory competition, where the richer states are forced to lower their standards to remain competitive. Faced with threats of such 'social dumping', social democratic governments in rich states prefer no agreement on common process standards to low standards being imposed, because the absence of an agreement would allow them to keep their high standards and compete over productivity. Poorer states, meanwhile, prefer their low standards to the high standards of the richer states, as common high standards would drive up their production costs without improving production. Also, common low standards would deprive them of their competitive advantage of lower production costs. As a result, both richer and poorer states prefer the existence of 'regulatory diversity' on workers' rights, and have resisted the extension of QMV in this area (Lange, 1993).

Supranational politics: interests, entrepreneurship, and preferences

A competing explanation focuses on the role of non-state actors (Sandholtz and Stone Sweet, 1998). Here, the variations in the development of regulatory policies at the EU level result from three sets of factors.

First, the variations stem from different degrees of influence of business and public interests in the EU policy process (see Chapter 7). Business interests are better organized at the European level than are environmentalists, consumer groups, and trade unions. According to the 'logic of collective action' (Olson, 1965), business interests, who are able to reap specific benefits from the EU policy process, are more able to secure from their members the resources needed to lobby the EU. In contrast, public interests are only able to obtain diffuse benefits from the EU policy process. Positive theories of regulation predict that business interests have a particular incentive to promote regulatory policies at the highest level possible as they will be more able than their opponents to influence policy at that level, and prefer to see regulatory competition at the lower levels in order to put downward pressure on national regulations (Dunleavy, 1997). As a result, business interests lobbied both national governments and the Commission for the single market programme (Sandholtz and Zysman, 1989).

In addition, business interests were less opposed to high product standards than process standards as the former are less costly, reduce market distortions, and could enable European products to be sold in the North American and Japanese markets. As with the governments, business interests are split over process standards. Businesses from richer states want process standards to be lowered to increase their competitiveness, while businesses in poorer states fear that expensive EU rules will drive up production costs. As a result, business interests have only been willing to allow voluntaristic process regulations.

Second, the Commission is not a perfect agent of the member states. The Commission has interests of its own and uses its delegated power selectively to obtain its objectives. Like all bureaucracies, the Commission has an incentive to increase its power and prestige in the policy process. Once power has been delegated, the Commission has discretion in how it exercises these powers (see Chapter 2). Framing of policy issues determines how actors order, update and act upon their policy preferences (Riker, 1986; Tversky and Kahneman, 1981). Strategically using its right of initiative to frame the proposal, the Commission is able to present new policy initiatives in a way that it is most likely to find support for the proposal. In other words, the Commission is a 'policy entrepreneur' (Kingdon, 1984): selecting the policies that promote its interests; restricting the available choices for governments; continually pressing and negotiating until it gets what it wants; and involving other actors in the policy process to force reluctant governments to accept its proposals (Cram, 1996; Majone, 1996; Peters, 1992, 1994; Young and Wallace, 2000).

For example, the white paper *Completing the Internal Market* was presented in a particular 'cultural frame', with a new method of harmonizing rules of exchange, mutual recognition of the establishment of property rights, and enforcement of these rules by national administrations (Fligstein and Mara-Drita, 1996). The Commission has engaged civic interests to promote high standards in environmental policies and selective social rights. Relying on the expertise of environmental interest groups, the Commission was able to increase its prestige among the 'green' member states and gain the support from the majority in the European Parliament (Eichener, 1997). The initiation of the 'social dialogue' facilitated the adoption of workers' rights despite a divided Council (Falkner, 1996). Furthermore, the Commission's use of scientific expertise in the area of health and safety at work won over reluctant governments and business interests (Eichener, 1997).

Third, the configuration of the policy preferences of the main political actors in the EU – the governments in the Council, the parties in the European Parliament and the Commission – determines what kind of policy changes are possible. As we see from Figure 8.2, there was a substantive shift in favour of more deregulation among the governments in the Council from 2000 to 2010 as well as in the Commission. The shift is substantively smaller in the case of environmental policy. Figure 8.2

Figure 8.2   *Locations of EU actors on regulatory issues*

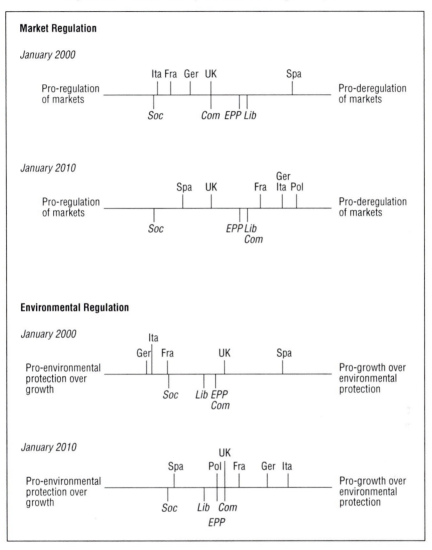

Note: The locations of the national governments are taken from expert judgements about party positions on a number of policy scales, as collected by Benoit and Laver (2006). The locations of the Commission are the median locations of the national parties of the Commissioners in the Prodi Commission and the second Barroso Commission, using the Benoit–Laver data. The locations of the EPP, Socialist (Soc), and Liberal (Lib) groups in the European Parliament are taken from the expert judgements about the positions of the political groups in the European Parliament collected by McElroy and Benoit (2010). The member state governments are shown above the lines and the supranational actors are shown below the lines and in italics.

also makes it clear that government preferences do not have stable national preferences on regulatory issues. If we compare the positions of Italy and Spain on deregulation as well as re-regulation over time, we see that they moved from one end of the scale to the other in this period.

With the increased legislative powers of the European Parliament,

Table 8.2   *Vote in the European Parliament on the Takeover Directive*

Group/member state	For	Against	Abstain	Absent	Total	Cohesion
Vote by political group						
EPP–ED	203	2	2	25	232	0.97
ELDR	43	1	0	7	51	0.97
UEN	21	1	0	8	30	0.93
Non-attached	15	8	3	1	27	0.37
EDD	3	11	0	2	16	0.68
G/EFA	9	35	0	4	48	0.69
PES	29	120	2	25	176	0.69
EUL/NGL	2	43	0	1	46	0.93
Vote by member state delegation						
Ireland	12	2	0	1	15	0.79
United Kingdom	65	14	0	8	87	0.73
Sweden	13	6	0	3	22	0.53
Italy	47	22	2	16	87	0.49
Finland	9	5	0	2	16	0.46
Netherlands	17	11	0	3	31	0.41
Germany	53	37	2	7	99	0.36
Austria	10	7	0	4	21	0.38
Spain	32	23	0	9	64	0.37
Denmark	8	6	0	2	16	0.36
Portugal	12	9	0	4	25	0.36
Luxembourg	3	3	0	0	6	0.25
Belgium	11	13	0	1	25	0.31
France	25	47	3	12	87	0.44
Greece	8	16	0	1	25	0.50
Total	325	221	7	73	626	0.38
%	59.5	40.5				

Note: The table shows the vote on the proposal to approve the directive on takeover bids, which took place on 16 December 2003. The political groups and member state delegations are sorted from most in favour of the proposal to most opposed. In the vote, 88.8 per cent of MEPs voted the same way as the plurality of their political group, while 64.6 per cent of MEPs voted the same way as the plurality of their member state delegation. See Chapter 6 for the calculation of cohesion scores.

Source: Calculated from data in Hix *et al.* (2007).

Table 8.3   *Vote in the European Parliament on the Services Directive*

Group/member state	For	Against	Abstain	Absent	Total	Cohesion
Vote by political group						
EUL/NGL	29	0	0	12	41	1.00
G/EFA	35	1	1	5	42	0.92
Non attached	11	5	4	11	31	0.33
IND/DEM	7	11	0	11	29	0.42
PES	34	116	6	45	201	0.62
UEN	3	18	0	14	35	0.79
ALDE	1	57	2	30	90	0.93
EPP–ED	0	200	1	64	265	0.99
Vote by member state delegation						
France	42	23	0	13	78	0.47
Cyprus	2	3	0	1	6	0.40
Belgium	5	12	2	5	24	0.45
Denmark	3	8	0	3	14	0.59
Czech Republic	6	16	1	1	24	0.54
Greece	4	11	4	5	24	0.37
Germany	19	58	0	22	99	0.63
Austria	4	13	0	1	18	0.65
Italy	10	38	0	31	79	0.69
Luxembourg	1	4	0	1	6	0.70
Netherlands	3	12	3	10	28	0.50
United Kingdom	10	44	2	22	78	0.68
Sweden	2	10	0	7	19	0.75
Portugal	2	12	0	10	24	0.79
Finland	1	7	0	6	14	0.81
Lithuania	1	8	0	4	13	0.83
Spain	4	33	0	17	54	0.84
Slovakia	1	9	2	2	14	0.63
Estonia	0	5	0	1	6	1.00
Malta	0	5	0	0	5	1.00
Latvia	0	6	0	3	9	1.00
Slovenia	0	7	0	0	7	1.00
Ireland	0	10	0	3	13	1.00
Hungary	0	17	0	7	24	1.00
Poland	0	37	0	17	54	1.00
Total	120	408	14	192	734	
%	22.7	77.3				

Note: The table shows the vote on the proposal to reject the directive on services in the internal market, which took place on 15 November 2006. The political groups and member state delegations are sorted from most in favour of the proposal to reject the directive to most opposed. There were only 734 MEPs at that time (instead of 735), as 1 MEP had resigned and had not yet been replaced. In the vote, 88.0 per cent of MEPs voted the same way as the plurality of their political group, while 78.8 per cent of MEPs voted the same way as the plurality of their member state delegation. See Chapter 6 for the calculation of cohesion scores.

Source: Compiled from VoteWatch.eu data (at: www.votewatch.eu/cx_vote_details. php?id_act=2171&lang=en).

particularly in the area of regulatory policies, politics in the European Parliament also matters. Table 8.2 shows how the MEPs voted on the controversial takeover directive in December 2003. Here, the two main political groups, the EPP and PES, voted against each other. A minority of the PES MEPs broke away to vote with the liberals (ELDR) and EPP. The minority of MEPs who defected from the PES line were predominantly from the UK, which has a liberal takeover regime, and the Nordic member states, who felt that the directive would allow them to continue with their national takeover policies. In contrast, the socialist MEPs from the coordinated market economies of continental Europe were opposed to the directive. Note, however, that even on this vote, cohesion was higher within the political groups than within the member states, hence indicating that political preferences played a larger role than national interests in guiding voting behaviour in the European Parliament on this issue.

Table 8.3 shows how MEPs voted on the services directive in November 2006. On this vote we see that the three main political groups, the EPP, PES, and ALDE, voted together against the other groups, although a minority within the PES again broke away from the group. On this vote, national interest clearly guided the behaviour of the MEPs from the new member states, while the national delegations from many the old 15 states were more split. This illustrates that even when issues unite MEPs from some member states, it is unlikely to cause the European Parliament to split purely along national lines. The increase in the power of the European Parliament has hence sharpened competition over regulatory policies along ideological rather than national lines (see Chapter 6).

Conclusion: Mostly Winners, But Some Losers

The single market has fundamentally changed Europe. The production, distribution, and exchange of goods, services, and capital are now predominantly regulated at the European level. The regime has both deregulatory and re-regulatory features. Deregulation is driven by the principle of mutual recognition and EU competition policy has led to a liberalization of most sectors of the European economy. National governments are no longer free to use trade barriers, state aids, or special operating licences to protect their industries from competition from firms from other member states. This has meant substantive gains as firms have access to bigger markets and taxpayers' money is not wasted on propping up uncompetitive national enterprises. Furthermore, this deregulation of markets has been matched with a re-regulation of product standards at the EU level, which offers consumers clearer product information, which is both more environmentally-friendly and cheaper.

This combination of de- and re-regulation also has distributive effects.

EU regulatory policies impose cost on producers and protect the values and interests of environmentalist and consumers. Also, while the EU has improved workers' rights in several respects, some employees and labour unions have lost from the single market. EU social policy has not developed to the same extent as environmental policy. A key reason for this is that labour unions in the richer old 15 states prefer to keep their high social standards rather than agree to common minimum European standards. Similarly, employers from the new, and poorer, member states are afraid that common high social standards would make them uncompetitive. In light of the recent economic crises it is nevertheless unclear to what extent the old 15 states will continue to see their rigid labour laws as sustainable.

For the development of strong EU social policy to materialize, it may be necessary to consider not only re-regulatory policy tools, but also expenditure. We hence investigate EU expenditure policies in the next chapter.

Chapter 9

Expenditure Policies

Theories of Public Expenditure and Redistribution
The Budget of the European Union
The Common Agricultural Policy
Cohesion Policy
Other Internal Policies
Explaining EU Expenditure Policies
Conclusion: a Set of Redistributive Bargains

The capacity of the EU to distribute resources through taxation and public spending is limited. The EU budget constitutes about 1 per cent of total EU GDP. However, for member states, farmers, regions, private organizations, or individual citizens who receive money from the EU budget, the absolute sums involved are considerable, and someone somewhere in the EU pays for this. To help understand how EU expenditure policies are made, and who gets what and why, we shall first look at some general theories of public finances and redistribution.

Theories of Public Expenditure and Redistribution

The traditional explanation for the development of public expenditure is normative: to achieve greater equality (Heidenheimer *et al.*, 1990; Marshall, 1950; Rawls, 1971; Wilensky, 1975). The theory of 'fiscal federalism' is also primarily normative (Oates, 1972, 1999). According to this theory, because the lower levels of government are constrained in respect of macroeconomic policy-making (since monetary policy is centralized), the central (federal) government should have basic responsibility for macroeconomic stabilization, for example by using the central budget to alleviate demand shocks (see Chapter 10). Local governments, in contrast, should be responsible for providing public services and redistributing incomes within their jurisdiction, according to the particular political preferences of their constituents. If the central government were to take over redistributive functions from the local governments, the general level of welfare would be reduced as the central government would replace tailor-made policies with a single, uniform level of expenditure (see Weingast, 1995). Nevertheless, decentralized public expenditure can lead to negative externalities (such as the consumption of public

218

goods in one locality by people living in another locality) and tax competition between welfare regimes (to attract investment) (Break, 1967). Fiscal decentralization also means that the burden of providing universal public services (from which everyone benefits regardless of income) will fall disproportionally on poorer localities. Consequently, in most federal systems, funds from the central government budget are used to reduce regional inequality as well as income inequality.

However, the growth of public spending policies can also be explained by positive theories (Mueller, 1989, pp. 445–6). Majority decision-making in a democracy results in the transfer of resources from the minority to the majority. One might expect that because there are more citizens on low incomes than on high incomes, governments would pursue progressive taxation and welfare programmes for the poor (Meltzer and Richard, 1981). Because the median voter in a democratic system is considerably poorer than the average member of the wealthy elite in a non-democratic system, democratic systems tend to have higher taxes and higher levels of public spending than do non-democratic polities (Acemoglu and Robinson, 2001; Boix, 2003). Nevertheless, because the pivotal voter (in the key electoral constituencies) is often considerably better off than the person with the median level of income – particularly in countries where voter turnout is low – political parties often advocate expenditure programmes that will disproportionately benefit higher income groups than the average citizen (Stigler, 1970; Tullock, 1971).

Furthermore, when voting on budgetary packages it is easier for legislators to increase the size of government spending than to reduce it. If government spending remains stable, a change in the structure of public expenditure will mean that some social groups will gain at the expense of others. However, if the budget is increased, benefits can be distributed in such a way that everyone gains at least something. For example, legislators from rural constituencies can vote for welfare programmes for the urban poor, in return for legislators from inner cities voting for welfare programmes for farmers. This 'vote trading' consequently leads to the expansion of public expenditure, and an increase in public deficits (see Weingast *et al.*, 1981).

However, budgetary expansion can be restricted by institutional mechanisms. First, a balanced-budget rule prevents expenditure from being increased without simultaneously raising revenue. If revenue cannot be increased, changes in the budget can only occur by removing expenditure from one programme (group of citizens) and giving it to another. Second, if the budget has to be adopted by unanimity, as is the case with multiannual budgetary packages in the EU, any decision-maker can veto a proposed change that redistributes resources away from their supporters. As a result of these two institutional constraints, all legislators can demand that contributions made by their supporters to the budget are exactly equal to the compensation they receive. This compensation (side-payment) can take two forms: direct benefits from expenditure programmes, or indirect benefits from non-expenditure programmes, such as other policy areas.

According to Olson's (1965) theory of collective action (see Chapter 7), different interest groups have different incentives to organize to secure benefits from government. The benefits of a welfare programme tend to be concentrated whereas the costs are diffuse. For example, the benefits of agricultural subsidies to each individual farmer are much larger than the costs to each individual consumer or taxpayer. Also, because of their lack of resources and information, low income citizens tend to be underrepresented in the policy process, whereas doctors and pensioners tend to be more powerful. Hence, public expenditure programmes tend to benefit concentrated minorities and well organized groups at the expense of diffuse and disorganized groups.

In sum, public expenditure is a core responsibility of government, and has traditionally been primarily used in liberal democracies to redistribute resources from one social group to another. At face value, redistributive policies aim to reduce inequalities in society, but the reality is often very different. Who gains from expenditure policies depends on the interests of political decision-makers, the power of organized interests, and the institutional rules of budgetary decision-making.

The Budget of the European Union

The Treaty of Rome originally established an annual budget. However, due to uncertainty on both the revenue and expenditure side, and growing multiannual spending commitments as a result of new policies and intergovernmental bargains, since 1988 the EU has operated through multiannual financial perspectives. These packages set the general levels of expenditure for each main budgetary category as well as the overall ceiling of the budget relative to the Gross National Product (GNP) of the EU member states and the structure of revenues. Within these multiannual frameworks, the precise amounts of revenue and expenditure are agreed in an annual budgetary cycle. The current multiannual financial framework runs from 2007 to 2013.

Revenue and expenditure

On the revenue side, the EU is funded through the four 'own resources':

1 *Agriculture levies:* under the Common Agricultural Policy (CAP), these are charges on imports of agricultural products from non-EU countries.
2 *Customs duties:* common customs tariffs and other duties are levied on imports from non-EU countries.

Figure 9.1 *Relative composition of the EU's revenue sources, 1980–2010*

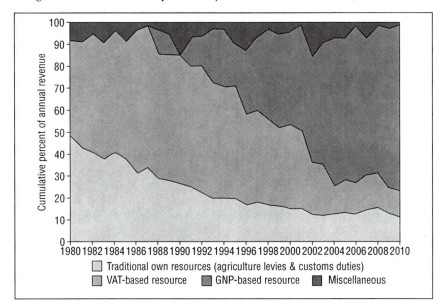

Source: Annual budget reports of the European Commission.

3 *Value added tax (VAT):* a harmonized rate is applied in all member states, and this should not exceed 1 per cent of EU GNP.

4 *GNP-based own resource:* based on the GNP of the member states, this covers the difference between planned expenditure and the amount yielded from the other three resources.

As Figure 9.1 shows, the balance between these sources of income has changed between 1980 and 2010. The Council established the first three resources in 1970 to replace the old system of financing the EU by direct contributions from the member states, based on their relative GNP. The member states expected that import levies and VAT would be sufficient to cover EU expenditure. However, as the EU became a net exporter in the 1980s, revenues from agricultural and other import duties fell. Also, in the early 1990s the EU budget grew as a percentage of EU GNP. In response, the Commission proposed the reintroduction of GNP-based contributions by national governments. This is calculated on an annual basis to cover the shortfall in revenues from import levies and the VAT levy. The increase in GNP-based contributions has continued after the 2004 enlargement, and now makes up more than 70 per cent of revenues.

On the expenditure side, the composition of EU expenditure has changed considerably since the 1980s, as Figure 9.2 shows. The two main expenditure categories are the CAP and cohesion funds. Expenditure under the CAP declined from almost 70 per cent of the EU

Figure 9.2   *Relative composition of EU expenditure, 1980–2010*

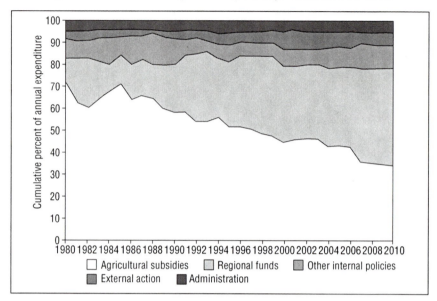

Source: Annual budget reports of the European Commission.

budget in 1980 to 37 per cent in 2010, while expenditure on structural and cohesion policies increased from 11 per cent of the budget to 45 per cent. Agriculture and regional policies today account for 82 per cent of the budget. The remainder is divided between internal policies (mostly research and development), external policies (mostly humanitarian and development aid), and the administrative costs of running the EU institutions.

Table 9.1 shows the actual amounts allocated to the different budget headings in the most recent multiannual financial framework. The budget headings are not as transparent as they could be. In particular, agricultural subsidies are contained under the heading 'preservation and management of nature' alongside several other policies (such as the environmental protection), while regional spending is contained under the heading 'sustainable growth' along with several other internal policies (such as research spending).

The annual budget procedure: the power of the purse

A traditional function of parliaments is to control the purse strings, and the European Parliament acquired a limited budgetary role through reforms to the annual budgetary procedure in 1970 and 1975.

Until the Lisbon Treaty, there was a distinction between 'compulsory' and 'non-compulsory' expenditure. The Council had the final say on

Table 9.1 *EU budget, financial perspective, 2007–13*

EUR million – current prices	2007	2008	2009	2010	2011	2012	2013
Sustainable growth	53,979	57,653	61,700	63,358	63,638	66,628	69,621
Preservation and management of nature	55,143	59,193	56,468	59,989	60,338	60,810	61,289
Citizenship, freedom, security, and justice	1,273	1,362	1,523	1,693	1,889	2,105	2,376
The EU as a global partner	6,578	7,002	7,440	7,893	8,430	8,997	9,595
EU administration	7,039	7,380	7,568	7,858	8,334	8,670	9,095
Compensations	445	207	210				
Total	124,457	132,797	134,909	140,791	142,629	147,210	151,976
Ceiling, appropriations for payment as % of gross national income (GNI) (ESA 95)	1.02	1.08	1.13	1.16	1.13	1.12	1.11

Source: Commission of the European Communities (2009) Communication from the Commission to the European Parliament and the Council concerning the revision of the multiannual financial framework.

'compulsory expenditure'; expenditure that was necessary under the treaties. This was mostly expenditure on the CAP and the small amount of expenditure arising from international agreements. The Council and the European Parliament together had the final say on non-compulsory expenditure, which included the annual expenditure on economic and social cohesion and most expenditure on other internal policies, such as research, education, and financial support for European-level interest groups. The Lisbon Treaty removed the distinction between compulsory and non-compulsory expenditure, and thus increase the European Parliament's influence over the annual budget.

The annual budgetary procedure can be simplified as follows (Benedetto and Høyland, 2007). The Commission proposes an annual budget, within the guidelines of the multiannual financial framework. The Council then adopts or amends the proposed budget by QMV and forwards it to the European Parliament. Unless an absolute majority of MEPs amends the budget, the Council version of the text is adopted. If the Parliament does amend the budget, a qualified majority in the Council must accept all the Parliament's amendments, otherwise a conciliation committee is convened (see Chapter 3 on the composition of conciliation). In the conciliation committee, a simple majority in the Parliament and QMV in the Council is required to adopt the budget. If there is no agreement at this stage, the budget fails and the Commission must submit a new proposal.

The annual budget is prepared by the Budget DG in the Commission, and is negotiated by the members of the Budget Committee in the European Parliament, the Budget Committee of the Committee of Permanent Representatives (COREPER) and the Budget Council (consisting of junior ministers from the national finance ministries).

In contrast to the annual budgetary procedure, the European Parliament has very little say in the agreement of multiannual financial framework, which is adopted via intergovernmental bargaining between finance ministers and heads of government in the European Council. Consequently, the redistributive capacity of the European Parliament is weak compared with that of national parliaments in Europe or the US Congress.

The Common Agricultural Policy

Agriculture may seem a minor issue compared with foreign affairs or the state of the economy. However, the CAP is the largest item of EU expenditure, was the first genuinely supranational policy of the EU, several member states maintain a romantic attachment to rural society, and the public is increasingly concerned about food safety and animal rights. As a result, the political stakes are high when it comes to the making and reform of the CAP.

Operation and reform of the CAP

The Treaty of Rome established the CAP as a central policy, and set out the CAP objectives as follows:

(a)   to increase agricultural productivity, by promoting technical progress and ensuring rational development of agricultural production and the optimum utilization of the factors of production, particularly labour;

(b)   to ensure a fair standard of living for the agricultural community, in particular by increasing the individual earnings of persons engaged in agriculture;

(c)   to stabilize markets;

(d)   to ensure the availability of supply; and

(e)   to ensure that supplies reach consumers at reasonable prices.

After protracted negotiations, in 1962 the governments agreed to achieve these objectives through three mechanisms:

1   protection against low internal prices: by buying surplus goods from farmers – paid out of the European Agricultural Guidance and Guarantee Fund (EAGGF) – when prices fall below an agreed guarantee price in the European market;

2   protection against low import prices: through import quotas and levies (paid into the EAGGF) on imported agricultural goods when the world price falls below an agreed price; and

3   subsidies to achieve a low export price: through refunds (paid out of the EAGGF) for the export of agricultural goods when the world price falls below an agreed price.

The result is a system of indirect income support for farmers, paid for by European taxpayers through the EU budget, and by European consumers through the extra prices charged on imported agricultural goods.

When the CAP was set up Europe was not self-sufficient in most agricultural goods. However, as agricultural production stabilized and Europe became a net exporter of agricultural goods, the CAP price-support mechanism created some intractable problems:

• Guaranteed prices encouraged overproduction and production grew faster than demand, resulting in 'wine lakes' and 'grain mountains'.

• These surpluses had to be stored thus imposing an additional cost on the CAP budget.

• Environmental destruction resulted from over-intensive farming and excessive use of herbicides, pesticides, and artificial fertilizers.

- The bulk of revenues went to larger farmers (who earned more because they produced more), but it was smaller farmers who were in need of the most support.
- Import quotas and levies created numerous trade disputes and prevented the development of global free trade in agricultural goods.
- Export subsidies depressed world prices, distorting agriculture markets in the Third World, thus contributing to global development problems.

The original goals of the CAP had been fulfilled, in that the EU quickly became self-sufficient in agricultural produces and agricultural goods could be supplied at cheap prices to consumers. However, price subsidies had made some farmers better off than others, and better off than many other sections of society. Moreover, agricultural markets no longer needed to be stabilized and although the CAP consumed ever-greater resources its utility to EU taxpayers and small farmers had fallen and its distortion of global agriculture markets increased. Consequently, by the early 1990s the CAP was no longer sustainable in its original form. Consumer and environmental groups, several EU governments and a number of foreign governments demanded reform.

In response to these problems there have been two major reforms of the CAP. The first reform was in 1992. This reform involved price cuts, particularly in the cereals and beef sectors, a system of direct income support for farmers to compensate for the reduction in price subsidies, a 'set-aside scheme' whereby farmers were paid to leave their land fallow instead of growing crops that would have to be bought by the EU, and aid programmes to promote rural development and environmentally-friendly agriculture.

The second reform was in 1999. This time, the price cuts on cereals and beef were extended to other sectors, including milk, olive oil, and wine. The reform also changed the guiding principle of the CAP from price support for agricultural products to income support for farmers. Furthermore, the reform strengthens the non-welfare objectives of the policy, such as environmental protection, food safety, and animal welfare. The original proposal from the Commission was watered-down in a Franco-German deal, as part of the agreement on the new multiannual financial framework (Akrill, 2000b; Galloway, 1999). While the basic elements of the reform remained intact, the French government managed to secure an agreement that price support would continue for key producers (such as dairy and cereal farmers) and that the transition to income support would happen at a slower rate.

The reform process continued with a mid-term review of the multi-annual budget in 2003, when intervention prices on several products were reduced and the Single Farm Payment (SFP) system was introduced. Under the SFP, farmers receive payments from the EU even if they produce nothing, provided that they comply with EU environmental, food safety, animal welfare, and occupational safety standards. Finally, in 2008 a 'health check' reform took place which aimed to base payments along three principles: (a) making farmers respond to market signals; (b) ensuring that farmers received the 'correct' level of support; and (c) enabling farmers to meet new challenges in areas related to climate change, water management, renewable energy, and biodiversity (Fouilleux, 2010).

As a result of these reforms, prices on agricultural goods in the EU are increasingly set by the free market. Through the shift to direct income support the CAP is now more clearly a 'welfare state for farmers' than it was in the beginning. Nevertheless, the 'new CAP' also aims to address market failures resulting from agricultural production (see Chapter 8). For example, environmental destruction and rural underdevelopment are negative externalities of transactions in the agriculture market, and in the supply of agricultural goods there is information asymmetry in respect of food quality and safety.

Making agricultural policy: can the iron triangle be broken?

Agricultural policy is made by an 'iron triangle' of agriculture ministers, agriculture officials in the Commission, and European-level farming interests (see Daugbjerg, 1999; Pappi and Henning, 1999).

First, the Agriculture Council, which meets at least every month, is the central decision-making body. Until the Lisbon Treaty, the part played by the European Parliament in the CAP was limited, as CAP legislation was passed under the consultation procedure (see Chapter 3). Agriculture ministers are often from political parties that are supported by farmers and/or represent rural regions. Also, the work of the Agriculture Council is supported by the Special Committee of Agriculture (SCA) rather than the usual Committee of Permanent Representatives (COREPER), and the SCA is staffed by officials from national agriculture ministries, whereas the members of COREPER are career diplomats.

Finance ministers, who are generally more in favour than agriculture ministers of reining-in agricultural subsidies, only intervene whenever there are major questions on the financing of the CAP, and the heads of government in the European Council are usually only called into play to negotiate the major reform packages. There are often disputes between agriculture and finance ministers. For example, on several occasions in the 1980s the German agriculture minister opposed proposals by the German finance minister to scale down the CAP subsidies.

Second, agricultural interests are protected by the Agriculture and Rural Development DG in the Commission. The Agriculture and Rural

Development DG is the largest DG in the Commission and is staffed predominantly by officials from the main farming member states. Also, the day-to-day management of the CAP is undertaken by the network of agriculture, veterinary, and food safety committees around the Commission, and these committees are staffed by 'national experts', most of whom are nominated by and answerable to national agriculture ministries.

Third, farming interests are strongly represented at the national and European levels (Keeler, 1996). In most member states, the close relationship between national farmers' associations and agriculture ministries ensures that farmers play a central role in the making of national agriculture policies. At the European level, the Confederation of Professional Agricultural Organizations (COPA) is the most well resourced, well staffed, and highly organized of all the supranational sectoral associations (see Chapter 7).

Each element of this triangle has a vested interest in defending the interests of the others: subsidies to farmers, the centrality of the CAP in the EU decision-making process for the Agriculture and Rural Development DG, and the protection of domestic supporters of the agriculture ministers. In contrast, there are few incentives for consumers to mobilize to attempt to break the iron triangle, as the cost of the CAP to each individual consumer or taxpayer is less than the cost of organizing an anti-CAP campaign (Nedergaard, 1995).

Nevertheless, the iron triangle has been undermined by several developments. First, social, economic, and political changes in Europe have reduced the power of agricultural interests. There has been a dramatic change in the status of agriculture in national economies since the 1970s. Between 1970 and 2004 the share of agriculture as a percentage of the labour force of the member states declined from over 20 per cent in some member states to less than 10 per cent in all but seven member states (only Portugal and Greece from the old 15, and Poland, Romania, Latvia, Lithuania, Estonia from the new 12). In most member states, the number of people employed in agriculture today is less than one-third of the 1970 level. Moreover, income from agriculture accounts for less than 5 per cent of GDP in all EU states except Romania and Bulgaria.

Furthermore, active farmers comprise less than 5 per cent of the electorate in most member states. This has forced many agricultural parties, and parties with traditional support in rural areas, such as Christian democrats, to appeal to urban middle-class voters, who are the ones paying for the CAP. Voters with a 'strong agricultural attribute' – including farmers, retired farmers, spouses of farmers, voting-age children of farmers, and former farmers in other occupations – may still constitute a significant proportion of the electorate in some member states (Keeler, 1996). Placed between the middle class and the urban working class, this constituency can be pivotal in determining electoral outcomes. But, in the 1990s, greens politicians obtained cabinet seats in government in several member states, which led to significant changes of the preferences of these governments towards the CAP.

Second, external pressures have created new incentives for the CAP to be reformed. These began with the negotiations in the Uruguay Round of the General Agreement on Tariffs and Trade (GATT) in 1987 and 1988. Without reform of the subsidies on European agriculture, a groundbreaking agreement on global trade liberalization could not have been achieved. Many of the non-EU signatories of GATT were not prepared to support the EU's trade liberalization agenda while the EU continued to subsidize the export of agricultural products to their domestic markets. The GATT agreement was finally signed when the EU trade ministers and heads of state promised to reform the CAP as part of the deal (Patterson, 1997).

A similar situation existed at the end of the 1990s, with the prospective enlargement of the EU to include Central and East European countries. One consequence of enlargement has been a 50 per cent increase in agricultural land in the EU and a 100 per cent increase in agricultural labour. Even with a move towards direct income support rather than price support, enlargement would have led to a dramatic increase in the cost of the CAP if the CAP had not been reformed (Daugbjerg and Swinbank, 2004). At the same time, global trade negotiations continued to put pressure on the EU to reform the CAP. The new member states are unlikely to stand as a single bloc on agricultural issues – against reform of the CAP for example – because the structure of agriculture and the relationship between agricultural interests, political parties, and bureaucrats vary among these states (Sharman, 2003).

Agriculture ministers and COPA may have preferred to delay enlargement in order to protect their interests, but this decision was out of their hands. Also, once international trade issues and enlargement became associated with reform of the CAP, an 'issue linkage' was established, which created specific incentives for non-agricultural industrial interests to lobby against the CAP (Coleman and Tangermann, 1999). For many industrial sectors, the benefits reaped from global trade liberalization and EU enlargement are greater than the costs of mobilizing to break the grip of the farming lobby at the national and European levels. Hence, the interest groups that supported the CAP have begun to be outnumbered by groups that recognized that failing to reform the CAP would jeopardize their policy goals elsewhere. Furthermore, as the Council of agriculture only needed QMV to adopt CAP reform, reluctant member state governments, such as the French and the Portuguese, were unable to block reforms (Daugbjerg and Swinbank, 2007).

Finally, with the Lisbon Treaty, the European Parliament is now a player in the CAP. The extension of the ordinary legislative procedure to the CAP means that the European Parliament now has a say on all CAP legislation. Agricultural interests are not as dominant in the European Parliament as they are in the Council, and the European Parliament has a history of promoting consumer rather than producer interests.

Cohesion Policy

Under the EU Treaty, one of the central aims of the EU is to promote 'economic and social cohesion' – that is, to reduce disparities between different regions and social groups in the EU. This is a classic normative redistributive goal. To this end an ever-larger proportion of the EU budget has been transferred to poorer and less-developed regions. However, the extent to which cohesion policy is a genuine welfare policy and how much it has been able to reduce social and economic disparities in Europe are open to question.

Operation of the policy

The EU has four structural funds:

1   the European Regional Development Fund (ERDF), which was set up in 1975 and is managed by the Regional Policy DG;
2   the European Social Fund (ESF), which was set up in 1960 and is managed by the Employment, Social Affairs and Equal Opportunities DG;
3   the Guidance Section of the EAGGF, which was set up as part of the CAP in 1962 and is managed by the Agriculture and Rural Development DG; and
4   the Financial Instrument for Fisheries Guidance (FIFG), which was set up in 1994 and is managed by the Maritime Affairs and Fisheries DG.

The 1988 reform of the structural funds introduced four key principles for the management of social and economic cohesion policies:

1   *Additionality:* the member states cannot use EU resources to reduce national spending on regional development, so EU resources go directly to regions or managing authorities rather than to national treasuries.
2   *Partnership:* the policy operates through close cooperation between the Commission, national governments and regional authorities

(which in some states had to be created for the purpose) in the process that runs from the preparation of projects to the implementation and monitoring of expenditure.

3   *Programming:* funding is delivered through multiannual development programmes.
4   *Concentration:* EU assistance measures are concentrated in a series of priority objectives.

The structural funds were then reformed again in 1999. One aspect of the reforms was a reduction and streamlining of the objectives, down to three:

1   *Objective 1:* to promote development and structural adjustment in regions that lag behind, defined as having a per capita GDP of below 75 per cent of the EU average.
2   *Objective 2:* to combat structural adjustment in regions with industrial, service, or fisheries sectors facing major change, rural areas in serious decline, and deprived urban areas.
3   *Objective 3:* (for regions not covered by Objectives 1 and 2) to modernize 'human resources' infrastructure, such as education and training systems.

The Commission also set up separate 'community initiatives', to be funded by the structural funds, such as Interreg (for planning and cooperation between border regions) and Urban (for urban regeneration).

In addition to the structural funds, a Cohesion Fund was established in 1994 as part of the implementation of the Maastricht Treaty, and linked to the specific goal of EMU. Because qualification for EMU involved meeting strict budgetary and fiscal criteria (see Chapter 10), the Cohesion Fund was geared to increasing the growth capacity of the four poorest member states: Greece, Ireland, Portugal, and Spain. Two types of project are supported by the fund: environmental protection, and transport and other infrastructure networks.

As a result of the 2004 and 2007 enlargements, the bulk of regional spending now goes to the new member states, although the main beneficiaries of regional spending prior to enlargement managed to keep substantial funds. Table 9.2 consequently shows how much each member state is due to receive under the 2007 to 2013 cohesion policy budget. The main beneficiaries are the states who joined in 2004. Estonia, the Czech Republic, and Hungary will each receive more than €2,500 per capita in cohesion policy income. In absolute terms, though, Poland will be the largest beneficiary, receiving almost one-fifth of the total budget, although Greece and Portugal are due to receive more funds per capita than Poland.

Table 9.2   *Member state receipts from cohesion policy, 2007–13*

Member state	Cohesion policy allocation 2007–13, €m, current prices	% of total funds	Cohesion policy income per capita, €
Estonia	3,456	1.00	2,579
Czech Republic	26,692	7.71	2,548
Hungary	25,307	7.31	2,523
Slovakia	11,588	3.35	2,142
Malta	855	0.25	2,072
Lithuania	6,885	1.99	2,055
Slovenia	4,205	1.21	2,048
Latvia	4,620	1.33	2,043
Portugal	21,511	6.22	2,023
Greece	20,420	5.90	1,813
Poland	67,284	19.44	1,765
Romania	19,668	5.68	915
Bulgaria	6,853	1.98	901
Cyprus	640	0.18	798
Spain	35,217	10.18	768
Italy	28,812	8.32	479
Finland	1,716	0.50	322
Germany	26,340	7.61	321
France	14,319	4.14	223
Belgium	2,258	0.65	210
Sweden	1,891	0.55	204
Ireland	901	0.26	199
Austria	1,461	0.42	175
United Kingdom	10,613	3.07	172
Luxembourg	65	0.02	132
Netherlands	1,907	0.55	116
Denmark	613	0.18	111

Source: Calculated from European Commission data.

Impact: a supply-side policy with uncertain convergence implications

EU cohesion policy is a combination of a classic redistributive policy and a policy which aims to improve the efficiency of the single market (see Behrens and Smyrl, 1999; De Rynck and McAleavey, 2001). Under the cohesion policies there are significant fiscal transfers from taxpayers in the North to the poorer counties in the East and South. For the main recipient regions, revenues from cohesion policies amount to 3 to 5 per cent of regional GDP. In other words, there is a certain amount of 'fiscal federalism', whereby fiscal transfers are made between territorial units through a central budget.

However, it is not only the poor member states who benefit from the cohesion policies. Over 50 per cent of EU citizens live in regions covered by the regional-based objectives. This is a product of the design of the policy. The policy is primarily a regional policy, whereby transfers are made at the sub-state level, rather than pure fiscal federalism, which would involve transfers between member states. Also, the objectives are designed in such a way that every member state can claim to have a region which qualifies for aid. When measured at the level of the member states, cohesion policy is as much about subsidies for the 'middle-income' member states as it is about improving the living standards of low-income member states.

Cohesion policy is also more about supply-side macroeconomic stabilization than demand-side income support. If it were a classic welfare policy subsidies would be given directly to low-income regions, families or individuals, to spend as they saw fit. Such a policy would increase the spending power of low-income groups, and hence the demand for goods and services in the single market. In contrast, cohesion resources are primarily spent on infrastructure projects, such as improving transport and telecommunications networks and education facilities. This increases the efficient supply of the factors of production (land, labour, and capital), and as a result improves the competitiveness (and comparative advantage) of recipient regions in the single market (Leonardi, 1993; Martin and Rogers, 1996). In other words, the basic aim of the cohesion policies is convergence between regional economies rather than between regional incomes (Anderson, 1995, Bufacchi and Garmise, 1995).

The extent to which the cohesion policies have reduced social and economic disparities is uncertain. At a theoretical level, there is a debate between convergence and divergence theories of regional growth (Leonardi, 1993). On the one hand, convergence in regional incomes may occur naturally in a free market, as capital flows to where land and labour are cheapest (see for example Krugman, 1991). On the other hand, economic integration in a free market could lead to regional divergence as capital flows from the periphery, where infrastructure is weak and demand is low, to the core, where infrastructure is plentiful and there is a high return on investment (Myrdal, 1957).

At an empirical level, in terms of per capita GDP, Leonardi (1993, 1995) found that if convergence is measured as the average deviation from the mean for all regions, between 1960 and 1992 there was considerable convergence in terms of per capita GDP. Because Leonardi accepts the divergence theory, he concludes that this convergence must have been due to the cohesion policies. However, cohesion is not purely about per capita GDP, it is also about reducing other socio-economic disparities. For example, some of the regions with the highest per capita

GDP, such as Hamburg and Bremen, have considerable socio-economic, infrastructural and unemployment problems (Keating, 1995). Steinle (1992) finds that the most competitive EU regions are those with intermediate levels of economic development, and Fagerberg and Verspagen (1996) found that cohesion policies may have actually increased disparities in certain important economic variables, such as access to research and development resources. Finally, Rodriguez-Pose (1998) claims that variations in social conditions and social infrastructure are key factors in determining variations in regional economic performance, and hence whether regions can effectively use EU resources to foster economic growth.

Making cohesion policy: Commission, governments, and regions

As with the CAP, EU cohesion policy is made through a triangular interaction between the main legislative body (the Council), the main executive actors in the Commission, and private interests (the regional authorities). However, unlike the CAP, these three actors do not have mutually reinforcing interests. This produces two competing policy logics rather than a unified iron triangle: intergovernmental bargaining in the Council on the basis of national costs and benefits, versus strategic behaviour by the Commission and the regions to undermine the autonomy of the national governments (Hooghe and Keating, 1994).

The volume of resources available through the structural funds, plus which member states should gain the most and which regions qualify for support, are decided by the governments in the Council. Also, in the implementation of the cohesion policies 90 per cent of funds are spent on 'national initiatives'. At the beginning of each programme period, each national government submits a proposal to the Commission in the form of a regional development plan or a single programming document, on the basis of which two- to six-year regional development programmes are negotiated between the Commission and the national governments, with significant input by the regional authorities concerned. Implementation of the programmes is supervised by monitoring committees which are made up of representatives of the regions, the national governments, and the Commission.

However, the member states are not in full control of cohesion policy as the Commission has introduced four principles, each of which constrains the autonomy of national governments. For example, the principle of 'additionality' has forced several member states to alter their accounting practices for managing the distribution of regional funds, and the principle of 'partnership' has enabled the Commission to bypass national governments and negotiate directly with representatives from the regions on the preparation and implementation of projects and encouraged several member states to set up new regional authorities. The

Commission has also deliberately developed expenditure and programmes under the community initiatives scheme, whereby projects to address European-wide concerns are initiated by the Commission rather than the member states.

Linked to the principle of partnership, representatives of sub-national authorities have sought to influence EU cohesion policies directly. There are approximately 200 offices of regions and local authorities in Brussels (see Chapter 7), many of which have established direct informal contacts with the Regional Policy DG. Senior officials in this directorate-general tend to come from regions that receive substantial resources under the structural funds, and are consequently connected to networks of sub-national elites (see Ansell *et al.*, 1997). Moreover, the Maastricht Treaty established the Committee of the Regions, which provides the representatives of sub-national authorities and assemblies with a formal consultation role in the making and implementation of regional policy (much like that of the European Parliament under the consultation procedure) and has institutionalized transnational contacts between governmental authorities below the level of the state (Loughlin, 1996).

The access to and influence of regions in the EU policy process varies considerably among the member states. In general, the regions in federal states such as Germany and Belgium, and regions with strong identities, as in parts of Spain, Italy, France, and the UK, tend to have the most influence in Brussels (see Conzelmann, 1995; Marks *et al.*, 1996). Nevertheless, several authors claim that EU regional policies have contributed to decentralization and devolution in states where there were no previously regional authorities, as in France, the UK, Portugal, Ireland, and Greece (Balme and Jouve, 1996; Hooghe, 1996b; Ioakimidis, 1996; Jones and Keating, 1995; Nanetti, 1996). There is also some evidence that the partisan composition of the regional authorities matter for the allocation of structural funds (Bouvet and Dall'Erba, 2010; Kemmerling and Bodenstein, 2006).

The EU may be some way from being a 'Europe of regions', where regions replace nation-states as the main territorial unit of the EU political system. But, cohesion policies have pushed the EU towards a 'Europe *with* the regions'. Regions are active players in the EU policy-making process, alongside national governments and the Commission, and the redistribution of resources directly to sub-national territorial units is an integral part of the EU political system.

Other Internal Policies

As noted earlier, approximately 7 per cent of the EU budget is spent on other internal policies. Table 9.3 shows the breakdown of these funds in

Table 9.3   *Expenditure on other internal policies, 2010*

Policy area	Budget in 2010, €m	Per cent of total EU budget	Per cent of other internal policies
Research	5,142.1	3.64	27.56
Energy and transport	4,950.5	3.50	26.53
Information society and media	1,628.3	1.15	8.73
Education and culture	1,500.1	1.06	8.04
Area of freedom, security, and justice	1,066.1	0.75	5.71
Maritime affairs and fisheries	1,001.2	0.71	5.37
Enterprise	795.2	0.56	4.26
Health and consumer protection	676.7	0.48	3.63
Environment	471.4	0.33	2.53
Economic and financial affairs	448.7	0.32	2.40
Direct research	383.3	0.27	2.05
Communication	217.7	0.15	1.17
Taxation and customs union	135.2	0.10	0.72
Competition	90.8	0.06	0.49
Fight against fraud	77.6	0.05	0.42
Internal market	74.0	0.05	0.40
Total	18,658.8	13.19	100.00

Source: Calculated from data in European Commission (2010) *General Budget of the European Union for the Financial Year 2010: The Figures* (Brussels: European Commission).

the 2010 budget. The two largest items of expenditure in this are research and energy and transport, with most of the remaining funds going to information society and media and education and culture.

Research

EU expenditure on research took off in the 1980s, primarily because of concerns that Europe was falling behind the level of technological development in the US and Japan. In 1982, the Commission and the 'big-12' European high-technology firms (including Philips, Siemens, Thomson, and Olivetti) persuaded the governments to agree to the ESPRIT programme (European Strategic Programme for Research and Development in Information Technologies) (see Sandholtz, 1992). The success of ESPRIT enabled the Commission to secure funding for a number of parallel programmes. In the seventh framework programme (2007–13), the budget for research has increased to a massive €50.5 billion over the seven-year period.

The funds for these programmes go to an agreed set of research categories and academic and private researchers bid for funding. In terms of the disciplines covered, the Seventh Framework Programme provided resources in the following areas:

- information and communication technologies (€9.1 billion);
- health (€6 billion);
- transport (including aeronautics) (€4.1 billion);
- nanoproduction (€3.5 billion);
- energy (€2.3 billion);
- food, agriculture and biotechnology (€1.9 billion);
- environment (including climate change) (€1.8 billion);
- security (€1.4 billion);
- space (€1.3 billion); and
- socio-economic sciences and the humanities (€0.6 billion).

The total amount of resources spent on research and the amount for each category is set via Commission–Council–European Parliament negotiations. Since the Maastricht Treaty, the research framework programmes have been adopted through the co-decision procedure (now the ordinary legislative procedure). In the Council, the governments seek to ensure funding for areas of research in which their own universities, public institutions and firms have a particular interest. For example, the UK and Germany, which are home to Europe's leading biotechnology firms, have consistently argued that investment in biotechnology research is essential if Europe is to catch up with Japan and the US. Nevertheless, governments are also careful to restrain the EU budget in this area, and usually reduce the amounts proposed by the Commission. The European Parliament, in contrast, usually reinstates the amounts proposed by the Commission.

Nevertheless, the Commission, in collaboration with the public and private sector elites in the pan-European research community, controls the setting of the overall research policy agenda, for example by determining which types of research should be funded by the EU (Peterson, 1995). When launching the Seventh Framework Programme in 2005 the European Research Council (ERC) was established. Modelled in part on the National Science Foundation in the United States and the various funding bodies in the EU member states, the ERC grants funds to researchers on a competitive basis, via a system of peer review. The ERC is a break from the traditional method of allocating EU research funds through the Commission. Nevertheless, the ERC budget for 2007 to 2013 is only €7.5 billion, and the remaining €43 billion will still be allocated by the Commission.

Other internal policies

Some of the EU budget is devoted to investment in infrastructure, in the broadest meaning of the word. The largest of the areas covered is the

Trans-European Networks (TENs) programme, which was established in 1993 to upgrade infrastructure and foster infrastructural links between the member states in terms of:

- *Information networks*, particularly telecommunications networks.
- *Transportation networks*, particularly high-speed train links.
- *Energy networks*, such as electricity supplies.

Other related areas are the promotion of information exchange between small firms (under 'internal market'), and the promotion of energy efficiency and renewable energy resources (under 'energy'). Many of the projects funded from this part of the EU budget are also supported by loans from the European Investment Bank.

In addition, since the 1970s a portion of the EU budget has been devoted to promoting social integration in Europe. For example the EU spends more than €500 million each year on educational exchanges, cross-border vocational training schemes, and cooperation on youth policies. A major part of this funding goes to the ERASMUS programme, which has enabled a significant proportion of university students (the future European intellectual and professional elite) to spend six months or more studying in another member state. The EU runs the European City of Culture project and helps with the production and distribution of European-made television programmes and films throughout the EU under the MEDIA programme (this comes under the heading of 'culture and audiovisual policy').

Finally, as Laffan (1997, pp. 129–30) points out, 'many obscure budgetary lines are used to create an embryonic civil society that is transnational in nature and to counteract the excessive representation of producer groups in the Union's governance structures'. For example, the EU funds the 'social dialogue' between European-level labour and employers' peak associations (listed under 'other social operations'), and the activities of the European associations representing consumers and environmental groups (see Chapter 7).

Several member states have questioned this use of EU resources, but the Commission argues that the funds are essential to establish a balanced policy community in Brussels, where public and private interests have equal access to decision-makers. Similarly the European Parliament has used its budgetary powers to secure funds for groups with close political links to the political groups or individual MEPs.

In sum, the primary justification for EU expenditure on research and infrastructure is not the redistribution of resources from rich to poor. These policies are mainly supply-side measures to foster macroeconomic stabilization in the EU (Sharp and Pavitt, 1993). On the one hand, they enable resources to be used more productively within the EU, and hence complement the macroeconomic goals of cohesion policy. On the other hand, they aim to increase EU competitiveness vis-à-vis the US and Japan. However, a by-product of EU expenditure on research is the creation of a supranational technocracy around the Commission. As a result, EU research policy also involves a redistribution of resources from taxpayers to the elite scientific community. Similarly, expenditure on civil society measures and social integration can be understood as redistribution from taxpayers to NGOs in Brussels and cultural and social interests in the member states.

Explaining EU Expenditure Policies

There are three interrelated questions about EU expenditure policies that need to be addressed:

1   Why does the EU tax and spend to the amount that it does – in particular, why is the EU budget so small?
2   Why is the bulk of expenditure in two main areas – agriculture and cohesion policy – and what explains the decline of agriculture and the rise of cohesion spending?
3   Why are some individuals, regions and member states net winners, while others are net losers?

When answering these questions, academic analyses have focused on two main explanations: (a) intergovernmental bargaining; and (b) supranational politics.

Intergovernmental bargaining: national cost–benefit calculations

The design of the EU budget is a product of a series of intergovernmental bargains between the governments (e.g. Carrubba, 1997; Mattila, 2006; Rodden, 2002; Webber, 1999). One ways of thinking about this is that the EU budget is an equilibrium outcome of a bargaining game between the governments, in which each government is willing to pay into/take out of the budget exactly how much it believes it will gain/lose from the EU's non-spending policies (such as the single market and monetary union). As a result, changes in the expenditure policies of the EU, and particularly expansions of the budget and increases in spending on the main policy areas, occur because the losers from the process of economic integration and regulation demand fiscal compensation (see Moravcsik, 1993, 1998; Pollack, 1995, pp. 363–73). Equally, cuts in EU expenditure, particularly on the CAP, proceed only if those states which benefit most from the budget – such as France in the case of the CAP – can be 'bought off' with other policies. If other policy benefits are not available, reform is virtually impossible (see Akrill, 2000b; Meunier, 1998; Sheingate, 2000).

From this perspective, the CAP was originally set up in the Treaty of Rome to support French farmers in return for German access to French industrial markets. Similarly, the ERDF was established as part of the package that secured British and Irish accession to the EU. In the Single European Act, the doubling of the structural funds was explicitly linked to the completion of the single market, which Spain, Ireland, Greece, and Portugal argued would primarily benefit the core economies of the EU at the expense of those on the periphery. And, in the Maastricht Treaty the cohesion fund was Spain's price for supporting the German-oriented design of EMU.

When bargaining over the budget in the multiannual financial frameworks, governments carefully calculate how much they will gain or lose from other EU policies, such as trade liberalization in the single market. If a member state is a net exporter to the rest of the EU, its industries will be able to secure new markets as a result of the single market and EMU (see Frieden, 1991). Conversely, if a state is net importer from the other member states, its production will be predominantly for the national market and its industries will suffer under competitive pressure from importers as a result of trade liberalization. Figure 9.3 consequently

Figure 9.3   *EU trade balances and net budgetary contributions, 2000–6*

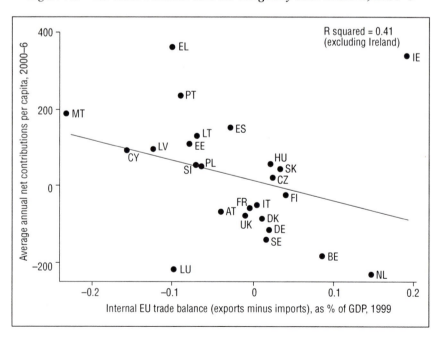

Source: Calculated from Commission annual budget reports and Eurostat data.

Figure 9.4   *Solidarity and net contributions, 2000–6*

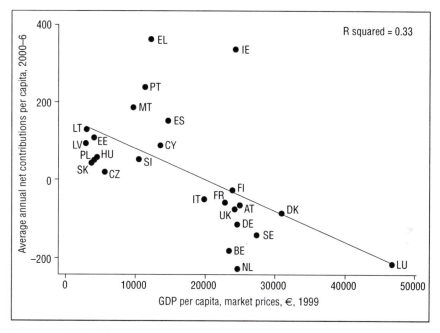

Source: Calculated from Commission annual budget reports and Eurostat data.

shows that the more a member state was a net importer from the rest of the EU in 1999 – when the 2000 to 2006 financial framework was agreed – the more it received from the EU budget in 2000 to 2006; while the more a member state was a net exporter to the rest of the EU in 1999, the more it paid in 2000 to 2006 – with the notable exception of Ireland, which is a large net exporter and a large budget recipient.

Figure 9.4 considers a traditional solidarity-based explanation of EU budget outcomes: that resources are primarily transferred from richer to poorer states (De La Fuente and Domenech, 2001). This also explains a significant amount of who gets what under the EU budget, which challenges a simple cost–benefit explanation.

The big outliers in both these explanations are Ireland and Greece. This can be explained by their bargaining power in budgetary negotiations (Mattila, 2004; Rodden, 2002). Because multiannual financial frameworks require unanimous agreement between all the governments, every state has equal bargaining power, regardless of how small they are. This means that any state which is a major net recipient can threaten to block agreement unless it continues to receive funds from the EU. Ireland and Greece were major recipients of EU cohesion funds prior to the 2000 to 2006 deal. As a result, when negotiating the new agreement they were able to secure benefits which far exceed how much these two states reasonable could have been expected to received given the GDP per capita or how well they do out of the single market. Hence, despite Ireland's dramatic increase in per capita GDP in the 1990s, which should have made it a net contributor rather than a recipient in the 2000 to 2006 budget, Ireland was able to maintain many of its subsidies in the negotiations in Berlin in 1999. Also, in these negotiations, the holders of the presidency may be able to use their proposal power to secure a larger share of the budget (Aksoy, 2010).

Supranational politics: private interests, policy entrepreneurship, and institutional rules

The main alternative explanation to the intergovernmental view focuses on the role of interest groups, the Commission, and decision-making rules in shaping EU expenditure policies.

Starting with interest groups, the benefits of EU expenditure policies are reaped at the individual level or by groups at a sub-state level. The benefits accruing to individual farmers under the CAP, individual recipient regions under cohesion policies, and individual scientists under EU research policy are far greater than the costs to individual taxpayers in the EU. As a result, farmers have a powerful lobbying voice in Brussels (through COPA), and have campaigned continuously against reform of the CAP (Keeler, 1996). Similarly, a key determinant of whether a regional authority sets up an office in Brussels is whether it comes under Objective 1, 2, or 3 (see Keating and Jones, 1995, pp. 1008; Marks *et al.*, 1996). However, some of the poorer and peripheral regions lack the bureaucratic capacity to lobby effectively in Brussels, and hence make the most of their opportunities to form 'partnerships' with the Commission (Bailey and De Propris, 2002). Non-European multinational firms have been able to secure participation in ESPRIT and other research and development programmes through continued lobbying of the Commission and member state governments (Wyatt-Walker, 1995). Also, private consultants and lobbying firms in Brussels sell advice to numerous private and public interest groups on securing a grant from the EU budget (Laffan, 1997, pp. 90–3).

Furthermore, the expenditure game is not simply a battle between governments or interest groups. As the referee of this game, the Commission can use its agenda-setting powers to shape policy outcomes and promote its institutional interests (Peters, 1992, 1994; Pollack, 1997; Tsebelis and Garrett, 1996). In the everyday bargaining process of EU politics, to secure the approval of its policy proposals by the Council and the European Parliament, the Commission has an incentive to support key governments and influential societal groups and private interests. The Commission has played a central role in shaping the two sets of CAP reforms as well as the development of cohesion and research policies (e.g. Coleman, 1998; Daugbjerg, 2003; Skogstad, 1998). For example, during the 1993 negotiations on reform of the structural funds the Commission successfully achieved a more substantial package of funds for the regions than most governments had in mind at the beginning of the negotiations (Hooghe, 1996a; Marks, 1996).

Finally, the decision-making rules governing expenditure policies have made a difference. The annual budgetary procedure provides for QMV in the Council. QMV gives the Commission more agenda-setting power than unanimity (see Chapter 3). As a result, within the overall constraints of the multiannual financial framework, this has enabled the Commission to have a significant influence over policy outcomes. For example, during the redesign of the structural funds in 1993 the French and British governments were opposed to the Commission's plan but were unable to block majority support for the reforms (Marks, 1996). Under the new annual budgetary procedure established by the Lisbon Treaty, the European Parliament will be equally influential under all budgetary headings, which could enable the political groups and MEPs shape policy outcomes in much the same way as the Commission was able to do under the old budgetary procedure.

Furthermore, the strict 'balanced-budget' rule – whereby EU expenditure must not exceed EU income – places a significant institutional constraint on the evolution of EU budgetary policies. Having to reach an agreement without such a rule would probably lead to a rapid expansion of the EU budget, as each member state would come to the table with a separate demand – rather like every cabinet ministers asking the finance minister for funds for their particular projects, which has led to budgetary expansion in many countries. When there is a tight fiscal constraint, competing budgetary claims have to be balanced in some way. For example, Akrill (2000a) points out that the balanced-budget rule and the expenditure ceiling of 1 per cent of EU GNP forced the member states to accept CAP reform in the early 1990s. Without the budgetary ceiling, it would have been easier for the member states to allow agriculture spending to continue to rise than to face up to the need for reform.

Conclusion: a Set of Redistributive Bargains

As in other democratic political systems, the dominant outcome of EU public expenditure policies is redistribution. This is an inevitable product of political bargaining in a democratic polity. Once redistributive policies are in place they are difficult to reform. Redistribution creates entrenched interests that are willing to spend resources to protect their subsidies. The CAP would be easier to reform if it were purely about price stability, as would cohesion policy if it were purely about infrastructure investment.

The fact that these policies have become welfare policies for farmers and regions, respectively, means that it is unlikely that the net contributor states and EU taxpayers will be able to secure a fundamental reform of these policies without a major external shock.

The result is a set of redistributive bargains: between the amount the recipient groups can gain, and how much contributor states and tax-payers are willing to pay. But, three such external shocks are now working their way through the system: EMU, the expansion of the EU to Central and Eastern Europe, and the fall-out from the global economic crisis in 2008 to 2010. These developments may unbalance the delicate equilibrium of EU expenditure policies and prompt new redistributive bargains.

Chapter 10

Economic and Monetary Union

Economic and monetary union (EMU) was launched on 1 January 1999 and euro notes and coins were introduced in 12 EU states on 1 January 2002, and by 2011 the eurozone had grown to 17 of the 27 EU states. This chapter seeks to explain why some member states decided to replace their national currencies with the euro, while other did not; and explain how the EMU works. We start by looking at some general theories of monetary union.

The Political Economy of Monetary Union

According to the theory of optimal currency areas (OCA), independent states form a currency union if the benefits of joining exceed the costs (Mundell, 1961). The main cost is the loss of the possibility of using the interest rate as a macroeconomic policy tool. In classical economic theory, this tool can be used to protect economies from varying economic conditions between states. A basic law of economics is the existence of cycles, times of high economic growth ('boom') are followed by recession ('bust'), which are followed by growth, and so on. If two states are in different stages of the cycle, they are likely to pursue different monetary policies. A government facing a recession would want to cut interest rates to stimulate demand or devalue the currency to make its export sector more competitive internationally. A government facing high growth would like to increase interest rates in order to dampen pressure on prices and wages or revaluate the currency to lower the cost of imports and increase the per-unit value of exports. These options do not exist in a monetary union as exchange rates are fixed and there are common interest rates.

However, asymmetries in economic cycles or asymmetric economic shocks can be addressed by other means, including:

245

- *Labour mobility:* the unemployed in the state where there is a recession could move to take up jobs in the state where there is high growth.
- *Wage flexibility/capital mobility:* workers in the state where there is low demand could reduce their wages, thereby attracting mobile capital from the high demand country.
- *Fiscal transfers:* the state in recession can run a budgetary deficit, spending the extra resources in policies that increase the domestic demand.

Fiscal transfers and budgetary deficits are only temporary solutions to asymmetric economic performance. If the fall in demand is due to changing fundamentals of the economy rather than a cyclical downturn, the state risks making a budget deficit a permanent feature or becoming dependent on fiscal transfers. Moreover, if fiscal transfers and budget deficits become permanent features, they risk becoming substitutes for wage and price changes and may prevent labour from moving to obtain jobs. According to the OCA theory, a state faced with asymmetric shocks should consider two alternative strategies: (a) to devalue its currency; or (b) to combine stable exchange rates with wage reductions and increased labour mobility. If the economic and social costs of the second strategy are more painful than the first, then Mundell (1961) concluded that a state should not join a monetary union.

However, there are three problems with this original formulation of the OCA theory. First, a single currency may have other benefits that can outweigh the cost of giving up floating exchange rates. Second, modern macroeconomic theory questions the value of currency devaluation as a macroeconomic policy tool. Third, the OCA theory ignores political calculations related to macroeconomic policy decisions.

Starting with the first of these issues, the main economic benefits of a single currency are as follows (De Grauwe, 2003; Eichengreen, 1990):

- *Lower transaction costs:* by removing the cost of exchanging currencies, firms involved in trade between states do not have to pay exchange rate commissions or insure themselves against currency fluctuations.
- *A more efficient market:* a common currency reduces the possibility of price discrimination, eliminates the information costs of consuming goods and locating businesses across borders, and hence promotes market integration and market efficiency.
- *Greater economic certainty:* exchange-rate stability increases the certainty of prices and revenues, which improves the quality of production, investment, and consumption decisions (which in turn increases collective welfare).

- *Lower interest rates:* greater economic certainty reduces the risk premium on interest rates and interest rates are hence more likely to be lower in a larger economy and in an economy that is less exposed to trade in a foreign currency.
- *Higher economic growth:* 'new growth' theorists argue that larger and more integrated economies with greater productivity, more capital accumulation, better information, more economies of scale and lower interest rates can maintain higher levels of economic growth.

Some of these benefits are disputed. Supporters of monetary union in Europe tend to overemphasize the potential for lower interest rates and higher growth rates. Reduction in exchange rate uncertainty does not necessarily reduce the systematic risk in the economy as political decision-makers may compensate for the loss of exchange rate manipulation by increased use of other monetary instruments (Poole, 1970). Furthermore, the empirical evidence supporting the new growth theory is weak in both Europe and the US, and the theoretical argument has been questioned (Krugman, 1998). The market efficiency gains are unlikely to materialize in the short term and the reduction in transaction costs arising from the elimination of currency exchange must be weighted against the loss to the banking industry of revenues from service charges on currency exchange, estimated to account for 5 per cent of European banks' total revenues before the launch of the EMU. Nevertheless, even if non-certain benefits are discounted, some transaction costs will disappear as a result of the removal of currency speculation and exchange for firms involved in cross-border trade in a currency union. The European Commission estimated, somewhat optimistically, that the benefits of removing these cost could amount to savings of 0.25 to 0.5 per cent of EU GDP (European Commission, 1990).

The second problem with the OCA theory relates to the feasibility of using the exchange rate as a shock absorber. Although devaluation will increase demand for exported goods by lowering their price in foreign markets, the long-term devaluation is an increase in the price of imported goods, which in turn raises the costs of production and provokes demand for higher domestic wages. Consequently, the long-term effects of manipulating the exchange rates are higher prices and lower output. The exchange rate is thus an inefficient fix for countries experiencing economic difficulties. The long-term benefits of a floating currency are hence less than the OCA assumes, which means that the costs of joining a currency union will be smaller as well.

As for the third weakness of the OCA theory, political considerations often override economic calculations. The ideological orientation of voters and elites may influence preferences over inflation, unemployment, welfare protection, and government debt. The centre-left may pursue a high level of employment and welfare protection by means of high taxes and public debt. A government of this political orientation may be unable to enforce wage reductions or labour market reforms to attract capital investments. Thus a government in a high-wage/low-growth state may conclude that the costs of the structural adjustment needed for monetary union are too high, and therefore opt for maintaining a separate currency. Alternatively, the public may support economic and political union for non-economic reasons. The public may have a high level of 'affective' support for political integration even if they perceive that it may make them economically worse off in the short term (see Chapter 5). In this case, a government in a low-growth state may use the promise of economic and political integration to implement structural adjustment programmes. Conversely, in a high-growth state, public support for currency union may enable a government to sanction fiscal transfers to other states to maintain the currency union.

Finally, there are two other political implications of currency union to consider alongside the potential economic costs and benefits:

1   *A single voice in the global economy*: a single currency has consequences for international political economy. In the case of the EU, the euro may rival the US dollar as the dominant global currency, which would give the EU political clout on global economic issues.
2   *A step towards political union*: a single currency is likely to facilitate further political integration, through pressures for fiscal transfers and tax harmonization, demands for political government over monetary policy, and the emergence of new allegiances towards the EU institutions.

Citizens in favour of political integration may view these as potential benefits of monetary union, while citizens opposed to political integration may view them as costs. These mass political preferences will influence the elite's calculations when deciding whether to establish or join a monetary union.

In sum, the main cost of monetary union is the inability to reduce the exchange rate or adjust the interest rate to absorb a demand shock. However, this cost must be weighted against the long-term ineffectiveness of devaluation and growth generated by artificially low interest rates and the potential economic benefits of a single currency, particularly lower transaction costs. In addition, these economic calculations may be constrained by publics' and governments' political preferences over inflation, the level of unemployment, wage levels, labour market policies, and the desirability of further political integration.

Development of Economic and Monetary Union in Europe

While the Maastricht Treaty set out the plan for EMU, the idea of an economic and monetary union was discussed during the negotiations on the Treaty of Rome back in 1956. Two precursors to the Maastricht plan were important for the preparation and design of EMU (Dyson, 1994). The first was the Werner Report of 1971, which proposed that EMU be introduced by 1980. This never materialized due to the recession of the mid-1970s. The second precursor was the Economic and Monetary System (EMS), set up in 1979. EMS had two elements: a basket of currencies (the ECU), weighted according to the strengths of the participating currencies; and an exchange-rate mechanism (ERM), consisting of a central ECU rate with permissible band of fluctuation of ±2.25 per cent and a system for trading currencies to ensure that they stayed within that band. The system collapsed during the international currency crises of 1992, when the Italian and British currencies were expelled from the EMS and the band of fluctuation widened to ±15 per cent for the remaining currencies.

The Delors Report

The 1985 Single European Act proposed that EMU should be an eventual goal of the EU, but did not set out how this could be achieved. In 1988 the governments set up a committee chaired by Commission President Jacques Delors to prepare a report on the best way to launch EMU. The committee was composed of two Commissioners, the central bank governors of the then 12 member states, and three independent experts. The final report of the committee, the Delors Report, was delivered to the European Council in June 1989 (Committee for the Study of Economic and Monetary Union, 1989).

The report argued that monetary union should involve the irrevocable fixing of exchange rates (not necessarily with a single set of notes and coins), complete liberalization of capital transactions, and the integration of banking and financial markets. It proposed that economic union should involve a single market, competition policies to strengthen market mechanisms, common policies aimed at structural change and regional development (with the possibility of significant fiscal transfers), and macroeconomic policy coordination with binding rules on budget deficits. The report set out a three-stage plan to achieve these goals:

1   Stage I: the introduction of free capital movement and the start of macroeconomic coordination between the member state governments by 1 July 1990.

2   Stage II: treaty reform to establish the institutional structure of EMU, including a European system of central banks and restricted fluctuation margins for national currencies.
3   Stage III: the fixing of exchange rates and the establishment of an independent European Central Bank, with the single goal of maintaining price stability.

The Delors Report suggested a phased approach, but was careful not to define it too precisely. Drawing on the experience from the EMS, the committee emphasized the importance of economic coordination and convergence as a precondition for monetary union. The plan also reflected a compromise. While Delors' aim was to design a project that would be irreversible, the governor of the German Bundesbank, Karl Otto Pöhl, wanted to be certain that the single currency would be as stable as the Deutschmark, arguing for constraints on national deficits and a fully independent European Central Bank.

The Delors Committee did not comment on whether the project was desirable. But under the direction of Delors, the Commission soon made its position clear. In October 1990, the Commission published a report entitled 'One Market, One Money', which argued that the full benefits of the single market could only be realized with a single currency (European Commission, 1990).

The Maastricht Treaty design

In June 1990 the governments decided to convene an Intergovernmental Conference (IGC) to prepare the treaty reforms needed to implement Delors' proposals. In October 1990 the government agreed by a majority (Margaret Thatcher voted against) that the IGC would propose a fixed timetable for Stage III. The IGC concluded in December 1991, when the governments signed the Maastricht Treaty.

The Maastricht Treaty provided the legal framework for launching EMU. First, the treaty set out the timetable. Stage II was set for January 1994, when the European Monetary Institute would be established to prepare the ground for Stage III. Stage III would then start in one of two ways: (a) by choice, in January 1997, if a majority of EU states met the set of required economic conditions; or (b) automatically, on 1 January 1999, with participation by those EU states which met the required criteria. The Maastricht Treaty indicated that EMU could not be cancelled or postponed without breach of the EU Treaty.

Second, the treaty set out four 'convergence criteria' for qualifying for membership of EMU:

1   *Price stability:* an average inflation rate of no greater than 1.5 per cent above the inflation rates in the three best-performing member states.

2 *Interest rates:* an average nominal long-term interest rate no greater than 2 per cent above the interest rates of the three best-performing member states.
3 *Government budgetary position:* an annual current account deficit not exceeding 3 per cent of GDP and a gross public debt ratio not exceeding 60 per cent of GDP.
4 *Currency stability:* membership of the narrow band of the ERM (with fluctuations of less than 2.5 per cent around the central rate) for at least two years, with no devaluations.

Third, the treaty set out the institutional structure of the European Central Bank (ECB) and the European System of Central Banks (ESCB), with a small executive board appointed by the European Council and a governing council comprising the executive board the governors of the national central banks.

Fourth, the treaty set out how monetary policy would operate in EMU:

- *An independent Central Bank:* 'neither the ECB, nor a national central bank, nor any member of the decision-making bodies shall seek or take instructions from Community institutions or bodies, from any government of a member state or from any other body' (Article 130).
- *A main goal of price stability:* 'the primary objective of the ESCB shall be to maintain price stability. Without prejudice to the objective of price stability, the ESCB shall support the economic policies in the Community with a view to contributing to the achievement of the objectives of the Community' (Article 127) (the 'objectives of the Communities' set out in Article 2 of the treaty include 'economic progress' and 'full employment').
- *The role of the ECB in monetary policy:* the basic tasks of the ECB and ESCB would be to define and implement monetary policy, conduct foreign exchange operations, hold and manage the official reserves of the member states, and promote the smooth operation of payment systems.
- *The role of the Council in monetary policy:* the Council of Economic and Finance Ministers (Ecofin) would have the final say on interventions in foreign exchange markets (by unanimity), could conclude monetary arrangements with third countries (by QMV), and would decide the position of the EU in international relations on issues relating to EMU (by QMV).
- *The role of the Council in economic policy:* Ecofin would conduct 'multilateral surveillance' through the adoption of common economic policy guidelines (drafted in cooperation with the Commission) and collective scrutiny of how the governments implemented these

guidelines; Ecofin would also be responsible for imposing fines on member states with excessive budget deficits.

Who qualifies? Fudging the convergence criteria

Before the Maastricht Treaty came into effect in November 1993 the EMS was hit by an international currency crisis. It soon became clear that the majority of the governments would not be able to meet the convergence criteria by the 1997 deadline. By 1996 a 'two-speed EMU' appeared the most likely outcome. A small set of states whose currencies were closely linked to the Deutschmark (Germany, France, the Netherlands, Luxembourg, Austria, and Belgium) could go ahead in 1999, while the states with weaker currencies (Spain, Italy, Portugal, Ireland, Greece, and Finland) could join at a later date. The Swedish, Danish, and British governments indicated that they were unlikely to join due to concerns about national sovereignty. Denmark and the UK had negotiated 'opt-outs' from EMU in the Maastricht Treaty, while Sweden had not.

The currency crisis had the effect of strengthening the belief among many elites that irrevocably fixing exchange rates and delegating the responsibility for monetary policy to a supranational central bank were essential to isolate the EU economy from the vagaries of international currency speculation (Henning, 1998). Rather than abandoning the project, the currency crisis made the likely second-tier governments more determined than ever to join EMU in order to constrain the power of international currency speculators (Cobham, 1996; Jones *et al.*, 1998; Sandholtz, 1996).

The Spanish, Portuguese, and Italian governments made huge budgetary cuts. The Italian government re-entered the ERM in November 1996 and introduced a one-off 'Europe tax' to reduce its budget deficit to below the 3 per cent target. The Finnish government joined the ERM and introduced a series of macroeconomic reforms. Ireland became the fastest growing economy in Europe, allowing the government to reduce its public debt and revalue the currency in the ERM. Consequently, in May 1998, the governments supported the Commission's proposal that EMU should be launched between 11 member states, even though only three had met all the convergence criteria.

The Commission argued that the gross public debt criterion was less important than the annual deficit criterion, and it was more important for the gross public debt figures to be falling. This was clearly not the case for Belgium and Italy. But Belgium was already in a currency union with Luxembourg, which would have to be broken up if Belgium could not join EMU. Moreover, the Belgian economy was small relative to the eurozone.

The Italian case was more problematic. Both the German Bundesbank and the German government were opposed to allowing Italy to join, believing that Italian entry would undermine the stability of the new currency and defeat the object of the convergence criteria. Nonetheless, with the backing of the Commission and the French government, which feared a devaluation of the lira if Italy remained outside EMU, the Italian prime minister Romano Prodi managed to persuade the other governments that he could implement a budgetary plan that would significantly reduce Italy's debt by 2002. The admittance of Italy to EMU was clearly a political compromise. Greece was the only member that wished to join in 1997 but was excluded for not meeting the convergence criteria. It eventually joined on 1 January 2001.

Denmark, Sweden, and the UK made a political decision not to join EMU at its launch. Denmark and the UK invoked their treaty opt-outs, while Sweden simply decided not to join. Denmark and Sweden held referendums on joining, in May 2000 and September 2003 respectively, but membership was rejected by the electorates in both states, despite campaigns in favour by the two governments and a majority of the public supporting euro membership when the referendums were called. However, as the euro fell in the currency markets in the run-up to the referendums, the public opted for holding onto their national currencies (Hobolt and Leblond, 2009; Jupille and Leblang, 2007). In the UK, in 1997 the newly elected Labour government promised to hold a referendum on the issue. But it soon became clear that the Chancellor of the Exchequer, Gordon Brown, was less enthusiastic about membership than prime minister Tony Blair. By 2004 the prospect of a referendum had receded, following a negative assessment of the economic case for EMU membership by Gordon Brown, the Scandinavian referendum results, and the shift of focus of the European debate in the UK to the proposed EU Constitution.

Then, several of the new Eastern and Southern European member states also joined the euro. Slovenia joined in 2007, Cyprus and Malta in 2008, Slovakia in 2009, and Estonia in 2011. In addition, Latvia and Lithuania have pegged their currencies to the euro via the ERM II arrangements, as has Denmark, and several of the other new member states are seeking to join.

In the end, the agreement to launch involved several political compromises. Since more member states looked set to join than the German government had expected, Germany proposed a 'Stability Pact' to prevent governments from running large deficits once EMU was launched. This was opposed by the French socialist government, which had been elected on a platform that was critical of the monetarist design of EMU. A Franco-German deal was eventually reached, which introduced fines for wayward governments (conditional on QMV in Ecofin) and for cosmetic reasons the agreement was called the 'Stability and Growth Pact'.

Furthermore, the French government managed to secure support for a political element to EMU, via a new 'Euro Committee' to oversee the management of the single currency, among the finance ministers of the participating member states. The intention behind this initiative became clear when the French finance minister described it as the 'economic government of the Euro'. The German government insisted that such a committee should not compromise the independence of the ECB, while the British government feared that it would gradually replace Ecofin as the main economic organ of the EU. As a further compromise, the governments agreed that the committee would focus on technical issues and policy questions specific to the eurozone states, and that Ecofin would remain the main forum for macroeconomic policy coordination. Unlike the Stability and Growth Pact, this was seen as a victory for the French government, as it soon became clear that the Euro Committee would be the main macroeconomic policy arena in EMU.

Finally, there was a compromise deal over the first President of the ECB. Until 1997 most member states had accepted that Wim Duisenberg, a former governor of the Dutch central bank and President of the EMI, would be given the job. But the French government proposed Jean-Claude Trichet, the French central bank governor as a rival candidate. The French government claimed that there was an informal agreement between François Mitterrand and Helmut Kohl that in return for the ECB being located in Frankfurt, the first President of the bank would be French. The German government disputed this interpretation, but the then French President, Jacques Chirac, threatened to veto Duisenberg. A deal was eventually struck in May 1998, that Duisenberg would be appointed as the first President with the understanding that he would retire halfway through his tenure. Trichet then took over as ECB President in November 2003.

Explaining Economic and Monetary Union

Several aspects of this story need to be explained. Why was monetary union launched at the time it was? Why was it designed in the way it was – with three stages, convergence criteria, an independent central bank, the goal of price stability, and the Stability and Growth Pact? Why did certain countries join but not others? Four main explanations have been proposed: (a) economic rationality; (b) intergovernmental bargaining; (c) supranational politics; and (d) the dominance of neo-liberal ideas about monetary policy.

Economic rationality: economic integration and a core optimal currency area

The cost and benefits of forming a single currency union vary according to the degree of economic integration of the states involved (Krugman,

1990). The benefits of monetary union increase as trade between the state increases (Cameron, 1997). More economic integration means removal of the transaction costs of currency exchange. Moreover, as trade increases, the cost of surrendering the exchange rate as an instrument of macroeconomic policy falls. As the structural conditions of the economy levels out, due to more efficient allocation of resources due to the single currency and the gradual synchronization of economic cycles, the likelihood of asymmetric shocks declines. Thus, as trade integration increases, the need to use an independent exchange rate recedes.

When the expected benefits increase and the expected costs fall, there will be a point where it makes rational economic sense to form or join a currency union. It is difficult to tell when this point was reached by the EU member states. In the mid-1990s, the level of imports and exports between the member states varied considerably. For the larger economies, intra-EU trade accounted for less than one-quarter of their GDP, while for many of the smaller economies intra-EU trade accounted for more than one-half of their GDP. Moreover, for Germany, the core economy of the EU, trade with the rest of the world was almost as large as trade with the rest of the EU. In other words, when the decision was taken to launch EMU, on the basis of simple economic cost–benefit calculations, the smaller states were more likely to benefit than the larger states.

The data show that between 1994 and 2003 trade integration proceeded faster for the eurozone states than for the non-eurozone states. However, between 2003 and 2008 many of the states in the eurozone experienced a substantive drop in intra-EU trade, while states outside the eurozone did not experience this drop. This suggests that once the decision to adopt a single the single currency was made, eurozone trade increased, but as the novelty faded other factors became more important for the trajectory of EU trade.

Nevertheless, empirical analysis of the EU economy suggests that the EU is not an optimal currency area, particularly compared with the US (Caporale, 1993; De Grauwe and Vanhaverbeke, 1993; Eichengreen, 1990; Feldstein, 1992). First, the economic performances of the member states differ markedly, so asymmetric economic cycles are likely to be frequent and persistent. Second, there is a relatively low degree of labour market flexibility in the European economy, both in terms of labour mobility between states and the flexibility of wages. However, an optimal currency area may exist between the core EU economies (Dornbusch, 1990). Although the labour markets of these states may not be sufficiently flexible, the economic cycles of Germany, France, and the Benelux countries are closely linked.

In sum, economic logic may be able to explain why EMU was launched in the 1990s, but it offers at best a partial explanation of why certain states joined and others did not. Economics suggests that EMU should have been launched only between a small number of closely integrated states. Economics cannot explain why Italy and Spain joined when they had comparatively low levels of trade integration and potentially divergent economic cycles, but Denmark did not despite its comparatively high level of trade integration. Most economists also accept that economics cannot explain the chosen design of EMU, with three stages, the convergence criteria, and a specific institutional structure (Artis, 1996; Crowley, 1996). These questions are more convincingly answered by politics than economics.

Intergovernmental bargaining: a Franco-German deal

The institutional design of EMU was the product of unanimous bargaining among the governments over the Maastricht Treaty (Eichengreen and Frieden, 2001; Hosli, 2000; Sandholtz, 1993; Moravcsik, 1998). Two inherently contradictory forces operate in this strategic context. First, the government with the least to lose from non-agreement on a policy stands the best chance to secure an outcome close to its most preferred policy, as this government does not need to compromise. In contrast, a government that stands to lose a lot from non-agreement will be willing to make concessions. Second, because agreement has to be reached by unanimity, the result is a package deal, where issues are added to the agenda so that each government can get something from the final agreement. In this situation, the government with the least to lose in one area may be willing compromise in order to secure its interests in other areas.

Both of these dynamics were important in the politics of EMU. First, the design of EMU was essentially a German plan (Moravcsik, 1993, 1998): the convergence criteria, the independence of the ECB, and the central goal of price stability were all demanded by the German government as conditions for its approval of EMU. By these means the German government hoped that EMU would be an optimal currency area, as only a few states would be likely to meet the conditions and therefore the euro would be as stable as the Deutschmark. The German government, backed by the Bundesbank, was prepared to veto the whole project and continue with the EMS, which was effectively run by the Bundesbank. The hegemony of Germany in the EMS was illustrated in the ERM crisis of 1992 to 1993, when the Bundesbank dictated which states should leave the ERM and the price to be paid by the remaining members (Cameron, 1993; Smith and Sandholtz, 1995). Meanwhile, the other governments were prepared to pay the German price to regain some say over monetary policy. In EMU, the common interest rate would be set for the European economy as a whole rather than just for Germany, and all the member states' central bank governors would have a say in the ECB.

However, certain aspects of the package deal and the final design of

EMU were not completely to Germany's liking. The French government extracted painful concessions from Germany. In the institutional design, Germany accepted the establishment of the ECB Governing Council, where the ECB Executive Board could potentially be outvoted by national central bank governors as well as a political role for Ecofin in the management of external exchange rate policy (Garrett, 1994). Also, while the German government got its way with the Stability and Growth Pact, the French government secured the creation of the Euro Committee and successfully politicized the choice of the ECB President.

Germany also had little to gain from monetary union with high inflation countries such as Italy, Spain, and even France. But, cross-border investors in and exporters of sophisticated manufactured goods and the trade unions that worked in these sectors – both of which are powerful economic interests in Germany – gained considerably from fixed exchange rates with their main export or investment markets and therefore strove to persuade the German government to support a broader membership of EMU (Frieden, 2002; Josselin, 2001). Some scholars also claim that Germany was willing to make concessions on the precise design of EMU because it had a political interest in maintaining the pace of political integration in Europe following German reunification and the collapse of the Soviet Union (Dyson *et al.*, 1994; Kaltenthaler, 2002; McKay, 1996; Woolley, 1994). In this view, EMU was part of a historic package deal between France and Germany, with France supporting German reunification in return for Germany giving up the Deutschmark.

Supranational politics: the Commission and central bankers

An alternative view is that the timing and institutional design of EMU were the result of supranational politics rather than intergovernmental bargaining. The most influential supranational actor in setting the agenda of EMU was the Commission (Dyson, 1994; Dyson and Featherstone, 1999; Sandholtz, 1993; Smith and Sandholtz, 1995). Since the 1960s, several Commissioners and prominent figures in the Commission's administration had argued for monetary union. But it was not until Jacques Delors took over as President that the Commission openly pursued a strategy to secure EMU. Delors had considerable experience in the field of monetary policy. In his capacity as French finance minister Delors had engineered the U-turn in French monetary policy in the early 1980s. He was also ideologically committed to the goal of monetary union. He successfully argued that the governments should set up a committee under his leadership to prepare a plan for EMU and his strategic use of expertise and information was crucial in changing the perceptions of EMU and the institutional preferences of central bankers, employer organizations, and trade unions (Jabko, 1999; Verdun, 2000).

For example, it was Delors' idea that EMU should progress in a series of stages, with economic convergence being pursued in parallel to the technical and institutional preparations for the launch of the single currency. Once each stage had been completed it would be politically very difficult to take a step backwards, as this would have a negative impact on the credibility of the EU as a whole. Most economists argued that Delors' strategy did not make sense, and few governments supported the idea at its inception. However, due to the absence of a coherent alternative plan, his model was institutionalized as the collective strategy.

The other main non-state actors to play an important role in EMU were the central bank governors, who shared common strategic interests in the project (Verdun, 1999). EMU would guarantee their independence from political interference by national finance ministers, and they would each participate in making EU monetary policy in the ECB Governing Council. These actors also shared similar ideas about how monetary policy should be managed, and were able to offer considerable expertise on numerous technical issues in the transition to EMU, such as how a payment system should be designed and run. Their national governments delegated particular responsibilities to them. All the central bank governors sat on the Delors Committee. It was also in the interest of governments to secure credible technical advice and ensure that EMU was supported by the people who would be running EU monetary policy, and once the governments had delegated important design issues to the governors, the governments had limited control over the actions of the central bankers and the ideas they put forwards.

The power of ideas: the monetarist policy consensus

Another key factor, according to McNamara (1998), was the emergence of a 'monetarist policy consensus' in Europe by the end of the 1980s. This consensus grew in response to the policy failure in the 1970s, when Keynesian demand management policies had proved inadequate for coping with slow growth, high unemployment, and high inflation. Monetarism emerged as an alternative economic paradigm which at the time seemed theoretically coherent and empirically successful. At a theoretical level, monetarism offered a convincing critique of why there was no inherent trade-off between unemployment and inflation, as predicted by the Phillips curve (Friedman, 1968). At an empirical level, meanwhile, the German economic growth of the 1970s and early 1980s provided a successful example of monetarist policies. Centre-right parties now had a 'big idea' against the Keynesian hegemony of the 1960s and 1970s. As Keynesian policies failed, monetarist policies became increasingly accepted by political parties and international organizations (McCracken, 1977), and as centre-right parties won elections across Europe in the 1980s, centre-left parties began to reject their old policies and accept these new economic ideas.

Monetarist economists argued that manipulating exchange rates (an aspect of Keynesian demand management) would only bring short-term benefits. The long-term effects would be wage and price inflation. They insisted that stable or even fixed exchange rates, combined with wage flexibility and labour market reforms, offered the only long-term cure for low productivity.

To understand what this meant for EMU, compare the Keynesian and monetarist interpretation of the cost and benefits of monetary union. The Keynesian view is that the world is full of rigidities – wages and prices are stable and labour is immobile – so the exchange rate is a powerful tool for macroeconomic management. This implies that the cost of fixing exchange rates falls slowly as trade integration increases (Minford, 1996). In contrast, the monetarist view is that the exchange rate is an ineffective tool, and the costs of losing this tool fall rapidly as trade integration increases. Hence, monetarists supported fixed exchange rates in a monetary union at considerably lower levels of economic and trade integration than Keynesians (Bofinger, 1994).

These ideas gradually gained force from the end of the 1970s and prevailed until the 1990s. As early as 1975 *The Economist* published an 'All Saints' Day Manifesto', written by several prominent monetarists, calling for a revival of the idea of EMU (*The Economist*, 1 November 1975: 33). The German government, supported by the Bundesbank – one of the primary architects of monetarism in Europe – used similar ideas to justify the EMS. And, the Commission DG in change of economic and monetary affairs was full of monetarists who prepared the Commission's strategy for the Delors Committee and wrote the 'One Market, One Money' report (European Commission, 1990).

In the 1980s and early 1990s governments across Europe introduced 'sound money' policies and made the central banks responsible for maintaining the stability of exchange rates. As this idea had been accepted, it was a small step to fixing exchange rates and delegating monetary policy to an independent supranational central bank. This made sense from a monetarist point of view on both economic grounds, in terms of increased individual and collective welfare, and political grounds, in terms of limiting macroeconomic policy uncertainty for national decision-makers (Cameron, 1997; Østrup, 1995).

How Economic and Monetary Union Works

We have until now focused on how and why EMU was established. The rest of the chapter focuses on how EMU works. The aim of this section is to evaluate to what extent the euro has managed to establish itself as a credible currency.

Independence of the ECB: establishing credibility and reputation

There is an inflationary bias in the making of monetary policy by elected politicians (Barro and Gordon, 1983; Lohmann, 1999; Nordhaus, 1975). Even if the main goal is price stability, finance ministers can gain in the short term from 'surprise inflation'. If governments can produce an inflation rate that is higher than expected by business and trade unions, there will be a short-term increase in output and employment. Growth and higher employment win votes, so in the run-up to an election there is an incentive for governments to 'pump up' the economy by cutting interest rates. Private actors will be aware that the government has an incentive to supply 'surprise inflation' and that the long-term effect will be an increase in interest rates to curb inflation. Allowing politicians to set interest rates may consequently lead to an economic cycle driven by political incentives rather than economic logic (a political business cycle), a higher than optimal rate of inflation, and a policy that is not credible with national and international currency traders.

A widely accepted solution is to delegate monetary policy to an independent central bank. By isolating interest rates from electoral politics, governments can commit to a credible level of inflation (Drazen, 2002). Central bank independence can be achieved through several mechanisms (Cukierman *et al.*, 1993; Grilli *et al.*, 1991). The central bank can be made responsible for setting interest rates and money supply targets. The goal of price stability can be set out in a constitution, rather than simply in a legislative act, to avoid alteration of the goal by a future electoral majority. The terms of office of the central bank officials can be made longer than the terms of office of the politicians who appoint them. And, sanctions can be used if the central bank fails to achieve price stability, for example by automatically dismissing the president of the bank if an inflation target is missed.

Empirical research finds significant correlation between the level of central bank independence and the average long-term inflation rate. In short, the most independent banks produce the lowest inflation rates (Alesina and Summers, 1993; Cukierman, 1992; Franzese, 1999).

The design of the ECB is highly independent (Kaufmann, 1995). The ECB is solely responsible for implementing monetary policy, without interference from the governments. The goal of price stability is set out in the treaty, so it is difficult for governments to revoke it. The ECB is free to decide monetary policy goals, such as an inflation target and a money supply target. The term of office for ECB officials is eight years. Finally, because unanimous agreement among the governments is required to change the institutional design of EMU, the independence of the ECB is highly credible (Keefer and Stasavage, 2002).

Yet, credibility is not enough to ensure stable monetary policy. A central bank also needs to be legitimate. It needs to possess what economists call reputation (Winkler, 1996). Reputation enables markets and the public to accept monetary policy decisions that might be unpopular in the short term. In the absence of a history of currency stability and economic growth as a result of a central bank's decisions, the markets and the public may be fickle in the face of inflation or recession. This was a potential problem for the ECB as a new institution managing a new currency. Without an established reputation, public opinion in states that suffer asymmetric shocks could potentially turn against the ECB more quickly than they would against a national central bank with a history of independence, such as the Bundesbank.

Several scholars consequently argued that the ECB's reputation would be enhanced if the ECB were more transparent, for example if the minutes of its meetings were made public and its inflation forecasts and assumptions were published (Buiter, 1999; Haan and Eijffinger, 2000; Verdun, 1998). Without transparent decision-making it is difficult for economic interests and the public to determine whether the central bank is responsible for a downturn in the economy or whether this is the result of unexpected economic shocks (Keefer and Stasavage, 2002). Hence, central banks that are transparent usually establish a reputation for sound monetary policies faster than central banks that act in secret (Stasavage, 2002).

In its defence, the ECB argues that publishing voting records would undermine the collective responsibility of the ECB and encourage political interference in its decision-making (Issing, 1999). Also, the ECB contends that because the inflation target is set out in the treaty (the goal of price stability), the basic goal is transparent and the ECB does not have much discretion in interpreting this mandate.

Furthermore, the claim that central bank independence is the best way to guaranteeing long-term economic benefits is not universally accepted (McNamara, 2002). The delegation of monetary policy to a central bank can suffer from the same problems as other principal–agent relations in politics (see Chapter 2). Central bankers may have different policy preferences to politicians and publics. In the short term this is precisely the aim of delegation: to prevent politicians from promoting growth today that citizens will have to pay for tomorrow. But locking in a restrictive monetary policy via central bank independence may not be in the long-term interests of large sections of society, and so may undermine the legitimacy of the EU as a whole.

The separation of monetary policy and fiscal policy can also cause coordination problems (Bini Smaghi and Casini, 2000; Buti *et al.*, 2001; Way, 2000). If the central bank pursues a restrictive monetary policy, politicians will be tempted to increase public debt to inflate the economy, which will prompt the central bank to raise interest rates further and politicians to borrow more money, and so on. Failure to coordinate fiscal and monetary policies can result in debt spiralling out of control. Hence, delegating monetary policy to an independent central bank may only be credible if there is a parallel agreement on how politicians should manage fiscal policy and public borrowing (Stasavage and Guillaume, 2002). Hence, the convergence criteria for EMU and the Stability and Growth Pact could be interpreted as 'contracts' between European-level monetary policy and national fiscal policies (Winkler, 1999). But, as we will see below, the Stability and Growth Pact proved not to be credible and the efforts of national governments to coordinate their economic policies has been questionable during the first decade of the euro.

ECB decision-making

The decisions taken by the ECB Executive Board are carefully scrutinized. The ECB President presents an annual report to Ecofin and the Economic and Monetary Affairs committee in the European Parliament. The European Parliament committee can ask to hear evidence from the ECB President as often as it likes. The media also carefully watch the weekly meetings of the ECB and analyse statements by the ECB President and the other members of the Executive Board. However, the minutes of Executive Board and Governing Council meetings are not available to the public.

Under the rules of the treaty, governments cannot instruct their central bank governors. Nevertheless, when the term of office of a national central bank governor ends (after five years), a government may appoint someone whose views are more representative of those of the national public. Also, with staggered terms of office in the ECB Executive Board, the governments may collectively decide to appoint inflation-averse people to the Board and gradually remove 'hawkish' monetarists.

Political scrutiny of ECB decisions is unlikely to conflict with the policy of the ECB if the national economic cycles are synchronized. In this situation the ECB Governing Council will have little difficulty agreeing to a 'one size fits all' interest rate. However, if there are asymmetric economic cycles, when some national economies are growing while others are declining, a common ECB position is more problematic. In this situation it is reasonable to assume that the six members of the Executive Board propose an interest rate that is considered ideal for the EMU economy as a whole, or slightly above that rate to establish a hawkish reputation. However, under pressure from national publics and governments, those central bank governors whose economies are in recession probably support lower interest rates, while those whose economies are booming probably support higher interest rates.

In the ECB Governing Council there is one vote per central bank governor and member of the ECB Executive Board. Decisions are by simple majority. With this voting rule we can assume that the Governing

Council agrees on the interest-rate preferences of the median member of the council, as this member is pivotal. The members of the Executive Board are likely to be decisive if the interest rates preferences of the central bank governors are split more or less evenly either side of the preferences of the Board. However, if there is public pressure in a large numbers of states for lower interest rates, the six members of the Executive Board can be outvoted by the central bank governors. The practice of 'one member, one vote' in the ECB Executive Board also causes problems if economic cycles are unevenly distributed between the large and small economies (Bindseil, 2001).

We saw an example of this in 2002 to 2003, when Germany, France, and Italy had growth rates of 1 to 2 per cent, while most of the smaller states (Ireland, Greece, Finland, Luxembourg, and Belgium) had growth rates of 2.0 to 4.5 per cent. The central bank governors from the three largest economies all preferred lower interest rates, but were easily outvoted by a coalition of small states and the ECB Executive Board. The design of the voting rules inside the ECB was consequently one of the reasons why the German and French governments had to run public deficits in this period, and hence break the rules of the Stability and Growth Pact.

As the enlargement of the EU in 2004 opened the possibility of more, and poorer, states in the eurozone, there was a need to reform the decision-making rules in the ECB so that voting rights reflected the balance of economic power in the eurozone. Hence, in 2003 the European Council adopted a new voting system in the ECB Governing Council. Under the new system, the number of central bank governors with voting rights is limited to 15, while the members of the Executive Board retain 6 votes. While the central bank governors all have a right to attend and speak at Governing Council meetings, the voting rights now rotate between the member state governors. There are two groups of states: a group of the five largest states (with 4 votes rotating annually between them), and all the other states (with 11 votes rotating between them). If the membership of EMU exceeds 21 members, there will be three voting groups: the five largest states (with 4 votes), a group of the average-size countries consisting of half the number of eurozone members (with 8 votes), and a group of the remaining smallest countries (with 3 votes). The membership of the groups is determined by GDP (five-sixths) and total assets in monetary and financial institutions (one-sixth). The classification of states into the groups is revised every five years (Bénassy-Quéré and Turkisch, 2009). Table 10.1 presents the likely classification of states based on ECB data from 2008.

The new system is designed to alleviate the problem of small states outvoting the larger states, but it may be politically damaging for a state suffering an economic shock in a year when it does not have voting rights on the Governing Council (Baldwin *et al.*, 2001). Nevertheless,

Table 10.1   *Voting weights of countries in the ECB*

	Euro 22 (EU 27 except UK, Sweden, Denmark, Bulgaria, Romania)	Euro 27 (EU 27)
Group 1 4 votes	Germany France Italy Spain Netherlands	Germany United Kingdom France Italy Spain
Group 2 8 votes	Luxembourg Belgium Ireland Austria Poland Greece Portugal Finland Czech Republic Hungary Slovakia	Netherlands Luxembourg Belgium Ireland Sweden Austria Denmark Poland Greece Portugal Finland Romania
Group 3 3 votes	Slovenia Lithuania Cyprus Latvia Estonia Malta	Slovakia Slovenia Bulgaria Lithuania Cyprus Latvia Estonia Malta

Source: Adapted from Bénassy-Quéré and Turkisch (2009). The order of the states in the table is determined by their economic weight, as measured by their GDP (five-sixths) and the size of their financial sectors (one-sixth).

Bénassy-Quéré and Turkisch (2009) show that the change in the system of rotating voting rights will have very little impact on the decisions made by the Governing Council, as the median desired interest rate is likely to continue to lie within the executive board. Both the old and new set of rules operate effectively as fully centralizing rules, where the Executive Board sets the interest rate. If the Executive Board takes the average position of eurozone into account when making proposals, then the voting rules serve the interests if the median economies in the eurozone.

Countries that are out of sync with the median economies are unlikely to be able to influence policy outcomes regardless of whether or not they are a voting member at the time. Nevertheless, a potential problem with the new voting rules is that the economic weights of the countries do not correspond to population size, and ECB decisions might not be seen as legitimate in a large member state with a relatively small economy (such as Poland) which finds itself out of sync with the rest of the eurozone.

Inflation targets: ECB–Ecofin relations

There is some room for political interpretation of the division of labour between the ECB and Ecofin (De Grauwe, 2002). The treaty states that the aim of the ECB is to maintain price stability. Price stability literally means zero inflation. Since a goal of zero inflation is impractical, the ECB has interpreted this to mean an annual inflation of 0 to 2 per cent. This interpretation has not been without criticism because the target is asymmetric, assuming that inflation above 2 per cent is worse than inflation below 2 per cent. The ECB has taken a conservative approach in order to establish its credibility in the financial markets. As the target inflation target is both low and asymmetric, the ECB runs a deflationary risk and negative growth. The experience of Japan shows that even negative interest rates may not be sufficient to escape such economic conditions.

Several central bankers and finance ministers advocated an alternative interpretation of the treaty based on a division of labour between the ECB and Ecofin, where the Ecofin could set the inflation target and the degree of asymmetry around the target (Buiter, 1999). The ECB could then set the interest rates to achieve this target. This would increase the transparency and accountability of monetary policy and would allow some political control of interest rate policy: what the French government likes to call 'economic government' of the eurozone. Critics of this alternative approach argue that separating inflation targets and interest rates decisions would defeat the purpose of an independent central bank, as politicians would have an incentive to set the inflation target at a high level in order to generate high growth, and thereby increase their political support in the short term. However, the danger of this happening would be lower under a separation of inflation targets and interest rates than under a system where these two policy tools are both held by the politicians. In a divided regime, to pump up the European economy the politicians would have to set the inflation target at an unreasonable high level, which would then by heavily criticized by economic interests and the public. The danger of a political business cycle is also smaller in the EU context than in most political systems, because the finance ministers in Ecofin have different electoral timetables. Hence, at a time when some governments would want to raise inflation (in the build-up to an election) others would want to keep it down (immediately after an election).

National fiscal policies and the eurozone crisis

Political pressures on the ECB also result from the constraints on national fiscal policies in EMU. A negative demand shock in one country will increase the government's budget deficit, due to a reduction in tax revenues and an increase in social security expenditure. Budget deficits may also lead to unsustainable long-term debts. Within EMU some governments may be tempted to free-ride on the sound monetary policies of the other states by running a high public deficit with only a moderate threat to the value of the common currency, and hence of the value of its bonds (Horstmann and Schneider, 1994). Consequently, the EU designed the convergence criteria to limit budget deficits prior to joining EMU. To give credibility to these constraints, the treaty includes provisions to combat excessive deficits. These constraints constituted a 'decisive structural break' in the development of European governments' fiscal policies (Freitag and Sciarini, 2001), although many European governments, both left and right, seemed to converge on sound fiscal policies prior to the Maastricht Treaty (Clark *et al.*, 2002; Cusack, 2001).

The Stability and Growth Pact, adopted in July 1997, significantly strengthen the constraints imposed on national fiscal autonomy by the Maastricht Treaty. The excessive deficit procedure of the pact gave the Ecofin Council the right to sanction a government that had run an excessive deficit, which the pact defined as exceeding 3 per cent of GDP (in normal economic conditions). This placed a severe constraint on a member state running a large enough deficit to threaten the stability of the euro. However, a political decision was needed to impose sanctions. Governments would have to cut spending rather than run large budget deficits when faced with an asymmetric shock (Buiter *et al.*, 1993; Eichengreen and von Hagen, 1996).

The main problem with restrictions on government deficits is that it locks in a particular mix of monetary and fiscal policies, whereby the ECB pursues a restrictive monetary policy (as defined by the price stability goal in the treaty), while national governments are forced to pursue restrictive monetary policies (government budgets must be close to balance or in surplus). While this policy mix is certainly anti-inflationary, if there are asymmetric economic cycles it is likely to be unpopular in the states with the lowest levels of growth. With divergent cycles, the interest rates set by the ECB will be higher than those needed for a state at the bottom of an economic cycle, but the state will not be able to borrow money to get the economy moving again.

Also, with a policy mix of tight monetary policies at the European level and constraints on national government budget deficits, states are unlikely to introduce structural reforms. EMU would work more efficiently if states reformed their labour markets and welfare states.

However, such structural reforms would produce higher unemployment in the short term. Consequently, the public would be unlikely to support such structural reforms unless they were balanced with monetary and fiscal policies to stimulate economic growth.

The contradictions of this policy mix in EMU came to a head in 2002 and 2003. At the time, the one-size-fits-all interest rate was higher than was needed for the French and Germen economies. The two governments chose to borrow money to tackle the problem of raising unemployment and a sluggish economy, knowing that raising taxes or introducing labour market reforms at the bottom of an economic cycle were politically unfeasible. As these governments increased their borrowing they exceeded the 3 per cent annual deficit criterion in the Stability and Growth Pact. Ironically, Germany, which had insisted on the pact in the first place because it feared that France and Italy would run high deficits, now found itself in the position of being one of the first member states to face the prospect of sanctions.

But in November 2003 France and Germany were able to secure the support from enough other member states to suspend the excessive deficits procedure. The Commission was so infuriated by the decision to effectively abandon the Stability and Growth Pact that it took a case to the ECJ. The ECJ ruled in support of the governments. As a result, for all practical purposes the Stability and Growth Pact is now moribund.

The viability of EMU was further tested following the global financial crises that started in 2008, when several eurozone governments had to run large deficits to ensure that their banking sectors did not collapse. As governments had to borrow in the international markets, it became apparent that several eurozone states, notably Portugal, Ireland, Italy, Greece, and Spain were experiencing problems financing their debts. It also became clear that the magnitude of the Greek debt and annual deficit were substantively larger than what the government had previously reported to its fellow EMU members. Since joining the eurozone, the Greek economy had benefited from low interest rates and experienced growth figures well above the eurozone average, as access to foreign capital improved. The low interest rates led to over-lending with the ratio of loans to savings exceeding 100 per cent in 2009. It also enabled the government to run large structural deficits. In the run-up to the 2009 Greek elections the reported deficit reached 13.6 per cent of GDP and debt levels rose to 115 per cent of GDP. In the aftermath of the elections, which the ruling centre-right New Democracy Party lost, it become clear that the Greek authorities had misreported official economic statistics. It also became clear that international banks had aided several Greek governments in their efforts to hide the actual levels of government deficit and debt. This led the markets to doubt the ability and willingness of the Greek government to honour its debt, in particular given the fact that most of the debt was held by foreign banks. In April

2010, the international credit agencies duly downgraded the Greek debt rating to 'junk' which dramatically increased the cost, leading analysts to speculate against Greece's ability to refinance its debt. The Greek government was forced to request EU and IMF for assistance. A loan agreement between Greece, the other eurozone countries and the IMF was negotiated in May 2010. The ECB also intervened to guarantee the Greek bonds. This effectively made the ECB the lender of last resort. The loan deal meant that the Greek government had to implement a series of austerity measures, including a freeze on public sector wages for three years, increase in the retirement age and tax increases. When the extent of the required reforms became known, large-scale and violent demonstrations erupted in Athens, with buildings and cars being set on fire, causing the death of three employees of a bank.

The bailout package was also unpopular in Germany, the largest contributor to the package. It was widely claimed in the German press that an EU rescue package for Greece would breach the 'no bailout' rules in the EMU provisions of the EU Treaty. Facing regional elections in North Rhine–Westphalia, the German Chancellor Angela Merkel was reluctant to offer Greece an easy way out, insisting on the IMF playing a central role in the restructuring of the Greek economy. Nevertheless, her hard bargain failed to impress voters in the cash-strapped region, as they defected to the social democratic opposition party, preferring their leaders to think less about Europe and more about their own financial burdens. The result of the elections meant that the Merkel's centre-right coalition lost its majority in the German upper house.

As markets speculated that other EU governments might follow the Greek tragedy, the EU finance ministers held an emergency meeting to adopt an EU-wide rescue package of €720 billion. The package consists of three elements: (a) a stabilization fund, intended to help a member of the eurozone struggling to finance its debts; (b) government backed loans to improve market confidence; (c) loans made available by the IMF. As this package primarily consisted of interest-bearing loans issued on the global financial markets, the governments claimed that they had not broken the no-bailout rules.

While the markets initially reacted positively to the news of the creation of this 'European Monetary Fund', the new credit does nothing to address the need for fiscal adjustment and structural reforms in the eurozone.

The political and economic costs of the bailout of the Greek economy may increase the demand for interstate fiscal transfers linked to the macroeconomic consequences of the EMU as well as improved monitoring of the fiscal discipline of the member states (Crowley, 2001; Eichengreen, 1994; Sala-i-Martin and Sachs, 1991; Wildasin, 2002). With a budget of only 1 per cent of EU GDP, the redistributive capacity of the EU is small, and in the 1970s it was widely felt that EMU would not be possible without a significant increase in the budget (McDougall, 1977). Also, in most currency unions an asymmetric economic shock has been tackled by greater centralization of budgets, as happened in the US in the 1930s and after the reunification of Germany in 1990.

Labour market flexibility: structural reforms and wage agreements

According to the OCA theory, a monetary union should be able to adapt to asymmetric economic cycles or exogenous shocks (such as the situation in Greece) either via labour mobility between states or via flexible wage and labour costs.

There is far less labour mobility across borders in the EU than in the US (see Chapter 11). In certain sectors – such as the building industry, the service sector, and the informal economy – migrant workers do follow capital investments (Eichengreen, 1993b). However, it is hard to imagine that the EU will experience a similar situation to that in the US in the 1930s and 1940s, when there was a mass movement of unemployed and underemployed people from the southern states to the north-eastern states and the rapidly expanding car industry in Detroit. There is also less labour mobility *within* European states than in the US. Political upheaval is avoided because European states have been able to manage internal demand-and-supply shocks through mechanisms other than labour movement, such as lower wages in low-demand regions and fiscal transfers from high-demand to low-demand regions (Eichengreen, 1993a).

However, the issue of labour mobility varies from state to state in the EU. For example, the success of the Irish economy in the 1990s was attributed to its open labour market, with high levels of immigration and emigration by workers in both low-wage and high-wage job categories – more like a regional economy in the US than a national economy in Europe (Krugman, 1997). Thus, although Ireland is a peripheral economy in EMU, and was already out of sync with the core economies at the start of monetary union, it was able to adjust its economy successfully, although suffering a severe setback during the financial crisis that started in 2008. Ireland contrasts starkly with Portugal. It is also a peripheral economy and was growing faster than the core economies when EMU was launched. But, unlike Ireland, Portugal has many unemployed skilled workers because they tend not to emigrate and a shortage of low-skilled workers because such workers have not immigrated from elsewhere in the EU (Munchau, 1998; Torres, 1998).

Furthermore, the EU is unlikely to be able to use wage flexibility to tackle the need for adjustments following from the global financial crisis. As Table 10.2 shows, there is considerable variation in labour costs in the eurozone, with labour being cheaper in the new member states. Labour costs are generally a reflection of productivity rates rather than the

Table 10.2   *Productivity, labour costs, and unemployment in the EU*

Member state	Labour productivity per person employed, 2008 (EU 27=100)	Hourly labour costs, 2006 (euros)	Unemployment 2007 (%)
Luxembourg	175.8	32.4	4.2
Ireland	130.2	–	4.6
Belgium	125.5	30.4	7.5
France	121.6	–	8.4
Netherlands	114.5	–	3.2
Austria	113.5	26.8	4.4
Sweden	110.6	30.2	6.2
United Kingdom	110.0	25.9	5.3
Finland	111.6	26.6	6.9
Italy	109.7	–	6.1
Germany	107.0	27.4	8.4
Spain	103.6	16.2	8.3
Greece	102.2	–	8.3
Denmark	102.5	31.8	3.8
Cyprus	87.3	13.1	4.0
Malta	87.4	8.7	6.4
Slovenia	84.4	12.1	4.9
Slovakia	79.2	5.2	11.1
Czech Republic	71.9	7.1	5.3
Portugal	71.2	12.1	8.1
Hungary	71.0	6.5	7.4
Estonia	63.8	5.5	4.7
Poland	62.0	6.3	9.6
Lithuania	62.0	4.3	4.3
Latvia	52.6	3.6	6.0
Romania	50.2	2.8	6.4
Bulgaria	37.2	1.7	6.9
EU 27	100.0	17.7	7.1

Source: Compiled from Eurostat data.

supply and demand of labour. However, it is worth noting that Denmark has some of the highest hourly labour costs, but is also among the least productive of the old 15 states, while Spanish workers are almost as productive as German workers at half the hourly cost. The most significant difference in both hourly labour costs and productivity is between the new and old member states, yet they have similar official unemployment rates.

To make wages flexible, wage-bargaining negotiations could be decentralized. This would allow trade unions in different economic situations to accept different wage settlement. However, decentralized wage bargaining can lead to inflationary pressures, as high settlements in one region or sector prompt demands for high settlements in other regions/sectors. And, empirical research suggests that economies perform best (in terms of relatively high growth with low inflation and low unemployment) when there is centralized wage bargaining, which allows for wage negotiations to respond directly to the centralized monetary and fiscal policies to balance inflation and employment objectives (Iversen, 1998a). Indeed, the danger for EMU is that the ECB will raise interest rates to pre-empt the inflationary pressures that could arise from separate wage settlements in each of the member states, which would then prompt trade unions to demand higher wages, and so on (Hall and Franzese, 1998; Iversen, 1998b). But, despite efforts to establish European-wide collective agreements within some sectors and some multinational companies, different national industrial relations traditions, and competing trade union interests undermine the prospect of a genuine coordination of wage demands at the European level (Marginson and Sisson, 1998).

Increasing labour market flexibility comes down to political commitment to EMU by governments and the public. If there is a high degree of public support for EMU, governments will be able to introduce labour market reforms, such as liberalizing the rules that govern the hiring and firing of employees by small businesses, and businesses and trade unions will be able to negotiate flexible wage rates. The problem for most governments is that deregulation of the labour market might be in the long-term interest of the eurozone as a whole, but it is against the short-term interest of large sections of the electorate. Moreover, the allocation of policy competences in the EU – whereby labour market policies are decided at the national level and monetary policy and fiscal policy constraints are imposed from the EU level – prevents an easy solution to the problem. As the Luxembourg Prime Minister, Jean-Claude Juncker, once put it: 'we all know what to do, but we just don't know how to get re-elected once we have done it'.

Conclusion: Testing Times for the Euro

Economic and Monetary Union has always been a political project. While the European Commission made the economic case for a common currency, few economists were convinced. Indeed, many warned that the EU was not an optimal currency area and lacked a common fiscal policy. Furthermore, it was pointed out that the criteria for entry into the monetary union seemed fairly arbitrary.

However, EMU is the flagship project of European integration. If the euro fails, Europe fails. There was a strong political commitment to monetary union and there has been a willingness to defend EMU in times of crisis. When the global financial crises caused several governments to run unsustainable deficits, the leaders of the EU agreed to provide a rescue package to a failing eurozone member while the ECB started to buy government bonds.

The problem in the eurozone, however, is that there is a clear need for major political reforms if the project is to be sustainable in the long term. These reforms, which include flexible labour markets and/or major fiscal transfers between states, will be unpopular with voters. While the financial crises may have demonstrated that there is a need for a stronger economic union, there are few signs that voters are keen on common economic policies and large fiscal transfers.

Chapter 11

Interior Policies

Theories of Citizenship and the State
EU Interior Policies: From Free Movement of Workers to an Emerging
    European State
Explaining EU Interior Policies
Conclusion: a Pan-European State?

One of the central aims of the modern state is to grant and protect citizens' rights and freedoms, via a range of 'interior policies', such as immigration policy, policing, internal security, and criminal justice policies. The EU has gradually established 'an area of freedom, security and justice', which touches on all these policy issues. This chapter seeks to analyse why the EU has developed these policies and how far these policies have changed existing rights and freedoms of citizens in Europe. To help in this task we shall first look at general theories of the relationship between citizens and the state.

Theories of Citizenship and the State

Citizens in liberal democracies are entitled to a variety of rights and freedom (see Berlin, 1969; Rawls, 1971; Walzer, 1983). The traditional view is that these rights and freedoms are inextricably linked to the emergence of the modern *state* (Moore, 1967; Tilly, 1990). Citizens' rights were initially the preserve of the privileged classes and were guaranteed and protected by means of the state's 'monopoly of the legitimate use of physical force' (Weber, 1946 [1919], p. 78). The expansion of citizenship went hand in hand with the expansion of the power of the state. Modern constitutions, courts, police forces, and border controls emerged in the nineteenth century in response to middle-class demands for the protection of private property from the state, criminal activity, and immigration.

The *nation* was also thought of as inherently connected to citizens' rights and freedoms. Democratic rights and freedoms were reinforced by a single national identity, because a democratic 'will' (public opinion) requires a single language and mass media, and majority rule was legitimatized by a single national culture (Smith, 1991). Also, with a common national destiny, the ruling classes were willing to allow economic redistribution and grant social rights to the working classes (Alesina and

Glaeser, 2005; cf. Marshall, 1950). As a result, in most European countries the welfare state only developed once the nation had been established as the dominant focus of political identification (Flora and Heidenheimer, 1981).

Consequently, the traditional connection between the nation-state and citizenship suggests that 'transnational citizenship' in the EU – which is neither a state nor a nation – is impossible (Aaron, 1974). However, this is not the case. At a theoretical level, the connection between the nation-state and citizenship is a particular geographical and historical ideal type. First, the classic, homogeneous nation-state only developed in a few countries in north-western Europe (such as France and Sweden) and the fully democratic welfare state only emerged in the middle of the twentieth century (Badie and Birnbaum, 1983). Citizenship rights existed in non-state, non-national settings well before this period. For example, in city-state Europe, economic rights, such as the right to trade, were granted to non-residents well before the nation-state was established, and in multi-ethnic polities, such as Belgium and Switzerland, redistributive welfare states were founded without strong sociocultural solidarity bonds.

Second, with regard to democracy and political and civil rights, it is not clear which came first: the nation-state or democracy. In most European systems as well as in the United States, democratic elections and practices preceded the emergence of the modern nation-state. In other words, national identity and the institutions of the nation-state were products of the development of universal democratic citizenship rights, and not vice-versa (Rokkan, 1973; Skowronek, 1982).

At an empirical level, citizens' rights today are very different from those in the mid-nineteenth century and even in the immediate post-Second World War period. The growth of political and economic migration in the late 1980s and throughout the 1990s has forced Western nation-states to reconfigure their traditional citizenship policies (e.g. Brubaker, 1992; Favell, 2001; Hollifield, 1992; Kymlicka, 1995). For example, as a result of global free trade and capital flows, economic rights have been extended to non-residents and non-nationals, such as guest workers. Also, the boundary of political rights has become increasingly blurred with the emergence of dual nationality and the extension of voting rights to first- and even second-generation expatriates. Finally, Western societies are not homogeneous nations. Successive waves of immigration have produced multi-ethnic and multi-religious polities and forced states to develop new definitions of citizenship and new social and political rights, such as racial equality and minority representation.

In other words, there is a tension in citizenship politics. On the one hand, citizenship requires the institutions of a state to guarantee positive freedoms (through the courts) and to secure and protect negative freedoms (through the police and security forces). For example, markets, including the European single market, cannot exist without the existence and protection of property rights. On the other hand, in the world of global capitalism, global migration, and multi-ethnic societies:

> the classical formal order of the nation-state and its membership is not in place. The state is no longer an autonomous and independent organization closed over a nationally defined population ... Rights, participation, and representation in the polity, are increasingly matters beyond the vocabulary of national citizenship. (Soysal, 1994, pp. 163–4)

This tension is central to the politics of citizenship in the EU: by establishing transnational citizenship rights the EU has undermined the traditional nation-state; and to define and secure transnational citizenship, new state powers and security mechanisms are being reinvented at the European level.

EU Interior Policies: From Free Movement of Workers to an Emerging European State

EU interior policies, which aim to establish certain rights and protections for citizens of the EU member states, fall into four main categories (see Geddes, 2008):

1   *the free movement of persons* between the EU member states, ranging from work and residency rights to the removal of border controls between the member states;
2   *fundamental rights* for EU nationals in other member states, such as equal economic, political, and civil rights;
3   *immigration and asylum policies*, involving cooperation on refugee policies and common policies towards third-country nationals; and
4   *police and judicial cooperation*, to combat drug-trafficking, terrorist activities, cross-border crime, and illegal immigration.

The first two of these confer rights on EU citizens who move between and/or live in other EU member states, while the second two relate to how the member states and the EU institutions decide who has access to national and EU citizenship rights, and how these rights should be guaranteed and protected.

From free movement of workers to 'an area of freedom, security and justice'

The Treaty of Rome established a basic citizenship right: the right of citizens from a member state to seek and take up work in any other member state. The Single European Act built on this foundation, with the aim of removing all physical barriers to the movement of services and labour as part of the single market. The Maastricht Treaty added a 'justice and home affairs' pillar (the so-called 'third pillar' of the EU), which covered free movement, immigration policies, and police and judicial cooperation. A major change then came with the Amsterdam Treaty. Which included a new section which aimed to create 'an area of freedom, security and justice' within five years of entry into force of the treaty, by 1 May 2004. This new area of freedom, security, and justice brought free movement, immigration policies, and police and judicial cooperation on civil matters into the main body of the treaty, but left police and judicial cooperation on criminal matters in the largely intergovernmental third pillar.

At the Tampere European Council October 1999 the governments adopted an action plan to bring about the area of freedom, security, and justice by 2004. The plan defined an 'area of freedom' as covering the free movement of persons, as well as protecting fundamental rights and combating all forms of discrimination. Meanwhile, an 'area of security' was defined as common policies to combat crime, particularly terrorism, trade in human beings, and arms, as well as drug trafficking, corruption, and fraud. And, an 'area of justice' was defined as equal access to justice for all EU citizens, via cooperation between the member states' authorities on civil matters, and the establishment of minimum common rules covering criminal acts, procedures, and penalties. The plan also set out a provisional timetable for achieving these policies.

For the five-year transition period, the treaty specified that decisions in this area would be made by unanimous agreement between the governments, with legislative initiative by the Commission and consultation of the European Parliament. However, the treaty also included a clause (known as the 'passerelle clause') which allowed the governments to decide after May 2004, acting by unanimity, to pass all the policy issues in this area over to QMV and the co-decision procedure. In October 2004, the governments signed the draft Constitutional Treaty, which proposed to transfer most policies covered by the area of freedom, security, and justice to majority voting and the new ordinary legislative procedure. Having agreed to this in the Constitutional Treaty, when the Tampere action plan was reviewed at the Hague European Council, in November 2004, the governments agreed to invoke the passerelle clause and so passed all policy issues over to QMV and co-decision.

The Hague Programme also called for the implementation of a common asylum policy by 2010 and the gradual expansion of the European Refugee Fund to €150 million per year by 2009. The governments also adopted SitCen, the Council's situation centre for strategic analysis of terrorist threats and called for the creation of a European External Borders Agency, with the possible creation of a European System of Border Guards. Following the adoption of the Hague

Programme, the area of interior policies became one of the most active areas of EU legislation between 2004 and 2010.

The Treaty of Lisbon entered into force in December 2009, which implemented all the proposed changes that had been envisaged in the draft Constitutional Treaty in this policy area. One of the key changes from the Amsterdam Treaty was to consolidate all policy issues in a single section of the treaty, hence bringing free movement, immigration, and police and judicial cooperation policies together under a single set of decision-making arrangements, although with a five-year transition period for police and judicial cooperation on criminal matters. In December 2009, the European Council adopted the Stockholm Programme, which set out how the Lisbon Treaty provisions in this area would be implemented between 2010 and 2014. The Stockholm Programme is a hugely ambitious programme, with provisions across the full gamut of justice and interior policies, such as the full implementation of the free movement persons, new instruments to tackle racism and xenophobia, guaranteeing personal data protection in the information society, mutual recognition of criminal and civil law, access of EU citizens to criminal and civil law, a new 'internal security strategy' which covers everything from terrorism and drug trafficking to the trafficking of persons and cyber crime, a more coherent EU disaster management policy, and more integrated management of the EU's external borders.

Free movement of persons

The Treaty of Rome established the free movement of persons as a fundamental objective of the European Economic Community, but this provision originally applied only to cross-border economic activity. Nationals of one member state would have the right to seek work, reside, and provide or receive a service in another member state. Secondary legislation and ECJ judgments have extended entry, residency, and working rights to non-EU nationals who are dependants of EU citizens (spouses and children of EU citizens) and to some economically independent non-EU citizens (people who have sufficient funds and resources not to be a burden on the recipient state, such as students, company employees and the self-employed).

The removal of physical barriers to the free movement of persons became a central part of the single market programme. The white paper *Completing the Internal Market* (European Commission, 1985) suggested that a single market implied the complete elimination of internal frontier controls and borders by 31 December 1992 (see Chapter 8). The Council adopted several measures to remove controls on the free movement of goods across internal borders by that date, but little progress was made on removing border controls on the free movement of persons. Most member states were reluctant to remove these internal controls without harmonized rules on the crossing of the EU's external borders, such as common visa requirements and asylum policies. Due to domestic sensitivities and the requirement for unanimity, the Council failed to reach agreement on such rules by the date in question.

In the meantime, in 1985 France, Germany, and the three Benelux countries signed the Schengen Accord. This was an intergovernmental agreement outside the EU Treaty, for the elimination of border controls between the signatory states. An implementation convention was eventually adopted in 1990. Italy, Spain, Portugal, and Greece signed the accord in 1992. The members of the Nordic passport union – Denmark, Sweden, Finland, and Norway (although not in the EU) – joined in 1995. In March 1995 the Schengen Convention entered into force, with only France refusing to remove all its border controls on the ground that Belgium and the Netherlands had not undertaken sufficient policies to prevent drug trafficking.

The Amsterdam Treaty introduced two major changes to the free movement of persons. First, the treaty committed the Council to removing 'controls on persons, be they citizens of the Union or nationals of third countries, crossing internal borders' within five years of the entry into force of the treaty. Second, through a protocol attached to the treaty, the Amsterdam Treaty incorporated the 3,000 pages of the Schengen *acquis* into the legal framework of the EU. The Council, acting by unanimity, became the main executive body under the Schengen rules, and the Schengen secretariat became part of the Council's general secretariat. While the ECJ was granted jurisdiction over some decisions, decision-making in this area remained relatively secretive. The European Parliament had no formal right of consultation, and the Schengen protocol explicitly excluded the ECJ from exercising jurisdiction on matters of law and order or internal security arising from the Schengen Convention.

In addition, the free movement of persons provisions do not apply to all the member states. Through a series of protocols attached to the treaty, the UK, Ireland, and Denmark have a series of 'opt-outs'. The UK and Ireland chose to be excluded from all aspects of the free movement of persons and the Schengen *acquis*, although they have chosen to opt in to individual proposals on an ad hoc basis. In a separate provision of the treaty, Ireland declared that it intended to participate as fully as possible while remaining in a passport union with the UK. Denmark, on the other hand, opted out of the free movement of persons provisions with no possibility of opting in to individual proposals. Nonetheless, Denmark is a member of Schengen (but reserves the right to opt out on any new policy proposal) and participates in the provisions on common visa policies. Of the 12 member states that joined the EU in 2004 and 2007, nine fully joined Schengen in 2007. Romania, Bulgaria, and Cyprus have applied to join, and Romania and Bulgaria expect to do so in 2011.

Meanwhile, two other non-EU countries, Iceland and Switzerland, have joined Schengen since the Amsterdam Treaty.

Despite the Schengen arrangements, the citizens of the member states that joined the EU in 2004 and 2007 did not immediately gain full freedom of movement rights throughout the EU. During the accession negotiations, several governments, particularly Germany and Austria, voiced their fear that they would be subjected to a huge influx of immigrants from Central and Eastern Europe. As a result, the applicant states were required to accept a transition period in which movement would be restricted. Until 2006 the old 15 were free to apply their own national rules to the citizens of the new member states. Sweden, Denmark, Ireland, the Netherlands, the UK, France, and Spain either applied relatively liberal access measures from 2004 or removed their transition measures in 2006. The transition measures were then reviewed and were extended for some member states until 2014, after which time the citizens of all the EU 27 member states will be free to reside and work in any other member state in the EU.

A similar transition period was imposed when Spain and Portugal joined the EU in the mid-1980s, but was quickly abandoned when the other member states realized that the number of Spanish and Portuguese workers seeking jobs elsewhere in the EU actually declined. There were two reasons for this decline. First, most people in Spain and Portugal who wished to emigrate to another EU state had done so in the years immediately prior to their countries' accession. Second, as the per capita GDP gap between Spain and Portugal and the rest of the EU declined, the incentive to emigrate declined.

Immediately after the 2004 enlargement, there was considerable migration from some Central and Eastern European states to several of the old 15 states who had decided to allow free movement from the new member states, particularly the UK and Ireland. For example, approximately 300,000 Polish citizens emigrated to the UK either immediately before or after Poland joined the EU (Favell, 2008b). However, as with the case of Spanish and Portuguese workers in the 1980s, as Polish GDP began to grow, and particularly after the economic crisis hit the UK and Ireland in 2008 and 2009 and the pound sterling began to decline against the Polish złoty, thousands of Polish workers decided to return home. Despite the media hysteria in some member states about the 'waves' of migrants from the new member states, the data on EU residents suggests that the largest intra-EU migrations are between the original 12 states, such as Italians in Germany, Portuguese in France, and Irish in the United Kingdom (Recchi and Favell, 2009).

Immigration is a salient political issue in a large number of EU member states. However, there is little evidence that these concerns are directed at migrants from other EU member states. Most opposition to immigrants has been aimed at ethnic minorities from Africa, South Asia, or the

Middle East, and Muslims from these parts of the world in particular. In contrast, the free movement of persons in the EU is a surprisingly non-salient issue, except for a few isolated cases, such as the treatment of Roma migrants in France, Italy, and Spain.

Fundamental rights and freedoms

In addition to freedom of movement, the Treaty of Rome established several economic rights for citizens of the signatory states. Through its rules on state aid, the common market, and competition policy, the treaty placed limits on the extent to which the state could intervene in private economic interactions. The treaty also outlawed economic discrimination (such as in the granting of contracts and in pay and conditions) on the grounds of nationality and gender. In combination with the establishment of the direct effect of EU law (see Chapter 4), these provisions turned EU nationals into 'market citizens', not only in other member states but also in their own countries (see Everson, 1995).

Nevertheless, citizens' identification with the EU could not be guaranteed by offering economic rights alone. In 1974, the Paris Summit first discussed the idea of adding political and civil rights to the economic rights. During the preparation of the Single European Act in 1984, the Adonnino Report argued that a 'People's Europe' – via cultural, educational, and identity policies – should be pursued in parallel to the completion of the single market. Then in 1990, at the Rome European Council that launched the Intergovernmental Conference (IGC) that negotiated the Maastricht Treaty, the governments agreed that the EU Treaty should establish 'EU citizenship'.

The citizenship provisions were then amended by the Lisbon Treaty in 2009. The section of the treaty on 'non-discrimination and citizenship of the union' specifies that an EU citizen is anybody who is a national of one of the EU member states, and that EU citizens have the following rights:

- to move and reside freely within the territory of the member states;
- to vote and stand as candidates in elections to the European Parliament and in municipal elections in their member state of residence;
- to enjoy, in the territory of a third country in which the member state of which they are nationals is not represented, the protection of the diplomatic and consular authorities of any EU member state;
- to petition the European Parliament, to apply to the European Ombudsman, and to address the institutions and advisory bodies of the Union in any of the Treaty languages and to obtain a reply in the same language.

Despite the symbolic value of declaring 'EU citizenship', these provisions are limited. First, they do not mean that all EU citizens have the same rights in every member state: each member state has its own set of civil, economic, political, and social rights and these are selectively granted to people from other member states. For example, EU nationals residing in another state do not automatically have a right to vote in national elections.

Second, EU citizenship rights only apply to EU nationals. One implication of this is that the member states retain the right to decide who is an EU citizen, and hence who has access to the economic and political rights granted under the EU Treaty. Moreover, by restricting the rights to EU nationals, millions of legal residents in the territories of the EU are excluded from receiving these rights. A third-country national who has the right to reside and work in one member state does not automatically have the same right in other member states.

Third, the citizenship provisions in the main body of the treaty do not define a set of fundamental rights for EU nationals or residents in the EU. There has been an ongoing discussion about whether the EU should have its own bill of rights or whether the EU should or could accede to the European Convention on Human Rights (ECHR). The ECJ stated in 1996 (Opinion 2/94) that the EU did not have the authority to accede to the ECHR, unless the treaty was amended to provide a mandate to do this. In response, in 1999 the governments set up a convention of representatives from the member states and the EU institutions to prepare a charter of rights for the EU. The convention reported in October 2000, and the Charter of Fundamental Rights of the EU was approved unanimously by the governments, the European Parliament, and the Commission in December 2000. The Nice Treaty did not refer to the Charter, but did introduce a mechanism for expelling a member state from the EU (by a four-fifths majority in the Council) for a breach of fundamental rights. Then, in June 2004 the Charter was included in the draft Constitutional Treaty of the EU, and it remained in the final Lisbon Treaty with some amendments and qualifications, and hence entered into force as a binding part of EU law in December 2009.

The Charter of Fundamental Rights of the EU brings together in a single text all the main personal, civil, political, economic, and social rights contained in the ECHR, the constitutions of the EU member states, the case law of the ECJ, and various other international conventions on fundamental rights. The Charter adds some provisions that are specific to the EU, namely the rights set out in under the citizenship provisions of the treaty (such as freedom of movement, the right of petition, and so on). The Charter also adds several new rights that reflect changes in society since 1950 (when the ECHR was adopted). For example, the Charter introduces a right to 'good administration', the right to protection of personal data, and certain rules governing bioethics.

Following the Lisbon Treaty, then, the EU has something akin to a 'bill of rights' – which, among other things, makes the EU more like a state than an international organization. Nevertheless, it is not yet clear how much of an impact the Charter will have. First, application of the Charter is restricted to EU laws and the EU institutions, and so is limited in its likely effect on national institutions and laws. Second, almost all the rights in the Charter already exist at the national level, as all EU member states have to be signatories of the ECHR to be members of the EU. Third, three member states – the UK, Poland, and the Czech Republic – secured a protocol attached to the Lisbon Treaty which limits the application of the Charter in these states. Specifically, the protocol precludes the domestic courts in these states and the ECJ from finding that 'laws, regulations or administrative provisions, practices or actions' in these states are inconsistent with the Charter, and also explicitly states that nothing in the Charter creates justiciable rights applicable to these states which these states have not already provided for in their national law. In other words, the Charter may be meaningless for three of the 27 member states!

In sum, EU citizenship is not exactly the same as national citizenship. EU citizenship does not establish full and equal economic, political, civil, and social rights for all individuals regardless of where they reside in the EU. Nevertheless, the citizenship provisions in the treaty are a significant step towards a genuine 'post-national citizenship' of Europe, where the right to reside, seek work, receive welfare benefits, pursue educational opportunities, participate in society and politics, and have one's culture and personal data protected, is no longer the independent preserve of the European nation-states but the subject of collective agreement between the member states and policy-making by the supranational EU institutions (e.g. Shaw, 2007; Wiener, 1998).

Immigration and asylum policies

Without internal borders, any person who is granted entry to, residence in, or citizenship of one member state can conceivably move freely within the territory of the EU. Consequently, the goal of removing physical barriers to the movement of persons inside the single market forced the member states to address the issue of the movement of persons across the external borders of the EU. This was initially done outside the framework of the EU treaties, via the Ad Hoc Working Group on Immigration (AWGI), which was set up by interior ministries in 1986. Through this informal cooperation the governments agreed two conventions: the Dublin Convention on Asylum in 1990, and the External Frontiers Convention in 1991.

The Dublin Convention aimed to prevent multiple asylum applications by mutual recognition of all states' asylum regulations and ensuring that asylum applications would only be processed by the member state in which the asylum seeker first arrived in the EU. The External Frontiers

Convention provided for the mutual recognition of visas for non-EU nationals, and abolished the need for third-country nationals residing legally in one member state to obtain a visa to travel to another EU state for a period of less than three months. However, these conventions had to be transposed into national legislation in all member states before they could enter into force, and several member states refused to ratify the Dublin Convention, while the UK and Spain refused to sign the External Frontiers Convention due to their ongoing disagreement over Gibraltar.

The Maastricht Treaty brought the work of the AWGI into the framework of the EU through its provisions for cooperation in the fields of justice and home affairs (JHA) – the third pillar of the EU. The JHA pillar established asylum policy, the crossing of external frontiers, immigration policy, and policy towards third-country nationals as areas of common interest to the member states. However, this development was more an institutionalization of the existing intergovernmental provisions than a new supranational competence: the AWGI simply became a subcommittee of the Council committee responsible for JHA issues, decision-making remained by unanimity, the Commission still had no right of initiative, and there was no role for the European Parliament or the ECJ.

Nevertheless, under the JHA provisions, justice and home affairs ministers began to meet on a more regular basis and to adopt common policies. These policies were still mainly non-binding resolutions and recommendations rather than directly effective joint actions or decisions. Decisions also tended to be on information-exchange issues, such as the decision in November 1992 to set up two clearing houses for data exchange on asylum rules, asylum applications, and immigration developments: the Centre for Information, Discussion and Exchange on Asylum (CIREA), and the Centre for Information, Discussion and Exchange on the Crossing of External Borders and Immigration (CIREFI).

The Amsterdam Treaty, however, marked a fundamental break from this intergovernmental framework, by bringing asylum and immigration policies into the main body of the treaty, under the goal of completing an area of freedom, security, and justice. The new framework covered the following areas:

- standards and procedures for checking on persons crossing the EU's external borders;
- rules on visas for stays of longer than three months, including a single list of countries whose citizens require visas to visit the EU;
- the conditions under which third-country nationals shall have freedom to travel in the EU for up to three months;
- standards and procedures for granting and withdrawing asylum and refugee status, including minimum standards for the reception of asylum seekers and refugees;

- minimum standards for the temporary protection of displaced persons (*de facto* refugees rather than asylum seekers);
- measures on immigration policy, including common conditions of entry and residence and common rules on illegal immigration and repatriation; and
- measures defining the rights and conditions under which third-country nationals can work and reside anywhere in the EU.

The Amsterdam Treaty specified that for the first five years after the treaty's entry into force (up to May 2004) these policies would be adopted through a mix of intergovernmental and supranational procedures. On the intergovernmental side, the Council was to act by unanimity, and legislation was to be initiated by the member state governments. On the supranational side, the Commission was given a right of legislative initiative, the Council could adopt legally binding and directly effective directives or regulations, the European Parliament would have to consulted, and the ECJ was granted jurisdiction (but only if all national legal remedies had been exhausted).

The Nice Treaty then reinforced the supranational procedures: legislation on checks at external borders, visas, third-country nationals, asylum, and the temporary protection of refugees would now have to be passed by the co-decision procedure. And, under the Lisbon Treaty all aspects of the EU asylum and immigration policy are now covered by QMV and the ordinary legislative procedure.

Since the Amsterdam Treaty the EU has taken several significant steps towards a 'common European asylum system'. This common asylum policy is based on four legal instruments:

1　the Dublin regulation, which establishes rules for which a member state is responsible for assessing an asylum application, to prevent multiple applications;
2　the reception conditions directive, which establishes minimum standards for the reception of asylum-seekers, including housing, education, and health care;
3　the qualification directive, which establishes criteria for defining who can qualify for refugee or subsidiary protection status and what rights are attached to each status (in other words a common EU approach to applying the Geneva Convention on the status of refugees); and
4　the asylum procedures directive, which ensures that throughout the EU, all asylum applicants at first instance are subject to the same minimum standards – such as a personal interview – as well as the basic principles and guarantees relating to interpretation, legal aid, and access to a court appeal.

In addition to the legislative work, the common asylum policy has a financial instrument: the European Refugee Fund (ERF). The ERF provides support to member states to enable them to grant adequate reception conditions to refugees. The ERF was allocated €628 million for the period 2008 to 2013.

The EU has also started to move beyond a common European asylum system to establish several elements of a 'common immigration policy'. These include several provisions on legal immigration into the EU, such as common rules on family reunification, the granting of long-term resident status to third-country nationals, and the admission of third-country nationals into the EU for the purpose of studying or conducting research. There are also ongoing discussions about a 'Blue Card' scheme, which would establish common rules for granting employment rights to skilled immigrations. As of 2010, however, such a scheme was still some way off.

The EU has also adopted several provisions on illegal immigration. These include the returns directive, which was adopted in 2008 and establishes common rules for the return of illegal immigrants to third countries. To facilitate the return of illegal immigrants, the EU has readmission agreements with several countries, including Albania, Bosnia and Herzegovina, the Former Yugoslav Republic of Macedonia, Hong Kong, Macao, Moldova, Montenegro, Russia, Sri Lanka, and Ukraine. And, in 2004 the EU established the European Agency for the Management of Operational Cooperation at the External Borders of the Member States of the EU (FRONTEX). FRONTEX was the first EU agency to be based in a new member state, in Warsaw. FRONTEX helps the member states implement EU rules on external border controls, coordinates operations between member states in the field of external border management, assists member states in training national border guards, carries out risk analysis, and provides support in organizing joint return operations. In addition to staff resources, FRONTEX has equipment at its disposal, including aeroplanes, helicopters, and sea vessels. In 2007 the EU established a team of rapidly deployable border guards to assist in controlling illegal immigration, particularly on Europe's southern coastlines and around the Canary Islands. These readmissions and external border control policies have forced the EU to start to think about the foreign policy aspects of common EU migration policies, such as how EU development policies can be used to reduce the demand for economic migration to Europe (Lavenex, 2006; Lavenex and Kunz, 2008; Lavenex and Ucarer, 2004).

In sum, immigration policy has been one of the most active areas of EU policy-making in the last decade, and the Commission, the European Parliament, and increasingly the ECJ play a major role in shaping these policies. The member states still control most aspects of immigration policy, such as who can be given citizenship and which workers should be given access to the national labour market to fill skills shortages. However, the EU now has policy competences in most areas of immigration policy, and there is growing pressure for a genuine common EU immigration policy, particularly to address labour market shortages and the problem of the ageing population, where many member states need to increase the number of people paying into the state pensions system.

Police and judicial cooperation

While supranational policy-making and binding legal instruments have developed rapidly in the area of immigration and asylum, in the area of police and judicial cooperation, in contrast, progress has been much slower and mainly via intergovernmental decision-making and non-binding instruments. Police and judicial cooperation began before cooperation on migration policy. Back in 1975, the European Council set up a forum for cooperation between interior ministries and police agencies to combat terrorism. This intergovernmental group, the Trevi group was not part of the EU. Its main activities involved information exchanges about terrorist activities, the security aspects of air traffic systems, nuclear plants, and other vulnerable targets, and cooperation in the development of tactics and equipment to fight terrorism. In the 1980s, Trevi's mandate was widened to include cooperation in fighting football hooliganism and serious international organized crime such as drug trafficking, arms trafficking, and bank robbery, and in 1988 the Trevi 1992 project was launched to study the consequences of the single market programme on cross-border security issues.

With the creation of the JHA pillar, the Maastricht Treaty brought the Trevi framework into the EU legal framework in the justice and home affairs provisions. In addition to the immigration and asylum provisions discussed above, the provisions covered judicial cooperation on civil matters, judicial cooperation on criminal matters, customs cooperation, police cooperation to prevent terrorism, drug trafficking, and other forms of serious international crime, and the creation of the European Police Office (EUROPOL). This was essentially the institutionalization of existing intergovernmental practices. The committees around the Trevi ministers meetings (such as the Ad Hoc Group on Organized Crime) simply became working groups of COREPER. Also, decision-making remained by unanimity, and the Commission, the European Parliament, and the ECJ were excluded.

Justice and home affairs ministers then adopted action plans to fight drug addiction, organized crime, trafficking in human beings, the exploitation of children, and the control of large groups of people who posed a threat to law and order (in other words, football hooligans). In most areas the action plans did not lead to the establishment of common European-wide practices. In December 1991, the Council passed the

EUROPOL Convention, but this was not signed by all member states until July 1995, and due to ratification problems EUROPOL only came into operation (in The Hague) in 1998.

Then in the Amsterdam Treaty, unlike with the immigration and asylum policies, the member states decided not to move police and judicial cooperation policies to the supranational first pillar. Instead these policies were left in a revamped third pillar: on 'police and judicial cooperation in criminal matters'. However, the Lisbon Treaty finally absorbed this separate pillar into the main body of the treaty, within the framework of the area of freedom, security, and justice, although it left the intergovernmental structure of decision-making in this policy area largely intact. Council decision-making is still by unanimity, but the Commission shares the right of policy initiation with the Council, and the European Parliament must be consulted before the Council can act.

Progress was initially slow. However, the events of 11 September 2001 spurred the EU into action (Den Boer and Monar, 2002; Bossong, 2008). In the area of police cooperation, in 2002 the Council established a European Police College (CEPOL) for training police officers at the European level, a European network to capture persons responsible for genocide, crimes against humanity and war crimes, a mechanism for evaluating the legal systems of the member states for fighting terrorism, and introduced a series of measures to promote police and judicial cooperation in the combating of terrorism. Similarly, in the area of judicial cooperation, the Council set up the European Justice Office (EURO-JUST) in The Hague, to improve cooperation between the member states in investigating and prosecuting people suspected of serious cross-border crime. Then in July 2003 the EU signed an agreement with the US on mutual legal assistance in the fight against terrorism and international organized crime.

In 2002 the EU adopted the European Arrest Warrant (EAW). The EAW replaces the previous bilateral extradition arrangements with a system derived from the concept of the 'mutual recognition' of legal rulings between the member states (Lavenex, 2007). An EAW is valid throughout the EU, and can be issued for offences carrying a maximum penalty of 12 months or more. Once a member state has issued an EAW, the receiving state has 90 days to arrest and transfer the suspect or sentenced person to the issuing state, for trial or to complete a detention period. An EAW can only be issued for the purposes of conducting a criminal prosecution (not merely an investigation), or enforcing a custodial sentence. The introduction of the EAW system was intended to increase the speed and ease of extradition throughout the EU by removing the political and administrative phases of decision-making which had characterized the previous system of extradition in Europe, and converting the process into a system run entirely by the judiciary.

Then, following the bombings in Madrid in March 2004 and in

London in July 2005, the EU appointed an Anti-Terrorism Coordinator. At the same time the governments added the office of European Public Prosecutor into the draft Constitutional Treaty, which remained in the Lisbon Treaty. A decision to establish the office of European Public Prosecutor requires unanimity in the Council, which may be difficult to achieve. If the member states can reach agreement, the European Public Prosecutor's role will initially be quite limited: to investigate, prosecute, and bring to judgment offences against the EU's financial interests. Nevertheless, the member states could, if they all agree, extend the powers of the Prosecutor to cover serious cross-border crime.

In sum, compared with EU socio-economic policies, and even asylum and immigration policies, the internal security powers of the EU are relatively limited. The EU is a long way from possessing a monopoly on the legitimate use of physical force. For example, EUROPOL is not a European FBI with independent powers of investigation, and EURO-JUST, even with a European Public Prosecutor, is not a European justice department with independent powers of prosecution and enforcement.

Explaining EU Interior Policies

There are several issues in the development of EU freedom and security policies that need to be explained, such as:

- Why are policies to promote the free movement of persons less advanced than policies to promote the free movement of goods, services, and capital?
- Why was there a move to supranational decision-making in immigration and asylum policies, with agenda-setting powers delegated to the Commission and binding policy instruments, in the late 1990s and a rapid acceleration in the adoption of policies since then?

The research in political science and sociology has produced three main explanations of the development of EU interior policies (see Niemann, 2008): (a) exogenous changes in European and global society; (b) intergovernmentalism; and (c) supranational politics.

Exogenous pressures: global migration, crime, and terrorism

It is often claimed that one of the side-effects of globalization is that states are less able to control the global movement of persons (Bhagwati, 2003; Cornelius *et al.*, 2005; Guiraudon and Lahav, 2000; Sassen, 1996). Even if the most extreme versions of this thesis exaggerate the openness of borders, since the mid-1980s most states in Western Europe have found it difficult to prevent the arrival and settlement of asylum seekers, refugees fleeing states suffering from economic or political collapse, family members of previous migrants and undocumented immigrants.

One consequence of this is that Europe is now a multi-ethnic continent. As Table 11.1 shows, in 2008 in a majority of EU states more than 10 per cent of residents were ethnic minorities, even excluding the states in Central and Eastern Europe where large linguistic minorities exist for historical reasons (such as Russians in Latvia and Estonia, or Hungarians in Romania and Slovakia). Moreover, in 2008, more than 6 per cent of EU residents had been born in a different country from the one in which

Table 11.1   *Minorities and migrants in the EU*

	Ethno-linguistic minorities as % of pop'n, 2008	Foreign born pop'n as % of pop'n, 2008	Residents from other EU27 states as % of pop'n, 2008	Asylum applications, 2009	
				Total	per million pop'n
Austria	8.9	10.0	3.5	15,475	485
Belgium	10.0	9.1	6.2	18,290	490
Bulgaria	16.1	0.3	0.0	750	25
Cyprus	–	15.9	10.3	–	–
Czech Republic	4.0	3.3	1.3	1,355	25
Denmark	9.9	5.5	1.7	3,340	165
Estonia	32.1	17.1	0.6	35	10
Finland	8.6	2.5	0.9	5,400	230
France	16.0	5.8	2.0	46,280	180
Germany	18.7	8.8	3.1	29,580	105
Greece	17.0	8.1	1.4	16,225	140
Hungary	7.7	1.8	1.0	4,760	140
Ireland	12.6	12.6	8.9	3,130	145
Italy	5.0	5.8	1.6	20,455	45
Latvia	42.3	18.3	0.3	60	10
Lithuania	16.5	1.3	0.1	475	40
Luxembourg	–	42.6	36.6	420	300
Malta	4.7	3.8	2.0	2,310	1,200
Netherlands	19.3	4.2	1.6	15,650	235
Poland	3.3	0.2	0.1	10,535	120
Portugal	8.0	4.2	1.1	145	14
Romania	10.5	0.1	0.0	1,210	10
Slovakia	14.2	0.8	0.5	840	50
Slovenia	16.9	3.4	0.2	245	25
Spain	11.0	11.6	4.7	3,455	15
Sweden	12.0	5.7	2.6	23,305	715
United Kingdom	14.3	6.6	2.6	32,055	100
Total EU27		6.2	2.3	258,605	125

Sources: Compiled from CIA World Factbook estimates from national population censuses and Eurostat data.

they were residing, of which approximately one-quarter were migrants from another member state (Favell, 2008a; Recchi and Favell, 2009). France, the UK, Belgium, and the Netherlands, which once had colonial empires, have had significant minority populations since the 1950s, and Germany welcomed successive generations of guest workers in the 1960s and 1970s. By the 1990s, it had become clear that these guest workers were permanent immigrants. Moreover, in the 1990s many other EU states became net-immigration states for the first time, including Italy, Spain, Portugal, Greece, and Ireland.

The 1990s also saw a new wave of refugees to Western Europe from Central and Eastern Europe, the former Yugoslavia, North Africa, the Horn of Africa (Ethiopia and Somalia), the Great Lakes region of Africa (especially Rwanda and Burundi), and Afghanistan. As Figure 11.1 shows, total asylum applicants to the EU member states peaked above 400,000 per year in 2001, with large inflows from Iraq, Afghanistan, and North Africa, but have since declined to approximately half that level. Some of these people were able to claim *de jure* asylum status under the 1951 UN Convention on Asylum, but many could not, as they were not able to prove personal persecution. Nevertheless, these people are *de facto* refugees, in flight from economic deprivation, environmental destruction,

Figure 11.1 *Asylum applications per year*

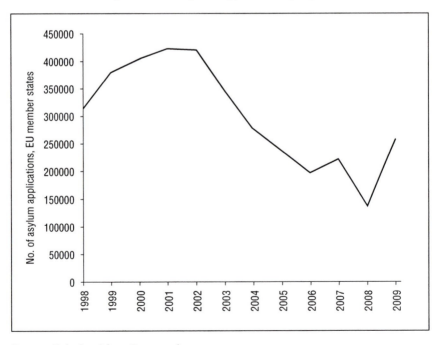

Source: Calculated from Eurostat data.

civil wars, or collapsed states, and therefore had to be offered some form of protection, either permanent or temporary. The EU states have not been equal recipients of these *de jure* and *de facto* refugees. For example, in the early 1990s Germany received almost 60 per cent of all asylum applications to the EU, in the early 2000s the UK received over 20 per cent of total applicants, and in 2009 Malta, Sweden, Belgium, and Austria received the greatest number of asylum applicants per capita of domestic population, as Table 11.1 shows.

In response to the changing patterns of global migration, European governments introduced new immigration, societal integration, and asylum policies (Baldwin-Edwards and Schain, 1994; Joppke, 1998). After the German government introduced more restrictive asylum procedures in the mid-1990s the number of asylum applications declined. Several other states followed the German lead (notably France and Denmark), in contrast to which the UK seemed to be a comparatively 'soft touch' for asylum seekers. Nevertheless, the variation in the burden of asylum applications can only be partially explained by government policies (Neumayer, 2005; Thielemann, 2003, 2004; Vink and Meijerink, 2003). Other factors played a much larger part in refugees' choice of destination, such as their country of origin, the size of the existing community of fellow nationals, and the second language of the refugee. For example, most asylum seekers in the early 1990s were from former Yugoslavia and preferred to go to Germany because it had a large Yugoslav population and was physically not too far from the Balkans. Similarly, in the late 1990s and early 2000s there was an explosion of asylum seekers from Afghanistan, who preferred to go to the UK. Because they either had family connections in the UK or spoke English as a second language, the relative distance of Afghanistan from the UK was not a determining factor.

The 1990s also saw a rise in international organized crime (Anderson *et al.*, 1995). This category of crime covers a variety of activities, ranging from serious crimes such as terrorism, drug trafficking, money laundering, Mafia activities, arms trafficking, and fraud against private corporations and governmental (national and EU) budgets, to lesser crimes such as football hooliganism, the smuggling of tax-free goods, and national cultural treasures, and the distribution of banned racist and pornographic publications. It is difficult to ascertain the exact extent to which international crime has increased, but the limited statistics that do exist suggest a moderate increase in all member states (Alvazzi del Frate *et al.*, 1993).

At the same time, the terrorist attacks on New York and Washington in September 2001, followed by the attacks on Madrid in 2004 and London in 2005, and the related 'global war on terrorism' forced governments in Europe to develop common external as well as internal policies to tackle the new global terrorist threats. On the external side, this involved discussions of a common EU strategy towards groups such as Al-Qaeda and potential terrorists entering the EU, while on the internal side the EU states began to coordinate their efforts to identify and deal with home-grown terrorist threats.

The removal of border controls in the single market has not necessarily facilitated the rise in migration, organized crime, and terrorist activities. Rather, migration rose after the collapse of communism, conflicts in the Balkans and Central Asia, and crises in Northern, Eastern, and Central Africa. Similarly, organized crime in Europe is a part of global criminal activities and is connected to the globalization of capital flows and national policies unrelated to the EU, for example the liberalization of laws on soft drugs such as cannabis. And, global terrorism has arisen as a result of failed states close to Europe's borders, the spread of radical Islam both outside and inside Europe, and growing resentment among Muslims in Europe and across the world about the policies of Western states towards the Islamic world and the Middle East.

Nevertheless, the removal of physical controls on the movement of goods, services, and persons has made it difficult for national governments in Europe to pursue independent policies to control migration, international crime, and global terrorism. Open internal borders means that one government's immigration policy has a potential impact on the number of migrants to other EU states. Such negative externalities of separate national immigration policies have forced the governments to accept that migration should be tackled collectively at the European level through some form of 'burden-sharing' – with the costs of common initiatives and public goods being shared by the member states (see Czaika, 2009; Dewan and Thielemann, 2006). The situation is not so clear in the case of cross-border crime and terrorist activities, as reducing crime or fighting terrorism in one state will not automatically increase criminal or terrorist activity in a neighbouring state.

Intergovernmentalism: high politics, voters' demands, and bureaucrats' interests

As part of the single market programme the EU governments were less willing to remove physical borders on the movement of persons – which is a salient 'high politics' issue – than barriers to the movement of goods, services, and capital – which are usually 'low politics' issues. It was not long, though, before the governments could not resist the pressure for common action, at which point they chose to cooperate through intergovernmental procedures – first through informal mechanisms and then in a separate intergovernmental (third) pillar in the EU. Under these arrangements, national sovereignty is preserved in two ways: decisions are taken by unanimity, which allows any government to veto a measure that threatens a vital national interest; and decisions do not have direct effect in domestic law – they need to be transposed into domestic law by parliaments and are justiciable only in domestic courts.

However, in the mid-1990s the political calculations of the governments changed. First, the governments were forced to face up to the failure of these intergovernmental methods for tackling migration and policing issues. As already noted, the single market produced negative externalities on immigration, asylum, and policing policies as governments were affected by each other's policies on refugees, border controls, and immigration. As a result, the governments had a collective interest in developing frameworks to discuss each other's policies and develop common strategies, despite this being an area of high politics, and they duly established institutions for collective decision-making with the Trevi framework, the Schengen Accord and the JHA provisions of the Maastricht Treaty.

Nevertheless, the intergovernmental nature of these institutions obstructed coherent policy development. In addition to the unanimity requirement, there was no independent agenda-setter. The governments had to rely on each other to come up with legislative proposals, and these inevitably tended to promote the individual interests of the government currently holding the Council Presidency, rather than the collective interests of the EU. Also, once a policy had been adopted there was no guarantee that non-binding actions (such as a convention) would ever be enforced. Each member state had an incentive not to implement agreements once they had been adopted as they were costly to force on unwilling publics, and their citizens could free-ride on the liberal policies of other states. The result was a classic collective action problem, with a suboptimal outcome: few collective policies and a low level of implementation (Ireland, 1995; Ugur, 1995). Put this way, the issue facing governments in the area of migration policies in the mid-1990s was similar to the issue they had faced on market regulation policies in the mid-1980s: there was a growing public and elite perception of policy failure, and the easiest way of tackling this crisis was to delegate agenda-setting to an independent agent – the Commission (Alink *et al.*, 2001; Stetter, 2000).

Second, governments were forced to respond to new voter concerns. A reason for governments not to delegate high politics issues to the supranational level is that voters might be opposed to external interference in these areas. However, voters can change their minds and concede to the erosion of national sovereignty to secure individual and collective goals, such as personal freedom, reduced immigration, or the control of crime. In the mid-1990s this was exactly what happened in the area of migration policy. For the first time, a majority of Europe's voters were in favour of more cooperation at the European level to stem migration flows (Lahav, 2004: 69–112; Turnbull and Sandholtz, 2001). Rather than complaining about interference from Brussels, voters recognized the ineffectiveness of national immigration policies and demanded collective action. As they shared the voters' (negative) attitude towards immigration, the governments were eager to oblige.

Figure 11.2   *Public support for EU action on crime and immigration*

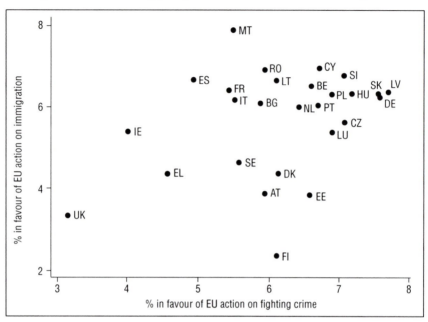

Note: The survey question was: 'For each of the following areas do you think the decision should be made by the [Nationality] government, or made jointly within the
European Union?'. The figure shows the per cent of respondents in each member state
who answered 'jointly within the European Union' for the issues of fighting crime and
immigration, separately.

Source: Calculated from Eurobarometer 69.2 (spring 2008) data.

With the growth in international criminal activity and the shock of the
terrorist attacks in the US on 11 September 2001, voters also started to
favour EU action on cross-border crime and fighting terrorism. For
example, Figure 11.2 shows the attitudes of publics across Europe in
spring 2008 to common EU action on immigration and fighting crime. At
the individual level, there is considerable variation in support for EU
policy-making on immigration and crime, with individuals with strong
national identities being less supportive of an EU role in migration policies, for example (Luedtke, 2005). At the aggregate national level,
however, a clear majority of citizens in a majority of member states is in
favour of common EU action in both these policy areas. Only in the UK
and Greece did less than a majority of respondents support common EU
action on both these policy issues.

Third, bureaucratic elites within interior ministries began to support
further EU-level cooperation (Bigo, 1994). Governments are not unitary
actors, and within governments, politicians and bureaucrats can have

different interests. Whereas politicians seek re-election, bureaucrats seek more influence over policy outcomes, for example through larger budgets (Niskanen, 1971) or greater freedom to shape their own organizational structures and policy choices (Dunleavy, 1990; see also Chapter 2). The single market posed a threat to the status and resources of interior and justice ministries. The removal of border controls on the movement of goods, services, capital, and labour implied that fewer resources would need to be spent in interior and justice ministries. Also, without customs and excise duties, these departments would receive fewer revenues. Interior and justice ministers across the EU produced reports designed to scare politicians into dedicating resources to their ministries to fight the spectre of 'Euro-crime' (Clutterbuck, 1990; Heidensohn and Farrell, 1993).

As part of their response to these threats, administrative elites in interior ministries sought to develop new networks and decision-making mechanisms at the European level. One of their motivations was the opportunity to share policy ideas with officials facing similar problems. Another motivation was that cooperation at the European level would to some extent free them from domestic political pressures, the attention of interest groups that were opposed to restrictive migration or security policies, competition from other ministries for resources and space in the policy agenda, and parliamentary and judicial scrutiny. Virginie Guiraudon (2000) calls this 'venue shopping', whereby interior ministry officials looked for the forum that offered them the greatest freedom to devise and implement policies that best suited their collective policy interests. The ad hoc intergovernmental settings at the European level were perfect for this, with no official records of meetings and beyond the attention of parliaments and publics.

Consequently, the actions taken by governments in the Amsterdam and Lisbon Treaties can be regarded as at least in part a response to self-interest and domestic public and administrative pressure. As the issues of illegal immigration, asylum seekers, cross-border crime, and terrorism rose on the domestic agenda, the governments took several decisive steps towards supranational decision-making on free movement and internal security issues: delegating agenda-setting powers to the Commission, replacing unanimity voting with QMV, using binding legal instruments, and granting monitoring and enforcement powers to the Commission and the ECJ.

Supranational politics: entrepreneurship, credibility, and actors' preferences

The institutional outcome in the Amsterdam Treaty and the development of policies since then are also products of deliberate strategies by supranational actors, outside the control of national governments. As a result of the activities and policy ideas promoted by the EU institutions and non-governmental organizations, the governments were persuaded that replacing intergovernmental procedures with supranational mechanisms would improve the credibility and accountability of policy-making, particularly in the case of immigration and asylum policies. And once the new agenda-setting powers were delegated to the Commission, supranational agents at the European level were eager to use them to their maximum extent.

The most influential of the supranational institutions was the Commission. Under the Maastricht Treaty the Commission was virtually excluded from influencing policy-making in the JHA field. But, following the ratification of the treaty, the Commission strengthened its ability to develop JHA policy ideas, with a new division in the secretariat-general, and a JHA policy portfolio with one of the Commissioners. This was a long-term strategy. Despite the absence of formal agenda-setting powers, the Commission sought to develop credible policy ideas in the expectation that this would tempt the governments to delegate this function to the Commission in the next round of treaty reform. As a result, between 1994 and 1996 the Commission undertook a series of policy initiatives, such as the funding of independent research on national immigration and social integration policies, and negotiations with the US State Department on possible US–European cooperation on international migration and crime issues (for example, on a transatlantic temporary protection regime for refugees from the former Yugoslavia). The Commission also argued that a central reason for the lack of policy development in this area was because it did not have an agenda-setting role.

This strategy paid off. Seeing that the Commission had developed expertise in these areas and could present credible policy ideas, the governments agreed (in the Amsterdam Treaty) to share the right of initiative with the Commission. Once this power had been delegated to the Commission, the new directorate-general for JHA set to work on legislative proposals across the full range of policy areas covered by the fields of freedom, security and justice. One example of the Commission's entrepreneurship in this field was its freedom, security, and justice scoreboard, which lists over 50 issues upon which the member states had promised to act, and for each issue sets out what action the Commission thinks is needed and the timetable the Commission thinks is necessary. This scoreboard has raised the profile of EU policies among interest groups and the media, and focused the minds of decision-makers in national ministries.

The second supranational actor with a vested interest in further policy integration in this area was the European Parliament. Since the establishment of the Trevi and Schengen groups, the European Parliament has been critical of the secretive nature of intergovernmental cooperation on migration and security issues. It was also critical of the Maastricht Treaty provisions, despite its new right to question the Council Presidency about JHA developments. The European Parliament argued that the decision procedures removed policy-making accountability from national parliaments without replacing it with effective powers of scrutiny for the European Parliament. In the intergovernmental conference which led to the Amsterdam Treaty the European Parliament argued that legislation in this policy domain should be adopted using the consultation procedure, initially, with the possibility of moving to the co-decision procedure at a later date. This was a minimalist strategy, as the European Parliament did not demand full legislative rights immediately, simply the right to issue opinions, which would give it a limited power of delay (see Chapter 3). The governments agreed, as it seemed a small price to pay to satisfy demands for greater transparency and accountability in policy-making, which the EU heads of government had established as one of the main aims of the intergovernmental conference in all policy areas.

The governments then moved to the co-decision procedure for almost all immigration and asylum policy issues at the same time as they shifted decision-making to QMV on these issues, with the adoption of the Hague Programme in 2004. This decision was partly a response to policy failure and domestic pressure, as discussed. However, many governments were also willing to move to the co-decision procedure on these issues as they trusted the European Parliament, having seen how the MEPs and political groups in the Parliament had operated when scrutinizing the large number of directives that were adopted between 1999 and 2004 under the consultation procedure. On most of these issues the majority in the European Parliament voted in favour of more liberal migration policies, with the liberal group voting with the socialists, greens, and radical left MEPs, against the centre-right and conservatives (Hix and Noury, 2007). As Figure 11.3 shows, most EU governments in the early 2000s also had relatively liberal attitudes towards immigrants, and so had little to fear from increasing the power of the majority in the European Parliament.

Nevertheless, by 2010 the centre of gravity on immigration policies in the EU institutions had shifted considerably to the right. The dominant coalition in the Council is now on the centre-right, and the Barroso Commission is dominated by politicians from parties who have relatively conservative views on immigration. The positions of the main groups in the European Parliament on migration and related issues may not have changed much over this period. However, on some key issues the liberal group has voted with the centre-right groups in support of more restrictive immigration policies, as it did in 2008 on the controversial returns directive. As Table 11.2 shows, the returns directive passed in the European Parliament by 367 votes in favour to 205 votes against, and the winning majority was composed of a centre-right coalition of national-conservatives (UEN), the Christian democrats/conservatives (EPP–ED),

Figure 11.3   *Politics of interior policies*

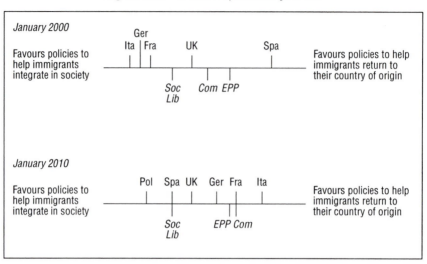

Note: The locations of the national governments are taken from expert judgements about party positions on a number of policy scales, as collected by Benoit and Laver (2006). The locations of the Commission are the median locations of the national parties of the Commissioners in the Prodi Commission and the second Barroso Commission, using the Benoit–Laver data. The locations of the EPP, Socialist (Soc), and Liberal (Lib) groups in the European Parliament are taken from the expert judgements about the positions of the political groups in the EP collected by McElroy and Benoit (2007). The member state governments are shown above the lines and the supranational actors are shown below the lines and in italics.

and liberals (ALDE), with the socialists (PES) opposed but divided. Voting on the returns directive, as on most issues in the European Parliament, was mainly along political group lines rather than along national lines. Nevertheless, Table 11.2 also reveals that the MEPs from Spain, Latvia, Slovakia, Slovenia, and Germany voted in a relatively cohesive way for the directive.

Another supranational institution, the ECJ, has also played a role. In its submission to the intergovernmental conference which led to the Amsterdam Treaty the ECJ was careful not to propose any concrete measures for reform. However, the ECJ did argue that there was a clear clash of jurisdictions in the Maastricht design in this policy area. Under the citizenship provisions in the first pillar the ECJ was required to protect the fundamental rights of EU citizens, yet although the policy areas tackled under the third pillar touched on this issue, neither it nor national courts had jurisdiction over Council decisions on justice and home affairs. The ECJ consequently argued that the treaties should be reformed to ensure consistent interpretation and application of Community law and the justice and home affairs provisions. A few

Table 11.2   *Vote in the European Parliament on the Returns Directive*

Group/member state	For	Against	Abstain	Absent	Total	Cohesion
Vote by political group						
UEN	39	0	3	2	44	0.89
EPP-ED	218	1	29	38	286	0.82
ALDE	57	8	21	14	100	0.49
Non attached	15	5	4	6	30	0.44
IND/DEM	6	11	3	2	22	0.33
PES	32	105	48	32	217	0.35
G/EFA	0	38	2	3	43	0.93
EUL/NGL	0	37	0	4	41	1.00
Vote by member state delegation						
Malta	2	0	2	1	5	0.25
Spain	39	4	3	8	54	0.77
Latvia	8	1	0	0	9	0.83
Slovakia	11	2	1	0	14	0.68
Slovenia	5	1	1	0	7	0.57
Lithuania	8	2	3	0	13	0.42
Poland	34	9	8	3	54	0.50
Hungary	13	4	5	2	24	0.39
Germany	62	24	2	11	99	0.56
Netherlands	13	6	6	2	27	0.28
Romania	17	8	2	7	34	0.44
Bulgaria	10	5	0	3	18	0.50
Czech Republic	12	6	2	4	24	0.40
Ireland	4	2	6	1	13	0.25
Italy	30	16	13	18	77	0.26
Finland	8	5	0	1	14	0.42
Cyprus	3	2	0	1	6	0.40
Denmark	4	3	6	1	14	0.19
Belgium	8	7	1	8	24	0.25
Luxembourg	3	3	0	0	6	0.25
Greece	10	10	1	3	24	0.21
Austria	6	6	0	6	18	0.25
Estonia	2	2	1	1	6	0.10
Sweden	9	10	0	0	19	0.29
France	27	37	4	10	78	0.32
Portugal	9	13	0	2	24	0.39
United Kingdom	10	17	43	8	78	0.42
Total	367	205	110	101	783	
%	64.2	35.8				

Note: The table shows the vote on the proposal for a directive on common standards and procedures in member states for returning illegally staying third-country nationals, which took place on 18 June 2008. The political groups and member state delegations are sorted from most in favour of the directive to most opposed. There were only 783 MEPs at that time (instead of 785), as two MEPs had resigned and had not yet been replaced. In the vote, 76.2 per cent of MEPs voted the same way as the plurality of their political group, while 61.4 per cent of MEPs voted the same way as the plurality of their member state delegation. See Chapter 6 for the calculation of cohesion scores.

Source: Compiled from VoteWatch.eu data (at: www.votewatch.eu/cx_vote_details. php?id_act=4418).

months later, in March 1996, the ECJ issued Opinion (2/94) on a request from the Council, arguing that the treaty base was insufficient for the accession of the EU to the European Convention on Human Rights. This opinion was against the views of a number of pro-integrationist member states, such as the Benelux countries. The ECJ's strategy – of critical analysis accompanied by moderation – paid off in the Amsterdam and Lisbon Treaties, which extended the ECJ's jurisdiction to all migration and security issues and also incorporated the Charter of Fundamental Rights into the treaty, under the jurisdiction of the ECJ.

Finally, a number of NGOs have lobbied for more supranational policy-making on migration and security issues (see Ireland, 1991; Niessen, 2000). These included Brussels-based groups such as the European Council of Refugees and Exiles, Migrants Forum, Migration Policy Group, and the Starting Line Group. They also included national groups such as the Dutch Standing Committee of Experts on International Immigration, Refugee and Criminal Law, and the British Commission for Racial Equality (CRE) and the Federal Trust. Despite their differing perspectives, these groups have been unanimous in their criticism of the secretive nature of intergovernmental decision-making, the lack of judicial and parliamentary control, and the subordination of migration issues to crime policies (Chopin and Niessen, 1998; Federal Trust, 1996; Meijers *et al.*, 1997). Their demands have been particularly effective in the case of centre-left governments. For example, under pressure from the CRE the British Labour government dropped its opposition to a general anti-racism clause in the treaty and accepted the idea of allowing the other member states to integrate their immigration policies.

Conclusion: a Pan-European State?

Through the development of EU interior policies a social contract is emerging between EU citizens and the EU polity. The EU does not have the exclusive right to decide who can be an EU citizen. However, with the completion of the single market, the EU institutions have established and are responsible for governing a set of common economic rights for nationals of the member states, based on the freedom to move between countries, seek employment, trade, and provide and consume services. Furthermore, with the establishment of EU citizenship, the member states are no longer independent from the EU polity in determining who may receive social, civil, and political rights in the domestic system.

The EU does not have a legitimate monopoly on the use of force to guarantee, protect, and secure individual and collective rights. Nevertheless, through the development of EU competences on immigration and asylum and on police and judicial cooperation, the EU governments have chosen to cooperate in deciding how domestic security forces operate to secure these goals. Furthermore, through the delegation of power of legislative initiative to the Commission, legislative rights for the European Parliament, and judicial review by the ECJ, the treaty reforms have established a new policy regime in which the EU institutions have a say in fighting cross-border crime and directing those domestic security agencies which make asylum and immigration decisions.

Chapter 12

Foreign Policies

Theories of International Relations and Political Economy
External Economic Policies: Free Trade, Not 'Fortress Europe'
Security and Defence Policies
Enlargement
Explaining EU Foreign Policies
Conclusion: a Major Player in Global Politics?

The EU pursues two main types of policies towards the rest of the world: economic policies, through trade agreements and development and humanitarian aid; and foreign and security policy, through the Common Foreign and Security Policy (CFSP) and the European Security and Defence Policy (ESDP). Nevertheless, the most important foreign policy of the EU since the end of the Cold War has been the process of integrating the Central and Eastern European countries into the EU, and managing its relations with its bordering non-member states. This chapter seeks to explain the development of EU foreign policy, in particular why it seems to be better able to play an important role in some policy areas than in others. To guide our explanation, we first review the main theoretical frameworks in international relations and international political economy.

Theories of International Relations and Political Economy

There are three central theoretical frameworks within contemporary international relations: realism, liberalism, and constructivism (Woods, 1996). Realism views international relations as a continuous struggle for power and domination between states in a system of anarchy (Morgenthau, 1948; Waltz, 2000). The contemporary neo-realist version of this approach has three core assumptions: (a) states are unitary actors; (b) their preferences are mainly geopolitical; and (c) states aim to maximize their security given the relative balance of power (Keohane, 1986; Waltz, 1979). Realists consequently argue that because states have stable territorial and socio-political structures, their geopolitical and security preferences are also stable. As a result, each of the rival actors in the international system can predict how the others are likely to behave. Moreover, because security interests are perceived to be in conflict rather than complementary, inter-state politics tends to be a zero-sum game. If one state wins, another must lose. Cooperation between states is thus unlikely as there is little oppor-tunity for the provision of a common public good, and there are no cred-ible enforcing agents in a system of anarchy. Hence, once created, international institutions (such as the United Nations and the EU) are instruments of states' preferences and powers, not constraints on their power. The intergovernmental theory of EU politics draws heavily on this approach to interstate relations.

Liberalism, on the other hand, sees international relations as driven by global economic interdependence. This approach starts from three differ-ent assumptions about state preferences and behaviour: (a) state prefer-ences are formed through competition between domestic groups; (b) the interests of these groups are primarily economic, not geopolitical; and (c) international and supranational institutions, as well as development in other parts of the international system, can shape the preferences of state officials (Evans *et al.*, 1993; Keohane and Nye, 1989; Milner, 1997; Rosecrance, 1986).

These assumptions lead liberals, unlike realists, to predict that states' preferences are unstable (Frieden, 1991; Moravcsik, 1997). First, inter-ests change if different societal actors win in domestic competition over national power, for example when the ruling political parties are replaced following national elections. Second, interests change when individual economic opportunities open up as a result of changes in the global system.

Liberals also predict more interstate cooperation and formation of international institutions than realists. Because states' interests are defined in terms of economics and economic interdependence increases with globalization, states have incentives to create institutions to help solve collective action problems, for example to coordinate product stan-dards or enforce trade rules (Grieco, 1990; Keohane, 1984; Krasner, 1983). This leads to the delegation of enforceable functions to interna-tional institutions. Liberalism questions the realist description of the international system as an anarchic system. Instead, they claim that the international system is best described as a series of international regimes. In the theories of EU politics, Andrew Moravcsik (1993, 1998) combines these ideas with the realist version of interstate bargain, to create what he calls the 'liberal–intergovernmental' theory.

The realist–liberal divide has specific application in the field of inter-national political economy (see Frieden and Lake, 1995). In global economic relations, realists assert the primacy of politics over economics. International economic policies are pursued to achieve geopolitical goals such as strengthening state security and political hegemony. Consequently, realists predict that states will sacrifice economic gains to strengthen their position in the global struggle for power. For example, trade protection often reduces a state's long-term welfare, but may increase its leverage in the international system. Although free trade agreements do emerge, realists consider that this is usually a result of 'hegemonic stability', in which a single dominant actor has the power to construct an economic regime to suit its own political interests at the expense of those of its partner.

Liberals, on the other hand, assert the primacy of economics and societal economic interests over politics and power relations. Most liberals accept the insight from neoclassical economics that the free market is the most efficient way of allocating resources. Rather than competing in the production of the same goods, total welfare will increase if states specialize in the production of goods in which they have a comparative advantage. Consequently, liberals argue that in a world where individual economic interests drive politics, states should recognize the potential gains from trade and pursue free trade rather than protectionist policies. Nevertheless, liberals accept that government is important for the provision of public goods – goods and services that would not be supplied in sufficient quantity by the market (see Chapter 8). Global governance institutions are hence necessary to provide the sufficient conditions for free trade and competitive global markets, such as stable property rights and rules against protectionism and unfair competition.

Liberals also think that domestic government institutions produce particular external economic policy outcomes. Historically, free trade policies developed as a result of trade policies being locked into a constitution, as in the case of the interstate commerce clause in the US constitution, or through the establishment of a parliamentary majority in favour of trade liberalization, as in the case of the Corn Laws in the mid-nineteenth century in the UK (McGillivray *et al.*, 2001). By forcing leaders to promote the interest of the median voter rather than a particular special interest, democratic regimes tend to promote free trade policies and the enforcement of international trade agreements (Mansfield *et al.*, 2002).

Finally, constructivism sees international relations as dominated by cultural, ideological, and ideational forces. This focus distinguishes constructivism from the interest-based focus of both realist and liberal approaches. Despite the fact that the constructivist research programme is rather heterogeneous, most scholars in this approach share three common assumptions (Ruggie, 1998): (a) preferences stem from ideological and/or cultural norms; (b) actors are not rational in the narrow instrumentalist sense, but instead are guided by symbolic or historical trajectories; and (c) preferences and behaviour evolve as a results of social interaction and socialization (Finnemore and Sikkink, 1998; Hill, 2003; Risse *et al.*, 1999).

These assumptions lead constructivists to argue that international institutions can have profound and unexpected consequences. Actors are forced to adapt their preferences and behaviour to the 'constitutive' norms of institutional organizations and society, such as the human rights clause of the United Nations Charter. International norms may be constructed and promoted by both states and non-state actors such as NGOs (Keck and Sikkink, 1998). Like liberals, constructivists do not accept the realist premise that states are the only relevant actors in international politics. Furthermore, through regular interactions in international institutions and shared knowledge communities, the preferences of foreign policy elites and the normative justifications for their actions are likely to converge. This logic is not dissimilar to the early neo-functionalist view of European integration (see Rosamond, 2000).

These three approaches predict different things about the EU's foreign policies. From the realist perspective, because the EU is not a state it will not have a clear and indivisible national interest. Instead, EU foreign policies will be dominated by the geopolitical and security concerns of the member states.

From a liberal perspective, in contrast, the battle between the member states will be between rival economic, not geopolitical, interests. While liberal theory predicts that EU external economic policies will determine how the EU acts in foreign and security policies, realist theory predicts the opposite. Also, while realists expect member states' foreign policy preferences to be stable, liberals and constructivists expect them to be changing. For liberals, states' preferences will change as the power of domestic economic forces changes.

For constructivists, EU diplomats' and negotiators' interests, and their understanding of their role and the question at hand, will change as a result of their interaction with and adaptation to the institutional and normative environment of EU foreign policy-making.

Finally, whereas realists predict that the institutional rules of EU foreign policies will be largely irrelevant, liberals and constructivists both think that institutions matter, but for different reasons. Liberals argue that institutions matter because the allocation of agenda-setting and decision-making powers shapes policy outcomes, while constructivists argue that institutions matter because the design of the rules determines the values and identities that emerge.

External Economic Policies: Free Trade, Not 'Fortress Europe'

The EU has developed common external policies in parallel to the development of internal economic integration. This development has been both out of necessity to preserve the coherence of the single market and out of the choice to promote EU economic interests in the global economy. This has resulted in three types of external economic policy: (a) a single set of rules on the importation of goods; (b) bilateral and multilateral trade agreements between the EU and other states and trading blocks; and (c) trade, aid and cooperation policies with developing countries.

Pattern of EU trade

The EU is the world's largest market. The EU's two largest trading partners are China and the US. The EU imports most goods from China. In 2008, Chinese exports to the EU amounted to €248 billion, while the EU only exported €78 billion to China. This means that the EU runs a large trade deficit with China. The trade deficit with China accounts for 65 per cent of the EU's total trade deficit. The largest external market for EU exporters is the US. EU exports to the US amount to €250 billion, while the EU market is worth €187 billion to US exporters. The EU hence runs a trade surplus with the US. In total, EU–US trade accounts for 15 per cent of total EU external trade, while trade with China accounts for 11 per cent. Other large trading partners are the EU's neighbouring states, particularly Russia, Switzerland, and Norway. Due to the EU's dependency on gas and oil from Russia and Norway, the EU runs large trading deficits with these countries. The EU also runs a substantial trade deficit with Japan.

In terms of the composition of EU trade, the bulk is intra-industry trade (in which the same products are imported and exported) in the manufacturing sector, for example in machinery, chemicals, and other manufacturing goods. Although services have been excluded from the statistics on commodities trade, EU trade in services such as financial services, tourism, and transport has risen to over 20 per cent of total EU trade. In terms of the trade balance by sector, the EU is a net importer of raw materials for manufacturing (such as minerals and fuels, and crude materials, oils, and fats) and a net exporter of finished products, although the trade surpluses in some manufacturing sectors have declined in recent decades.

As a result of the CAP, the EU is almost self-sufficient in agriculture products, and consequently exports almost as much food products, beverages, and tobacco as it imports. The current imbalance in the EU external trade is mainly due to energy. While the EU exports energy products worth €81 billion, it imports energy worth €456 billion. As access to energy is essential for a functioning economy, and a major source of the EU's trading budget, there are both security and economic rationales for EU foreign policy initiatives in the area of energy policy.

The Common Commercial Policy

The EU has a single external trade policy, known as the Common Commercial Policy (CCP). The objective of the CCP is essentially liberal: to promote development of world trade, progressive abolition of restrictions on international trade and lowering of customs barriers. Nonetheless, the CCP operates through several protectionist policy instruments. The four main ones are as follows:

1   *The Common External Tariff.* With the establishment of the common market, the EU states agreed to apply the same tariffs on goods entering their country from any state outside the EU. As part of the multilateral GATT, in 2000 the EU reduced tariffs by approximately one-third, to an average of 18 per cent on agricultural goods and zero per cent on many manufactured goods.
2   *Import quotas.* Due to the single market, member states were obliged to replace national quotas with EU-wide restrictions on the import of certain goods (as monitoring national quotas would be impossible without border controls on goods). These quotas currently apply to a wide variety of products, including agricultural products as well as iron and steel.
3   *Anti-dumping measures.* The Commission has the power to impose import tariffs and minimum price levels if exporters to the EU sell at discriminatory prices that are likely to harm domestic producers. According to the WTO, the EU is a frequent user of anti-dumping measures.
4   *Voluntary Export Restraints (VERs).* VERs are arrangements between an exporter state and an importer state, whereby the exporter agrees to limit the volume of goods consigned to the importer. VERs usually result from political pressure, such as the threat of anti-dumping measures by an importer. However, they can also be established to protect the interests of both exporters and import-competing domestic producers at the expense of consumers in the importing country.

In addition to these measures, the EU uses several minor measures to restrict free trade. These include: export-promoting measures, where the Commission organizes EU trade fairs and coordinates national initiatives; trade sanctions, which are usually imposed for political reasons and are based on decisions by the UN Security Council; countervailing duties, which the EU imposes if there is evidence of export subsidies in third countries; safeguard clauses, which allow the members of the WTO to suspend normal rules to protect a vital interest; and rules of origin, which determine the proportion of a product that must be added locally for a product to qualify as originating from the EU or from a state covered by a preferential trade agreement.

Under the decision-making rules of the CCP, the Commission has a monopoly of legislative initiative, and is also responsible for managing the execution of the CCP. The Commission negotiates all external trade agreements related to goods and in areas there the EU has competence, on behalf of the Council (rather like the US President's 'fast track' mandate from the US Congress). Moreover, the Commission has the power of executive decree. That means that the Commission can adopt anti-dumping measures, countervailing duties, and other import restrictions. These measures have to be reviewed by the Council and the European Parliament after a set time. Following the Lisbon Treaty, the Council and the European Parliament can act under the ordinary legislative procedure, to issue negotiation mandates to the Commission or to approve agreements negotiated by the Commission.

Multilateral trade agreements: GATT and WTO

The EU has been a key player in the negotiation and establishment of the global trading regime that has gradually led to liberalization of world trade. GATT was first agreed in 1948. Since the Dillon Round in 1960 to 1962, the EU has attempted to coordinate a common stance in successive negotiations to reform the GATT. With the Commission as the EU's negotiator, the EU managed to act with a single voice in subsequent negotiations: the Kennedy Round in 1964 to 1967, the Tokyo Round in 1973 to 1979, and the Uruguay Round in 1986 to 1994, which established the World Trade Organization (WTO). Finally, the Doha Round started in 2001 and is still ongoing.

Since the establishment of the WTO, the EU has been one of its strongest defenders. Successive EU trade Commissioners have argued to their colleagues in the Commission and the governments that because the EU is the world's largest trading block it has the most to gain from the liberalization of world trade. Moreover, if the EU does not abide by the WTO rules, there is little incentive for the US to do so. As the US, at least prior to Obama becoming President, has become increasingly isolationist on trade policy, its commitment to the WTO rules has been a concern for the EU. However, the US supports multilateral trade bargaining, and criticizes the EU for its various anti-free-trade policies, in particular in the field of agriculture. The Bush administration was keener than previous administrations to protect particular industrial sectors from external competitions. Although Obama made some promises along those lines in the electoral campaign in 2008, he did not let such promises guide his economic stimulus packages adopted to cope with the financial crises in 2009, which mainly went to banking and manufacturing. When the WTO has ruled against the US protectionist measures and authorized the EU to introduce tariffs on US goods as compensation, US trade negotiators have deliberately challenged other EU policies before the WTO to strengthen their hand in bilateral EU–US negotiations.

While the EU may be able to use its trade muscle to force the US to abide by multilateral trade rules, this policy is not without costs. The US has challenged EU rules in a number of areas, such as on the permitted percentage of genetically modified organisms (GMOs) in foodstuffs and the geographical origin of foodstuff. It is not clear whether the EU was in breach of the WTO rules on these issues. However, the US actions demonstrate that the US does not like to be defeated by the EU and that the EU is equally as willing as the US to protect certain industrial sectors (agriculture) and to use consumer preferences (such as in the GMO case) as non-tariff barriers. Due to fear of US retaliation or isolationism, when the WTO has looked set to rule against the EU on a high-profile issue, the Commission has urged the Council to reform the offending policy or law before the WTO has had a chance to act.

Bilateral preferential trade agreements

The EU has many different types of preferential trade agreements with a wide range of countries and regions of the world. These agreements grant varying degree of access to the single market. The hierarchy is as follows (with the most privileged at the top):

- the European Economic Area (EEA) with Norway, Iceland, and Liechtenstein;
- stabilization and association agreements with the Balkan states;
- free-trade agreements with Switzerland, Turkey, Island, Egypt, Jordan, Morocco, Tunisia, Algeria, Lebanon, and Syria;
- Partnership Agreements with African, Caribbean, and Pacific former colonies of European countries;
- the Generalized System of Preferences, which gives privileged access to the single market for certain products from developing countries;
- mutual recognition agreements with the US and Canada;
- Partnership and Cooperation Agreements with the ten members of the Commonwealth of Independent States;
- Inter-Regional Association Agreements with the Andean Pact, Mercosur, the Central American Customs Union, the Gulf Cooperation Council, and the Association of Southeast Asian Nations; and
- a variety of trade agreements with other countries, including China, Australia, New Zealand, South Africa, Argentina, Brazil, India, Pakistan, Mexico, and South Korea.

The different degrees of access to the single market provided by these agreements reflect the political priorities of the EU. The EEA agreement allows states that would be eligible to join the EU but have at least for now chosen to remain outside of the EU, to gain access to the EU single market – a similar relationship to that between a 'commonwealth' of the US (such as Puerto Rico) and the US market. The level of integration between the EU and the EEA economies became painfully clear to both

Icelanders and the EU customers of Icelandic banks in the wake of the collapse of the Icelandic banks during the financial crises in 2009.

The Commission has argued that the agreements with the US and Canada for the 'mutual recognition' of product standards in a number of product areas (based on the same principles as in the EU single market) could be the basis for a general free-trade agreement between the EU and the North American Free Trade Area (NAFTA). Lower down the hierarchy of access are the general members of the WTO (such as Japan), and at the bottom are non-members of the WTO (for example Iran and North Korea).

European development policy

The EU uses its external economic policies to promote political and economic progress in the developing world. The EU, via the EU budget and the member states' budgets, is the world's largest aid donor, accounting for over 50 per cent of the world's official development assistance. In 2006, the total value of EU development assistance was €47 billion. This is almost €100 per citizen. This is a high figure compared to the US (€53 per citizen) and Japan (€69 per citizen) (EU Commission, 2007:13). This gives the EU a powerful position in international development policy. The EU has adopted the UN Millennium Development Goals as the key development aims to achieve by 2015, which include eradicating extreme poverty and hunger, universal primary education, gender equality, reducing infant mortality, combating AIDS and other diseases, and environmental sustainability.

In 2005 the EU adopted 'the European Consensus on Development' which sets out the EU's vision in the field of development policy. In addition to the Millennium Development Goals, the EU stresses Europe's democratic values and the responsibility of developing countries responsibility for their own development. At the same time, the EU is through its 'policy coherence for development' aiming to achieve synergies from other policy fields in the understanding that development policies cannot be successful if pursued in isolation from other policy-areas such as agriculture, trade, migration, security, and climate change.

Security and Defence Policies

Development of foreign policy cooperation and decision-making

The West European Union (WEU) was set up in 1948 between the European members of the North Atlantic Treaty Organization (NATO) including the UK, which was not a signatory of the Treaty of Rome. The six founding states subsequently agreed a plan for a European Defence

Community (EDC) in 1952. However, the French National Assembly rejected the latter because of concerns about national sovereignty. It was not until the attempt to relaunch European integration at the Hague Summit in 1969 that the governments sought to add a political dimension to the process of economic integration. The Hague Summit set up the European Political Cooperation (EPC) outside the legal structure of the treaties. EPC enabled foreign ministers and heads of government to debate broader political and security issues in the General Affairs Council, alongside their regular meetings in the European Council. The day-to-day business of EPC was managed by a network of committees composed of national bureaucrats and headed by 'political directors' – senior officials from the member states' foreign ministries.

EPC actions were taken through 'common positions' of the foreign ministers or heads of government. These were not binding, but the governments agreed that they would try not to undertake national actions that would contradict a common position. In 1981, the governments strengthened the structure by providing a new role for the rotating Presidency of the Council, formalizing a 'troika' system (of the previous, current, and next Presidencies), establishing a consultation role for the Commission, and allowing common positions to be adopted in a number of new areas (such as economic and trade sanctions).

The institutionalization of foreign policy cooperation was further enhanced when EPC was brought into the treaty framework in the Single European Act (SEA). While EPC remained separate from the institutions and policies of the EC, linking it to the treaty framework provided a legal framework for EPC actions, formalized the relationship between EPC and the General Affairs Council, and gave more freedom to the European Parliament to scrutinize the actions of national officials and foreign ministers. Also, the governments introduced a new decision-making norm for foreign policy: that decisions should be by consensus, and that if a consensus could not be reached, governments in the minority should abstain rather than vote against an agreement. This became known as 'constructive abstention' and has remained a central decision-making norm in the area of foreign policy cooperation.

However, at the beginning of the 1990s foreign and security policy issues were pushed to the top of the agenda with the revolutions in Central and Eastern Europe, the collapse of the Soviet empire and the sudden end of the Cold War. The inadequacy of the EPC structure, even within the SEA framework, was further highlighted by the outbreak of the Gulf crisis in August 1990 and the civil war in Yugoslavia in June 1991. In response, Europe's leaders agreed in June 1990 that an IGC on political union should be convened in parallel to the one preparing institutional reforms for economic and monetary union. The political union IGC, which concluded in December 1991 with the Maastricht Treaty, transformed EPC into the Common Foreign and Security Policy (CFSP):

the so-called 'second pillar' of the EU. The second pillar set out five CFSP objectives:

1   To strengthen the common values, fundamental interests and independence of the EU.
2   To strengthen the security of the EU and its member states in all ways.
3   To preserve peace and strengthen international security, in accordance with the principles of the United Nations Charter.
4   To promote international cooperation.
5   To develop and consolidate democracy and the rule of law, including human rights.

To achieve these goals the decision-making procedures and instruments of foreign policy cooperation were reformed. Foreign policy issues became a normal part of Council business: the EPC meetings of foreign ministers were subsumed within the General Affairs Council; the Political Committee (of the political directors) became part of the Committee of Permanent Representatives (COREPER); and the EPC secretariat joined the Council secretariat. The Commission consequently created a new External Political Affairs DG (now called the External Relations DG) to manage these responsibilities.

The European Parliament was not given a role in CFSP decision-making, but the Presidency of the Council is required to consult the European Parliament on the main aspects of the CFSP to ensure that the Parliament's views are taken into account, and to answer Parliament's questions related to CFSP. In addition, the European Parliament's Foreign Affairs committee has special colloquia four times a year with the chair of the Political Committee (the political director from the member state holding the Council Presidency).

The Maastricht Treaty also established two CFSP policy instruments:

1   *Common positions:* these are adopted in the Council by unanimity (but with the informal constructive abstention rule applying) and require the member states to implement national policies that comply with the position defined by the EU on a particular issue, for example in international organizations such as the UN Security Council. However, there are no legal sanctions for failing to comply with common positions.
2   *Joint actions:* these are operating actions to implement common positions, are adopted by the Council after the European Council has agreed that a matter should be subject of a joint action, and may be adopted by QMV (following a decision by unanimity that QMV can be used). This was the first time that a treaty provided for the use of QMV in the foreign policy field. Also, joint actions are more binding

than common positions. As with common positions, the member states are required to change their policies in accordance with a joint action, but under joint actions they must also inform and consult the Council on how joint actions have been implemented. If a member state is unable or unwilling to implement a joint action, it must justify its position to the other member states.

In addition, the Maastricht Treaty brought the issue of defence policy into the EU framework for the first time. Here, there was a compromise between the Atlanticists, who favoured strong ties with the US (for example the UK and the Netherlands), the Europeanists, who favoured a European defence policy independent of NATO (mainly France), and the neutral member states (Ireland at the time). The treaty recognized the WEU as 'an integral part of the development of the EU' and provided for the foreign and defence ministers of the WEU member states to discuss defence issues within the framework of the European Council. But, to address the fears of the Atlanticists, the treaty asserted that the aim was to 'strengthen the European pillar of the Atlantic Alliance'.

Having accepted this bargain, the EU heads of government decided that the reform of the CFSP should be a central issue for the 1996–7 IGC. The resulting Amsterdam Treaty made several significant changes:

- *Common strategies:* a new foreign policy instrument was established: the 'common strategy', whereby the European Council sets out a particular issue's objectives, duration, and means, to be made available by the EU and the member states. These goals are then implemented through common positions, joint actions (in the CFSP) or legislation (in the other EU policies). The intention is to give a clearer focus to EU foreign policy, and to combine all the external policies of the EU into a single framework.
- *Distinction between common positions and joint actions:* joint actions are supposed to be used when specific operational action is required, while common positions are meant for less clearly defined situations 'of a geographic or thematic nature'.
- *Constructive abstention:* the use of 'constructive abstention' was formalized in the treaty: all CFSP decisions are taken by unanimity, but abstentions do not count as votes against. Also, to encourage member state governments to abstain rather than veto, governments are allowed to explain an abstention in a formal declaration, and governments that abstain are not bound to participate in the implementation of a decision, although they must still refrain from taking an action directly contrary to the decision.
- *Qualified-majority voting:* the Treaty formalized the use of QMV in two areas: (a) for common positions or joint actions to implement a common strategy adopted (by unanimity) in the European Council;

and (b) for any decision to implement a joint action or common position already adopted by the Council. However, if a member state objects to the use of QMV for 'important and stated reasons of national policy', it can request that the matter to be referred to the European Council for a decision by unanimity.

- *High Representative for the CFSP:* the treaty established a new post: High Representative for the CFSP, fused with the office of the secretary-general of the Council. The treaty prescribes that the high representative will 'assist the Council in matters coming within the scope of the CFSP, in particular through contributing to the formulation, preparation and implementation of policy decisions, and, when appropriate and acting on behalf of the Council at the request of the Presidency, through conducting political dialogue with third countries'. A new troika was also established between the High Representative for the CFSP, the Commissioner for external relations, and the foreign minister of the member state holding the Council Presidency.

- *Enhanced strategic planning:* a new planning and early-warning unit, the Policy Unit, was established in the secretariat-general of the Council Presidency. It was granted several new powers: to convene an extraordinary Council meeting with 48 hours' notice (or shorter in an emergency); the possibility of being mandated to negotiate of the EU in international negotiations; and enhanced responsibility for ensuring the implementation of EU actions.

- *European Security and Defence Policy (ESDP):* the Amsterdam Treaty strengthened defence policy cooperation by granting the European Council the competence to elaborate and implement common defence policies, particularly with regard to armaments. However, the treaty explicitly stated that these policies must not jeopardize NATO, and it granted the right to remain neutral, as demanded by Sweden, Austria, Finland, and Ireland.

Since the Amsterdam Treaty entered into force in 1999 the EU has been very active in the area of foreign policy. Indeed, the General Affairs Council has become so dominated by foreign policy business that it rarely has time to resolve disputes in other policy areas, which was its original purpose at the pinnacle of the Council hierarchy (see Chapter 2). The European Council agreed three common strategies in quick succession: on Russia in June 1999, Ukraine in December 1999, and the Mediterranean in June 2000. However, frustration with the vagueness of common strategies meant that the European Council quickly abandoned this path.

The post of High Representative has generally been considered to be a success. The first holder of the post, Javier Solana, a former Spanish foreign minister, quickly established a high profile on the international stage. He played an active part in the Middle East peace process and in the resolution of the conflict in former Yugoslavia. He also drafted and negotiated a 'European Security Strategy', which was unanimously approved by the EU foreign ministers in 2003 and set out how and why EU security policies differ from the Bush administration's 'pre-emptive strike' security doctrine.

There was also significant development in the area of defence policy. Even before the implementation of the Amsterdam Treaty, in December 1998 the French and British governments (the two European nuclear powers and members of the UN Security Council) agreed on the St Malo defence initiative. This Franco-British initiative aimed to create an operational defence capacity for the EU. This would be done by merging the WEU into the EU structure to become the 'European pillar' of the NATO alliance. The EU would have access to national assets committed to NATO, and it would be able to act without US participation.

Frustrated with the failure of the EU in the Yugoslav region and the fact that NATO was the primary actor, all governments, include the neutrals, agreed that the core features of the defence capacity of the EU should be humanitarian and rescue operations, peacekeeping, and military crisis management – the so-called 'Petersburg tasks'. In 1999 the governments set 2003 as the deadline by which the ESDP would be fully operational. To ensure that this deadline could be met, the governments made specific commitments to personnel, equipment, and other resources.

The EU's incapability to act decisively in the Balkans was repeated during the Kosovo war in 1998 to 1999 when the European Council stressed the EU's 'moral obligation' to respond to the humanitarian catastrophe in the 'middle if Europe' while depending on the American-led NATO operation to put an end to the Serb offensive (Shepherd, 2009: 513). The failings of the EU in the Balkans combined with the challenges of the Eastern and Southern enlargements prompted the EU to take some decisive steps towards developing a credible ESDP. In December 1999, the European Council agreed to make troops available for EU missions by 2003. They proposed to deploy within 60 days, and be capable of sustaining for at least a year, a military force of up to 60,000 troops capable of the full range of the Petersburg tasks. However, by 2004 the focus turned instead to the concept of battle groups: battalion-sized units of 1,500 troops, deployable within 5 to 10 days, and sustainable for up to 30 days, with the possible extension of up to 120 days. The EU battle groups became fully operational in 2007. By 2010, the EU had taken on six military missions. In addition to the missions on the Balkans, the EU also provided troops to missions in Congo, Somalia, Chad, and the Central African Republic.

So far, the perhaps greatest display of the EU as a serious diplomatic actor came in the autumn of 2008 when the French European Council Presidency played a significant role in reaching a settlement in the five-day

Table 12.1 *EU military missions*

Where	Name of operation	Mandate
Republic of Macedonia	CONCORDIA (FYROM)	–
Congo, RDC	ARTEMIS	–
Bosnia and Herzegovina	EUFOR ALTHEA	In December 2004, ALTHEA took over from SFOR, a NATO-led mission. The preparatory work for a possible evolution towards a non-executive capacity-building and training operation was under progress and the planning work under regular review.
Congo, RDC	EUFOR RD Congo	–
Chad/Central African Republic	EUFOR TCHAD/RCA	–
Coast of Somalia	EU NAVFOR ATLANTA	Launched on 8 December 2008 and planned for a period of 12 months. Extended **until December 2010.** The area of operation is comparable to that of the Mediterranean.
Bosnia and Herzegovina	EUPM BiH	Initiated in January 2003. EUPM I extended into EUPM II (Jan. 2006–31 Dec. 2007) with a refocused mandate on the above-mentioned objectives. EUPM II was extended into EUPM III (1 Jan. 2008–31. Dec 2009). Another extension of another two years was foreseen for the end of the year.
Republic of Macedonia	EUPOL Proxima (Fyrom)	–
Georgia	EUJUST Themis	–
Congo, RDC	EUPOL Kinshasa	–
Congo, RDC	EUSEC DR Congo	Launched in June 2005, extended in July 2007 for 12 months. The mandate ran until 30 September 2009. A new mandate was adopted by the Council on 15 September 2009
Sudan	AMIS II Support (Darfur Province, Sudan)	–
Iraq	EUJUST LEX	Launched in March 2005 for an initial period of 12 months. Extended three times **until 30 June 2010.** For the first time, pilot projects to be carried out in Iraq, as and where conditions allow, to follow up and make the results achieved so far more sustainable.

Indonesia	AMM (Acheh province, Indonesia)	On 11 May 2006 in Brussels, favourable consideration was given by the EU to the government of Indonesia's request for AMM to continue its mandate until the date of the local elections (Pilkada) in Aceh, but no later than 15 September 2006.
Palestinian Territories	EUBAM Rafah	Operational phase began on 25 November 2005 with a duration of 12 months. **Extended three times,** EUBAM was to run **until 24 November 2009. operations were suspended** and the mission maintained its full operational capability and remained on standby, **ready to re-engage in 15 days**, awaiting a political solution. Nevertheless member states could decide to reduce it to the minimum establishment strictly necessary for maintenance of premises and equipment.
Republic of Macedonia	EUPAT (FYROM)	–
Palestinian Territories	EUPOL–COPPS	The aim of the Mission was to contribute to the establishment of sustainable and effective policing arrangements and to advise Palestinian counterparts on criminal justice and rule-of-law-related aspects under Palestinian ownership, in accordance with the best international standards and in cooperation with the EU institution-building programmes conducted by the European Commission and with other international efforts in the wider context of the security sector, including criminal justice reform.
Kosovo Afghanistan Congo, RDC	EUPT Kosovo EUPOL Afghanistan EUPOL RD Congo	– Launched in June 2007 and established for a period of at least three years, **up to 15 June 2010.** EUPOL RD Congo builds on EUPOL Kinshasa (2005–7, the first EU mission in Africa).Launched 1 July 2007 initially for a year, it was extended twice, up to the end of June 2010. The Force HQs are located in **Kinshasa** and an 'East antenna' was established in 2008 with mission deployment in Goma (North Kivu) and Bukavu (South Kivu). Head of Mission: **Superintendent Adilio Ruivo Custodio.**
Guinea Bissau	EU SSR Guinea-Bissau	Launched in June 2008, after a three-month preparatory phase, for an initial period of 12 months. The mandate of the initial period to run to May 2009 and was been extended **until 30 November 2009.**
Kosovo	Eulex Kosovo	EULEX KOSOVO was launched on 4 February 2008 (Joint Action) and reached initial operational capability on 9 December 2008 and **full operational capability by 6 April 2009**. The initial mandate was for **two years** but the mission was foreseen to be terminated according to real progresses and achievements in the rule of law.
Georgia	EUMM	The mission was launched on 1 October 2008. The expected initial duration is 12 months. Mandate extended **until 14 September 2010.**

Source: Compiled from information on the website of Europa.eu (at: http://europa.eu/).

war between Russian and Georgia in Abkhazia and South Ossetia. This could be considered as the first significant display of the EU's newfound capacity to act in the area of international crisis management. The Germany Chancellor and the Commission President followed up the efforts of the French Council Presidency and the Finnish OSCE chair. In an extraordinary European Council meeting, the EU managed to give full backing to the ceasefire agreement and agreed to deploy a civilian monitoring mission (EUMM) (Whitman and Wolff, 2010). Since 2003, the EU has deployed 16 civilian missions across three continents. Table 12.1 lists the impressive range of military and civilian missions undertaken by the EU since 2003.

The Lisbon Treaty made two further significant changes to the framework established by the Amsterdam:

1   *High Representative of the Union for Foreign Affairs and Security Policy:* the office of High Representative for CFSP in the Council was fused with the office of External Relations Commissioner into a new single office, the holder of which would both chair the meetings of the Foreign Affairs Council (the meetings of EU foreign ministers) and be a Vice-President of the Commission.

2   *European External Action Service (EEAS):* the treaty created a 'diplomatic service' for the EU, under the authority of the new High Representative. The EEAS incorporates officials from the Council and the Commission in the foreign affairs field (for example in the Delegations of the Commission around the world) as well as staff seconded from national diplomatic services. The EEAS would be set up by a decision of the Council, acting on a proposal from the High Representative and after consulting the Commission.

Regarding the first of these changes, the creation of the new post aimed to resolve the conflicts that had emerged between the responsibilities of the High Representative for CFSP and the External Relations Commissioner. The Constitutional Treaty had originally termed the post 'Union Minister for Foreign Affairs', but this was rephrased in response to several governments, particularly the UK, who felt that the proposed term made the EU sound too much like a federal state. Nevertheless, significant proportions of the media continue to refer to the new position as the 'EU foreign minister'.

Lady Catherine Ashton, a former leader of the British House of Lords and minister in a UK Labour government, was appointed as the first holder of the new High Representative post in December 2009. To many commentators this seemed an odd choice as she had not had any previous experience in foreign affairs, except for a few months as the EU Trade Commissioner (after Lord Mandelson had resigned from the post). The reason she was chosen, though, was the package deal that came together amongst the heads of government on the appointment of the Commission President, the new President of the European Council, and the new High Representative. As Barroso and Van Rompuy had been chosen for the former two posts, who were both centre-right politicians, the socialists in the European Parliament and in several governments demanded that the High Representative come from their side of the political fence. There was also pressure from the public, the European Parliament, and several of the women Commissioners that a woman be appointed to one of these three positions. Finally, a number of governments felt that the new post should go to someone from one of the big member states, as this would give the holder of the post more clout on the international stage. But, immediately after the decision to appoint Ashton had been taken she came under attack from centre-right and green MEPs for missing an opportunity to make the EU more visible at the global stage by failing to visit Haiti in the immediate aftermath of the devastating earthquake in the country in January 2010.

Lady Ashton submitted her proposal for the European External Action Service in April 2010, which was then approved with some minor changes by the governments in July 2010. The decision established that: one-third of the EEAS staff would come from the diplomatic services of the member states; that the EEAS would be autonomous from the Commission and the Council; that the EEAS would consist of a central administration based in Brussels plus the staff in the EU delegations around the world (except for the delegation staff working on trade issues, who would still report directly to the Commission); and that the budget of the EEAS would be approximately €10 million per year.

Hence, there has been a gradual establishment of foreign and defence policy competences at the European level and a progressive movement towards supranational decision-making an increased role for supranational actors and institutions in Brussels, and instruments to ensure that the EU acts as a united force in world affairs.

Enlargement

In some respects the most significant foreign policy of the EU has been to secure its relations with its neighbours. With the collapse of the Berlin Wall in 1989, the EU's relations with Eastern and Central Europe changed dramatically. Two decades later ten of these countries have become members of the EU and several other countries in the region are pursuing membership of the Union. The 2004 and 2007 enlargement of the EU to include a total of 12 new members that were significantly poorer and, with the exception of Malta and Cyprus, less experienced with democracy. These enlargements put a definite end to the times when the EU could be considered as a wealthy club of West European states.

Why did the existing members of the EU agree to expand the union and how can we understand the process of enlargement?

The EU uses trade barriers and other legal instruments to restrict non-members access to the single market, as we discussed. Furthermore, the EU's internal policies have redistributive effects that can create divisible and rival benefits. First, the design of the EU's regulatory regime means that the expansion of the EU benefits some actors more than others. Second, EU expenditure policies redistribute resources from relative rich members of the EU to relative poor members (see Chapter 9). Depending on the economic development of applicants, enlargements may provide economic benefits or impose economic costs in budgetary terms. A successful enlargement process needs to balance the additional gains against these costs.

Throughout its history, EU enlargements have included relatively rich as well as relatively poor applicants:

- the 1973 enlargement to include Britain, Denmark and Ireland;
- the 1981 enlargement to include Greece;
- the 1986 enlargement to include Spain and Portugal;
- the 1995 enlargement to include Austria, Sweden, and Finland;
- the 2004 enlargement to include Cyprus, the Czech Republic, Estonia, Hungary, Latvia, Lithuania, Malta, Poland, Slovakia, and Slovenia; and
- the 2007 enlargement to include Bulgaria and Romania.

In all of these enlargements the existing EU members had to trade off the benefits of a larger market, increased influence in the political development of potential new members and a larger role in global politics against the costs of having to share its distributive policies amongst more member states, decision-making, and administrative costs as a function of more actors to be heard and more languages to translate. The 1973 and 1995 enlargements included new states that were slightly below (1973) or slightly above (1995) the average level of economic development of the existing members. The increased market and standing in world politics made these enlargements lucrative for both the new and old member states. The 1981 and 1986 enlargements were more problematic because the applicants were relatively poor, with a short democratic history and were eligible for large transfers under the CAP and the regional policy. Nevertheless, these enlargements included only one or two countries. Hence, they did not put large additional strains on either the EU budget or the decision-making and administrative capabilities of the EU.

The 2004 and 2007 enlargements were a different story altogether. The 2004 enlargement increased the membership of the EU from 15 to 25. Most of these countries were substantively poorer than the existing member states, with large agricultural sectors and with most of the regions qualifying for funds under the regional development funds. They were also all relatively small states, with the exception of Poland, which could have a dramatic effect on EU decision-making.

While the leaders of the EU offered encouraging speeches about the uniting of Europe in the aftermath of the events in 1989, initially these speeches were not followed up with actions. The EU attempted to stop short of offering full membership to these countries, but it became clear rather quickly that the former communist countries would not be content with anything but full membership. In the Copenhagen European Council in June 1993 the EU adopted the criteria for membership that allowed the EU substantive influence over the policy and polity development in the applicant countries in exchange for the promise of a membership once the conditions are fulfilled. These 'Copenhagen Criteria' were fairly general (see Mayhew, 1998: 162):

- the stability of institutions guaranteeing democracy, the rule of law, human rights, and respect for and protection of minorities;
- the existence of a functioning market economy;
- the capacity to cope with competitive pressures and market forces within the Union; and
- the ability to take on the obligations of membership, including adherence to the aims of political, economic, and monetary union.

The criteria also included a clause concerning the EU's ability to absorb new members. The negotiation process evolved around assessing the extent to which the prospective member states have implemented the existing EU rules and regulations, the *acquis communautaire*, as well as costs from and contributions to the EU budget. Schimmelfenning (2003) argues that the Eastern enlargement imposed so many costs to some of the current members, in terms of the EU budget and the influx of economic migrants, that the Eastern enlargement cannot be explained by rationalist self-interest of the existing members. Instead, he uses the concept of 'rhetorical action' to explain how existing members were trapped by the use of pro-enlargement arguments based on liberal democratic community-building, which emphasize the collective identity, norms, and values across Europe. Those hostile to Eastern enlargement found themselves unable to argue against these norms.

Schneider (2009), in contrast, finds that the enlargement process can be explained through the self-interest and strategic behaviour of both the existing EU members and the prospective member states. Drawing on models from political economy (Drazen, 2002), she demonstrates how differentiated integration has been used throughout the history of EU enlargements to distribute the costs and benefits among all actors in a pareto-efficient manner, by either making the benefiters from enlargement contribute more to the EU budget or by delaying the rights of accession states to some of the common EU policies, such as the CAP, fisheries, or the free movement of labour.

The politics of foreign policy

The power of the EU institutions varies across the different areas of EU foreign policy. Under the Lisbon Treaty, the EU has its own legal personality, which means that it can sign international treaties, and the role of the Commission in foreign and security policies has been strengthened. In most political systems the executive is given sweeping powers in the execution of foreign policy, although its actions may be subject to budget constraints or scrutinized *ex post*, and the signing of international treaties may be subject to national ratification and implementation. The development of a common foreign policy may thus strengthen the Commission at the expense of national governments. The challenge for the Commission, though, is to convince the governments that they are better served by the Commission acting on their behalf on the international stage, than they would be by pursuing their own foreign policy interests.

The unwillingness of national governments to give up their right to act independently in foreign policies was illustrated during the 2002–4 Iraq crisis. After the events of 11 September 2001, the EU governments took the unprecedented step of declaring their solidarity with the US by invoking the self-defence clause of the NATO Charter: in other words, they declared that the attack on the US was also an attack on Europe. While the semblance of a common European position just about held together during the US-led military offensive to oust the Taliban regime in Afghanistan, this united front collapsed when the Bush administration turned its attention to regime change in Iraq. On one side, the UK, Spain, Italy, Poland, Portugal, and Denmark were prepared to support US military action in Iraq, even without full UN endorsement. On the other side, France, Germany, and Belgium – which Donald Rumsfeld infamously described as 'Old Europe' – insisted that the proposed war was illegal under international law.

Following the rapid takeover of Iraq and the capture of Saddam Hussein, it appeared that the 'hawks' had been vindicated. However, by 2004, as Iraq descended into chaos, and as the US seemed unwilling to hand over authority for the stabilization and management of Iraq to the United Nations, the pro-US coalition started to collapse in the face of strong public opposition to the military occupation and the policies of the Bush administration. The clearest illustration of this was the dramatic electoral removal of the right-wing Spanish government in March 2004, just days after a terrorist bombing by Al-Qaeda in Madrid. Also, the British and Italian governments' support for Bush eroded as they feared that they too would be punished by their voters in the forthcoming elections.

Explaining EU Foreign Policy

A number of questions arise from this survey of EU foreign policies:

- Why did it take the EU longer to develop a voice in the area of foreign and security policies than in economic policies?
- Why has the EU pursued a relative liberal global economic policy despite pressures for and fear of a 'fortress Europe'?
- Why has the EU been able to adopt and implement common foreign and defence policies on some issues but not others?

The various answers to these questions broadly fall into three main types of explanation: (a) the global economic and geopolitical interdependence of the EU; (b) intergovernmentalism, and (c) supranational politics.

Global economic and geopolitical interdependence

The EU has until now been mainly a responder to global economic and geopolitical developments rather than a shaper of these developments. Global developments have tended to determine the agenda and timetable of the EU's policies and the options available to EU policy-makers. For example, in recent decades the EU has been forced to react to three major exogenous developments: economic globalization, the end of the Cold War, and the war on terror.

With regard to economic globalization, since the mid-1970s there has been a dramatic increase in cross-border trade and capital movements. First, import volumes as a percentage of the GDP of advanced industrial countries, which remained steady at 10 to16 per cent between 1880 and 1972, rose to almost 22 per cent between 1973 and 1987 (McKeown, 1991, p. 158). Also, whereas internal demand grew at approximately 2 per cent per year in this period, international trade grew at almost 5 per cent per year. In other words, between the 1970s and 1990s global trade grew at a rate that was about 66 per cent greater than the growth in domestic demand. Second, cross-border capital flows have increased faster than domestic demand for capital. International capital flows to the advanced industrial countries rose from an annual average of $99 billion in 1975 to 1977 to $463 billion in 1985 to 1989 (Turner, 1991, p. 23). Also, total net lending in world markets grew from $100 billion per year in the late 1970s to $342 billion in 1990, and foreign exchange trading more than quadrupled between 1982 and 1992, to $1,000 billion per day, or 40 times the average daily volume of world trade.

This economic globalization has had two main effects (Garrett and Lange, 1995; Milner and Keohane, 1996). First, globalization has facilitated global convergence in the price of goods, services, and capital. This has put pressure on the EU to reform its internal policies to allow convergence with its global competitors. Second, globalization has benefited financial services, importing firms and firms producing for global markets at the expense of the producers of goods for the domestic market (Frieden, 1991; Frieden and Rogowski, 1996). As trade and capital flows have grown, there has been pressure from organized interests for policies to promote free trade. In the Uruguay Round of the GATT negotiations, the linkage between trade liberalization and CAP reform meant that pro-free-trade EU states and domestic economic interests argued for CAP reform as a means of promoting greater trade liberalization (Devuyst, 1995; Hennis, 2001; Landau, 2001; Meunier, 1998; Patterson, 1997; see also Chapter 9). Similarly, the liberalization of world trade meant that the new ACP–EU Partnership Agreement had to be based on free trade rather than preferential trade (Forwood, 2001).

Meanwhile, the fall of the Berlin Wall, the democratic revolutions in Central and Eastern Europe, and the collapse of the Soviet Union and its empire created a new strategic environment in Western Europe (Knudsen, 1994; Sperling and Kichner, 1997). The EU governments were immediately forced to address a series of interrelated security, political, and economic issues that previously had been absent from the EU agenda. These included how to stabilize democracy and the free market in the new democracies in Central and Eastern Europe, how to involve these states in a broader 'European house' without antagonizing Russia, and how to tackle the potentially large influx of economic migrants (Heiberg, 1998; Smith, 1996).

The end of the Cold War has also thrown up new global political and security challenges that were suppressed by the previous balance-of-power relations. India and Pakistan have been added to the list of countries that possess nuclear weapons, against the terms of the international nuclear weapons treaties, and a number of other 'rogue states' seem intent on developing a nuclear capability, such as Iran and North Korea. Furthermore, the new spectre of global terrorism in the name of Islamic fundamentalism has emerged, centred on the Al-Qaeda network and the personality cult of Osama bin Laden. The number of terrorist attacks on Western targets increased dramatically from mid-1990s onwards, and the attacks on New York and Washington on 11 September 2001 profoundly demonstrated the vulnerability of Western democracies to attack by well-coordinated, well-funded terrorists who are willing to give their lives for the cause. The growing perception in both the Muslim world and the West of a 'clash of civilizations' has also presented problems for many European societies. For example, the UK, France, and Spain have sizeable and growing Muslim communities, who contain significant numbers of people who sympathize with the anti-Western movements in the Middle East. As a result, the connection between foreign and internal security issues is now much closer than at any time during the Cold War.

In other words, EU foreign policies are essentially reactive rather than proactive: responding to global events rather than shaping them. This is particularly true in comparison to the position of the US, with the EU invariably being forced to follow the lead of whichever administration is in Washington. When developing a policy towards Central and Eastern Europe, for example, the EU has had to take into account how many troops the US would pull out of Europe, whether the US Congress would retreat into isolationism, and how fast the US administration wanted to enlarge NATO to the East (Ullrich, 1998). Even in the negotiations on the Maastricht and Amsterdam Treaties the US government was instrumental in determining the shape of the proposed rules on defence cooperation (Duke, 1996; van Staden, 1994).

Intergovernmentalism: geopolitical and economic interests

In contrast, intergovernmental explanations of EU foreign policy tend to focus on the geopolitical or the economic interests of the EU member states themselves rather than global events. Emphasizing geopolitics over economics, Hoffmann (1966) distinguished between two types of issues: 'high politics', which touch on the fundamental definition, identity, security, and sovereignty of the nation-state; and 'low politics', which address issues that are not as threatening to the viability of the nation-state, such as European economic integration and regulatory policies. Because foreign and security policies are central to the concept of national identity and security, the EU governments have been reluctant to agree to supranational forms of decision-making in these policy areas while at the same time agreeing to use supranational decision-making for external economic and trade policies, more recently, international environmental policies.

The history of the development of the EU's common foreign and defence policies is perhaps best described as a competition between rival nation-states' interpretations of how best to defend their security (Hill, 1996; Pfetsch, 1994). At least until the Lisbon Treaty, the West European nation-state remained the sovereign actor in foreign policy issues. So instead of the EU developing an autonomous identity and capacity on the global stage, the EU was simply a vehicle for the member states to pursue their own foreign policies. When the interests of the states diverged, the EU hence becomes incapacitated and the member states pursue their interests independently of the EU. In this view, the institutional design of the CFSP is largely irrelevant (Stavridis, 1997). What matters is the political commitment of the member states, which cannot be obtained merely by introducing more effective decision-making procedures. The only hope for the EU is that the individual security interests of the member states will gradually converge, and that this will be facilitated by the development of EU foreign policies and institutions. However, from a realist perspective this is unlikely as national security interests tend not to vary over time.

Moreover, there is some evidence that the member states' security interests also determine the global economic policies of the EU. The member states allow supranational institutions and common policies in the case of external economic affairs because they share certain common economic interests. However, when security interests diverge, external trade policy preferences also diverge. For example, states that favour an independent European defence capability are also reluctant to allow the European economy to become dependent on transatlantic trade. Conversely, states that favour a transatlantic defence community have been at the forefront of attempts to tie the EU economy into a broader transatlantic economic community. Hence, the free-trade–protectionism cleavage between the member states on trade policies follows the Atlanticist–Europeanist cleavage on security policies.

However, the instrumental promotion of national interest can go hand in hand with the establishment of supranational modes of decision-making on foreign policy issues. In the case of crisis management, the EU governments were willing to agree to use QMV because in this area the need to reach a quick decision was more important than the preservation of national sovereignty (Wagner, 2003). More generally, the desire to preserve national sovereignty varies among the member states. The traditionally weaker states often feel that their national interest may be enhanced by delegating powers to the EU. As a results, 'all else being equal, governments of weaker countries are more likely to support supranational CFSP institutions than governments of stronger countries' (Koenig-Archibugi, 2004b: 167). The UK and France have traditionally been most eager to preserve the intergovernmental nature of foreign policy decision-making. Some of the larger states prefer to delegate contentious issues to the European level, to promote policy outcomes that would be difficult to bring about domestically. Amongst big states, executives in coalition-government systems (Germany and Italy) tend to be more in favour of supranational decision-making on foreign policy issues than are executives in single-party government systems (the UK, France, and Spain) (Koenig-Archibugi, 2004a).

Nevertheless, the liberal variant of the intergovernmentalist approach to the EU argues that economic interests trump geopolitical interests (Moravcsik, 1998). From this perspective, security interests are in fact derived from economic interests. These interests may be defined at the national level, where governments adjust their preferences to cater to the median voter or the most powerful domestic economic interests

(Rogowski, 1990). Alternatively, domestic interests may be defined and articulated at the European level by private economic actors that have no specific national allegiance, such as multinational corporations and sectoral associations (Junne, 1994). In either case, EU global policies change as the balance of power shifts among domestic economic interests, or the latter change their preferences in light of exogenous developments, such as globalization and the emergence of new markets.

Economic interests have played a vital part in shaping the external economic policies of the EU (Hofhansel, 1999; Ugur, 1998). Multinational corporations help shaped the EU's agenda in the Uruguay Round of the GATT negotiations. The European Round Table of Industrialists and the EU Committee of the American Chamber of Commerce have campaigned extensively to persuade anti-free-trade governments to support trade liberalization, and supplied the Commission with arguments to strengthen its position in Council bargaining. Similarly, a group of European and American multinational corporations formed the Trans-Atlantic Business Dialogue (TABD) in 1994 to campaign for greater transatlantic free trade. The TABD also drew up detailed proposals for the mutual recognition of standards in a number of product areas. The Commission and the US government subsequently adopted these proposals almost in their entirety.

Economic interests are a key factor in explaining the EU's external political and security policies (Praet, 1987) as well as the Eastern enlargement (Schneider, 2009). German businesses were the largest investors in Central and Eastern Europe following the collapse of communism, so Germany had both an economic and strategic interest in promoting the development of stable markets in its neighbours. In this instance, economic interest went hand in hand with security interests. On other issues, collective economic interests have overridden security concerns. The need to defend the credibility of GATT and the WTO is forcing the French and British governments to redefine and reform their historical relations with their former colonies, many of which relations have been maintained for security and military reasons. Administrative elites may oppose any perceived threat to national identity and security interests, but domestic economic groups are less interested in these concerns than in their own material well-being, and governments are ultimately accountable to the voters. Hence, in the liberal interpretation, if a state is faced with a choice between free trade and protecting a security interest, and if a large proportion of the electorate is employed in globally competitive industries, the government will choose free trade.

In almost direct contrast to claims of the determinacy of security interests, from this perspective the external economic implications of the single market and the EU's interest in promoting global free trade have been major determinants of the pace of institutional integration and the nature of policy outcomes in the foreign and security policy field. Part of the reason for this is that EU trade policy is largely managed by the Commission, in cooperation with trade ministers. When external economic issues touch on political and security concerns they are passed onto foreign ministers. However, this forces governments to tackle many political/security issues on an agenda and timetable that is set by the EU's single market and external economic policy agenda (Smith, 1998). It will be interesting to see how the establishment of the High Representative for Common Foreign and Security Policy inside the Commission changes this.

Supranational politics: institutional rules and supranational agenda-setting

The supranational politics view holds that the EU's foreign policies are determined by the institutional context at the EU level. Against the scepticism of realists, this perspective maintains that the supranational institutional framework shapes EU foreign policies in three ways: (a) through the existence of a supranational actor with certain agenda-setting powers (the Commission), which has a vested interest in promoting political integration and collective EU policy outcomes; (b) through the institutional design of trade policy-making, which limits the ability of anti-free-trade states to block a liberal policy outcome; and (c) through the decision-making rules and institutional norms in the CFSP field, which have promoted policy movement despite conflicting security interests.

First, the Commission has particular policy preferences in the foreign policy field (Nugent and Saurugger, 2002; Smith, 1997). On the one hand, the Commission has institutional interests: further economic and political integration in treaty reforms, and rules that grant it significant agenda-setting power and policy discretion (see Chapter 2). On the other hand, the Commission has political preferences: there has tended to be a free-trade majority in the college of Commissioners, but the Commission is also in favour of the EU playing a greater (interventionist) role in global affairs.

In the making of EU trade policy the Commission has used its agenda-setting and policy implementation powers to maximal effect. The Commission has successfully promoted multilateral and bilateral free-trade agreements against the preferences of important member states (notably France), and has been able to place new issues on the agenda, such as the mutual recognition agreements with the US and the organization and promotion of the EU–Asia summits. In some respects the Commission has successfully captured the external trade policy of the EU (Bilal, 1998).

Recognizing the ability of the Commission to shape trade policy outcomes, during the Amsterdam Treaty negotiations the governments refused to agree to the Commission's request to delegate negotiating authority to the Commission in the 'new trade issues' of services and intellectual property, preferring instead to allow the Council to decide whether and when to delegate this authority (Meunier and Nicolaïdis, 1999).

In the making of foreign and security policies the Commission did not have the same agenda-setting capability until the Lisbon Treaty in 2009. Following the Lisbon Treaty, the Commission, together with the High Representative for Foreign and Security Affairs, has been equipped with the institutional tools to potentially shape EU foreign and security policies. But, even prior to the Lisbon Treaty the Commission was able to influence policy outcomes through informal agenda-setting, such as the generation of policy ideas (Nuttall, 1997). The Commission has also used its powers in external trade policy to promote explicitly political goals, as in the development of the EU's policy towards the Mediterranean (Gomez, 1998; Nuttall, 1996; Piening, 1997).

Second, in the field of external economic policies, Hanson (1998: 81) argues 'that [EU] trade policy liberalization is largely the result of changes in the institutional context of trade policy-making' (see also Ugur, 1998; Young, 2000). By delegating trade policy-making to the EU level and trade policy negotiations to the Commission, the EU governments have consciously chosen to constrain the range of possible policy options available to them and are effectively locked in a liberal trade policy (Meunier and Nicolaïdis, 1999). The rules for adopting trade policy deals make it difficult for protectionist member states to reject international agreements negotiated by the Commission. As the Commission is able to make a take-it-or-leave-it proposal to the Council, which the Council cannot amend, the only choice for the governments is either to accept a proposed package or veto a carefully negotiated international deal. Faced with this choice, even the most protectionist member states are forced to accept global free-trade deals negotiated by the Commission on the governments' behalf (Jupille, 1999; Meunier, 2000).

Third, the design of decision-making in foreign and security policies has promoted some policy convergence between the EU governments. Bulmer (1991) argues that even the limited institutional structure of European Political Cooperation created a relationship between the member states that was akin to 'cooperative federalism', whereby the member states recognized that foreign policy-making should be 'shared' between the European and national levels. Similarly, the establishment of a new institutional framework for the CFSP immediately produced several policy changes, such as use of the new joint action policy instrument and the integration of CFSP issues in the general EU timetable (Cameron, 1998). Furthermore, the development of ESDP shows the same trend. The EU battle groups are now taking on missions in the Balkans, Middle East and Africa. The institutionalization of the security and defence policy fields has led the EU to take on a role as an international actor that was almost unthinkable when the idea was launched by the governments in 1999 (Matlary, 2009; Menon, 2009). Finally, the EU is increasingly acting as a party in international diplomatic controversies such as the nuclear programme of Iran, the Israeli–Palestinian conflict and in the six-party talks with North Korea.

Conclusion: a Major Player in Global Politics?

The EU is developing towards being a major, yet unevenly balanced, player in global politics. The EU is now one of the leading actors in international trade and development aid. Yet, its military role is mainly limited to low-profile peacekeeping missions. While recent developments in security and defence would have been difficult to imagine only a decade ago, the EU governments have been reluctant to use these capabilities, and have tended to focus more on the development of institutions than the capabilities required for resolute action.

Nevertheless, there is a gradual, albeit slow, development towards a stronger foreign policy identity of the EU which goes beyond the 'soft power' instruments of trade and aid. Ironically, the main drivers behind these developments have been the member states with their own independent military capabilities, such as the UK and France. While it is not realistic to believe that the EU will be able to challenge the hegemony of the US as the only military superpower in world, recent developments suggest that the EU may be on its way towards becoming a more credible partner for the US in world politics.

This concludes our review of EU policies. As we have seen, some policy areas are more developed than others. While there are clear differences between policy areas, our presentation has highlighted the similarities and attempted to show how EU policy-making can be analysed using two main theoretical frameworks: intergovernmentalism, and supranational politics. Next, in the Conclusion, we summarize the key insights of the book and highlight what we believe research on the EU has learned from mainstream political science as well as what EU research has contributed to this field of knowledge.

Chapter 13

Conclusion: Rethinking the European Union

What Political Science Teaches Us about the EU
What the EU Teaches Us about Political Science

This book has looked at the EU in a different way from the traditional approaches to European integration and EU studies. It has not proposed a new integration theory, nor has it provided a detailed description of particular events or developments in Brussels. Instead it has argued that we can improve our understanding of how the EU works by applying to the EU our general understanding of the main processes in modern political systems. The key assumption is that the EU is a political system. Because of this, political science has a lot to teach us about the EU. Conversely, studying the EU helps us to re-evaluate some of our general theories of how politics works.

What Political Science Teaches Us about the EU

Operation of government, politics, and policy-making in the EU

Political science tells us a considerable amount about each of the processes analysed in this book. In the area of executive politics, the Council delegates agenda-setting and policy implementation tasks to the Commission, primarily to reduce transaction costs and facilitate policy bargains. However, the Commission is not a neutral actor. Like all political executives, commissioners have their own career and political goals, and like all bureaucracies the Commission administration has incentives to expand its fiscal resources, political, and regulatory powers, and autonomy from political control. But, the EU governments can predict this. To pre-empt policy drift, the Council has established mechanisms to constrain the Commission, such as control over the appointment of commissioners and the comitology system.

With regard to legislative politics, both the Council and the European Parliament have established internal institutions to improve legislative decision-making: the Council Presidency and the European Parliament leadership structures improve agenda organization; and sectoral Councils and European Parliament committees facilitate bargaining on an issue-by-issue basis. As expected, different legislative coalitions have formed on different policy dimensions, and actors have different powers under the various legislative rules (QMV/unanimity and consultation/ordinary legislative procedure).

In the field of judicial politics, the governments established the ECJ to enforce treaty agreements and legislation. Having established the ECJ to achieve this goal, several actors then had incentives to promote the gradual constitutionalization of the EU. The ECJ developed doctrines to increase its institutional autonomy and influence over policy outcomes, national courts accepted EU law to strengthen their powers against national parliaments and governments, and private litigants sought EU norms to further their private interests. Meanwhile, the institutional design of the EU made it difficult for anti-integrationist forces to rein in the ECJ.

In the area of public opinion, citizens no longer trust their governments to go off to Brussels and represent a single 'national interest'. Citizens in different countries have different attitudes towards the EU. Nevertheless, within each member state, individuals form their attitudes towards the EU on the basis of personal economic interests and political values. In general, more highly skilled and highly educated groups are more supportive of the EU, while less skilled and less educated groups are less supportive. However, there are some key differences among lower skilled groups: for example, low-paid unskilled workers in the new members see more benefits of economic integration in Europe than more highly paid unskilled workers in the old 15 states.

Turning to democratic processes in the EU system, European Parliament elections do not allow voters to throw out the EU executive or choose the direction of the EU policy agenda. This is not because the European Parliament lacks the power over the Commission or in the legislative process. Rather, European Parliament elections are not about EU policies or candidates for EU political office because national parties have an incentive to use these elections as part of the ongoing contest for national government office. Nevertheless, as the powers of the European Parliament have grown, the incentive for MEPs with similar policy preferences to cooperate and organize together has led to growing organizational power and cohesion in the transnational political groups in the European Parliament.

With regard to interest representation, Brussels has a vibrant civil society – more like Washington, DC than London, Paris, or Berlin. In general, groups that can secure selective benefits from the EU (such as businesses and farmers) have more of an incentive to lobby the EU than do groups for whom the benefits and costs of EU policies are diffuse (such as consumers, taxpayers, workers, and environmentalists). Nevertheless, diffuse interests are well organized in Brussels and fully capable of mounting successful lobbying campaigns. This is helped by the fact that Commission officials and MEPs have provided access to under-represented groups, to use the policy expertise of these groups to gain advantage in the legislative process.

On regulatory policies, the single market programme is a combination of deregulatory and re-regulatory policies, which balances the interests of producers, consumers, and workers. In general, the removal of national rules and regulations favours producer groups, while the establishment of new European-wide standards aims to protect workers, environmentalists, and consumers. Nevertheless, on some regulatory issues the governments prefer any EU regulation to none, and as a result the EU has been more able to adopt deregulatory policies (such as privatization) and common product standards (such as environmental labelling) than common process standards (such as workers' rights and social policies).

Regarding expenditure policies, intergovernmental bargaining over the EU budget facilitates careful cost–benefit calculations by the governments. The member states who benefit most from trade integration in Europe have been willing to grant side-payments to those member states who benefit least. Nevertheless, because budgetary receipts are concentrated whereas payments are diffuse, social groups who benefit from EU programmes have more of an incentive to mobilize to protect their subsidies than do groups that pay into the budget. Also, expenditure policies tend to cause executive officials (in the Commission), legislators (such as agriculture ministers) and private interests (such as the farm lobby) to join forces to promote and protect expenditure in their policy area.

In the operation of EMU, the EU is not an optimum currency area, and as a result the eurozone has experienced asymmetric shocks. The EU is ill equipped to address these shocks. There is little labour movement between the states. Fiscal transfers through the EU budget are small. Governments' fiscal policies are restricted. However, the institutional design of EMU allows for some policy flexibility. The member states can implement labour market reforms, although this is politically very difficult. The ECB is not completely immune from political pressure. And, finance ministers have shown that they can relax the fiscal constraints and even bailed-out states that are not able to meet their fiscal commitments, even at the expense of risking the collapse of the eurozone.

In the area of interior policies, governments have responded to external pressures and voters' demands for action to combat the perceived threat of illegal immigration and cross-border crime and terrorism that can result from the free movement of persons in the single market. Meanwhile, the EU institutions have demanded institutional reforms to improve policy accountability and increase their influence over policy outcomes. As a result, the governments have instituted QMV, established new European Parliament and ECJ powers, and delegated agenda-setting powers to the Commission. These institutional changes have allowed the

EU to adopt a large number of laws in this policy area, some of which have been more liberal than domestic status quos, others of which have been more conservative – depending on the coalition that has formed in the EU's legislative institutions on each particular issue.

Finally, in the area of foreign policies, the governments have found it easier to agree common external economic policies than common political and security policies. On economic issues, policies tend to be driven by economic interests. As the world's largest trader, global free trade is in the EU's collective economic interest, and multinational firms, who benefit from free trade and are more able to lobby the EU than are domestic producers, who gain from protectionist policies. On political and security issues, in contrast, the governments have competing geopolitical interests, and therefore have been reluctant to delegate agenda-setting power to the Commission or to introduce QMV in this policy area. Nevertheless, the governments have agreed to equip the EU with some military and diplomatic capabilities.

Connections between government, politics, and policy-making in the EU

Political science also teaches us about how the processes of government, politics, and policy-making are connected in the EU. With regard to the *connection between politics and government*, EU governments are composed of political parties whose primary goal is to be re-elected. This has two effects. First, governments seek EU policies that are in line with their electoral commitments, accord with domestic public opinion, or benefit their voters and supporting interest groups. Second, governments have limited time horizons as the long-term impact of EU decisions is less important than their short-term political goals.

In contrast to national governments, the supranational institutions – the Commission, the European Parliament, and the ECJ – are isolated from short-term electoral considerations. Individual commissioners may wish to have their terms renewed. This encourages commissioners to remain connected to their domestic governing and party elites. However, renomination is uncertain as governments and party elites change. Similarly, because European Parliament elections are fought as national contests, the re-election of MEPs depends on the electoral success of their domestic party rather than their personal or party group performance in the European Parliament.

However, the supranational institutions are not completely isolated from public opinion. If the governments are to grant them more powers they need the support and confidence of the EU citizens. Consequently, the Commission has often proposed populist measures, the ECJ has become less activist since the rise of Euro-scepticism in several member states, and the European Parliament is increasingly concerned about the low turnout in, and 'second-order' nature of, European Parliament elections.

With regard to the *connection between politics and policy-making*, public opinion and party competition shape the preferences and strategies of actors in the policy-making process. For example, governments are reluctant to delegate powers to the Commission and the ECJ in areas where their electorates oppose EU action. And on highly salient issues, such as key pieces of legislation and the candidacy for the post of Commission President, parties in government put pressure on their MEPs to back the position their government has taken in the Council. Conversely, on issues for which there is strong public support for EU action (as in the environmental field) and on low-saliency issues (such as some regulatory issues), governments are more willing to allow policy outcomes that might strengthen the powers of the EU institutions in the long term.

The structure of interest representation also shapes policy outcomes. Groups that can secure selective or concentrated benefits from the EU policy process have the greatest incentives to mobilize. Thus, business interests lobby against high environmental and social regulations, regions lobby to maintain cohesion expenditure, and farmers lobby to maintain the CAP. Nevertheless, diffuse interests (such as environmentalists, consumers, and trade unions) have secured policies when the Commission has had an incentive to promote the interests of these groups, when centre-left parties have been powerful in the Council, and when the centre-left in the European Parliament has been able to set the legislative agenda.

In addition, transnational social divisions, domestic party competition, and interest group organization have all contributed to the emergence of a new left-right dimension in the EU policy process. The traditional European integration dimension remains: between groups and institutions seeking further integration and groups in favour of maintaining national sovereignty. Nevertheless, on many socio-economic policy issues – such as macroeconomic questions in EMU, and regulation of the single market – the battle lines are between 'regulated capitalism' (supported by parties on the left) and neo-liberalism (supported by parties on the right). A similar conflict has emerged on interior policies, between more liberal attitudes towards immigration and individual liberties (supported by parties on the left) and more conservative attitudes towards immigration and protecting the state against crime and terrorism (supported by parties on the right). On these new political dimensions at the EU level, the liberals in the Commission, the European Parliament and the Council have often been the kingmakers: able to form a winning majority with either the centre-left (social democrats and greens) or the centre-right (Christian democrats and conservatives).

With regard to the *connection between government and policy-making*, the EU's institutional rules facilitate particular policy outcomes. The delegation of executive and judicial powers to the Commission and the ECJ, respectively, has enabled these institutions to promote and protect their own institutional interests in the EU system and to secure the interests of their support groups. The governments may have failed to predict these outcomes because of a lack of information about the long-term consequences of treaty agreements at the start of the process of European integration as well as their ongoing short-time horizons. Also, because treaty reform requires unanimity, this delegation has tended to be 'one-way traffic'.

The legislative rules have also shaped policy outcomes. QMV in the Council has facilitated agreement on deregulatory policies and EU-wide product standards. In contrast, unanimity voting has undermined efforts to adopt common process standards. Similarly, the European Parliament has used its powers under the cooperation procedure and co-decision/ordinary legislative procedure to promote the policies preferred by the majority of MEPs.

However, as governments have come to understand the long-term relationship between institutional rules and policy outcomes they have consciously chosen institutional designs to promote or prevent particular policy outcomes. For example, most governments have been reluctant to delegate executive and judicial powers in areas of fundamental national sovereignty, such as foreign policy and police and judicial cooperation. Similarly, anti-integration and centre-right governments have fought to maintain the consultation procedure and unanimity voting in policy areas that are likely to result in federalist and left-wing outcomes, such as tax harmonization. Furthermore, the EU governments have usually only moved from unanimity/consultation procedure to QMV/co-decision in a particular policy area once a certain amount of policy has already been adopted. The reason for this is that once policy has been adopted under unanimity and consultation it is difficult to change unless QMV is introduced, and the risk of QMV is lessened by introducing co-decision at the same time, which allows the European Parliament to be a check on the majority among the governments.

Finally, the *connection between government/policy-making and politics* has generally been weaker than the connections in the opposite direction. Developments at the EU level have only had a limited impact on domestic politics. EU citizens remain ill-informed about the EU, and domestic parties remain focused on the battle for national government office. As a result, whereas new issues that arise in domestic politics are often placed on the EU agenda (such as the need to combat cross-border crime and illegal immigration in the late 1990s), issues at the EU level are rarely debated at the domestic level, as the absence of domestic debates on treaty reforms or major legislative initiatives have repeatedly shown.

What the EU Teaches Us About Political Science

At the *micro level*, research on the EU has produced some important findings on the relationship between actors and their institutional environment. In particular the development and operation of the EU seems to confirm some of the core propositions of the institutional rational choice approach in political science.

As in all systems, policy outcomes in the EU are the result of strategic interaction between actors. The location of actors in the EU policy space determines which actors are pivotal in turning minority coalitions into winning coalitions, be this in the Commission, the European Parliament, or the Council. However, the formal and informal institutions of the EU system are also crucially important in shaping political outcomes. The EU is a complex political system with numerous rules and procedures. These determine the order in which decisions are tackled, the time horizons of the actors, the types of payoff that can be achieved in the policy process, who has agenda-setting power (and under what conditions), whether or not actors can exercise a veto, and consequently under which conditions actors are pivotal (independently of their policy preferences). The informal norms of the EU system – such as the need to achieve a broad political consensus – are as important in determining political outcomes as the formal rules. Put another way, equilibria in the EU system are often 'structure induced'.

The formal and informal rules of EU politics have not developed randomly. Institutional choices are policy choices by other means. In the recurring institutional game of EU politics, the actors have developed highly sophisticated institutional preferences, such as which policies should be tackled at the EU level, who should have the right to initiate proposals under each of these policies, whether majority voting or unanimity should be used in the Council, whether the consultation procedure or the co-decision/ordinary legislative procedure should be used, which internal rules of procedure should be used inside the EU institutions, which private actors should be included in the policy process, and which procedures should be used to implement policies. At certain points in time actors are able to choose between rules or to choose new ones. Actors will try to change rules to secure outcomes that are closer to their ideal preferences.

Extrapolating this to the *meso level*, research on the EU tells us something interesting about each of the processes of government, politics, and policy-making. In the area of government, once executive, legislative, or judicial powers have been delegated to independent agents – be they governmental agencies or courts – these powers are difficult to rescind. As in the US and at the domestic level in the EU, this has generally led to a strengthening of the power of bureaucrats and judges at the expense of directly elected legislative representatives. However, the growing power of the European Parliament in the legislative process and in scrutinizing the activities of the Commission may be an important exception to this general rule.

In the area of politics, the EU tells us that citizens' opinions matter, but not as much as we might like. Governing elites in the EU are only forced to respond to public opinion when issues become highly salient, and as a result elites often have an incentive to collude to keep issues off the political agenda. However, events in the EU illustrate that in political systems with multiple points of access there are numerous opportunities for interest groups to become key intermediaries between society and decision-makers. When agendas become politicized, political parties and interest groups begin to drive the policy agenda and link the processes of mass politics, governmental bargaining, and policy outputs.

In the area of policy-making, the EU shows how regulation has become the key instrument of modern governance. The redistributive bargains of the democratic welfare state were struck in the immediate post-Second World War period. The current policy battles relate to the degree of state regulation of private economic and social interactions, and competing agendas on these issues have begun to emerge. Those on the centre-right tend to support freedom from regulatory red tape and the delegation of regulatory policies to agencies that are independent from political majorities. In opposition, the 'old left' agenda of wealth redistribution is being replaced by a 'new left' agenda of strong protection against social and economic risk, political accountability, and control of independent regulators.

Finally, extrapolating to the *macro level*, the EU shows that a highly developed political system can emerge without the full-blown apparatus of the state and/or strong popular support and mass political participation. The key reason for this is that the main achievements of the EU have been the single market, the single currency, regulatory rather than redistributive policies, and limited encroachment into the traditional areas of state power (internal and external security). These policies tend to be positive-sum rather than zero-sum: there are few permanent losers in the EU political system. If the outcomes were highly redistributive, the EU would require a greater use of force to impose its policies and a greater degree of democratic participation to legitimize redistributive outcomes.

However, the EU is unlikely to be able to meet the new policy challenges in Europe without greater state capacity or more democratic legitimacy. Hence, there is an ongoing debate about how to strengthen the leadership and executive capacity of the EU while at the same time increasing the accountability of EU office-holders. A powerful constraint, however, is that the allocation of policy powers between the national and European levels and the balance of powers between the EU institutions is already a highly stable equilibrium which is unlikely to be changed without a dramatic shift in voters' preferences or a major exogenous shock.

In sum, the key contention of this book is that to understand how the EU works we need to think about it in a more systematic and scientific way. Only by doing so can we begin to answer the vital theoretical and normative questions that surround the construction of this new and important political system. And along the way we may learn some new things about the world of politics.

Bibliography

Aaron, R. (1974) 'Is Multinational Citizenship Possible', *Social Research*, 41(4): 638–56.

Acemoglu, D. and Robinson, J. A. (2001) 'A Theory of Political Transitions', *American Economic Review*, 91(4): 938–63.

Achen, C. H. (2006) 'Evaluating Political Decision-Making Models', in R. Thomson, F.N. Stokman, C.H. Achen and T. König (eds), *The European Union Decides* (Cambridge: Cambridge University Press).

Akrill, R.W. (2000a) 'The European Union Budget, the Balanced Budget Rule and the Development of Common European Policies', *Journal of Public Policy*, 20(1): 1–19.

Akrill, R.W. (2000b) 'CAP Reform 1999: A Crisis in the Making?', *Journal of Common Market Studies*, 38(2): 343–53.

Aksoy, D. (2010) 'Who Gets What, When, and How Revisited: Voting and Proposal Power in the Allocation of the EU Budget', *European Union Politics*, 11(2):171–94.

Aldrich, J.H. (1995) *Why Parties? The Origin and Transformation of Party Politics in America* (Chicago, IL: University of Chicago Press).

Alesina, A. and E.L. Glaeser (2005) *Fighting Poverty in the US and Europe: A World of Difference* (Oxford: Oxford University Press).

Alesina, A. and L. Summers (1993) 'Central Bank Independence and Macroeconomic Performance: Some Comparative Evidence', *Journal of Money, Credit, and Banking*, 25(2): 151–62.

Alford, D. (2006) 'The Lamfalussy Process and EU Bank Regulation: Another Step on the Road to Pan-European Regulation?', *Review of Banking and Financial Law*, 25(1): 389–442.

Alink, F., A. Boin and P. t'Hart (2001) 'Institutional Crisis and Reforms in Policy Sectors: The Case of Asylum Policy in Europe', *Journal of European Public Policy*, 8(2): 286–306.

Almond, G.A. (1956) 'Comparing Political Systems', *Journal of Politics*, 18(2): 391–409.

Alter, K.J. (1996) 'The European Court's Political Power', *West European Politics*, 19(3): 458–87.

Alter, K.J. (1998a) 'Explaining National Court Acceptance of European Court Jurisprudence: A Critical Evaluation of Theories of Legal Integration', in A.-M. Slaughter, A. Stone Sweet and J.H.H. Weiler (eds), *The European Court and National Courts – Doctrine and Jurisprudence: Legal Change in Its Social Context* (Oxford: Hart).

Alter, K.J. (1998b) 'Who Are the "Masters of the Treaty?": European Governments and the European Court of Justice', *International Organization*, 52(1): 121–47.

Alter, K.J. (2000) 'The European Union's Legal System and Domestic Policy: Spillover or Backlash?', *International Organization*, 54(3): 489–518.

Alter, K.J. (2001) *Establishing the Supremacy of European Law: The Making of an International Rule of Law in Europe* (Oxford University Press).

Alter, K.J. (2008) 'The European Court and Legal Integration: An Exceptional Story or Harbinger of the Future?', in K.E. Whittington, R.D. Kelemen and G.A. Caldeira (eds), *The European Court and Legal Integration: An Exceptional Story or Harbinger of the Future?* (Oxford: Oxford University Press).

Alter, K.J. and S. Meunier-Aitsahalia (1994) 'Judicial Politics in the European Community: European Integration and the Pathbreaking *Cassis de Dijon* Decision', *Comparative Political Studies*, 26(4): 535–61.

Alvazzi del Frate, A., U. Zvekic and J.J.M. van Dijk (eds) (1993) *Understanding Crime: Experiences of Crime and Crime Control* (Rome: United Nations Interregional Crime and Justice Research Institute).

Andersen, S.S. and T.R. Burns (1996) *The European Union and the Erosion of Parliamentary Democracy: A Study of Post-parliamentary Governance* (London: Sage).

Anderson, C.J. (1995) 'Economic Uncertainty and European Solidarity Revisited: Trends in Public Support for European Integration', in C. Rhodes and S. Mazey (eds), *The State of the European Union*, 3 (London: Longman).

Anderson, C.J. (1998) 'When in Doubt, Use Proxies: Attitudes Towards Domestic Politics and Support for European Integration', *Comparative Political Studies*, 31(5): 569–601.

Anderson, C.J., A. Blais, S. Bowler, T. Donovan, and O. Listhaug (2005) *Losers' Consent: Elections and Democratic Legitimacy* (Oxford: Oxford University Press).

Anderson, C.J. and K. Kaltenthaler (1996) 'The Dynamics of Public Opinion Toward European Integration, 1973–93', *European Journal of International Relations*, 2(2): 175–99.

Anderson, C. and M.S. Reichert (1996) 'Economic Benefits and Support for Membership in the EU: A Cross-National Analysis', *Journal of Public Policy*, 15(3): 231–49.

Anderson, M., M. den Boer, P. Cullen, W. Gilmore, C. Raab, and N. Walker (1995) *Policing the European Union* (Oxford: Clarendon Press).

Ansell, C.K., C.A. Parsons, and K.A. Darden (1997) 'Dual Networks in European Regional Development Policy', *Journal of Common Market Studies*, 35(3): 347–76.

Apeldoorn, B. van (2002) 'The European Round Table of Industrialists: Still a Unique Player?', in J. Greenwood (ed.), The *Effectiveness of EU Business Associations* (London: Palgrave).

Artis, M. (1996) 'Alternative Transitions to EMU', *Economic Journal*, 106(437): 1005–15.

Aspinwall, M. (2002) 'The Dimensionality of the EU Policy Space', *European Union Politics*, 3(2): 81–111.

Attinà, F. (1990) 'The Voting Behaviour of the European Parliament Members and the Problem of Europarties', *European Journal of Political Research*, 18(3): 557–79.

Austen-Smith, D. (1993) 'Information and Influence: Lobbying for Agendas and Votes', *American Journal of Political Science*, 37(3): 799–833.

Austen-Smith, D. and J.R. Wright (1994) 'Counteractive Lobbying', *American Journal of Political Science*, 38(1): 25–44.

Axelrod, R. (1970) *Conflict of Interest: A Theory of Divergent Goals with Application to Politics* (Chicago, IL: Markham Publishing).

Bache, I. and M. Flinders (eds) (2004) *Multi-level Governance* (Oxford: Oxford University Press).

Badie, B. and P. Birnbaum (1983) *The Sociology of the State* (Chicago, IL: University of Chicago Press).

Bagehot, W. (1987 [1865]) *The English Constitution* (London: C.A. Watts.)

Bailey, I. (1999) 'Flexibility and Harmonization in EU Environmental Policy', *Journal of Common Market Studies*, 37(4): 549–71.

Bailey, I. and De Propris, L. (2002) 'The 1988 Reform of the European Structural Funds: Entitlement or Empowerment', *Journal of European Public Policy*, 9(3): 408–28.

Baldwin, R., E. Berglöf, F. Giavazzi, and J. Widgren (2001) 'Eastern Enlargement and ECB Reform', *Swedish Economic Policy Review*, 89(1): 15–50.

Baldwin-Edwards, M. and M. Schain (eds) (1994) *The Politics of Immigration in Western Europe* (London: Frank Cass).

Balme, R. and B. Jouve (1996) 'Building the Regional State: Europe and Territorial Organization in France', in L. Hooghe (ed.), *Cohesion Policy and European Integration: Building Multi-Level Governance* (Oxford: Oxford University Press).

Banks, J.S. and J. Duggan (2006) 'A General Bargaining Model of Legislative Policy-Making', *Quarterly Journal of Political Science*, 1(1): 49–85.

Banzhaf, J.F. (1965) 'Weighted Voting Doesn't Work: A Mathematical Analysis', *Rutgers Law Review*, 19(2): 317–43.

Baron, D.P. (1989) 'A Noncooperative Theory of Legislative Coalitions', *American Journal of Political Science*, 33(4): 1048–84.

Barr, J. and F. Passarelli (2009) 'Who has the power in the EU?', *Mathematical Social Sciences*, 57(3): 339–66.

Barro, R.J. and D.B. Gordon (1983) 'A Positive Theory of Monetary Policy in a Natural Rate Model', *Journal of Political Economy*, 91(4): 589–610.

Baumgartner, F.R. and B.L. Leech (1996) 'The Multiple Ambiguities of "Counteractive Lobbying"', *American Journal of Political Science*, 40(2): 521–42.

Becker, G.S. (1983) 'A Theory of Competition Among Pressure Groups for Political Influence', *Quarterly Journal of Economics*, 98(3): 371–400.

Behrens, P. and M. Smyrl (1999) 'A Conflict of Rationalities: EU Regional Policy and the Single Market', *Journal of European Public Policy*, 6(3): 419–35.

Bell, D. (1960) *The End of Ideology* (New York: Free Press).

Bellamy, R. (2010) 'Democracy Without Democracy? Can the EU's Democratic "Outputs" be Separated from the Democratic "Inputs" Provided by Competitive Parties and Majority Rule?', *Journal of European Public Policy*, 17(1): 2–19.

Bénassy-Quéré, A. and E. Turkisch (2009) 'The ECB Governing Council in an Enlarged Euro Area', *Journal of Common Market Studies*, 47(1): 25–53.

Benedetto, G. (2005) 'Rapporteurs as Legislative Entrepreneurs: The Dynamics of the Codecision Procedure in Europe's Parliament', *Journal of European Public Policy*, 12(1): 67–88.

Benedetto, G. and B. Høyland (2007) 'The EU Annual Budgetary Procedure: the Existing Rules and Proposed Reforms of the Convention and

Intergovernmental Conference, 2002–2004', *Journal of Common Market Studies*, 45(3): 565–87.

Benoit, K. and Laver, M. (2006) *Party Policy in Modern Democracies* (London: Routledge).

Bentley, A. F. (1908) *The Process of Government* (Chicago, IL: University of Chicago Press).

Bergman, T. (1997) 'National Parliaments and EU Affairs Committees: Notes on Empirical Variation and Competing Explanations', *Journal of European Public Policy*, 4(3): 373–87.

Berlin, I. (1969) *Four Essays on Liberty* (Oxford: Oxford University Press).

Bernhagen, P. and N.J. Mitchell (2009) 'The Determinants of Direct Corporate Lobbying in the European Union', *European Union Politics*, 10(2): 155–76.

Bernitz, U. (2001) 'Sweden and the European Union: On Sweden's Implementation and Application of European Law', *Common Market Law Review*, 38(4): 903–34.

Beyers, J. (2004) 'Voice and Access: Political Practices of European Interest Associations', *European Union Politics*, 5(2): 211–40.

Beyers, J. (2008) 'Policy Issues, Organisational Format and the Political Strategies of Interest Organisations', *West European Politics*, 31(6): 1188–211.

Bhagwati, J. (2003) 'Borders Beyond Control', *Foreign Affairs*, 82(1): 98–101.

Bigo, D. (1994) 'The European Security Field: Stakes and Rivalries in a Newly Developing Area of Policy Intervention', in M. Anderson and M. den Boer (eds), *Policing Across National Boundaries* (London: Pinter).

Bilal, S. (1998) 'Political Economy Considerations on the Supply of Trade Protection in Regional Integration Agreements', *Journal of Common Market Studies*, 36(3):1–32.

Bindseil, U. (2001) 'A Coalition–Form Analysis of the "One Country – One Vote" Rule in the Governing Council of the European Central Bank', *International Economic Journal*, 15(1): 141–64.

Bini Smaghi, L. and C. Casini (2000) 'Monetary and Fiscal Policy Co-operation in EMU', *Journal of Common Market Studies*, 38(3): 375–91.

Black, D. (1958) *The Theory of Committees and Elections* (Cambridge: Cambridge University Press).

Blom-Hansen, J. (2008) 'The Origins of the EU Comitology System: A Case of Informal Agenda-Setting by the Commission', *Journal of European Public Policy*, 15(2): 208–26.

Blondel, J., R. Sinnott, and P. Svensson (1997) 'Representation and Voter Turnout', *European Journal of Political Research*, 32(2): 243–72.

Blondel, J., R. Sinnott, and P. Svensson (1998) *People and Parliament in the European Union: Participation, Democracy and Legitimacy* (Oxford: Clarendon Press).

Bobbio, N. (1996) *Left and Right: The Significance of a Political Distinction*, trans. A. Cameron (Cambridge: Polity).

Bofinger, P. (1994) 'Is Europe an Optimal Currency Area', Discussion Paper No. 915 (London: Centre for Economic Policy Research).

Boix, C. (2003) *Democracy and Redistribution* (Cambridge: Cambridge University Press).

Boockmann, B. (1998) 'Agenda Control by Interest Groups in EU Social Policy', *Journal of Theoretical Politics*, 10(2): 215–36.

Boomgaarden, H.G. and A. Freire (2009) 'Religion and Euroscepticism: Direct, Indirect or No Effects?', *West European Politics*, 32(6): 1240–65.

Börzel, T. (2000) 'Why there is no "Southern Problem": on Environmental Leaders and Laggards in the European Union', *Journal of European Public Policy*, 8(5): 803–24.

Börzel, T. (2001) 'Non-Compliance in the European Union: Pathology or Statistical Artefact?', *Journal of European Public Policy*, 8(5): 803–24.

Börzel, T. (2003) *Environmental Leaders and Laggards in Europe: Why There is (not) a 'Southern Problem'* (Aldershot: Ashgate).

Bossong, R. (2008) 'The Action Plan on Combating Terrorism: A Flawed Instrument of EU Security Governance', *Journal of Common Market Studies*, 46(1): 27–48.

Bouvet, F. and S. Dall'Erba (2010) 'European Regional Structural Funds: How Large is the Influence of Politics on the Allocation Process?', *Journal of Common Market Studies*, 48(3): 501–28.

Bouwen, P. (2002) 'Corporate Lobbying in the European Union: the Logic of Access', *Journal of European Public Policy*, 9(3): 365–90.

Bouwen, P. (2004a) 'Exchanging Access Goods for Access: A Comparative Study of Business Lobbying in the European Union Institutions', *European Journal of Political Research*, 43(3): 337–69.

Bouwen, P. (2004b) 'The Logic of Access to the European Parliament: Business Lobbying in the Committee on Economic and Monetary Affairs', *Journal of Common Market Studies*, 42(3): 473–95.

Bowler, A. and D.M. Farrell (1993) 'Legislator Shirking and Voter Monitoring: Impact of European Parliament Electoral Systems upon Legislator–Voter Relationships', *Journal of Common Market Studies*, 31(1): 45–69.

Bradley, K. St. Clair (1997) 'The European Parliament and Comitology: On the Road to Nowhere?', *European Law Journal*, 3(3): 230–54.

Brams, A.J. and P.J. Affuso (1985) 'New Paradoxes of Voting Power on the EC Council of Ministers', *Electoral Studies*, 4(2): 135–9.

Branch, A. and J. Greenwood (2001) 'European Employers: Social Partners?', in H. Compston and J. Greenwood (eds), *Social Partnership in the European Union* (London: Palgrave).

Break, G. (1967) *Intergovernmental Fiscal Relations in the United States* (Washington, DC: Brookings Institution).

Brinegar, A.P. and S.K. Jolly (2005) 'Location, Location, Location: National Contextual Factors and Public Support for European Integration', *European Union Politics*, 6(2): 155–80.

Brinegar, A.P., A.K. Jolly, and H. Kitschelt (2002) 'Varieties of Capitalism and Political Divides over European Integration', in G. Marks and M. Steenbergen (eds), *European Integration and Political Conflict* (Cambridge: Cambridge University Press).

Broscheid, A. and D. Coen (2003) 'Insider and Outsider Lobbying of the European Commission: An Informational Model of Forum Politics', *European Union Politics*, 4(2): 165–89.

Broscheid, A. and D. Coen (2007) 'Lobbying Activity and Fora Creation in the EU: Empirically Exploring the Nature of the Policy Good', *Journal of European Public Policy*, 14(3): 346–65.

Brubaker, R. (1992) *Citizenship and Nationhood in France and Germany* (Cambridge, MA: Harvard University Press).

Budden, P. (2002) 'Observations on the Single European Act and "Relaunch of Europe"', *Journal of European Public Policy*, 9(2): 76–97.

Budzinski, O. and A. Christiansen (2005) 'Competence Allocation in the EU Competition Policy System an Interest-Driven Process', *Journal of Public Policy*, 25(3): 313–37.

Bufacchi, V. and S. Garmise (1995) 'Social Justice in Europe: An Evaluation of European Regional Policy', *Government and Opposition*, 30(2): 179–97.

Buiter, W., G. Corsetti and N. Roubini (1993) 'Excessive deficits: Sense and Nonsense in the Treaty of Maastricht', *Economic Policy*, 16(8): 57–100.

Buiter, W.H. (1999) 'Alice in Euroland', *Journal of Common Market Studies*, 37(2): 181–209.

Bulmer, S. (1991) 'Analysing European Political Co-operation: The Case for Two-Tier Analysis', in M. Holland (ed.) *Analysing European Political Co-operation: The Case for Two-Tier Analysis* (London: Macmillan).

Bulmer, S. and W. Wessels (1987) *The European Council: Decision-making in European Politics* (London: Macmillan).

Bush, E. and P. Simi (2001) 'European Farmers and Their Protest', in D. Imig and S. Tarrow (eds), *Contentious Europeans: Protest and Politics in an Emerging Polity* (Lanham, MD: Rowman & Littlefield).

Buti, M., W. Roeger, and J. In't Veld (2001) 'Stabilizing Output and Inflation: Policy Conflicts and Co-operation under a Stability Pact', *Journal of Common Market Studies*, 39(5): 801–28.

Butt Philip, A. (1985) *Pressure Groups in the European Community* (London: Universities Association of Contemporary European Studies).

Caldeira, G.A. and J.L. Gibson (1995) 'The Legitimacy of the Court of Justice in the European Union: Models of Institutional Support', *American Political Science Review*, 89(2): 356–76.

Cameron, D.R. (1992) 'The 1992 Initiative: Causes and Consequences', in A.M. Sbragia (ed.), *The 1992 Initiative: Causes and Consequences* (Washington, DC: Brookings Institution).

Cameron, D.R. (1993) 'British exit, German voice, French loyalty: defection, domination, and cooperation in the 1992–93 ERM crisis', paper presented at the annual meeting of the American Political Science Association, Washington, DC, September.

Cameron, D.R. (1997) 'Economic and Monetary Union: Underlying Imperatives and Third-Stage Dilemmas', *Journal of European Public Policy*, 4(3): 455–85.

Cameron, F. (1998) 'Building a Common Foreign Policy: Do Institutions Matters?', in J. Peterson and H. Sjursen (eds), *Building a Common Foreign Policy: Do Institutions Matters?* (London: Routledge).

Caporale, G.M. (1993) 'Is Europe an Optimal Currency Area? Symmetric Versus Asymmetric Shocks in the EC', *National Institute Economic Review*, 144(1): 95–113.

Cappelletti, M., M. Seccombe, and J.H.H. Weiler (eds) (1986) *Integration Through Law*, vols 1 and 2 (Berlin: De Gruyter).

Carey, J.M. and M.S. Shugart (1995) 'Incentives to Cultivate a Personal Vote: A Rank Ordering of Electoral Formulas', *Electoral Studies*, 14(4): 417–39.

Carey, S. (2002a) 'The impact of political parties on public support for European integration', doctoral thesis, University of Essex.

Carey, S. (2002b) 'Undivided Loyalties: Is National Identity an Obstacle to European Integration?', *European Union Politics*, 3(4): 387–413.

Carrubba, C.J. (1997) 'Net Financial Transfers in the European Union: Who Gets What and Why?', *Journal of Politics*, 59(2): 469–96.

Carrubba, C.J. (2001) 'The Electoral Connection in European Union Politics', *Journal of Politics*, 63(1): 141–58.

Carrubba, C.J., M. Gabel and C. Hankla (2008) 'Judicial Behavior under Political Constraints: Evidence from the European Court of Justice', *American Political Science Review*, 102(4): 435–52.

Cawson, A. and P. Saunders (1983) 'Corporatism, Competitive Politics and Class Struggle', in R. King (ed.), *Capital and Politics* (London, Routledge).

Cernat, L. (2004) 'The Emerging European Corporate Governance Model: Anglo-Saxon, Continental, or Still the Century of Diversity?', *Journal of European Public Policy*, 11(1): 47–166.

Chalmers, D. (1995) 'The Single Market: From Prima Donna to Journeyman', in J. Shaw and G. More (eds), *New Legal Dynamics of European Union* (Oxford: Clarendon Press).

Chalmers, D. (1997) 'Judicial Preferences and the Community Legal Order', *Modern Law Review*, 60(2): 164–99.

Chang, E.C.C. and M.A. Golden (2006) 'Electoral Systems, District Magnitude and Corruption', *British Journal of Political Science*, 37(1): 115–37.

Chopin, I. and J. Niessen (eds) (1998) *Proposals for Legislative Measures to Combat Racism and to Promote Equal Rights in the European Union* (Brussels: Starting Line Group).

Christiansen, T., G. Falkner, and K.E. Jørgensen (2002) 'Theorizing EU Treaty Reform: Beyond Diplomacy and Bargaining', *Journal of European Public Policy*, 9(1): 12–32.

Christiansen, T. and C. Reh (2009) *Constitutionalizing the European Union* (London: Palgrave).

Christin, T. (2005) 'Economic and Political Basis of Attitudes Towards the EU in Central and Eastern European Countries in the 1990s', *European Union Politics*, 6(1): 29–57.

Christin, T. and S. Hug (2002) 'Referendums and Citizen Support for European Integration', *Comparative Political Studies*, 35(5): 586–617.

Cichowski, R.A. (2000) 'Western Dreams, Eastern Realities: Support for the European Union in Central and Eastern Europe', *Comparative Political Studies*, 33(10): 1243–78.

Clark, W.R., M. Golder, and S.N. Golder (2002) 'Fiscal Policy and the Democratic Process in the European Union', *European Union Politics*, 3(2): 205–30.

Clift, B. (2009) 'The Second Time as Farce? The EU Takeover Directive, the Clash of Capitalisms and the Hamstrung Harmonization of European (and French) Corporate Governance', *Journal of Common Market Studies*, 47(1): 55–79.

Clutterbuck, R.L. (1990) *Terrorism, Drugs and Crime in Europe after 1992* (London: Routledge).

Cobham, D. (1996) 'Causes and Effects of the European Monetary Crisis of 1992–93', *Journal of Common Market Studies*, 34(4): 585–604.

Coen, D. (1997) 'The Evolution of the Large Firm as a Political Actor in the European Union', *Journal of European Public Policy*, 4(1): 91–108.

Coen, D. (1998) *The Large Firm as a Political Actor in the European Union* (London: Routledge).

Coen, D. (2007) 'Empirical and Theoretical Studies in EU Lobbying', *Journal of European Public Policy*, 14(3): 333–45.

Coen, D. (2010) 'European Business and Government Relations', in D. Coen, W. Grand and G. Wilson (eds.), *The Oxford Handbook of Business and Government* (Oxford: Oxford University Press).

Coen, D. and G. Richardson (2009a) 'Learning to Lobby the European Union: 20 Years of Change', in D. Coen and J. Richardson (eds), *Lobbying the European Union: Institutions, Actors, and Issues* (Oxford: Oxford University Press).

Coen, D. and J. Richardson (eds) (2009b) *Lobbying the European Union: Institutions, Actors, and Issues* (Oxford: Oxford University Press).

Cohen, M.A. (1992) 'The Motives of Judges: Empirical Evidence from Antitrust Sentencing', *International Review of Law and Economics*, 12(1): 13–30.

Cole, J. and Cole, F. (1997) *A Geography of the European Union*, 2nd edn (London: Routledge).

Coleman, W.D. (1998) 'From Protected Development to Market Liberalism: Paradigm Change in Agriculture', *Journal of European Public Policy*, 5(4): 632–51.

Coleman, W.D. and S. Tangermann (1999) 'The 1992 CAP Reform, the Uruguay Round and the Commission', *Journal of Common Market Studies*, 37(3): 385–405.

Committee for the Study of Economic and Monetary Union (1989) *Report on Economic and Monetary Union in Europe* (the Delors Report) (Luxembourg: Office for Official Publications of the European Union).

Compston, H. and J. Greenwood (eds) (2001) *Social Partnership in the European Union* (London: Palgrave).

Conant, L. (2002) *Justice Contained: Law and Politics in the European Union* (Ithaca, NY: Cornell University Press).

Conzelmann, T. (1995) 'Networking and the Politics of EU Regional Policy: Lessons from North Rhine–Westphalia, Nord–Pas de Calais and North West England', *Regional and Federal Studies*, 5(2): 134–72.

Cooper, I. (2006) 'The Watchdogs of Subsidiarity: National Parliaments and the Logic of Arguing in the EU', *Journal of Common Market Studies*, 44(2): 281–304.

Cooter, R. and J. Drexl (1994) 'The Logic of Power in the Emerging European Constitution: Game Theory and the Division of Powers', *International Review of Law and Economics*, 14(2): 307–26.

Cooter, R. and T. Ginsburg (1997) 'Comparative Judicial Discretion: An Empirical Test of Economic Models', in D. Schmidtchen and R. Cooter (eds), *Constitutional Law and Economics of the European Union* (Cheltenham: Edward Elgar).

Corbett, R., F. Jacobs, and M. Shackleton (1995) *The European Parliament* (London: Catermill).

Cornelius, W.A., P.L. Martin, and J.F. Hollifield (eds) (2005) *Controlling Illegal Immigration: A Global Perspective*, second edition (Stanford, CA: Stanford University Press).

Court of Justice (1999) *The Future of the Judicial System of the European Union (Proposals and Reflections)* (Luxembourg: Court of Justice of the European Union).

Cowles, M.G. (1995) 'Setting the Agenda for a New Europe: The ERT and EC 1992', *Journal of Common Market Studies*, 33(4): 501–26.

Cowles, M.G. (1997) 'Organizing Industrial Coalitions: A Challenge for the Future?', in H. Wallace and A.R. Young (eds), *Participation and Policy-Making in the European Union* (Oxford: Clarendon Press).

Cowles, M.G. (1998) 'The Changing Architecture of Big Business', in J. Greenwood and M. Aspinwall (eds), *Collective Action in the European Union* (London: Routledge).

Cowles, M.G. (2002) 'Large Firms and the Transformation of EU Business Associations: A Historical Perspective', in J. Greenwood (ed.), *The Effectiveness of EU Business Associations* (London: Palgrave).

Cox, G.W. and M.D. McCubbins (1993) *Legislative Leviathan: Party Government in the House* (Berkeley, CA: University of California Press).

Craig, P. (1998) 'Report on the United Kingdom', in A.-M. Slaughter, A. Stone Sweet and J.H.H. Weiler (eds), *The European Court and National Courts – Doctrine and Jurisprudence: Legal Change in Its Social Context* (Oxford: Hart).

Craig, P. (2001) 'The Jurisdiction of the Community Courts Reconsidered', in G. de Búrca and J.H.H. Weiler (eds), *The European Court of Justice* (Oxford: Oxford University Press).

Cram, L. (1996) 'Theories of Integration', in J. Richardson (ed.), *Policy-Making in the EU: Conceptual Lenses and the Integration Process* (London: Routledge).

Cram, L. (1998) 'The EU Institutions and Collective Action: Constructing a European Interest?', in J. Greenwood and M. Aspinwall (eds), *Collective Action in the European Union* (London: Routledge).

Crombez, C. (1996) 'Legislative Procedures in the European Community', *British Journal of Political Science*, 26(2): 199–218.

Crombez, C. (1997) 'Policy Making and Commission Appointment in the European Union', *Aussenwirtshaft*, 52(6): 3–82.

Crombez, C. (1997) 'The Co-Decision Procedure in the European Union', *Legislative Studies Quarterly*, 22(1): 97–119.

Crombez, C. (2000) 'Institutional Reform and Co-Decision in the European Union', *Constitutional Political Economy*, 11(1): 41–57.

Crombez, C. (2001) 'The Treaty of Amsterdam and the Co-decision Procedure', in G. Schneider and M. Aspinwall (eds), *The Rules of Integration: Institutional Approaches to the Study of Europe* (Manchester: Manchester University Press).

Crombez, C. (2002) 'Information, Lobbying and the Legislative Process in the European Union', *European Union Politics*, 3(1): 7–32.

Crombez, C. (2003) 'The Democratic Deficit in the European Union: Much Ado about Nothing?', *European Union Politics*, 4(1): 101–20.

Crouch, C. and A. Menon (1997) 'Organised Interests and the State', in M. Rhodes, P. Heywood and V. Wright (eds), *Developments in West European Politics* (London: Macmillan).

Crowley, P. (1996) 'EMU, Maastricht and the 1996 Intergovernmental Conference', *Contemporary Economic Policy*, 14(2): 41–55.

Crowley, P. (2001) 'The Institutional Implications of EMU', *Journal of Common Market Studies*, 39(3): 385–404.

Crum, B. (2007) 'Party Stances in the Referendums on the EU Constitution: Causes and Consequences of Competition and Collusion', *European Union Politics*, 8(1): 61–82.

Cukierman, A. (1992) *Central Bank Strategy, Credibility and Independence: Theory and Evidence* (Cambridge, MA: Massachusetts Institute of Technology Press).

Cukierman, A., S. B. Webb, and B. Neyapti (1992) 'The Measurement of Central Bank Independence and its Effect on Policy Outcomes', *The World Bank Economic Review*, 6(3): 353–98.

Curtice, J. (1989) 'The 1989 European Election: Protest or Green Tide?', *Electoral Studies*, 8(3): 217–30.

Cusack, T.R. (2001) 'Partisanship in the Setting and Coordination of Fiscal and Monetary Policies', *European Journal of Political Research*, 40(1): 93–115.

Czaika, M. (2009) 'Asylum Cooperation among Asymmetric Countries: The Case of the European Union', *European Union Politics*, 10(1): 89–113.

Dahrendorf, R. (1959) *Class and Class Conflict in Industrial Society* (London: Routledge).

Dali, M. (2006) 'EU Social Policy after Lisbon', *Journal of Common Market Studies*, 44(3): 461–81.

Dalton, R.J. (1988) *Citizen Politics in Western Democracies: Public Opinion and Political Parties in the United States Great Britain, West Germany and France* (Chatham: Chatham House).

Dalton, R.J. and M. Kuechler (eds) (1990) *Challenging the Political Order: New Social and Political Movements in Western Democracies* (Oxford: Oxford University Press).

Damro, C. (2001) 'Building an External Identity: The EU and Extraterritorial Competition Policy', *Journal of European Public Policy*, 8(2): 208–26.

Daugbjerg, C. (1999) 'Reforming the CAP', *Journal of Common Market Studies*, 39(3): 407–28.

Daugbjerg, C. (2003) 'Policy Feedback and Paradigm Shift in EU Agricultural Policy: The Effects of the MacSharry Reform on Future Reform', *Journal of European Public Policy*, 10(3): 421–37.

Daugbjerg, C. and A. Swinbank (2004) 'The CAP and EU Enlargement: Prospects for an Alternative Strategy to Avoid the Lock-in of CAP Support', *Journal of Common Market Studies*, 42(1): 99–119.

Daugbjerg, C. and A. Swinbank (2007) 'The Politics of CAP Reform: Trade Negotiations, Institutional Settings and Blame Avoidance', *Journal of Common Market Studies*, 45(1): 1:22.

De Grauwe, P. (2002) 'Challenges for Monetary Policy in Euroland', *Journal of Common Market Studies*, 40(4): 563–80.

De Grauwe, P. (2003) *The Economics of Monetary Integration* (Oxford: Oxford University Press).

De Grauwe, P. and W. Vanhaverbeke (1993) 'Is Europe an Optimal Currency Area? Evidence from Regional Data', in P.R. Masson and M.P. Taylor (eds), *Policy Issues in the Operation of Currency Unions* (Cambridge: Cambridge University Press).

De Haan, J. and C.W. Eijffinger (2000) 'The Democratic Accountability of the European Central Bank', *Journal of Common Market Studies*, 38(3): 393–8.

De La Fuente, A. and R. Domenech (2001) 'The Redistributive Effects of the EU Budget: An Analysis and Proposal for Reform', *Journal of Common Market Studies*, 39(2): 307–30.

De Rynck, S. and P. McAleavey (2001) 'The Cohesion Deficit in Structural Fund Policy', *Journal of European Public Policy*, 8(4): 541–57.

De Visscher, C., O. Maiscocq, and F. Varone (2008) 'The Lamfalussy Reform in the EU Securities Markets: Fiduciary Relationships, Policy Effectiveness and Balance of Power', *Journal of Public Policy*, 28(1): 19–47.

De Vreese, C.H. and H.G. Boomgaarden (2006) 'Media Effects on Public Opinion about the Enlargement of the European Union', *Journal of Common Market Studies*, 44(2): 419–36.

De Vreese, C.H. and A. Kandyla (2009) 'News Framing and Public Support for a Common Foreign and Security Policy', *Journal of Common Market Studies*, 47(3): 453–81.

De Winter, L. and M. Swyngedouw (1999) 'The Scope of EU Government', in H. Schmitt and J. Thomassen (eds), *Political Representation and Legitimacy in the European Union* (Oxford: Oxford University Press).

Dedman, N. (2009) *The Origins and Development of the European Union, 1945–2008*, 2nd edn (London: Routledge).

Dehousse, R. (1995) 'Constitutional Reform in the European Community: Are there Alternatives to the Majoritarian Avenue?', in J. Hayward (ed.), *The Crisis of Representation in Europe* (London: Frank Cass).

Dehousse, R. and G. Majone (1994) 'The Institutional Dynamics of European Integration: From the Single Act to the Maastricht Treaty', S. Martin (ed.), *The Construction of Europe – Essays in Honour of Emile Noël* (Dordrecht: Kluwer).

Den Boer, M. and J. Monar (2002) '11 September and Global Terrorism as a Challenge to the EU as a Security Actor', *Journal of Common Market Studies*, 40(1): 11–28.

Devuyst, Y. (1995) 'The European Community and the Conclusion of the Uruguay Round', in C. Rhodes and S. Mazey (eds), *The State and the European Union*, 3 (London: Longman).

Dewan, T. and E. Thielemann (2006) 'The Myth of Free-Riding: Refugee Protection and Implicit Burden-Sharing', *West European Politics*, 29 (2): 351–69.

Díez Medrano, J. (2003) *Framing Europe: Attitudes to European Integration in Germany, Spain, and the United Kingdom* (Princeton, NJ: Princeton University Press).

Díez Medrano, J. and P. Gutiérrez (2001) 'Nested Identities: National and European Identity in Spain', *Ethnic and Racial Studies*, 24(5): 753–78.

Dinan, D. (1994) *Ever Closer Union? An Introduction to the European Community* (London: Palgrave).

Docksey, C. and Williams, K. (1997) 'The Commission and the Execution of Community Policy', in G. Edwards and D. Spence (eds), *The European Commission*, 2nd edn (London: Catermill).

Dogan, R. (1997) 'Comitology: Little Procedures with Big Implications', *West European Politics*, 20(3): 31–60.

Dogan, R. (2001) 'A Cross-Sectional View of Comitology: Incidence, Issues and Implications', in T. Christiansen and E. Kirchner (eds), *Committee Governance in the European Union* (Manchester: Manchester University Press).

Dølvik, J.E. and J. Visser (2001) 'ETUC and European Social Partnership: A Third Turning-Point?', in H. Compston and J. Greenwoods (eds), *Social Partnership in the European Union* (London: Palgrave).

Donnelly, M. and Ritchie, E. (1997) 'The College of Commissioners and the Cabinets', in G. Edwards and D. Spence (eds), *The European Commission*, 2nd edn (London: Catermill).

Döring, H. (2007) 'The Composition of the College of Commissioners: Patterns of Delegation', *European Union Politics*, 8(2): 207–28.

Dornbusch, R. (1990) 'Two-Track EMU, Now!', in K.O. Pöhl *et al.*, *Britain and EMU* (London: Centre for Economic Performance).

Downs, A. (1957) *An Economic Theory of Democracy* (New York, NY: Harper & Row).

Downs, W.M. (2001) 'Denmark's Referendum on the Euro: The Mouse that Roared ... Again', *West European Politics*, 24(1): 222–6.

Drazen, A. (2002) *Political Economy in Macroeconomics* (Princeton, NJ: Princeton University Press).

Drewry, G. (1993) 'Judicial Politics in Britain: Patrolling the Boundaries', in M.L. Volcansek (ed.), *Judicial Politics and Policy-Making in Western Europe* (London: Frank Cass).

Duke, S. (1996) 'The Second Death (or Second Coming?) of the WEU', *Journal of Common Market Studies*, 34(2):167–190.

Dunleavy, P. (1991) *Democracy, Bureaucracy and Public Choice: Economic Explanations in Political Science* (London: Harvester Wheatsheaf).

Dunleavy, P. (1997) 'Explaining the Centralization of the European Union: A Public Choice Analysis', *Aussenwirtschaft*, 52(I/II):183–212.

Dunleavy, P. and B. O'Leary (1987) *Theories of the State: The Politics of Liberal Democracy* (London: Macmillan).

Dyson, K. (1994) *Elusive Union: The Process of Economic and Monetary Integration in Europe* (London: Longman).

Dyson, K. and K. Featherstone (1999) *The Road to Maastricht: Negotiating Economic and Monetary Union* (Oxford: Oxford University Press).

Dyson, K., K. Featherstone, and G. Michalopoulis (1994) 'The politics of EMU: the Maastricht Treaty and the relevance of bargaining models', paper presented at the annual meeting of the American Political Science Association, New York, September.

Earnshaw, D. and D. Judge (1995) 'Early Days: the European Parliament, Co-Decision and the European Union Legislative Process Post-Maastricht', *Journal of European Public Policy*, 2(4): 624–49.

Earnshaw, D. and D. Judge (1997) 'The Life and Time of the Co-operation Procedure', *Journal of Common Market Studies*, 35(4): 543–64.

Earnshaw, D. and D. Judge (2002) 'No Simple Dichotomies: Lobbyists and the European Parliament', *Journal of Legislative Studies*, 8(4): 62–79.

Easton, D. (1957) 'An Approach to the Study of Political Systems', *World Politics*, 9(5): 383–400.

Easton, D. (1965) *A Framework for Political Analysis* (Englewood Cliffs, NJ: Prentice-Hall).

Easton, D. (1975) 'A Reassessment of the Concept of Political Support', *British Journal of Political Science*, 5(4): 435–57.

Egan, M. (2001) *Constructing a European Market: Standards, Regulation, and Governance* (Oxford: Oxford University Press).

Egeberg, M. and A. Heskestad (2010) 'The Denationalisation of the Cabinets in the European Commission', *Journal of Common Market Studies*, 48(4): 775–86.

Ehlermann, C.-D. and L. Hancher (1995) 'Comments on Streit and Mussler', *European Law Journal*, 1(1): 84–8.

Eichenberg, R.C. and R.J. Dalton (1993) 'Europeans and the European Community: The Dynamics of Public Support for European Integration', *International Organization*, 47(4): 507–34.

Eichener, V. (1997) 'Effective European Problem-Solving: Lessons from the Regulation of Occupational Safety and Environmental Protection', *Journal of European Public Policy*, 4(4): 591–608.

Eichengreen, B. (1990) 'Costs and Benefits of European Monetary Unification', Discussion Paper No. 453 (London: Centre for Economic Policy Research).

Eichengreen, B. (1993a) 'Labor Markets and European Monetary Unification', in P. Masson and M. Taylor (eds), *Policy Issues in the Operation of Currency Unions* (Cambridge: Cambridge University Press).

Eichengreen, B. (1993b) 'Thinking About Migration: Notes on European Migration Pressures at the Dawn of the Next Millennium', in H. Siebert (ed.), *Migration: A Challenge for Europe* (Ann Arbor, MI: University of Michigan Press).

Eichengreen, B. (1994) 'Fiscal Policy in EMU', in B. Eichengreen and J. Frieden (eds), *The Political Economy of European Monetary Unification* (Boulder, CO: Westview).

Eichengreen, B. and J.A. Frieden (2001) 'The Political Economy of European Monetary Unification: An Analytical Introduction', in B. Eichengreen and J.A. Frieden (eds), *The Political Economy of European Monetary Unification*, 2nd edn (Boulder, CO: Westview).

Eichengreen, B. and J. von Hagen (1996) 'Fiscal Policy and Monetary Union: Federalism, Fiscal Restrictions, and the No-Bailout Rule', in H. Siebert (ed.), *Monetary Policy in an Integrated World Economy* (Mohr: Tubingen).

Eijk, C. van der and M. Franklin (eds) (1996) *Choosing Europe? The European Electorate and National Politics in the Face of Union* (Ann Arbor, MI: University of Michigan Press).

Eijk, C. van der, M. Franklin, and W. van der Brug (2001) 'Policy Preference and Party Choice', in H. Schmitt and J. Thomassen (eds), *Political Representation and Legitimacy in the European Union* (Oxford: Oxford University Press).

Eising, R. (2007a) 'Institutional Context, Organizational Resources and Strategic Choices: Explaining Interest Group Access in the European Union', *European Union Politics*, 8(3): 329–62.

Eising, R. (2007b) 'The Access of Business Interests to EU Institutions: Towards Elite Pluralism', *Journal of European Public Policy*, 14(3): 384–403.

Eising, R. (2008) 'Logics, Patterns and Power: Clientelism, Committees, Pluralism and Protests in the European Union: Matching Patterns?', *West European Politics*, 31(6): 1166–87.

Epstein, D. and S. O'Halloran (1999) *Delegating Powers: A Transaction Cost Politics Approach to Policy Making Under Separate Powers* (Cambridge: Cambridge University Press).

Eskridge, W.N. Jr. (1991) 'Reneging on History? Playing the Court/ Congress/President Civil Rights Game', *California Law Review*, 38: 613–84.

Esping-Andersen, Gøsta (1990) *The Three Worlds of Welfare Capitalism* (Oxford: Polity Press).

European Commission (1985) *Completing the Internal Market: White Paper of the Commission to the European Council*, COM(85) 310 (Luxembourg: Office of Official Publications of the European Communities).

European Commission (1990) 'One Market, One Money: An Evaluation of the Potential Benefits and Costs of Forming an Economic and Monetary Union', *European Economy* 44.

European Commission (1992) *An Open and Structured Dialogue Between the Commission and Special Interest Groups*, SEC (92) 2272 final (Brussels: European Commission, 2 December).

European Commission (2007) *The EU in the World: The Foreign Policy of the European Union* (Brussels: European Commission).

Evans, P.B., H.K. Jacobson and R.D. Putnam (1993) *Double-Edge Diplomacy: International Bargaining and Domestic Politics* (Berkeley, CA: University of California Press).

Everson, M. (1995) 'The Legacy of the Market Citizen', in J. Shaw and G. More (eds), *New Legal Dynamics of European Union* (Oxford: Clarendon Press).

Fagerberg, J. and B. Verspagen (1996) 'Heading for Divergence? Regional Growth in Europe Reconsidered', *Journal of Common Market Studies*, 34(3): 431–48.

Falkner, G. (1996) 'European Works Councils and the Maastricht Social Agreement: Towards a New Policy Style?', *Journal of European Public Policy*, 3(2): 192–208.

Falkner, G. (2000) 'The Council and the Social Partners? EC Social Policy Between Diplomacy and Collective Bargaining', *Journal of European Public Policy*, 7(5): 705–24.

Falkner, G. (2002) 'How Intergovernmental and Intergovernmental Conferences? An Example from the Maastricht Treaty Reform', *Journal of European Public Policy*, 9(1): 98–119.

Farrell, D.M. and R. Scully (2005) 'Electing the European Parliament: How Uniform are "Uniform" Electoral Systems?', *Journal of Common Market Studies*, 43(5): 969–84.

Farrell, D.M. and R. Scully (2007) *Representing Europe's Citizens: Electoral Institutions and the Failure of Parliamentary Representation* (Oxford: Oxford University Press).

Farrell, D., S. Hix, M. Johnson and R. Scully (2006) 'EPRG 2000 and 2006 MEP Surveys Dataset', mimeo (at: www.lse.ac.uk/collections/EPRG).

Farrell, H. and A. Heritier (2004) 'Interorganizational Negotiation and Intraorganizational Power in Shared Decision Making: Early Agreements Under Codecision and Their Impact on the European Parliament and Council', *Comparative Political Studies*, 37(10): 1184–212.

Favell, A. (2001) *Philosophies of Integration: Immigration and the Idea of Citizenship in France and Britain*, second edition (London: Palgrave).

Favell, A. (2008a) *Eurostars and Eurocities: Free Movement and Mobility in an Integrating Europe* (Oxford: Blackwell).

Favell, A. (2008b) 'The New Face of East–West Migration in Europe', *Journal of Ethnic and Migration Studies*, 34(5): 701–16.

Fearon, J. (1999) 'Electoral Accountability and the Control of Politicians: Selecting Good Types Versus Sanctioning Poor Performance', in A. Przeworksi, S.C. Stokes and B. Manin (eds), *Democracy, Accountability and Representation* (Cambridge: Cambridge University Press).

Federal Trust (1996) *Justice and Fair Play: Intergovernmental Conference of the European Union 1996*, Federal Trust Papers 6 (London: Federal Trust).

Feldstein, K. (1992) 'Europe's Monetary Union: The Case Against EMU', *The Economist*, 13 June, 19–22.

Felsenthal, D.S. and M. Machover (2001) 'The Treaty of Nice and Qualified Majority Voting', *Social Choice and Welfare*, 18(3): 431–64.

Ferejohn, J.A. and B.R. Weingast (1992) 'A Positive Theory of Statutory Interpretation', *International Review of Law and Economics*, 12(2): 263–79.

Ferrara, F. and J.T. Weishaupt (2004) 'Get Your Act Together: Party Performance in European Parliament Elections', *European Union Politics*, 5(3): 283–306.

Fierke, K. and A. Wiener (1999) 'Constructing Institutional Interests: EU and NATO Enlargement', *Journal of European Public Policy*, 6(5): 712–42.

Finer, S.E. (1987) 'Left and Right', in V. Bogdanor (ed.), *The Blackwell Encyclopaedia of Political Institutions* (Oxford: Blackwell).

Finnemore, M. and K. Sikkink (1998) 'International Norm Dynamics and Political Change', *International Organization*, 52(4): 887–917.

Fiorina, M.P. (1982) 'Legislative Choice of Regulatory Forms: Legal Process or Administrative Process?', *Public Choice*, 39(1): 33–66.

Fligstein, N. and I. Mara-Drita (1996) 'How the Make a Market: Reflections on the Attempt to Create a Single Market in the European Union', *American Journal of Sociology*, 102(1): 1–33.

Flora, P. and A.J. Heidenheimer (eds) (1981) *The Development of the Welfare State in Europe and America* (New Brunswick, NJ: Transaction Books).

Føllesdal, A. and S. Hix (2006) 'Why There is a Democratic Deficit in the EU: A Response to Majone and Moravcsik', *Journal of Common Market Studies*, 44(3): 533–62.

Forwood, G. (2001) 'The Road to Cotonou: Negotiating a Successor to Lomé?', *Journal of Common Market Studies*, 39(3): 423–42.

Fouilleux, E. (2010) The Common Agriculture Policy. In M. Cini and N. P.-S. Borragán. *European Union Politics* (Oxford: Oxford University Press).

Franchino, F. (2004) 'Delegating Powers in the European Community', *British Journal of Political Science*, 34(2): 449–76.

Franchino, F. (2007) *The Powers of the Union: Delegation in the EU* (Cambridge: Cambridge University Press).

Franchino, F. (2009) 'Experience and the distribution of portfolio payoffs in the European Commission', *European Journal of Political Research*, 48(1): 1–30.

Franchino, F. and B. Høyland (2009) 'Legislative Involvement in Parliamentary Systems', *American Political Science Review*, 103(4): 607–21.

Franklin, M. (1992) 'The Decline of Cleavage Politics', in M. Franklin, T. Mackie and H. Valen (eds), *Electoral Change: Responses to Evolving Social and Attitudinal Structures in Western Countries* (Cambridge: Cambridge University Press).

Franklin, M. (2001) 'How Structural Factors Cause Turnout Variations at European Parliament Elections', *European Union Politics*, 2(3): 309–28.

Franklin, M. (2002) 'Learning from the Danish Case: A Comment on Palle Svensson's Critique of the Franklin Thesis', *European Journal of Political Research*, 41(6): 751–7.

Franklin, M., C. van der Eijk, and M. Marsh (1995) 'Referendum Outcomes and Trust in Government: Public Support for Europe in the Wake of Maastricht', in J. Hayward (ed.), *The Crisis of Representation in Europe* (London: Frank Cass).

Franklin, M., M. Marsh, and C. Wlezien (1994) 'Attitudes Towards Europe and Referendum Votes: A Response to Siune and Svensson', *Electoral Studies*, 13(2): 117–21.

Franklin, M., M. Marsh, and L. McLaren (1994) 'Uncorking the Bottle: Popular Opposition to European Unification in the Wake of Maastricht', *Journal of Common Market Studies*, 32(4): 101–17.

Franzese, R.J., Jr. (1999) 'Partially Independent Central Banks, Politically Responsive Governments, and Inflation', *American Journal of Political Science*, 43(3): 681–706.

Freitag, M. and P. Sciarini (2001) 'The Political Economy of Budget Deficits in the European Union: The Role of International Constraints and Domestic Structure', *European Union Politics*, 2(2): 163–89.

Frieden, J.A. (1991) 'Invested Interests: The Politics of National Economic Policies in a World of Global Finance', *International Organization*, 45(4): 425–51.

Frieden, J.A. (2002) 'Real Sources of European Currency Policy: Sectoral Interests and European Monetary Integration', *International Organization*, 56(4): 831–60.

Frieden, J.A. and D.A. Lake (1995) 'Introduction: International Politics and International Economics', in J.A. Frieden and D.A. Lade (eds), *International Political Economy: Perspectives on Global Power and Wealth* (London: Routledge).

Frieden, J.A. and R. Rogowski (1996) 'The Impact of the International Political Economy on National Policies: An Overview', in R.O. Keohane and H.V. Milner (eds), *Internationalization and Domestic Politics* (Cambridge: Cambridge University Press).

Friedman, M. (1968) 'The Role of Monetary Policy', *American Economic Review*, 58(1): 1–17.

Gabel, M.J. (1998) *Interests and Integration: Market Liberalization, Public Opinion, and European Union* (Ann Arbor, MI: University of Michigan Press).

Gabel, M.J. and C.J. Anderson (2002) 'The Structure of Citizens Attitudes and the European Political Space', *Comparative Political Studies*, 35(8): 893–913.

Gabel, M.J. and S. Hix (2002) 'The European Parliament and Executive Politics in the EU: Voting Behaviour and the Commission President Investiture Procedure', in M. Hosli, A. Van Deemen and M. Widgrén (eds), *Institutional Challenges in the European Union* (London: Routledge).

Gabel, M.J. and S. Hix (2003) 'Defining the EU Political Space: An Empirical Study of the European Elections Manifestos, 1979–1999', *Comparative Political Studies*, 35(8): 934–64.

Gabel, M.J. and H. Palmer (1995) 'Understanding Variation in Support for European Integration', *European Journal of Political Research*, 27(1): 3–19.

Gabel, M.J. and K. Scheve (2007) 'Mixed Messages: Party Dissent and Mass Opinion on European Integration', *European Union Politics*, 8(1): 37–60.

Gabel, M.J. and G. Whitten (1997) 'Economic Conditions, Economic Perceptions, and Public Support for European Integration', *Political Behaviour*, 19(1): 81–96.

Galbraith, J.K. (1953) *American Capitalism and the Concept of Countervailing Power* (Boston, MA: Houghton Mifflin).

Galloway, D. (1999) 'Agenda 2000 – Packaging the Deal', *Journal of Common Market Studies*, 37 (Annual Review): 9–35.

Galloway, D. (2001) *The Treaty of Nice and Beyond: Realities and Illusions of Power in the EU* (Sheffiled: Sheffield Academic Press).

Garman, J. and L. Hiditch (1998) 'Behind the Scenes: An Examination of the Importance of the Informal Processes at Work in Conciliation', *Journal of European Public Policy*, 5(2): 271–84.

Garrett, G. (1992) 'International Cooperation and Institutional Choice: the European Community's Internal Market', *International Organization*, 46(2): 533–60.

Garrett, G. (1994) 'The Politics of Maastricht', in B. Eichengreen and J.A. Frieden (eds), *The Political Economy of European Monetary Unification* (Boulder, CO: Westview).

Garrett, G. (1995) 'The Politics of Legal Integration in the European Union', *International Organization*, 49(1): 171–81.

Garrett, G., R.D. Kelemen, and H. Schulz (1998) 'The European Court of Justice, National Governments, and Legal Integration in the European Union', *International Organization*, 52(1): 149–76.

Garrett, G. and P. Lange (1995) 'Internationalisation, Institutions, and Political Change', *International Organization*, 49(4): 627–55.

Garrett, G. and Weingast, B.R. (1993) 'Ideas, Interests and Institutions: Constructing the European Community's Internal Market', in J. Goldstein and R.O. Keohane (eds), *Ideas and Foreign Policy: Beliefs, Institutions and Political Change* (Ithaca, NY: Cornell University Press).

Garry, J. and J. Tilley (2009) 'The Macroeconomic Factors Conditioning the Impact of Identity on Attitudes towards the EU', *European Union Politics*, 10(3): 361–80.

Garry, J., M. Marsh, and R. Sinnott (2005) 'EU Referendums Evidence from the Irish Nice Treaty Referendums', *European Union Politics*, 6(2): 201–21.

Geddes, A. (2000) 'Lobbying for Migrant Inclusion in the European Union: New Opportunities for Transnational Advocacy', *Journal of European Public Policy*, 7(4): 632–49.

Geddes, A. (2003) *The Politics of Migration and Immigration in Europe* (London: Sage).

Geddes, A. (2008) *Immigration and European Integration: Beyond Fortress Europe?* Second edition (Manchester: Manchester University Press).

Gely, R. and P.T. Spillar (1992) The Political Economy of Supreme Court Constitutional Decisions: The Case of Roosevelt's Court Packing Plan', *International Review of Law and Economics*, 12(1): 45–67.

Geyer, R. (2001) 'Can EU Social NGOs Co-operate to Promote EU Social Policy?', *Journal of Social Policy*, 7(4): 632–49.

Gibson, J.L. and G.A. Caldeira (1995) The Legitimacy of Transnational Legal Institutions: Compliance, Support, and the European Court of Justice', *American Journal of Political Science*, 39(2): 459–98.

Gibson, J.L. and G.A. Caldeira (1998) 'Changes in the Legitimacy of the European Court of Justice: A Post-Maastricht Analysis', *British Journal of Political Science*, 28(1): 63–91.

Glarbo, K. (1999) 'Wide-Awake Diplomacy: Reconstructing the Common Foreign and Security Policy of the European Union', *Journal of European Public Policy*, 6(4): 634–51.

Glencross, A. and A.H. Trechsel (2011) 'First or Second Order Referendums? Understanding the Votes on the EU Constitutional Treaty in Four EU Member States', *West European Politics*, forthcoming.

Golub, J. (1996) 'The Politics of Judicial Discretion: Rethinking the Interaction Between National Courts and the European Court of Justice', *West European Politics*, 19(2): 360–85.

Golub, J. (1999) 'In the Shadow of the Vote? Decision Making in the European Community', *International Organization*, 53(4): 733–64.

Gomez, R. (1998) 'The EU's Mediterranean Policy: Common Foreign Policy by the Back Door?', in J. Peterson and H. Sjursen (eds), *A Common Foreign Policy for Europe? Competing Visions of the CFSP* (London: Routledge).

Gourevitch, P.A. (1989) 'The Politics of Economic Policy Choice in the Post-War Era', in P. Guerrieri and P.C. Padoan (eds) *The Political Economy of European Integration: States, Markets and Institutions* (London: Harvester Wheatsheaf).

Grant, W., D. Matthews, and P. Newell (2000) *The Effectiveness of European Union Environmental Policy* (London: Macmillan).

Green, A.W. (1969) *Political Integration by Jurisprudence* (Leyden: Sijthoff).

Greenwood, J. (2007a) *Interest Representation in the European Union*, 2nd edn (London: Palgrave).

Greenwood, J. (2007b) 'Organized Civil Society and Democratic Legitimacy in the European Union', *British Journal of Political Science*, 37(2): 333–57.

Greenwood, J. and M. Aspinwall (eds) (1998) *Collective Action in the European Union* (London: Routledge).

Greenwood, J., J.R. Grote, and K. Ronit (eds) (1992) *Organized Interests and the European Community* (London: Sage).

Greve, M. F. and K.E. Jørgensen (2002) 'Treaty Reform as Constitutional Politics: A Longitudinal View', *Journal of European Public Policy*, 9(1): 54–75.

Grieco, J.M. (1990) *Cooperation Among Nations: Europe, America and Non-Tariff Barriers to Trade* (Ithaca, NY: Cornell University Press).

Grilli, V., D. Masciandro, and G. Tabellini (1991) 'Political and Monetary Institutes and Public Financial Policies in the Industrial Countries', *Economic Policy*, 13(1): 341–92.

Grossman, E. (2004) 'Bringing Politics Back In: Rethinking the Role of Economic Interest Groups in European Integration', *Journal of European Public Policy*, 11(4): 637–54.

Guiraudon, V. (2000) 'European Integration and Migration Policy: Vertical Policy Making as Venue-Shopping', *Journal of Common Market Studies*, 38(2): 251–71.

Guiraudon, V. (2001) 'Weak Weapons of the Weak? Transnational Mobilization around Migration in the European Union', in D. Imig and S. Tarrow (eds), *Contentious Europeans: Protest and Politics in an Emerging Polity* (Lanham, MD: Rowman & Littlefield).

Guiraudon, V. (2003) 'The Constitution of a European Immigration Policy Domain: A Political Sociology Approach', *Journal of European Public Policy*, 10(2): 263–82.

Guiraudon, V. and G. Lahav (2000) 'A Reappraisal of the State Sovereignty Debate: The Case of Migration Control', *Comparative Political Studies*, 33(2): 163–95.

Haas, E.B. (1958) *The Uniting of Europe: Political, Social and Economic Forces 1950–1957* (London: Stevens and Sons).

Häge, F. (2007) 'Committee Decision-making in the Council of the European Union', *European Union Politics*, 8(3): 299–328.

Häge, F. (2008) 'Who Decides in the Council of the European Union?', *Journal of Common Market Studies*, 3(3): 533–58.

Hagemann, S. and B. Høyland (2008) 'Parties in the Council?', *Journal of European Public Policy*, 15(8): 1205–21.

Hagemann, S. and B. Høyland (2010) 'Bicameral Politics in the European Union', *Journal of Common Market Studies*, 48(4): 811–33.

Hall, P.A. and R. Franzese (1998) 'Mixed Signals: Central Bank Independence, Coordinated Wage-Bargaining and European Monetary Union', *International Organization*, 52(3): 505–36.

Hall, P.A. and D. Soskice (eds) (2001) *Varieties of Capitalism: The Institutional Foundations of Comparative Advantage* (Oxford: Oxford University Press).

Hallstein, W. (1972) *Europe in the Making* (London: Allen & Unwin).

Hanson, B.T. (1998) 'What Happened to Fortress Europe? External Trade Policy Liberalization in the European Union', *International Organization*, 52(1): 55–85.

Hartley, T.C. (1986) 'Federalism, Courts and Legal Systems: The Emerging Constitution of the European Community', *American Journal of Comparative Law*, 34(2): 229–47.

Hausemer, P. (2006) 'Participation and Political Competition in Committee Report Allocation: Under What Conditions Do MEPs Represent Their Constituents?', *European Union Politics*, 7(4): 505–30.

Haxell, H. (2010) *European Public Affairs Directory 2010* (London: Dod's Parliamentary Communications).

Hayes-Renshaw, F. and H. Wallace (2006) *The Council of Ministers* (London: Macmillan).

Heiberg, E.O. (1998) 'Security Implications of EU Expansion to the North and East', in K.A. Eliassen (ed.), *Foreign and Security Policy in the European Union* (London: Sage).

Heidenheimer, A.J., H. Heclo, and C.T. Adams (1990) *Comparative Public Policy: The Politics of Social Choice in America, Europe, and Japan*, 3rd edn (New York, NY: St Martin's Press).

Heidensohn, F. and M. Farrell (eds) (1993) *Crime in Europe*, 2nd edn (London: Routledge).

Heisenberg, D. (2005) 'The Institution of "Consensus" in the European Union: Formal versus Informal Decision-Making in the Council', *European Journal of Political Research*, 44(1): 65–90.

Hellström, J. (2008) 'Who Leads, Who Follows? Re-examining the Party-Electorate Linkages on European Integration', *Journal of European Public Policy*, 15(8): 1127–44.

Hennis, M. (2001) 'Europeanization and Globalization: The Missing Link', *Journal of Common Market Studies*, 39(5): 829–50.

Hervey, T. (2001) 'Community and National Competence in Health after Tobacco Advertising', *Common Market Law Review*, 38(6): 1421–46.

Hill, C. (ed.) (1996) *The Actors in Europe's Foreign Policy* (London: Routledge).

Hill, C. (1988) 'The Capability-Expectations Gap, or Conceptualizing Europe's International Role', *Journal of Common Market Studies*, 31(3): 305–28.

Hinich, M.J. and M.C. Munger (1997) *Analytical Politics* (Cambridge: Cambridge University Press).

Hix, S. (1994) 'The Study of the European Community: The Challenge to Comparative Politics', *West European Politics*, 17(1): 1–30.

Hix, S. (1999) 'Dimensions and Alignments in European Union Politics: Cognitive Constraints and Partisan Responses', *European Journal of Political Research*, 35(1): 69–106.

Hix, S. (2000) 'Parliamentary Oversight of Executive Power: What Role for the European Parliament in Comitology', in T. Christiansen and E. Kirchner (eds), *Committee Governance in the European Union* (Manchester: Manchester University Press).

Hix, S. (2001) 'Legislative Behaviour and Party Competition in the EU: An Application of Nominate in the Post 1999 European Parliament', *Journal of Common Market Studies*, 39(4): 663–88.

Hix, S. (2002a) 'Constitutional Agenda-Setting Through Discretion in Rule Interpretation: Why the European Parliament Won at Amsterdam', *British Journal of Political Science*, 32(2): 259–80.

Hix, S. (2002b) 'Parliamentary Behavior with Two Principals: Preferences, Parties, and Voting in the European Parliament', *American Journal of Political Science*, 46(3): 688–98.

Hix, S. (2004) 'Electoral Institutions and Legislative Behavior: Explaining Voting-Defection in the European Parliament', *World Politics*, 56(1): 194–223.

Hix, S. (2007) 'Euroscepticism as Anti-Centralization: A Rational Choice Institutionalist Perspective', *European Union Politics*, 8(1): 131–50.

Hix, S. (2008a) *What's Wrong with the European Union and How to Fix It* (Oxford: Polity).

Hix, S. (2008b) 'Towards a Partisan Theory of EU Politics', *Journal of European Public Policy*, 15(8): 1254–65.

Hix, S. and S. Hagemann (2009) 'Could Changing the Electoral Rules Fix European Parliament Elections?', *Politique Européenne*, 28: 27–41.

Hix, S., A. Kreppel, and A. Noury (2003) 'The Party System in the European Parliament: Collusive or Competitive?', *Journal of Common Market Studies*, 41(2): 309–31.

Hix, S. and C. Lord (1995) 'The Making of a President: The European Parliament and the Confirmation of Jacques Santer as President of the Commission', Government and Opposition, 31(1): 62–76.

Hix, S. and C. Lord (1997) *Political Parties in the European Union* (London: Palgrave).

Hix, S. and M. Marsh (2007) 'Punishment or Protest? Understanding European Parliament Elections', *Journal of Politics*, 69(2): 495–510.

Hix, S. and M. Marsh (2011) 'Second-Order Effects Plus Pan-European Political Swings: An Analysis of European Parliament Elections Across Time', *Electoral Studies*, forthcoming.

Hix, S. and A. Noury (2007) 'Politics not Economic Interests: Determinants of Migration Policies in the European Union', *International Migration Review*, 41(1): 182–205.

Hix, S. and A. Noury (2009) 'After Enlargement: Voting Patterns in the Sixth European Parliament', *Legislative Studies Quarterly*, 34(2): 159–74.

Hix, S., A. Noury, and G. Roland (2005) 'Power to the Parties: Cohesion and Competition in the European Parliament, 1979–2001', *British Journal of Political Science*, 35(2): 209–34.

Hix, S., A. Noury, and G. Roland (2006) 'Dimensions of Politics in the European Parliament', *American Journal of Political Science*, 50(2): 494–511.

Hix, S., A. Noury, and G. Roland (2007) *Democratic Politics in the European Parliament* (Cambridge: Cambridge University Press).

Hix, S., A. Noury, and G. Roland (2009) 'Voting Patterns and Alliance Formation in the European Parliament', *Philosophical Transactions of the Royal Society B*, 364: 821–31.

Hobolt, S.B. (2009) *Europe in Question: Referendums on European Integration* (Oxford: Oxford University Press).

Hobolt, S.B. and P. Leblond (2009) 'Is My Crown Better than Your Euro? Exchange Rates and Public Opinion on the European Single Currency', *European Union Politics*, 10(2): 202–25.

Hobolt, S.B., J. Spoon, and J. Tilley (2009) 'A Vote Against Europe? Explaining Defection at the 1999 and 2004 European Parliament Elections', *British Journal of Political Science*, 39(1): 93–115.

Hoffmann, S. (1966) 'Obstinate or Obsolete? The Fate of the Nation State and the Case of Western Europe', *Daedalus*, 95(4): 862–915.

Hoffmann, S. (1982) 'Reflections on the Nation-State in Western Europe Today', *Journal of Common Market Studies*, 21(1–2): 21–37.

Hoffmann, S. (1989) 'The European Community and 1992', *Foreign Affairs*, 68(4): 27–47.

Hofhansel, C. (1999) 'The Harmonization of EU Export Control Policies', *International Organization*, 32(2): 229–56.

Holland, M. (1988) 'The European Community and South Africa: In Search for a Policy for the 1990s', *International Affairs*, 64(3): 415–60.

Holland, M. (1995) 'Bridging the Capability-Expectations Gap: A Case Study of the CFSP Joint Action on South Africa', *Journal of Common Market Studies*, 33(4): 555–72.

Holland, S. (1980) *Uncommon Market: Capital, Class and Power in the European Community* (London: Macmillan).

Hollifield, J.F. (1992) *Immigrants, Markets and the State* (Cambridge, MA: Harvard University Press).

Hooghe, L. (1996a) 'Building a Europe With the Regions: The Changing Role of the European Commission', in L. Hooghe (ed.), *Cohesion Policy and European Integration: Building Multi-Level Governance* (Oxford: Oxford University Press).

Hooghe, L. (ed.) (1996b) *Cohesion Policy and European Integration: Building Multi-Level Governance* (Oxford: Oxford University Press).

Hooghe, L. (2002) 'The Mobilization of Territorial Interests and Multilevel Governance', in R. Balme, D. Chabanet and V. Wright (eds), *Collective Action in Europe* (Paris: Presses de Sciences Po).

Hooghe, L. (2003) 'Europe Divided? Elites vs. Public Opinion on European Integration', *European Union Politics*, 4(3): 281–304.

Hooghe, L. and Keating, M. (1994) 'The Politics of European Union Regional Policy', *Journal of European Public Policy*, 1(3): 367–93.

Hooghe, L. and G. Marks (1996) '"Europe With the Regions": Channels of Regional Representation in the European Union', *Publius*, 26(1): 1–20.

Hooghe, L. and G. Marks (1998) 'The Making of a Polity: The Struggle over European Integration', in H. Kitschelt, P. Lange, G. Marks and J. Stephens (eds), *The Politics and Political Economy of Advanced Industrial Societies* (Cambridge: Cambridge University Press).

Hooghe, L. and G. Marks (2001) *Multi-Level Governance and European Integration* (Lanham, MD: Rowman & Littlefield).

Hooghe, L. and G. Marks (2003) 'Unraveling the Central State, But How? Types of Multi-Level Governance', *American Political Science Review*, 97(2): 233–43.

Hooghe, L. and G. Marks (2005) 'Calculation, Community and Cues: Public Opinion and European Integration', *European Union Politics*, 6(4): 419–43.

Hooghe, L. and G. Marks (2009) 'A Postfunctionalist Theory of European Integration: From Permissive Consensus to Constraining Dissensus', *British Journal of Political Science*, 39(1): 1–23.

Hooghe, L., G. Marks and C. Wilson (2003) 'Does Left/Right Structure Party Positions on European Integration?', *Comparative Political Studies*, 35(8): 965–89.

Horn, M.J. (1995) *The Political Economy of Public Administration* (Cambridge: Cambridge University Press).

Horstmann, W. and F. Schneider (1994) 'Deficits, Bailout and Free Riders: Fiscal Elements of a European Constitution', *Kyklos*, 47(3): 355–83.

Hosli, M.O. (1995) 'The Balance Between Small and Large: Effects of a Double-Majority System on Voting Power in the European Union', *International Studies Quarterly*, 39(3): 351–70.

Hosli, M.O. (2000) 'The Creation of the European Economic and Monetary Union (EMU): Intergovernmental Negotiations and Two-level Games', *Journal of European Public Policy*, 7(5): 744–66.

Hotelling, H. (1929) 'Stability in competition', *Economic Journal*, 39(1): 41–57.

Høyland, B. (2006) 'Allocation of Codecison Reports in the Fifth European Parliament', *European Union Politics*, 7(1): 30–50.

Høyland, B. (2010) 'Procedural and Party Effects in European Parliament Roll Call Votes', *European Union Politics*, 11(4): 597–613.

Huber, J.D. and C.R. Shipan (2002) *Deliberate Discretion? The Institutional Foundations of Bureaucratic Autonomy* (Cambridge: Cambridge University Press).

Huber, J.D. and N. McCarty (2004) 'Bureaucratic Capacity, Delegation, and Political Reform', *American Political Science Review*, 98(3): 481–94.

Hubschmid, C., and P. Moser (1997) 'The Co-operation Procedure in the EU: Why Was the European Parliament Influential in the Decision on Car Emission Standards?', *Journal of Common Market Studies*, 35(2): 225–42.

Hug, S. (1997) 'Integration Through Referendums?', *Aussenwirtschaft*, 52(1–2): 287–310.

Hug, S. (2002) *Voices of Europe: Citizens, Referendums, and European Integration* (Lanham, MD: Rowman Littlefield).

Hug, S. (2003) 'Endogenous Preferences and Delegation in the European Union', *Comparative Political Studies*, 36(1/2): 41–74.

Hug, S. and T. König (2002) 'In View of Ratification: Governmental Preferences and Domestic Constraints at the Amsterdam Intergovernmental Conference', *International Organization*, 56(2): 447–76.

Hug, S. and P. Sciarini (2000) 'Referendums on European Integration: Do Institutions Matter in the Voter's Decision', *Comparative Political Studies*, 33(1): 3–36.

Imig, D. (2002) 'Contestation in the Streets: European Protest and the Emerging Euro-Polity', *Comparative Political Studies*, 35(8): 914–33.

Imig, D. and S. Tarrow (eds) (2001) *Contentious Europeans: Protest and Politics in an Emerging Polity* (Lanham, MD: Rowman & Littlefield).

Inglehart, R. (1970a) 'Cognitive Mobilization and European Identity', *Comparative Politics*, 3(1): 45–70.

Inglehart, R. (1970b) 'Public Opinion and Regional Integration', *International Organization*, 24(4): 764–95.

Inglehart, R. (1977a) *The Silent Revolution: Changing Values and Political Styles Among Western Publics* (Princeton, NJ: Princeton University Press).

Inglehart, R. (1977b) 'Long Term Trends in Mass Support for European Unification', *Government and Opposition*, 12(2): 150–77.

Inglehart, R. (1991) 'Trust Between Nations: Primordial Ties, Societal Learning and Economic Development', in K. Reif and R. Inglehart (eds), *Eurobarometer: The Dynamics of European Public Opinion: Essays in Honour of Jacques-René Rabier* (London: Macmillan).

Inglehart, R. and J.-R. Rabier (1978) 'Economic Uncertainty and European Solidarity: Public Opinion Trends', *Annals of the American Academy of Political and Economic Science*, 440: 66–97.

Inglehart, R. and K. Reif (1991) 'Analyzing Trends in Western European Opinion: The Role of the Eurobarometer Surveys', in K. Reif and R. Inglehart (eds), Eurobarometer: *The Dynamics of European Public Opinion: Essays in Honour of Jacques-René Rabier* (London: Macmillan).

Ioakimidis, P.C. (1996) 'EU Cohesion Policy in Greece: The Tensions Between Bureaucratic Centralism and Regionalism', in L. Hooghe (ed.), *Cohesion*

Policy and European Integration: Building Multi-Level Governance (Oxford: Oxford University Press).

Ireland, P. (1991) 'Facing the True "Fortress Europe": Immigrant Politics in the EC', *Journal of Common Market Studies*, 29(5): 457–80.

Ireland, P. (1995) 'Migration, Free Movement, and Immigrant Integration in the EU: A Bifurcated Policy Response', in S. Leibfried and P. Pierson (eds), *European Social Policy: Between Fragmentation and Integration* (Washington, DC: Brookings Institution).

Issing, O. (1999) 'The Eurosystem: Transparent and Accountable, or "Willem in Euroland"', *Journal of Common Market Studies*, 37(3): 503–19.

Iversen, T. (1998a) 'Wage Bargaining, Central Bank Independence and the Real Effects of Money', *International Organization*, 52(3): 469–504.

Iversen, T. (1998b) 'Wage Bargaining, Hard Money and Economic Performance: Theory and Evidence for Organized Market Economies', *British Journal of Political Science*, 28(1): 31–61.

Jabko, N. (1999) 'In the Name of the Market: How the European Commission Paved the Way for Monetary Union', *Journal of European Public Policy*, 6(3): 475–95.

Janssen, J.I.H. (1991) 'Postmaterialism, Cognitive Mobilization and Public Support for European Integration', *British Journal of Political Science*, 21(4): 443–68.

Jeffery, C. (2000) 'Sub-National Mobilization and European Integration', *Journal of Common Market Studies*, 38(1): 1–23.

Jensen, C.B. (2007) 'Implementing Europe: A Question of Oversight', *European Union Politics*, 8(4): 451–77.

Joerges, C. (1994) 'European Economic Law, the Nation-State and the Maastricht Treaty', in R. Dehousse (ed.), *Europe After Maastricht: An Ever Closer Union?* (Munich: Law Books on Europe).

Joerges, C. and J. Neyer (1997) 'Transforming Strategic Interaction into Deliberative Problem-solving: European Comitology in the Foodstuffs Sector', *Journal of European Public Policy*, 4(4): 609–25.

Johnston, A. (2001) 'Judicial Review and the Treaty of Nice', *Common Market Law Review*, 38(3): 499–523.

Jones, E., J.A. Frieden, and F. Torres (1998) *Joining Europe's Monetary Club: The Challenges for Smaller Member States* (London: Macmillan).

Joppke, C. (ed.) (1998) *Challenge to the Nation-State: Immigration in Western Europe and the United States* (Oxford University Press).

Jordan, A., R. Brouwer, and E. Noble (1999) 'Innovative and Responsive? A Longitudinal Analysis of the Speed of EU Environmental Policy-Making', *Journal of European Public Policy*, 6(3): 376–98.

Jordan, W.A. (1972) 'Producer Protection, Prior Market Structure and the Effects of Government Regulation', *Journal of Law and Economics*, 15(2): 151–76.

Joskow, P.L. and R.G. Noll (1981) *Regulation in Theory and Practice: An Overview* (Cambridge, MA: Massachusetts Institute of Technology Press).

Josselin, D. (2001) 'Trade Unions for EMU: Sectoral Preferences and Political Opportunities', *West European Politics*, 24(1): 55–74.

Judge, D., D. Earnshaw, and N. Cowan (1994) 'Ripples or Waves: The European Parliament in the European Community Policy Process', *Journal of European Public Policy*, 1(1): 27–52.

Junne, G. (1994) 'Multinational Enterprises as Actors', in W. Carlsnaes and S. Smith (eds), *European Foreign Policy: The EC and Changing Perspectives in Europe* (London: Sage).

Jupille, J. (1999) 'The European Union and International Outcomes', *International Organization*, 53(2): 409–25.

Jupille, J. (2004) *Procedural Politics: Issues, Influence and Institutional Choice in the European Union* (Cambridge: Cambridge University Press).

Jupille, J. and D. Leblang (2007) 'Voting for Change: Calculation, Community, and Euro Referendums', *International Organization*, 61(4): 763–82.

Justesen, M.K. (2007) 'The Social Choice of EU Treaties: Discrepancies between Voter Preferences and Referendum Outcomes in Denmark', *European Union Politics*, 8(4): 537–53.

Kaeding, M. (2004) 'Rapporteurship Allocation in the European Parliament: Information or Distribution?', *European Union Politics*, 5(3): 353–78.

Kaeding, M. (2005) 'The World of Committee Reports: Rapporteurship Assignment in the European Parliament', *Journal of Legislative Studies*, 11(1): 82–104.

Kaltenthaler, K. (2002) 'German Interests in European Monetary Integration', *Journal of Common Market Studies*, 40(1): 69–87.

Kaltenthaler, K. and C.J. Anderson (2001) 'Europeans and Their Money: Explaining Public Support for the Common European Currency', *European Journal of Political Research*, 40(2): 139–70.

Kardasheva, R. (2009) 'The Power to Delay: The European Parliament's Influence in the Consultation Procedure', *Journal of Common Market Studies*, 47(2): 385–409.

Kasack, C. (2004) 'The Legislative Impact of the European Parliament under the Revised Co-Decision Procedure: Environmental, Public Health and Consumer Protection Policies', *European Union Politics*, 5(2): 241–60.

Katz, R.S. (2001) 'Models of Democracy: Elite Attitudes and the Democratic Deficit in the European Union', *European Union Politics*, 2(1): 53–79.

Kaufmann, H.M. (1995) 'The Importance of Being Independent: Central Bank Independence and the European System of Central Banks', in C. Rhodes and S. Mazey (eds), *The State of the European Union*, vol. 3 (London: Longman).

Keating, M. (1995) 'A Comment on Robert Leonardi, "Cohesion in the European Community: Illusion or Reality?"', *West European Politics*, 18(2): 408–12.

Keating, M. and B. Jones (1995) 'Nations, Regions, and Europe: The UK Experience', in B. Jones and M. Keating (eds), *The European Union and the Regions* (Oxford: Clarendon Press).

Keck, M. and K. Sikkink (1998) *Activists Beyond Borders: Advocacy Networks in International Politics* (Ithaca, NY: Cornell University Press).

Keefer, P. and D. Stasavage (2002) 'Checks and Balances, Private Information, and the Credibility of Monetary Commitments', *International Organization*, 56(4): 751–74.

Keeler, J.T.S. (1996) 'Agricultural Power in the European Community: Explaining the Fate of CAP and GATT Negotiations', *Comparative Politics*, 28(2): 127–49.

Kelemen, R.D. (2000) 'Regulatory Federalism: EU Environmental Regulation in Comparative Perspective', *Journal of Public Policy*, 20(3): 133–67.

Kelemen, R.D. (2001) 'The Limits of Judicial Power: Trade–Environment Disputes in the GATT/WTO and the EU', *Comparative Political Studies*, 34(6): 622–50.

Kemmerling, A. and T. Bodenstein (2006) 'Partisan Politics in Regional Redistribution: Do Parties Affect the Distribution of EU Structural Funds across Regions?', *European Union Politics*, 7(3): 373–92.

Keohane, R.O. (1984) *After Hegemony: Cooperation and Discord in the World Political Economy* (Princeton, NJ: Princeton University Press).

Keohane, R.O. (ed.) (1986) *Neo-Realism and Its Critics* (New York, NY: Columbia University Press).

Koehane, R.O. and J.S. Nye (1989) *Power and Interdependence* (Glenview, IL: Pearson Scott Foresman).

Key, V.O. (1961) *Public Opinion and American Democracy* (New York, NY: Knopf).

Kiewiet, D.R. and M. McCubbins (1991) *The Logic of Delegation* (Chicago, IL: University of Chicago Press).

King, A. (1981) 'What do Elections Decide?', in D. Butler, H.R. Penniman and A. Ranney (eds), *Democracy at the Polls: A Comparative Study of National Elections* (Washington, DC: American Enterprise Institute).

Kingdon, J.W. (1984) *Agendas, Alternatives, and Public Policies* (Boston, MA: Little, Brown).

Kirchner, E. (1992) *Decision Making in the European Community: The Council Presidency and European Integration* (Manchester: Manchester University Press).

Kitschelt, H. (1994) *The Transformation of European Social Democracy* (Cambridge: Cambridge University Press).

Kitschelt, H. (1995) *The Radical Right in Western Europe: A Comparative Analysis* (Ann Arbor, MI: University of Michigan Press).

Knill, C. and A. Lenschow (1998) 'Coping with Europe: the Impact of British and German Administrations on the Implementation of EU Environmental Policy', *Journal of European Public Policy*, 5(4): 595–614.

Knill, C. and A. Lenschow (2000) *Implementing EU Environmental Policy: New Directions and Old Problems* (Manchester: Manchester University Press).

Knudsen, O.F. (1994) 'Context and Action in the Collapse of the Cold War European System', in W. Carlsnaes and S. Smith (eds), *European Foreign Policy: The EC and Changing Perspectives in Europe* (London: Sage).

Koenig-Archibugi, M. (2004a) 'Explaining Government Preferences for Institutional Change in EU Foreign and Security Policy', *International Organization*, 58(1): 137–74.

Koenig-Archibugi, M. (2004b) 'International Governance as New Raison D'Etat? The Case of the EU Common Foreign and Security Policy', *European Journal of International Relations*, 10(2): 147–88.

Koepke, J.R. and N. Ringe (2006) 'The Second-Order Election Model in an Enlarged Europe', *European Union Politics*, 7(3): 321–46.

Kohler-Koch, B. (1997) 'Organized Interests in the EC and European Parliament', *European Integration On-line Papers*, 1(9) (at: http://eiop.or.atieiop/texte/1997-009a.htm).

Kohler-Koch, B. (2010) 'Civil Society and EU Democracy: "Astroturf" Representation?', *Journal of European Public Policy*, 17(1): 100–16.

Kohler-Koch, B. and R. Eising (eds) (1999) *The Transformation of Governance in the European Union* (London: Routledge).

Kokott, J. (1998) 'Report on Germany', in A.-M. Slaughter, A. Stone Sweet and J.H.H. Weiler (eds), *The European Court and National Courts – Doctrine and Jurisprudence: Legal Change in Its Social Context* (Oxford: Hart).

König, T. (2007) 'Divergence or Convergence? From Ever-Growing to Ever-Slowing European Legislative Decision-Making', *European Journal of Political Research*, 46(3): 417–44.

König, T. and S. Hug (2000) 'Ratifying Maastricht: Parliamentary Votes on International Treaties and Theoretical Solution Concepts', *European Union Politics*, 1(1): 93–124.

König, T. and B. Luetgert (2009) 'Troubles with Transposition? Explaining Trends in Member-State Notification and the Delayed Transposition of EU Directives', *British Journal of Political Science*, 39(1): 163–94.

König, T. and M. Pöter (2001) 'Examining the EU Legislative Process: The Relative Importance of Agenda and Veto Power', *European Union Politics*, 2(3): 329–51.

König, T. and J.B. Slapin (2004) 'Bringing Parliaments Back In: The Sources of Power in European Treaty Negotiations', *Journal of Theoretical Politics*, 16(3): 357–94.

König, T., B. Lindberg, S. Lechner, and W. Pohlmeier (2007) 'Bicameral Conflict Resolution in the European Union: An Empirical Analysis of Conciliation Committee Bargains', *British Journal of Political Science*, 37(2): 281–312.

Krasner, S. (ed.) (1983) *International Regimes* (Ithaca, NY: Cornell University Press).

Krehbiel, K. (1990) 'Are Congressional Committees Composed of Preference Outliers', *American Political Science Review*, 84(1): 149–63.

Krehbiel, K. (1991) *Information and Legislative Organization* (Ann Arbor, MI: University of Michigan Press).

Krehbiel, K. (2007) 'Supreme Court Appointments as a Move-the-Median Game', *American Journal of Political Science*, 51(2): 231–40.

Kreppel, A. (1999) 'What Affects the European Parliament's Legislative Influence? An Analysis of the Success of EP Amendments', *Journal of Common Market Studies*, 37(3): 521–38.

Kreppel, A. (2000) 'Rules, Ideology and Coalition Formation in the European Parliament: Past, Present and Future', *European Union Politics*, 1(3): 340–62.

Kreppel, A. (2002a) *The European Parliament and Supranational Party System: A Study of Institutional Development* (Cambridge: Cambridge University Press).

Kreppel, A. (2002b) 'Moving Beyond Procedure: An Empirical Analysis of European Parliament Legislative Influence', *Comparative Political Studies*, 35(7): 784–813.

Krugman, P. (1990) 'Policy Problems of a Monetary Union', in P. De Grauwe and L. Papademos (eds), *The European Monetary System in the 1990s* (London: Longman).

Krugman, P. (1991) *Geography and Trade* (Cambridge, MA: Massachusetts Institute of Technology Press).

Krugman, P. (1997) 'Good News from Ireland: A Geographic Perspective', in A.W. Gray (ed.), *International Perspectives on the Irish Economy* (Dublin: Indecon Economic Consultants).

Krugman, P. (1998) *The Accidental Theorist and Other Dispatches from the Dismal Science* (London: Norton).

Kymlicka, W (1995) *Multicultural Citizenship: A Liberal Theory of Minority Rights* (Oxford: Clarendon Press).

Laffan, B. (1997) *The Finances of the European Union* (London: Macmillan).

Lahav, G. (2004) *Immigration and Politics in the New Europe: Reinventing Borders* (Cambridge: Cambridge University Press).

Lahusen, C. (2002) 'Commercial Consultancies in the European Union: the Shape and Structure of Professional Interest Intermediation', *Journal of European Public Policy*, 9(5): 695–714.

Lahusen, C. (2003) 'Moving Into the European Orbit: Commercial Consultancies in the European Union', *European Union Politics*, 4(2): 191–218.

Landau, A. (2001) 'The Agricultural Negotiations in the WTO: The Same Old Story', *Journal of Common Market Studies*, 39(5): 913–25.

Lange, P. (1993) 'Maastricht and the Social Protocol: Why Did They Do It?', *Politics and Society*, 21(1): 5–36.

Lasswell, H.D. (1936) *Politics: Who Gets What, When and How* (New York, NY: McGraw-Hill).

Lavenex, S. (2006) 'Shifting Up and Out: The Foreign Policy of European Immigration Control', *West European Politics*, 29(2): 329–50.

Lavenex, S. (2007) 'Mutual Recognition and the Monopoly of Force; Limits of the Single Market Analogy', *Journal of European Public Policy*, 14(5): 762–79.

Lavenex, S. and R. Kunz (2008) 'The Migration–Development Nexus in EU External Relations', *Journal of European Integration*, 30(3): 439–57.

Lavenex, S. and E.M. Ucarer (2004) 'The External Dimension of Europeanization: The Case of Immigration Policies', *Cooperation and Conflict*, 39(4): 417–43.

Lehmbruch, G. (1967) *Proporzdemokratie: Politisches System und politische Kultur in der Schweiz und in Österreich* (Tubingen: Mohr).

Leibfried, S. and Pierson, P. (1996) 'Social Policy', in H. Wallace and W. Wallace (eds), *Policy-Making in the European Union*, 3rd edn (Oxford: Oxford University Press).

Leonardi, R. (1993) 'Cohesion in the European Community: Illusion or Reality?', *West European Politics*, 16(4): 492–517.

Leonardi, R. (1995) *Convergence, Cohesion and Integration in the European Union* (London: Macmillan).

Lewis, J. (1998) 'In the Hard Bargaining Image of the Council Misleading? The Committee of Permanent Representatives and the Local Elections Directive', *Journal of Common Market Studies*, 36(4): 475–504.

Lijphart, A. (1977) *Democracy in Plural Societies: A Comparative Exploration* (New Haven, CT: Yale University Press).

Lijphart, A. (1984) *Democracies: Patterns of Majoritarian and Consensus Government in Twenty-One Countries* (New Haven, CT: Yale University Press).

Lijphart, A. (1994) *Electoral Systems and Party Systems: A Study of Twenty-Seven Democracies, 1945–1990* (Oxford: Oxford University Press).

Lindberg, B. (2008) 'Are Political Parties Controlling Legislative Decision-making in the European Parliament? The Case of the Services Directive', *Journal of European Public Policy*, 15(8): 1184–204.

Lindberg, L.N. (1963) *The Political Dynamics of Economic Integration* (Oxford: Oxford University Press).

Lindberg, L.N. and S.A. Scheingold (1970) *Europe's Would-Be Polity: Patterns of Change in the European Community* (Cambridge, MA: Harvard University Press).

Lindblom, C. (1977) *Politics and Markets* (New York, NY: Basic Books).

Lindgren, K.-O. and T. Persson (2008) 'The Structure of Conflict over EU Chemicals Policy', *European Union Politics*, 9(1): 31–58.

Lipset, S.M. (1959) *Political Man* (London: Heinemann).

Lipset, S.M. and S. Rokkan (1967) 'Cleavage Structures, Party Systems and Voter Alignments: An Introduction', in S.M. Lipset and S. Rokkan (eds), *Party Systems and Voter Alignments: Cross-national Perspectives* (New York, NY: Free Press).

Lohmann, S. (1998) 'An Information Rationale for the Power of Special Interests', *American Political Science Review*, 92(4): 809–27.

Lohmann, S. (1999) 'What Price Accountability? The Lucas Island Model and the Politics of Monetary Policy', *American Journal of Political Science*, 43(2): 396–430.

Long, T. and L. Lörinczi (2009) 'NGOs as Gatekeepers: A Green Vision', in D. Coen and J. Richardson (eds), *Lobbying the European Union: Institutions, Actors, and Issues* (Oxford: Oxford University Press).

Loughlin, J (1996) 'Representing Regions in Europe: The Committee of the Regions', *Regional and Federal Studies*, 6(2): 147–65.

Lowi, T.J. (1964) 'American Business, Public Policy, Case-Studies, and Political Theory', *World Politics*, 16(4): 677–715.

Lowi, T.J. (1969) *The End of Liberalism* (New York, NY: Knopf).

Lubbers, M. (2008) 'Regarding the Dutch "Nee" to the European Constitution: A Test of the Identity, Utilitarian and Political Approach to Voting "No" ', *European Union Politics*, 9(1): 59–86.

Luce, D.R. and H. Raiffa (1957) *Games and Decisions* (New York, NY: Wiley).

Luedtke, A. (2005) 'European Integration, Public Opinion and Immigration Policy: Testing the Impact of National Identity', *European Union Politics*, 6(1): 83–112.

Luetgert, B. and T. Dannwolf (2009) 'Mixing Methods A Nested Analysis of EU Member State Transposition Patterns', *European Union Politics*, 10(3): 307–34.

Maduro, M.P. (1997) 'Reforming the Market or the State? Article 30 and the European Constitution: Economic Freedom and Political Rights', *European Law Journal*, 3(1): 55–82.

Maher, I. (1998) 'Community Law in the National Legal Order: A Systems Analysis', *Journal of Common Market Studies*, 36(2): 237–54.

Maier, J. and B. Rittberger (2008) 'Shifting Europe's Boundaries: Mass Media, Public Opinion and the Enlargement of the EU', *European Union Politics*, 9(2): 243–67.

Mair, P. (2000) 'The Limited Impact of Europe on National Party Systems', *West European Politics*, 23(4): 27–51.

Majone, G. (1993) 'The European Community Between Social Policy and Social Regulation', *Journal of Common Market Studies*, 31(2): 153–70.

Majone, G. (1996) *Regulating Europe* (London: Routledge).

Majone, G. (1998) 'Europe's "Democratic Deficit": The Question of Standards', *European Law Journal*, 4(1): 5–28.

Majone, G. (2000) 'The Credibility Crisis of Community Regulation', *Journal of Common Market Studies*, 38(2): 273–302.

Majone, G. (2002) 'The European Commission: The Limits of Centralization and the Perils of Parliamentarization', *Governance*, 15(3): 375–92.

Mamadouh, V. and T. Raunio (2003) 'The Committee System: Powers, Appointments and Report Allocation', *Journal of Common Market Studies*, 41(2): 333–51.

Mancini, F. (1989) 'The Making of a Constitution for Europe', *Common Market Law Review*, 26(4): 595–614.

Manners, I. and R.G. Whitman (2003) 'The "Difference Engine": Constructing and Representing the International Identity of the European Union', *Journal of European Public Policy*, 10(3): 477–513.

Manow, P. and H. Döring (2008) 'Electoral and Mechanical Causes of Divided Government in the European Union', *Comparative Political Studies*, 41(10): 1349–70.

Manow, P., A, Schäfer and H. Zorn (2008) 'Europe's Party-Political Centre of Gravity, 1957–2003', *Journal of European Public Policy*, 15(1): 20–39.

Mansfield, E.D., H.V. Milner and P.B. Rosendorff (2002) 'Why Democracies Cooperate More: Electoral Controls and International Trade Agreements', *International Organization*, 56(3): 477–513.

Marginson, P. and K. Sisson (1998) 'European Collective Bargaining: A Virtual Prospect?', *Journal of Common Market Studies*, 36(4): 505–28.

Marks, G. (1993) 'Structural Policy and Multilevel Governance in the EC', in A.W. Cafruny and G.G. Rosenthal (eds), *The State of the European Community*, 2 (London: Longman).

Marks, G. (1996) 'Decision-Making in Cohesion Policy: Describing and Explaining Variation', in L. Hooghe (ed.), *Cohesion Policy and European Integration: Building Multi-Level Governance* (Oxford: Oxford University Press).

Marks, G. and D. McAdam (1996) 'Social Movements and the Changing Structure of Political Opportunity in the European Union', in G. Marks, F.W. Scharpf, P.C. Schmitter and W. Streeck (eds), *Governance in the European Union* (London: Sage).

Marks, G., L. Hooghe, and K. Blank (1996) 'European Integration from the 1980s: State-Centric v. Multi-Level Governance', *Journal of Common Market Studies*, 34(3): 341–78.

Marks, G., F.W. Scharpf, P.C. Schmitter, and W. Streeck (eds) (1996) *Governance in the European Union* (London: Sage).

Marks, G. and C. Wilson (2000) 'The Past in the Present: A Cleavage Theory of Party Response to European Integration', *British Journal of Political Science*, 38(3): 433–59.

Marks, G., C. Wilson, and L. Ray (2002) 'National Political Parties and European Integration', *American Journal of Political Science*, 46(3): 585–94.

Marquand, D. (1978) 'Towards a Europe of Parties', *Political Quarterly*, 49(4): 425–45.

Marsh, M. (1998) 'Testing the Second-Order Election Model after Four European Elections', *British Journal of Political Science*, 28(4): 591–607.

Marshall, D. (2010) 'Who to Lobby and When: Institutional Determinants of Interest Group Strategies in European Parliament Committees', *European Union Politics*, 11(4): 533–52.

Marshall, T.H. (1950) *Citizenship and Social Class* (Cambridge: Cambridge University Press).

Martin, A. and G. Ross (2001) 'Trade Union Organizing at the European Level: The Dilemma of Borrowed Resources', in D. Imig and S. Tarrow (eds), *Contentious Europeans: Protest and Politics in an Emerging Polity* (Lanham, MD: Rowman & Littlefield).

Martin, P. and C.A. Rogers (1996) 'Trade Effects of Regional Aid', in R. Baldwin, P. Haaparanta and J. Kiander (eds), *Expanding the Membership of the European Union* (Cambridge: Cambridge University Press).

Martinotti, G. and S. Stefanizzi (1995) 'Europeans and the Nation State', in O. Niedermayer and R. Sinnott (eds) *Public Opinion and Internationalized Governance* (Oxford: Oxford University Press).

Mastenbroek, E. (2005) 'EU Compliance: Still a "Black Hole"?', *Journal of European Public Policy*, 12(6): 1103–20.

Matlary, J.H. (2009) *European Union Security Dynamics: In the New National Interest* (London: Routledge).

Mattila, M. (2004) 'Contested Decisions: Empirical Analysis of Voting in the European Union Council of Ministers', *European Journal of Political Research*, 43(1): 29–50.

Mattila, M. (2006) 'Fiscal Transfers and Redistribution in the European Union: Do Smaller Member States Get More Than Their Share?', *Journal of European Public Policy*, 13(1): 34–51.

Mattila, M. (2009) 'Roll Call Analysis of Voting in the European Union Council of Ministers after the 2004 Enlargement', *European Journal of Political Research*, 48(6): 840–57.

Mattila, M. and T. Raunio (2006) 'Cautious Voters – Supportive Parties: Opinion Congruence between Voters and Parties on the EU Dimension', *European Union Politics*, 7(4): 427–49.

Mattli, W. and A.-M. Slaughter (1995) 'Law and Politics in the European Union: A Reply to Garrett', *International Organization*, 49(1): 183–90.

Mattli, W. and A.-M. Slaughter (1998a) 'The Role of National Courts in the Process of European Integration: Accounting for Judicial Preferences and Constraints', in A.-M. Slaughter, A. Stone Sweet and J.H.H. Weiler (eds), *The European Court and National Courts – Doctrine and Jurisprudence: Legal Change in Its Social Context* (Oxford: Hart).

Mattli, W. and A.-M. Slaughter (1998b) 'Revisiting the European Court of Justice', *International Organization*, 52(1): 177–209.

Mayhew, A. (1998) *Recreating Europe: The European Union's Policy Towards Central and Eastern Europe* (Cambridge: Cambridge University Press).

Mazey, S. and J. Richardson (eds) (1993) *Lobbying in the European Community* (Oxford: Oxford University Press).

Mazey, S. and J. Richardson (1997) 'The Commission and the Lobby', in G. Edwards and D. Spence (eds), *The European Commission*, 2nd edn (London: Catermill).

Mbaye, H.A.D. (2001) 'Why National States Comply with Supranational Law', *European Union Politics*, 2(3): 259–81.

McCarty, N. (2000) 'Proposal Rights, Veto Rights, and Political Bargaining', *American Journal of Political Science*, 44(3): 506–22.

McCormick, J. (2001) *Environmental Policy in the European Union* (London: Palgrave).

McCracken, P. (1977) *Towards Full Employment and Price Stability (McCracken Report)* (Paris: Organization for Economic Cooperation and Development).

McCubbins, M.D., R.G. Noll, and B.R. Weingast (1990) 'Positive and Normative Models of Procedural Rights: An Integrative Approach to Administrative Procedures', *Journal of Law, Economics, and Organization*, 6: 307–32.

McCubbins, M.D. and T. Schwartz (1984) 'Congressional Oversight Overlooked: Police Patrols versus Fire Alarms', *American Journal of Political Science*, 28(1): 165–79.

McDonagh, B. (1998) *Original Sin in a Brave New World: An Account of the Negotiation of the Treaty of Amsterdam* (Dublin: Institute of European Affairs).

McDonald, M.D. and I. Budge (2005) *Elections, Parties, Democracy: Conferring the Median Mandate* (Oxford: Oxford University Press).

McDougall, D. (1977) *Report of the Study on the Role of Public Finance in European Integration* (Brussels: European Commission).

McElroy, G. (2006) 'Committee Representation in the European Parliament', *European Union Politics*, 7(1): 5–29.

McElroy, G. and K. Benoit (2010) 'Party Policy and Group Affiliation in the European Parliament', *British Journal of Political Science*, 40(2): 377–98.

McGillivray, F., I. McLean, R. Pahre, and C. Schonhardt-Bailey (2001) *International Trade and Political Institutions: Instituting Trade in the Long Nineteenth Century* (Cheltenham: Edward Elgar).

McGowan, L. (2005) 'Europeanization Unleashed and Rebounding: Assessing the Modernization of EU Cartel Policy', *Journal of European Public Policy*, 12(6): 986–1004.

McGowan, L. and M. Cini (1999) 'Discretion and Politicization in EU Competition Policy: The Case of Merger Control', *Governance*, 12(2): 175–200.

McKay, D. (1996) *Rush to Union: Understanding the European Federal Bargain* (Oxford: Oxford University Press).

McKelvey, R.D. (1976) 'Intransitivities in Multidimentional Voting Models and Some Implications for Agenda Control', *Journal of Economic Theory*, 12(3): 472–82.

McKeown, T.J. (1991) 'A Liberal Trade Order: The Long-Run Pattern of Imports to the Advanced Capitalist States', *International Studies Quarterly*, 35(2): 151–72.

McLaren, L.M. (2002) 'Public Support for the European Union: Cost/Benefit Analysis or Perceived Cultural Threat?', *Journal of Politics*, 64(2): 551–66.

McLaren, L.M. (2004) 'Opposition to European Integration and Fear of Loss of National Identity: Debunking a Basic Assumption Regarding Hostility to the Integration Project', *European Journal of Political Research*, 43(6): 895–912.

McLaughlin, A.M. and J. Greenwood (1995) 'The Management of Interest Representation in the European Union', *Journal of Common Market Studies*, 33(1): 143–56.

McNamara, K.R. (1998) *The Currency of Ideas: Monetary Politics in the European Union* (Ithaca, NY: Cornell University Press).

McNamara, K.R. (2002) 'Rational Fictions: Central Bank Independence and the Social Logic of Delegation', *West European Politics*, 25(1): 47–76.

Meijers, H. *et al.* (1997) *Democracy, Migrants and Police in the European Union: The 1996 IGC and Beyond* (Utrecht: Standing Committee of Experts in International Immigration, Refugee and Criminal Law).

Meltzer, A.H. and S.F. Richard (1981) 'A Rational Theory of the Size of Government', *Journal of Political Economy*, 89(5): 914–27.

Menon, A. (2009) 'Empowering Paradise? The ESDP at Ten', *International Affairs*, 85(2): 227–46.

Meunier, S. (1998) 'Divided But United: European Trade Policy Integration and EU–US Agricultural Negotiations in the Uruguay Round', in C. Rhodes (ed.), *The European Community in the World Community* (Boulder, CO: Lynne Rienner).

Meunier, S. (2000) 'What Single Voice? European Institutions and EU–US Trade Negotiations', *International Organization*, 54(1): 103–35.

Meunier, S. and K. Nicolaïdis (1999) 'Who Speaks for Europe? The Delegation of Trade Authority in the EU', *Journal of Common Market Studies*, 37(1): 477–501.

Michalowitz, I. (2007) 'What Determines Influence? Assessing Conditions for Decision-Making Influence of Interest Groups in the EU', *Journal of European Public Policy*, 14(1): 132–65.

Middlemas, K. (1995) *Orchestrating Europe: The Informal Politics of the European Union, 1943–95* (London: Fontana Press).

Miller, G.J. and T.H. Hammond (1989) 'Stability and Efficiency in a Separation-of-Powers Constitutional System', in B. Grofman and D. Wittman (eds), *The Federalist Papers and the New Institutionalism* (New York, NY: Agathon).

Milner, H. (1997) *Interests, Institutions, and Information: Domestic Politics and International Relations* (Princeton, NJ: Princeton Univeristy Press).

Milner, H.V. and Keohane, R.O. (1996) 'Internationalization and Domestic Politics: An Introduction', in R.O. Keohane and H.V. Milner (eds), *Internationalization and Domestic Politics* (Cambridge: Cambridge University Press).

Minford, P. (1996) 'The Price of Monetary Unification', in M. Holmes (ed.), *The Eurosceptical Reader* (London: Macmillan).

Mitnick, B.M. (1980) *The Political Economy of Regulation: Creating, Designing and Removing Regulatory Forms* (New York, NY: Columbia University Press).

Moe, T.M. (1987) 'An Assessment of the Positive Theory of Congressional Dominance', *Legislative Studies Quarterly*, 12(4): 475–520.

Moe, T. (1989) 'The Politics of Bureaucratic Structure', in J. Chubb and P. Peterson (eds), *Can Government Govern?* (Washington, DC: Brookings Institution).

Monar, J. (1995) 'Democratic Control of Justice and Home Affairs: The European Parliament and National Parliaments', in R. Bieber and J. Monar (eds), *Justice and Home Affairs in the European Union: The Development of the Third Pillar* (Brussels: Interuniversity Press).

Monnet, J. (1978) *Memoirs* (Garden City: Doubleday).

Moore, B. (1967) *Social Origins of Dictatorship and Democracy: Lord and Peasant in the Making of the Modern World* (Harmondsworth: Penguin).

Moravcsik, A. (1991) 'Negotiating the Single European Act: National Interests and Conventional Statecraft in the European Community', *International Organization*, 45(1): 19–56.

Moravcsik, A. (1993) 'Preferences and Power in the European Community: A Liberal Intergovernmentalist Approach', *Journal of Common Market Studies*, 31(4): 473–524.

Moravcsik, A. (1997) 'Taking Preferences Seriously: A Liberal Theory of International Politics', *International Organization*, 51(4): 513–53.

Moravcsik, A. (1998) *The Choice for Europe: Social Purpose and State Power from Messina to Maastricht* (Ithaca, NY: Cornell University Press).

Moravcsik, A. (1999) 'A New Statecraft? Supranational Entrepreneurs and International Cooperation', *International Organization*, 53(2): 267–306.

Moravcsik, A. (2002) 'In Defense of the "Democratic Deficit": Reassessing the Legitimacy of the European Union', *Journal of Common Market Studies*, 40(4): 603–34.

Moravcsik, A. (2008) 'The Myth of Europe's "Democratic Deficit"', *Intereconomics: Journal of European Economic Policy*, 43(6): 331–40.

Moravcsik, A. and K. Nicolaïdis (1999) 'Keynote Article: Federal Ideals and Constitutional Realities in the Treaty of Amsterdam', *Journal of Common Market Studies: Annual Review*, 36: 13–38.

Moravcsik, A. and K. Nicolaïdis (1999) 'Explaining the Treaty of Amsterdam: Interests, Influence, Institutions', *Journal of Common Market Studies*, 37(1): 59–85.

Morgenthau, H.J. (1948) *Politics Among Nations: The Struggle for Power and Peace* (New York, NY: Knopf).

Moser, P. (1996) 'The European Parliament as a Conditional Agenda Setter: What are the Conditions? A Critique of Tsebelis (1994)', *American Political Science Review*, 90(4): 834–8.

Moser, P. (1997) 'A Theory of the Conditional Influence of the European Parliament in the Cooperation Procedure', *Public Choice*, 91(3–4): 333–50.

Mueller, D.C. (1989) *Public Choice II* (Cambridge: Cambridge University Press).

Munchau, W. (1998) 'Emu's First Boom and Bust', *Financial Times*, 8 October.

Mundell, R. (1961) 'A Theory of Optimal Currency Areas', *American Economic Review*, 51(4): 657–65.

Musgrave, R.A. (1959) *Public Finance in Theory and Practice* (New York, NY: McGraw-Hill).

Myrdal, G. (1957) *Economic Theory and the Underdeveloped Regions* (London: Duckworth).

Nanetti, R.Y. (1996) 'EU Cohesion and Territorial Restructuring in the Member States', in L. Hooghe (ed.), *Cohesion Policy and European Integration: Building Multi-Level Governance* (Oxford: Oxford University Press).

Nedergaard, P. (1995) 'The Political Economy of CAP Reform', in F. Laursen (ed.), *The Political Economy of European Integration* (The Hague: Kluwer).

Nelson, B.F. and J.L. Guth (2003) 'Religion and Youth Support for the European Union', *Journal of Common Market Studies*, 41(1): 89–112.

Nelson, B.F., J.L. Guth, and C.R. Fraser (2001) 'Does Religion Matter? Christianity and Public Support for the European Union', *European Union Politics*, 2(2): 191–217.

Neumayer, E. (2005) 'Bogus Refugees? The Determinants of Asylum Migration to Western Europe', *International Studies Quarterly*, 49(4): 389–409.

Nicolaïdis, K. and S.K. Schmidt (2007) 'Mutual Recognition "On Trial": The Long Road to Services Liberalization', *Journal of European Public Policy*, 14(5): 717–34.

Niedermayer, O. (1995) 'Trust and Sense of Community', in O. Niedermayer and R. Sinnott (eds), *Public Opinion and Internationalized Governance* (Oxford: Oxford University Press).

Niemann, A. (2008) 'Dynamics and Countervailing Pressures of Visa, Asylum and Immigration Policy Treaty Revision: Explaining Change and Stagnation from the Amsterdam IGC to the IGC of 2003–04', *Journal of Common Market Studies*, 46(3): 559–91.

Niessen, J. (2000) 'The Amsterdam Treaty and NGO Responses', *European Journal of Migration and Law*, 2(2): 203–14.

Niskanan, W.A. (1971) *Bureaucracy and Representative Government* (Chicago, IL: Aldine, Atherton).

Nordhaus, W.D. (1975) 'The Political Business Cycle', *Review of Economic Studies*, 42(2): 169–90.

Norris, P. and M. Franklin (1997) 'Social Representation', *European Journal of Political Research*, 32(2): 153–64.

Norton, P. (ed.) (1996) *National Parliaments and the European Union* (London: Frank Cass).

Nugent, N. and S. Saurugger (2002) 'Organizational Structuring: The Case of the European Commission and Its External Policy Responsibilities', *Journal of European Public Policy*, 9(3): 345–64.

Nuttall. S. (1996) 'The Commission: The Struggle for Legitimacy', in C. Hill (ed.), *The Actors in Europe's Foreign Policy* (London: Routledge).

Nuttall, S. (1997) 'The Commission and Foreign Policy-Making', in G. Edwards and D. Spence (eds), *The European Commission*, 2nd edn (London: Catermill).

Oates, W.E. (1972) *Fiscal Federalism* (New York: Harcourt Brace Jovanovich).

Oates, W.E. (1999) 'An Essay on Fiscal Federalism', *Journal of Economic Literature*, 37(4): 1120–49.

Obradovic, D. (1996) 'Prospects for Corporatist Decision-Making in the European Union: the Social Policy Agreement', *Journal of European Public Policy*, 2(2): 261–83.

Olson, M. (1965) *The Logic of Collective Action: Public Goods and the Theory of Groups* (Cambridge, MA: Harvard University Press).

Oppenhuis, E., C. van der Eijk, and M. Franklin (1996) 'The Party Context: Outcomes', in C. van der Eijk and M. Franklin (eds), *Choosing Europe? The European Electorate and National Politics in the Face of Union* (Ann Arbor, University of Michigan Press).

Ordershook, P.C. (1992) A *Political Theory Primer* (London: Routledge).

Ostrom, E. (1990) *Governing the Commons* (Cambridge University Press).

Østrup, F. (1995) 'Economic and Monetary Union', in F. Laursen (ed.), *The Political Economy of European Integration* (The Hague: Kluwer).

Owen, G. and L.S. Shapley (1989) 'Optimal Location of Candidates in Ideological Space', *International Journal of Game Theory*, 18(3): 339–56.

Pappi, F.U. and C.H.C.A. Henning (1999) 'The Organization of Influence on the EC's Common Agricultural Policy: A Network Approach', *European Journal of Political Research*, 36(2): 257–81.

Parsons, C. (2002) 'Showing Ideas as Causes: The Origins of the European Union', *International Organization*, 56(1): 47–84.

Patterson, L.A. (1997) 'Agricultural Policy Reform in the European Community: A Three-Level Game Analysis', *International Organization*, 51(1): 135–65.

Pedlar, R. (ed.) (2002) *European Union Lobbying: Changes in the Arena* (London: Palgrave).

Pedlar, R. and M.P.C.M. van Schendelen (eds) (1994) *Lobbying the European Union: Companies, Trade Associations and Interest Groups* (Aldershot: Dartmouth).

Pelkmans, J. (1990) *Regulation and the Single Market: An Economic Perspective* (Tübingen: Mohr).

Pelkmans, J. and L.A. Winters (1988) *Europe's Domestic Market* (London: Royal Institute of International Affairs).

Peltzman, S. (1976) 'Toward a More General Theory of Regulation', *Journal of Law and Economics*, 19(2): 211–40.

Peltzman, S. (1989) 'The Theory of Economic Regulation after a Decade of Deregulation', *Brookings Papers on Economic Activity – Microeconomics* (Washington, DC: Brookings Institution).

Peter, J., H.A. Semetko, and C.H. De Vreese (2003) 'EU Politics on Television News: A Cross-National Comparative Study', *European Union Politics*, 4(3): 305–27.

Peters, B.G. (1992) 'Bureaucratic Politics and the Institutions of the European Community', in A.M. Sbragia (ed.), *Euro-Politics: Institutions and Policymaking in the 'New' Europe* (Washington, DC: Brookings Institution).

Peters, B.G. (1994) 'Agenda-Setting in the European Community', *Journal of European Public Policy*, 1(1): 9–26.

Peterson, J. (1995) 'EU Research Policy: The Politics of Expertise', in C. Rhodes and S. Mazey (eds), *The State of the European Union*, 3 (London: Longman).

Petracca, M.P. (ed.) (1994) *The Politics of Interests: Interest Groups Transformed* (Boulder, CO: Westview).

Pfetsch, F. (1994) 'Tensions in Sovereignty: Foreign Policies of the EC Members Compared', in W. Carlsnaes and S. Smith (eds), *European Foreign Policy: The EC and Changing Perspectives in Europe* (London: Sage).

Piening, C. (1997) *Global Europe: The European Union in World Affairs* (Boulder, CO: Lynne Rienner).

Pierson, P. (1996) 'The Path to European Integration: A Historical Institutionalist Analysis', *Comparative Political Studies*, 29(2): 123–63.

Pochet, P. (2003) 'Subsidiarity, Social Dialogue and the Open Method of Co-ordination: The Role of Trade Unions', in D. Foster and P. Scott (eds), *Trade Unions in Europe: Meeting the Challenge* (Brussels: Peter Lange).

Pollack, M.A. (1995) 'Regional Actors in an Intergovernmental Play: The Making and Implementation of EC Structural Policy', in C. Rhodes and S. Mazey (eds), *The State of the European Union*, 3 (London: Longman).

Pollack, M.A. (1997) 'Representing Diffuse Interests in EC Policy-Making', *Journal of European Public Policy*, 4(4): 572–90.

Pollack, M.A. (2003) *The Engines of Integration: Delegation, Agency, and Agency Setting in the European Union* (Oxford: Oxford University Press).

Poloni-Staudinger, L.M. (2008) 'The Domestic Opportunity Structure and Supranational Activity: An Explanation of Environmental Group Activity at the European Level', *European Union Politics*, 9(4): 531–58.

Poole, W. (1970) 'Optimal Choice of Monetary Policy Instruments in a Simple Stochastic Macro Model', *Quarterly Journal of Economics*, 84(2):197–216.

Praet, P. (1987) 'Economic Objectives in European Foreign Policy Making', in J.K. de Vree, P. Coffey and R.H. Lauwaars (eds), *Towards a European Foreign Policy: Legal, Economic and Political Dimensions* (Dordrecht: Martinus Nijhoff).

Pridham, G. and P. Pridham (1979) 'The New Party Federations and Direct Elections', *The World Today*, 35(2): 62–70.

Princen, S. and B. Kerremans (2008) 'Opportunity Structures in the EU Multi-Level System', *West European Politics*, 31(6): 1129–46.

Proksch, S.-O., and J.B. Slapin (2011) 'Parliamentary Questions and Oversight in the European Union', *European Journal of Political Research*, 50(1):53–79.

Przeworski, A., M.E. Alvarez, J.A. Cheibub, and F. Limongi (2000) *Democracy and Development: Political Institutions and Well-Being in the World, 1950–1990* (Cambridge: Cambridge University Press).

Putnam, R. (1988) 'Diplomacy and Domestic Politics: the Logic of Two-level Games', *International Organization*, 42(3): 427–60.

Quaglia, L. (2007) 'The Politics of Financial Services Regulation and Supervision Reform in the European Union', *European Journal of Political Research*, 46(2): 269–90.

Quaglia, L. (2008) 'Financial Sector Committee Governance in the European Union', *Journal of European Integration*, 30(4): 563–78.

Raunio, T. (1996) 'Parliamentary Questions in the European Parliament: Representation, Information and Control', *Journal of Legislative Studies*, 2(4): 356–82.

Raunio, T. (1997) *The European Perspective: Transnational Party Groups in the 1989–1994 European Parliament* (London: Ashgate).

Raunio, T. (1999) 'Always One Step Behind National Legislatures and the European Union', *Government and Opposition*, 34(2): 180–202.

Raunio, T. and M. Wiberg (1998) 'Winners and Losers in the Council: Voting Power Consequences of EU Enlargements', *Journal of Common Market Studies*, 36(4): 549–62.

Raunio, T. and S. Hix (2000) 'Backbenchers Learn to Fight Back: European Integration and Parliamentary Government', *West European Politics*, 23(4): 142–68.

Rawls, J. (1971) *A Theory of Justice* (Cambridge, MA: Harvard University Press).

Ray, L. (1999) 'Measuring Party Orientations Towards European Integration: Results from an Expert Survey', *European Journal of Political Research*, 36(2): 283–306.

Recchi, E. and A. Favell (eds) (2009) *Pioneers of European Integration: Citizenship and Mobility in the EU* (Cheltenham: Edward Elgar).

Reif, K. (1984) 'National Election Cycles and European Elections, 1979 and 1984', *Electoral Studies*, 3(3): 244–55.

Reif, K. and H. Schmitt (1980) 'Nine Second-Order National Elections: A Conceptual Framework for the Analysis of European Election Results', *European Journal of Political Research*, 8(1): 3–45.

Rhinard, M. (2002) 'The Democratic Legitimacy of the European Union Committee System', *Governance*, 15(2): 185–210.

Riker, W.H. (1962) *The Theory of Political Coalitions* (New Haven, CT: Yale University Press).

Riker, W.H. (1980) 'Implications from the Dis-equilibrium of Majority Rule for the Study of Institutions', *American Political Science Review*, 74(2): 432–46.

Riker, W.H. (1986) *The Art of Political Manipulation* (New Haven, CT: Yale University Press).

Riker, W.H. (1992) 'The Justification of Bicameralism', *International Political Science Review*, 13(1): 101–16.

Ringe, N. (2005) 'Policy Preference Formation in Legislative Politics: Structures, Actors, and Focal Points', *American Journal of Political Science*, 49(4): 731–45.

Ringe, N. (2009) *Who Decides, And How? Preferences, Uncertainty, and Policy Choice in The European Parliament* (Oxford: Oxford University Press).

Risse, T., S. Ropp, and K. Sikkink (eds) (1999) *The Power of Human Rights: International Norms and Domestic Change* (Cambridge: Cambridge University Press).

Rittberger, B. (2000) 'Impatient Legislators and New Issue–Dimensions: A Critique of the Garrett–Tsebelis "Standard Version" of Legislative Politics', *Journal of European Public Policy*, 7(4): 554–75.

Rittberger, B. (2001) 'Which Institutions for Post-War Europe? Explaining the Institutional Design of Europe's First Community', *Journal of European Public Policy*, 8(5): 673–708.

Rodden, J. (2002) 'Strength in Numbers? Representation and Redistribution in the European Union', *European Union Politics*, 3(2): 151–75.

Rodriguez-Pose, A. (1998) *Dynamics of Regional Growth in Europe: Social and Political Factors* (Oxford: Oxford University Press).

Rogers, J.R. (2001) 'Information and Judicial Review: A Signaling Game of Legislative–Judicial Interaction', *American Journal of Political Science*, 45(1): 84–99.

Rogers, J.R. and G. Vanberg (2002) 'Judicial Advisory Opinions and Legislative Outcomes in Comparative Perspective', *American Journal of Political Science*, 46(2): 379–97.

Rogowski, R. (1990) *Commerce and Coalitions: How Trade Affects Domestic Political Alignments* (Princeton, NJ: Princeton University Press).

Rohrschneider, R. (2002) 'The Democratic Deficit and Mass Support for an EU-Wide Government', *American Journal of Political Science*, 46(2): 463–75.

Rokkan, S. (1973) 'Cities, States, and Nations: A Dimensional Model for the Study of Contrasts in Development', in S.N. Eisenstadt and S. Rokkan (eds), *Building States and Nations: Models and Data Resources, vol. 1* (London: Sage).

Rokkan, S. (1999) *State Formation, Nation-Building, and Mass Politics in Europe: The Theory of Stein Rokkan*, selected and rearranged by P. Flora, S. Kuhnle and D. Urwin (Oxford: Oxford University Press).

Romer, T. and H. Rosenthal (1978) 'Political Resource Allocation, Controlled Agendas, and the Status Quo', *Public Choice*, 33(4): 27–43.

Rootes, C. (2002) 'The Europeanisation of Environmentalism', in R. Balme, D. Chabanet and V. Wright (eds), *Collective Action in Europe* (Paris: Presses de Sciences Po).

Rosamond, B. (2000) *Theories of European Integration* (London: Palgrave).

Rosecrance, R. (1986) *The Rise of the Trading State* (New York, NY: Basic Books).

Rucht, D. (2001) 'Lobbying or Protest? Strategies to Influence EU Environmental Policies', in D. Imig and S. Tarrow (eds), *Contentious Europeans: Protest and Politics in an Emerging Polity* (Lanham, MD: Rowman & Littlefield).

Ruggie, J.G. (1998) *Constructing the World Polity: Essays on International Institutionalization* (London: Routledge).

Saalfeld, T. (2000) 'Members of Parliament and Governments in Western Europe: Agency Relations and Problems of Oversight', *European Journal of Political Research*, 37(3): 353–76.

Saglie, J. (2000) 'Values, Perceptions and European Integration: The Case of the Norwegian 1994 Referendum', *European Union Politics*, 1(2): 227–49.

Sala-i-Martin, X. and J. Sachs (1991) 'Fiscal Federalism and Optimum Currency Areas: Evidence from Europe and United States', *NBER Working Paper 3855.*

Sánchez-Cuenca, I. (2000) 'The Political Basis of Support for European Integration', *European Union Politics*, 1(2): 147–71.

Sandholtz, W. (1992) 'ESPRIT and the Politics of International Collective Action', *Journal of Common Market Studies*, 30(1): 1–39.

Sandholtz, W. (1993) 'Choosing Union: Monetary Politics and Maastricht', *International Organization*, 47(1): 1–39.

Sandholtz, W. (1996) 'Money Troubles: Europe's Rough Road to Monetary Union', *Journal of European Public Policy*, 3(1):84–101.

Sandholtz, W. and A. Stone Sweet (1998) *European Integration and Supranational Governance* (Oxford: Oxford University Press).

Sandholtz, W. and J. Zysman (1989) '1992: Recasting the European Bargain', *World Politics*, 42(1): 95–128.

Sassen, S. (1996) *Losing Control* (New York, NY: Columbia University Press).

Saurugger, S. (2008) 'Interest Groups and Democracy in the European Union', *West European Politics*, 31(6): 1274–91.

Scarrow, S.E. (1997) 'Political Career Paths and the European Parliament', *Legislative Studies Quarterly*, 22(2): 253–63.

Scharpf, F.W. (1996) 'Negative and Positive Integration in the Political Economy of European Welfare States', in G. Marks, F.W. Scharpf, P.C. Schmitter and W. Streeck (eds), *Governance in the European Union* (London: Sage).

Scharpf, F.W. (1997) 'Economic Integration, Democracy and the Welfare State', *Journal of European Public Policy*, 4(1): 18–36.

Scharpf, F.W. (1999) *Governing in Europe: Effective and Democratic?* (Oxford: Oxford University Press).

Schattschneider, E.E. (1960) *The Semi-Sovereign People: A Realist's View of Democracy in America* (New York, NY: Holt, Rinehart & Winston).

Schild, J. (2001) 'National v. European Identities: French and Germans in the European Multi-Level System', *Journal of Common Market Studies*, 39(2): 331–51.

Schimmelfennig, F. (2003) *The EU, NATO and the Integration of Europe: Rules and Rhetoric* (Cambridge: Cambridge University Press).

Schmitter, P.C. (1974) 'Still the Century of Corporatism?', *Review of Politics*, 36(1): 85–131.

Schmitter, P.C. (2000) *How to Democratize the European Union ... and Why Bother?* (Lanham, MD: Rowman & Littlefield).

Schmitter, P.C. and G. Lehmbruch (eds) (1979) *Trends Towards Corporatist Intermediation* (London: Sage).

Schneider, C.J. (2009) *Conflict, Negotiation and European Union Enlargement* (Cambridge: Cambridge University Press).

Schneider, G. and P.A. Weitsman (1996) 'The Punishment Trap: Integration Referendums as Popularity Contests', *Comparative Political Studies*, 28(4): 582–607.

Schofield, N. (1978) 'Instability of simple dynamic games', *Review of Economic Studies*, 45(3): 575–94.

Schulz, H. and T. König (2000) 'Institutional Reform and Decision-Making Efficiency in the European Union', *American Journal of Political Science*, 44(4): 653–66.

Schumpeter, J. (1943) *Capitalism, Socialism and Democracy* (London: Allen & Unwin).

Segal, J.A. (2008) 'Judicial Behavior', in K.E. Whittington, R.D. Kelemen and G.A. Caldeira (eds), *The European Court and Legal Integration: An Exceptional Story or Harbinger of the Future?* (Oxford: Oxford University Press).

Shapiro, M.J. (1981) *Courts: A Comparative and Political Analysis* (Chicago, IL: University of Chicago Press).

Shapiro, M.J. (1992) 'The European Court of Justice', in A.M. Sbragia (ed.), *Euro-Politics: Institutions and Policymaking in the 'New' European Community* (Washington, DC: Brookings Institution).

Shapley, L.S. and M. Shubik (1954) 'A Method for Evaluating the Distribution of Power in a Committee System', *American Political Science Review*, 48(4): 787–92.

Sharman, J.C. (2003) 'Agrarian Politics in Eastern Europe in the Shadow of EU Accession', *European Union Politics*, 4(4): 447–71.

Sharp, M. and K. Pavitt (1993) 'Technology Policy in the 1990s: Old Trends and New Realities', *Journal of Common Market Studies*, 31(2): 131–51.

Shaw, J. (1996) *Law of the European Union*, 2nd edn (London: Macmillan).

Shaw, J. (2007) *The Transformation of Citizenship in the European Union: Electoral Rights and the Restructuring of Political Space* (Cambridge: Cambridge University Press).

Sheingate, A.D. (2000) 'Agricultural Retrenchment Revisited: Issue Definition and Venue Change in the United States and European Union', *Governance*, 13(3): 335–63.

Shepherd, A.J.K. (2009) ' "A milestone in the history of the EU": Kosovo and the EU's International Role', *International Affairs*, 83(3): 513–30.

Shepsle, K.A. (1979) 'Institutional Arrangement and Equilibrium in Multidimensional Voting Models', *American Journal of Political Science*, 23(1): 27–59.

Shepsle, K.A. and B.R. Weingast (1987) 'Why Are Congressional Committees Powerful?', *American Political Science Review*, 81(3): 929–45.

Shipan, C.R. (2000) 'The Legislative Design of Judicial Review: A Formal Analysis', *Journal of Theoretical Politics*, 12(3): 269–304.

Shonfield, S. (1973) *Europe: Journey to an Unknown Destination* (London: Allen Lane).

Shugart, M.S., M.E. Valdini, and K. Suominen (2005) 'Looking for Locals: Voter Information Demands and Personal Vote-Earning Attributes of Legislators Under Proportional Representation', *American Journal of Political Science*, 49(2): 437–49.

Siune, Karen and Palle Svensson (1993) 'The Danes and the Maastricht Treaty: The Danish EC Referendum of June 1992', *Electoral Studies*, 12(2): 117–21.

Siune, K., P. Svensson, and O. Tongsgaard (1994) 'The European Union: The Danes Said "No" in 1992 but "Yes" in 1993: How and Why?', *Electoral Studies*, 13(2): 107–16.

Sjursen, H. (2002) 'Why Expand? The Question of Legitimacy and the Justification in the EU's Enlargement Policy', *Journal of Common Market Studies*, 40(3): 491–513.

Skogstad, G. (1998) 'Ideas, Paradigms and Institutions: Agricultural Exceptionalism in the European Union and the United States', *Governance*, 11(4): 463–90.

Skowronek, S. (1982) *Building a New American State: The Expansion of National Administrative Capacities* (Cambridge: Cambridge University Press).

Slapin, J.B. (2006) 'Who is Powerful? Examining Preferences and Testing Sources of Bargaining Strength at European Intergovernmental Conferences', *European Union Politics*, 7(1): 51–76.

Slater, M. (1982) 'Political Elites, Popular Indifference and Community Building', *Journal of Common Market Studies*, 21(1/2): 69–87.

Smith, A.D. (1991) *National Identity* (London: Penguin).

Smith, D.L. and J. Wanke (1993) 'Completing the Single European Market: An Analysis of the Impact on the Member States', *American Journal of Political Science*, 37(2): 529–54.

Smith, M. (1996) 'The European Union and a Changing Europe: Establishing the Boundaries of Order', *Journal of Common Market Studies*, 34(1): 5–28.

Smith, M. (1997) 'The Commission and External Relations', in G. Edwards and D. Spence (eds), *The European Commission*, 2nd edn (London: Catermill).

Smith, M. (1998) 'Does the Flag Follow Trade?: "Politicisation" and the Emergence of a European Foreign Policy', in J. Peterson and H. Sjursen (eds), *A Common Foreign Policy for Europe? Competing Visions of the CFSP* (London: Routledge).

Smith, M.E. (2000) 'Conforming to Europe: The Domestic Impact of EU Foreign Policy Co-operation', *Journal of European Public Policy*, 7(4): 613–31.

Smith, M.E. and W. Sandholtz (1995) 'Institutions and Leadership: Germany, Maastricht and the ERM Crisis', in C. Rhodes and S. Mazey (eds), *The State of the European Union*, vol. 3 (London: Longman).

Smith, M.E. (2003) *Europe's Foreign and Security Policy: The Institutionalization of Cooperation* (Cambridge: Cambridge University Press).

Soysal, Y. (1994) *Limits of Citizenship: Migrants and Postnational Membership in Europe* (Chicago, IL: University of Chicago Press).

Sperling, J. and E. Kichner (1997) 'The Security Architectures and Institutional Features of Post-1989 Europe', *Journal of European Public Policy*, 4(2): 155–70.

Stasavage, D. (2002) 'Transparency, Democratic Accountability, and the Economic Consequences of Monetary Institutions', *American Journal of Political Science*, 32(1): 119–46.

Stasavage, D. and D. Guillaume (2002) 'When are Monetary Commitments Credible? Parallel Agreements and the Sustainability of Currency Unions', *British Journal of Political Science*, 32(1): 119–46.

Stavridis, S. (1997) 'The Common Security Policy of the European Union: Why Institutional Arrangements Are Not Enough', in S. Stavridis, E. Mossialos, R. Morgan and H. Machin (eds), *New Challenges to the European Union: Policies and Policy-Making* (Aldershot: Dartmouth).

Steenbergen, M.R., E.E. Edwards, and C.E. de Vries (2007) 'Who's Cueing Whom? Mass–Elite Linkages and the Future of European Integration', *European Union Politics*, 8(1): 39–49.

Stein, E. (1981) 'Lawyers, Judges and the Making of a Transnational Constitution', *American Journal of International Law*, 75(1): 1–27.

Steinle, W.J. (1992) 'Regional Competitiveness in the Single Market', *Regional Studies*, 26(4): 307–18.

Stetter, S. (2000) 'Regulating Migration: Authority Delegation in Justice and Home Affairs', *Journal of European Public Policy*, 7(1): 80–103.

Steunenberg, B. (1994) 'Decision Making under Different Institutional Arrangements: Legislation by the European Community', *Journal of Institutional and Theoretical Economics*, 150(4): 642–69.

Steunenberg, B. (1997a) 'Codecision and its Reform: A Comparative Analysis of Decision-Making Rules in the European Union', in B. Steunenberg and F. van Vught (eds), *Political Institutions and Public Policy* (Amsterdam: Kluwer).

Steunenberg, B. (1997b) 'Courts, Cabinet, and Coalition Parties: The Politics of Euthanasia in a Parliamentary Setting', *British Journal of Political Science*, 27(4): 551–71.

Stigler, G.J. (1970) 'Director's Law of Public Income Redistribution', *Journal of Law and Economics*, 13(1): 1–10.

Stigler, G.J. (1971) 'The Theory of Economic Regulation', *Bell Journal of Economics and Management Science*, 2(1): 1–21.

Stigler, G.J. and C. Friedland (1962) 'What Can Regulators Regulate? The Case of Electricity', *Journal of Law and Economics*, 5(1): 1–16.

Stone, A. (1993) 'Where Judicial Politics Are Legislative Politics: The French Constitutional Council', in M.L. Volcansek (ed.), *Judicial Politics and Policy-Making in Western Europe* (London: Frank Cass).

Stone Sweet, A. (1998) 'Constitutional Dialogues in the European Community', in A.-M. Slaughter, A. Stone Sweet and J.H.H. Weiler (eds), *The European Court and National Courts – Doctrine and Jurisprudence: Legal Change in Its Social Context* (Oxford: Hart).

Stone Sweet, A. (2002) 'Constitutional Courts and Parliamentary Democracy', *West European Politics*, 25(1): 77–100.

Stone Sweet, A. and T.L. Brunell (1998a) 'Constructing a Supranational Constitution: Dispute Resolution and Governance in the European Community', *American Political Science Review*, 92(1): 63–81.

Stone Sweet, A. and T.L. Brunell (1998b) 'The European Court and National Courts: A Statistical Analysis of Preliminary References, 1961–95', *Journal of European Public Policy*, 5(1): 66–97.

Stone Sweet, A. and T.L. Brunell (2000) 'The European Court, National Judges, and Legal Integration: A Researcher's Guide to the Data Set on Preliminary References in EC Law, 1958–98', *European Law Journal*, 6(2): 117–27.

Stone Sweet, A. and W. Sandholtz (1997) 'European Integration and Supranational Governance', *Journal of European Public Policy*, 4(3): 297–317.

Stone Sweet, A. and W. Sandholtz (eds) (1998) *European Integration and Supranational Governance* (Oxford University Press).

Stone Sweet, A., W. Sandholtz and N. Fligstein (eds) (2001) *The Institutionalization of Europe* (Oxford: Oxford University Press).

Story, J. (1996) 'Strategy, Ideology and Politics: The Relaunch of Social Europe, 1987–1989', in O. Cadot, H.L. Gabel, J. Story and D. Webber (eds), *European Casebook on Industrial and Trade Policy* (Hemel Hempstead: Prentice-Hall).

Streeck, W. (1996) 'Neo-Voluntarism: A European Social Policy Regime?', in G. Marks, F. W. Scharpf, P.C. Schmitter and W. Streeck (eds), *Governance in the European Union* (London: Sage).

Streeck, W. and P.C. Schmitter (1991) 'From National Corporatism to Transnational Pluralism: Organized Interests in the Single European Market', *Politics and Society*, 19(2): 133–64.

Streit, M.E. and W. Mussler (1995) 'The Economic Constitution of the European Community: From "Rome" to "Maastricht"', *European Law Journal*, 1(3): 5–30.

Svensson, P. (2003) 'Five Danish Referendums on the European Community and European Union: A Critical Assessment of the Franklin Thesis', *European Journal of Political Research*, 41(6): 733–50.

Taggart, P. (1998) 'A Touchstone of Dissent: Euroscepticism in Contemporary Western European Party Systems', *European Journal of Political Research*, 33(3): 363–88.

Tallberg, J. (2000) 'The Anatomy of Autonomy: An Institutional Account of Variation in Supranational Influence', *Journal of Common Market Studies*, 38(5): 843–64.

Tallberg, J. (2006) *Leadership and Negotiation in the European Union* (Cambridge: Cambridge University Press).

Tallberg, J. and K.M. Johansson (2008) 'Party politics in the European Council', *Journal of European Public Policy*, 15(8): 1222–42.

Tarrow, S. (1995) 'The Europeanisation of Conflict: Reflections from a Social Movement Perspective', *West European Politics*, 18(2): 223–51.

Taylor, M. (1976) *Anarchy and Cooperation* (New York, NY: Wiley).

Taylor, P. (1991) 'The European Community and the State: Assumptions, Theories and Propositions', *Review of International Studies*, 17(2): 109–25.

Teasdale, A. (1993) 'The Life and Death of the Luxembourg Compromise', *Journal of Common Market Studies*, 31(4): 567–79.

Thielemann, E. (2003) 'Does Policy Matter? On Governments' Attempts to Control Unwanted Migration', IIIS Discussion Paper No. 9, Trinity College Dublin.

Thielemann, E. (2004) 'Why Asylum Policy Harmonisation Undermines Refugee Burden-Sharing', *European Journal of Migration and Law*, 6(1): 43–61.

Thomson, R (2009) 'Actor Alignments in the European Union Before and After Enlargement', *European Journal of Political Research*, 48(6): 756–81.

Thomson, R., F.N. Stokman, C.H. Achen, and T. König (eds) (2006) *The European Union Decides* (Cambridge: Cambridge University Press).

Thomson, R., J. Boerefijn, and F. Stokman (2004) 'Actor Alignments in European Union Decision Making', *European Journal of Political Research*, 43(2): 237–61.

Tilley, J., J. Garry, and T. Bold (2008) 'Perceptions and Reality: Economic Voting at the 2004 European Parliament Elections', *European Journal of Political Research*, 47(5): 665–86.

Tillman, E.R. (2004) 'The European Union at the Ballot Box. European Integration and Voting Behaviour in the New Member states', *Comparative Political Studies*, 27(5): 590–610.

Tilly, C. (1990) *Coercion, Capital and European States, AD 990–1990* (Oxford: Blackwell).

Titmus, R.M. (1974) *Social Policy* (London: Allen & Unwin).

Tonra, B. (2003) 'Constructing the Common Foreign and Security Policy: The Utility of a Cognitive Approach', *Journal of European Public Policy*, 41(1): 731–56.

Torres, F. (1998) 'Portugal Toward EMU: A Political Economy Perspective', in E. Jones, J. Frieden and F. Torres (eds), *Joining Europe's Monetary Club: The Challenges for Smaller Member States* (London: Macmillan).

Toshkov, D. (2007) 'In Search of the Worlds of Compliance: Culture and Transposition Performance in the European Union', *Journal of European Public Policy*, 14(6): 933–59.

Toshkov, D. (2008) 'Embracing European Law: Compliance with EU Directives in Central and Eastern Europe', *European Union Politics*, 9(3): 379–402.

Treib, O. and G. Falkner (2009) 'Bargaining and Lobbying in the EU Social Policy', in D. Coen and J. Richardson (eds), *Lobbying the European Union: Institutions, Actors, and Issues* (Oxford University Press).

Truman, D. (1951) *The Governmental Process: Political Interests and Public Opinion* (New York, NY: Knopf Press).

Tsebelis, G. (1994) 'The Power of the European Parliament as a Conditional Agenda Setter', *American Political Science Review*, 88(1): 128–42.

Tsebelis, G. (1995) 'Conditional Agenda-Setting and Decision-Making Inside the European Parliament', *Journal of Legislative Studies*, 1(1): 65–93.

Tsebelis, G. (1997) 'Maastricht and the Democratic Deficit', *Aussenwirtshaft* 52(I/II): 29–56.

Tsebelis, G. (1999) 'Veto Players and Law Production in Parliamentary Democracies: An Empirical Analysis', *American Political Science Review*, 93(3): 591–608.

Tsebelis, G. (2000) 'Veto Players and Institutional Analysis', *Governance*, 13(5): 441–74.

Tsebelis, G. (2002) *Veto Players: How Political Institutions Work* (Princeton, Princeton University Press).

Tsebelis, G. and G. Garrett (1996) 'An Institutional Critique of Intergovernmentalism', *International Organization*, 50(2): 269–99.

Tsebelis, G. and G. Garrett (1997) 'Agenda Setting, Vetoes and the European Union's Co-decision Procedure', *Journal of Legislative Studies*, 3(3): 74–92.

Tsebelis, G. and G. Garrett (2000) 'Legislative Politics in the European Union', *European Union Politics*, 1(1): 9–36.

Tsebelis, G. and G. Garrett (2001) 'The Institutional Foundations of Intergovernmentalism and Supranationalism in the European Union', *International Organization*, 55(2): 357–90.

Tsebelis, G., C.B. Jensen, A. Kalandrakis, and A. Kreppel (2001) 'Legislative Procedures in the European Union: An Empirical Analysis', *British Journal of Political Science*, 31(4): 573–99.

Tsebelis, G. and A. Kalandrakis (1999) 'The European Parliament and Environmental Legislation: The Case of Chemicals', *European Journal of Political Research*, 36(1): 119–54.

Tsebelis, G. and A. Kreppel (1998) 'The History of Conditional Agenda-Setting in European Institutions', *European Journal of Political Research*, 33(1): 41–71.

Tsebelis, G. and J. Money (1997) *Bicameralism* (Cambridge: Cambridge University Press).

Tsebelis, G. and X. Yataganas (2002) 'Veto Players and Decision-making in the EU After Nice: Policy Stability and Bureaucratic/Judicial Discretion', *Journal of Common Market Studies*, 40(2): 283–307.

Tucker, J.A., A. Pacek, and A.J. Berinsky (2002) 'Transitional Winners and Losers: Attitudes Toward EU Membership in Post-Communist Countries', *American Journal of Political Science*, 46(3): 557–71.

Tullock, G. (1971) 'The Charity of the Uncharitable', *Western Economic Journal*, 9(4): 379–92.

Turnbull, P. and W. Sandholtz (2001) 'Policing and Immigration: The Creation of New Policy Spaces', in A. Stone Sweet, W. Sandholtz and N. Fligstein (eds), *The Institutionalization of Europe* (Oxford: Oxford University Press).

Turner, P. (1991) 'Capital Flows in the 1980s', *BIS Economic Papers* 30.

Turner, C. and R. Muñoz (2000) 'Revising the Judicial Architecture of the European Union', *Yearbook of European Law*, 19: 1–93.

Tversky, A. and T. Kahneman (1981) 'The Framing of Decisions', *Science*, 211(3):453–58.

Ugur, M. (1995) 'Freedom of Movement vs. Exclusion: A Reinterpretation of the 'Insider' – 'Outsider' Divide in the European Union', *International Migration Review*, 29(4): 964–99.

Ugur, M. (1998) 'Explaining Protectionism and Liberalization in European Union Trade Policy: The Case of Textiles and Clothing', *Journal of European Public Policy*, 29(4): 652–70.

Ullrich, H. (1998) 'Transatlantic Relations in the Post-Cold War Era', *Journal of European Public Policy*, 10(1): 200–5.

van Hees, M. and B. Steunenberg (2000) 'The Choice Judges Make: Court Rulings, Personal Values, and Legal Constraints', *Journal of Theoretical Politics*, 12(3): 305–23.

van Keesbergen, C. (2000) 'Political Allegiance and European Integration', *European Journal of Political Research*, 37(1): 1–17.

van Schendelen, M.P.C.M. (1996) 'EC Committees: Influence Counts More Than Legal Powers', in R.H. Pedler and G.F. Schaefer (eds), *Shaping European Law and Policy. The Role of Committees and Comitology in the Political Process* (Maastricht: European Institute of Public Administration).

van Staden, A. (1994) 'After Maastricht: Explaining the Movement towards a Common European Defence Policy', in W. Carlsnaes and S. Smith (eds),

European Foreign Policy: The EC and Changing Perspectives in Europe (London: Sage).

Vanberg, G. (1998) 'Abstract Judicial Review, Legislative Bargaining, and Policy Compromise', *Journal of Theoretical Politics*, 10(3): 299–326.

Vanberg, G. (2001) 'Legislative-Judicial Relations: A Game–Theoretic Approach to Constitutional Review', *American Journal of Political Science*, 45(2): 346–61.

Verdun, A. (1998) 'The Institutional Design of EMU: A Democratic Deficit?', *Journal of Public Policy*, 18(2): 107–32.

Verdun, A. (1999) 'The Role of the Delors Committee in Creating EMU: An Epistemic Community?', *Journal of European Public Policy*, 6(2): 308–28.

Verdun, A. (2000) *European Responses to Globalization and Financial Market Integration: Perceptions of Economic and Monetary Union in Britain, France and Germany* (London: Macmillan).

Vink, M. and F. Meijerink (2003) 'Asylum Applications and Recognition Rates in EU Member States 1982–2001: A Quantitative Analysis', *Journal of Refugee Studies*, 16(3): 297–315.

de Vries, C.E. (2007) 'Sleeping Giant: Fact or Fairytale? How European Integration Affects Vote Choice in National Elections', *European Union Politics*, 8(3): 363–85.

Wagner, W. (2003) 'Why the EU's Common Foreign and Security Policy will Remain Intergovernmental: A Rationalist Institutional Choice Analysis of European Crisis', *Journal of European Public Policy*, 10(4): 576–95.

Waltz, K.N. (1979) *Theory of International Politics* (New York, NY: McGraw-Hill).

Waltz, K.N. (2000) 'Structural Realism after the Cold War', *International Security*, 25(1): 5–41.

Walzer, M. (1983) *Spheres of Justice: A Defense of Pluralism and Equality* (New York, NY: Basic Books).

Warleigh, A. (2000) 'The Hustle: Citizenship Practice, NGOs and "Policy Coalitions" in the European Union – the Cases of Auto Oil, Drinking Water and Unit Pricing', *Journal of European Public Policy*, 7(2): 229–43.

Warleigh, A. (2001) ' "Europeanizing" Civil Society: NGOs as Agents of Political Socialization', *Journal of Common Market Studies*, 39(4): 619–39.

Warntjen, A. (2008) 'The Council Presidency: Power Broker or Burden? An Empirical Analysis', *European Union Politics*, 9(3): 316–338.

Warntjen, A., S. Hix and C. Crombez (2008) 'The Party Political Make-up of EU Legislative Bodies', *Journal of European Public Policy*, 15(8): 1243–53.

Way, C. (2000) 'Central Banks, Partisan Politics and Macroeconomic Outcomes', *Comparative Political Studies*, 33(2): 196–224.

Weale, A. (1996) 'Environmental Rules and Rule-Making in the European Union', *Journal of European Public Policy*, 3(4): 594–611.

Weatherill, S. and S. Beaumont (2004) *EU Law: The Essential Guide to the Legal Workings of the European Union*, 4th edn (London: Penguin).

Webber, D. (1999) 'Franco-German Bilateralism and Agricultural Politics in the European Union', *West European Politics*, 22(1): 45–67.

Weber, K. and M. Hallerberg (2001) 'Explaining Variation in Institution Integration in the European Union: Why Firms May Prefer European Solutions', *Journal of European Public Policy*, 8(2): 171–91.

Weber, M. (1946 [1919]) 'Politics as a Vocation', in H.H. Gerth and C. Wright Mills (eds), *From Max Weber: Essays in Sociology* (Oxford: Oxford University Press).

Weber, T. (2007) 'Campaign Effects and Second-Order Cycles: A Top-Down Approach to European Parliament Elections', *European Union Politics*, 8(4): 509–36.

Webster, R. (1998) 'Environmental Collective Action: Stable Patterns of Cooperation and Issue Alliances at the European Level', in J. Greenwood and M. Aspinwall (eds), *Collective Action in the European Union* (London: Routledge).

Weiler, J.H.H. (1991) 'The Transformation of Europe', *Yale Law Journal*, 100(8): 2403–83.

Weiler, J.H.H. (1993) 'Journey to an Unknown Destination: A Retrospective and Prospective of the European Court of Justice in the Area of Political Integration', *Journal of Common Market Studies*, 31(4): 417–46.

Weiler, J.H.H. (1994) 'A Quiet Revolution: The European Court of Justice and Its Interlocutors', *Comparative Political Studies*, 26(4): 510–34.

Weiler, J.H.H. (1995) 'Does Europe Need a Constitution? Reflections on Demos, Telos and the German Maastricht Decision', *European Law Journal*, 1(3): 219–58.

Weiler, J.H.H. (1997) 'The Reformation of European Constitutionalism', *Journal of Common Market Studies*, 35(1): 97–131.

Weiler, J.H.H., U.R. Haltern, and F. Mayer (1995) 'European Democracy and its Critique', *West European Politics*, 18(3): 4–39.

Weingast, B.R. (1995) 'The Economic Role of Political Institutions: Market-Preserving Federalism and Economic Development', *Journal of Law and Economic Organization*, 11(1): 1–31.

Weingast, B.R. (1996) 'Political Institutions: Rational Choice Perspectives', in R.E. Goodin and H.-D. Klingeman (eds), *A New Handbook of Political Science* (Oxford: Oxford University Press).

Weingast, B.R., and M.J. Moran (1983) 'Bureaucratic Discretion or Congressional Control? Regulatory Policymaking by the Federal Trade Commission', *Journal of Political Economy*, 91(5): 765–800.

Weingast, B.R., K.A. Shepsle, and C. Johnson (1981) 'The Political Economy of Benefits and Costs: A Neoclassical Approach to Distributive Politics', *Journal of Political Economy*, 89(4): 642–64.

Wessels, B. (1999) 'European Parliament and Interest Groups', in R.S. Katz and B. Wessels (eds), *The European Parliament, National Parliaments, and European Integration* (Oxford: Oxford University Press).

Westlake, M. (1998) 'The European Parliament's Emerging Appointment Powers', *Journal of Common Market Studies*, 36(3): 431–44.

Whitman, R.G. and S. Wolff (2010) 'The EU as a conflict manager? The Case of Georgia and Its Implications', *International Affairs*, 86(1): 87–107.

Whittington, K.E., R.D. Kelemen, and G.A. Caldeira (eds) (2008) *The Oxford Handbook of Law and Politics* (Oxford: Oxford University Press).

Widgren, M. (1994) 'The Relationship Between Voting Power and Policy Impact in the European Union', Centre for Economic Policy Research Discussion Paper (1033).

Widgren, M. (1995) 'Probabilistic Voting Power in the EU Council: The Cases of Trade Policy and Social Regulation', *Scandinavian Journal of Economics*, 97(2): 345–56.

Wiener, A. (1998) *'European' Citizenship Practice: Building Institutions of a Non-State* (Boulder, CO: Westview Press).

Wiener, A. and T. Diez (2009) *European Integration Theory*, 2nd edn (Oxford: Oxford University Press).

Wildasin, D.E. (2002) 'Fiscal Policy in Post-EMU Europe', *European Union Politics*, 3(2): 251–60.

Wilensky, H. (1975) *The Welfare State and Equality* (Berkeley, CA: University of California Press).

Wilks, S. (2005) 'Agency Escape: Decentralization or Dominance of the European Commission in the Modernization of Competition Policy?', *Governance*, 18(3): 431–52.

Wilson, J.Q. (1980) *The Politics of Regulation* (New York, NY: Basic Books).

Wincott, D. (1995) 'The Role of Law or the Rule of the Court of Justice? An 'Institutional' Account of Judicial Politics in the European Community', *Journal of European Public Policy*, 2(4): 583–602.

Winkler, B. (1996) 'Towards a Strategic View on EMU: A Critical Survey', *Journal of Public Policy*, 16(1): 1–28.

Winkler, B. (1999) 'Is Maastricht a Good Contract?', *Journal of Common Market Studies*, 37(1): 39–58.

de Witte, B. (1998) 'Sovereignty and European Integration: The Weight of Legal Tradition', in A.-M. Slaughter, A. Stone Sweet and J.H.H. Weiler (eds), *The European Court and National Courts – Doctrine and Jurisprudence: Legal Change in Its Social Context* (Oxford: Hart).

Wonka, A. (2007) 'Technocratic and Independent? The Appointment of European Commissioners and Its Policy Implications', *Journal of European Public Policy*, 14(2): 171–91.

Wonka, A. (2008) Decision-making Dynamics in the European Commission: Partisan, National or Sectoral?', *Journal of European Public Policy*, 15(8): 1145–63.

Woods, N. (1996) 'The Use of Theory in the Study of International Relations', in N. Woods (ed.), *Explaining International Relations Since 1945* (Oxford: Oxford University Press).

Woolley, J.T. (1994) 'Linking Political and Monetary Union: The Maastricht Agenda and German Domestic Politics', in B. Eichengreen and J. Frieden (eds), *The Political Economy of European Monetary Unification* (Boulder, CO: Westview).

Wyatt-Walker, A. (1995) 'Globalization, Corporate Identity and European Technology Policy', *Journal of European Public Policy*, 2(3): 427–46.

Yordanova, N. (2009) 'The Rationale behind Committee Assignment in the European Parliament: Distributive, Informational and Partisan Perspectives', *European Union Politics*, 10(2): 226–52.

Young, A.R. (1997) 'Consumption Without Representation? Consumers in the Single Market', in H. Wallace and A.R. Young (eds), *Participation and Policy-Making in the European Union* (Oxford: Clarendon Press).

Young, A.R. (1998) 'European Consumer Groups: Multiple Levels of Governance and Multiple Logics of Collective Action', in J. Greenwood and M. Aspinwall (eds), *Collective Action in the European Union* (London: Routledge).

Young, A.R. (2000) 'The Adaptation of European Foreign Economic Policy', *Journal of Common Market Studies*, 38(1): 93–116.

Young, A.R. and H. Wallace (2000) *Regulatory Policies in the Enlarging European Union: Weighing Civic and Producer Interests* (Manchester: Manchester University Press).

Zhelyazkova, A. and R. Torenvlied (2009) 'The Time-Dependent Effect of Conflict in the Council on Delays in the Transposition of EU Directives', *European Union Politics*, 10(1): 35–62.

Zimmer, C., G. Schneider, and M. Dobbins (2005) 'The Contested Council: The Conflict Dimension of an Intergovernmental Institution', *Political Studies*, 53(2): 403–22.

Index

CPSIA information can be obtained at www.ICGtesting.com
Printed in the USA
BVOW040430120912

299932BV00002B/3/P

9 780230 249813